Menergy

Menergy

San Francisco's Gay Disco Sound

LOUIS NIEBUR

OXFORD
UNIVERSITY PRESS

Oxford University Press is a department of the University of Oxford. It furthers
the University's objective of excellence in research, scholarship, and education
by publishing worldwide. Oxford is a registered trade mark of Oxford University
Press in the UK and certain other countries.

Published in the United States of America by Oxford University Press
198 Madison Avenue, New York, NY 10016, United States of America.

© Oxford University Press 2022

All rights reserved. No part of this publication may be reproduced, stored in
a retrieval system, or transmitted, in any form or by any means, without the
prior permission in writing of Oxford University Press, or as expressly permitted
by law, by license, or under terms agreed with the appropriate reproduction
rights organization. Inquiries concerning reproduction outside the scope of the
above should be sent to the Rights Department, Oxford University Press, at the
address above.

You must not circulate this work in any other form
and you must impose this same condition on any acquirer.

Library of Congress Cataloging-in-Publication Data
Names: Niebur, Louis, 1971– author.
Title: Menergy : San Francisco's gay disco sound / Louis Niebur.
Description: [First.] | New York : Oxford University Press, 2022. |
Includes bibliographical references and index.
Identifiers: LCCN 2021036239 (print) | LCCN 2021036240 (ebook) |
ISBN 9780197511084 (paperback) | ISBN 9780197511077 (hardback) |
ISBN 9780197511107 (epub)
Subjects: LCSH: Disco music–California–San Francisco–History and
criticism. | Electronic dance music–California–San Francisco–History
and criticism. | Sound recording industry—California—San
Francisco–History–20th century. | Gay men–California–San
Francisco–Social life and customs–20th century. | Castro (San Francisco, Calif.)
Classification: LCC ML3526 .N54 2022 (print) | LCC ML3526 (ebook) |
DDC 781.648155409794/61–dc23
LC record available at https://lccn.loc.gov/2021036239
LC ebook record available at https://lccn.loc.gov/2021036240

DOI: 10.1093/oso/9780197511077.001.0001

To my dancing brothers never forgotten

To my darling brother, never forgotten

Contents

Acknowledgments	ix
Introduction: Setting Up the Sound	1
1. Disco, the Castro, and Gay Liberation	11
2. Liberation for Some: The Continued Expansion of Gay San Francisco in the Late 1970s	31
3. Sylvester's Fantasy Comes True	48
4. The First Wave of the San Francisco Sound	61
5. Blecman and Hedges	78
6. Disco's Dead/Not Dead	96
7. The San Francisco Sound Thrives	116
8. New Heights	139
9. Trouble in Paradise	165
10. Dancing with AIDS	184
11. Everything Falls Apart	205
12. In Retrospect	223
Notes	233
Suggested Reading	261
Selected Discography	263
Index	267

Acknowledgments

This book has been a long time coming, and there are many people who made it possible. At the University of Nevada, Reno (UNR), I would like to thank the College of Liberal Arts and the Department of Music, who generously funded my research. I couldn't have written this book without the clerical assistance of Vicki Bell, Cynthia Prescott, and Neva Sheehan, the support of department chairs Dmitri Atapine and Peter Epstein, and the invaluable staff at the UNR Knowledge Center, especially Amy Hunsaker, Maggie Ressel, Rayla Tokarz, and Jennifer Wykoff. Thank you to Michael C. Oliveira at the ONE National Gay and Lesbian Archives at the USC Libraries, and Isaac Fellman, Alex Barrows, and Joanna Black at the GLBT Historical Society in San Francisco. Thank you to the Oral History Center, the Bancroft Library at the University of California at Berkeley. Huge thanks to my editor, Norm Hirschy, at Oxford University Press for again making this process run so smoothly. His wisdom, experience, and most of all friendship over the last decade has been essential to this project and I can't imagine how different this book would be without his guidance.

Special thanks to my amazing colleagues Julianne Lindberg, Ruthie Meadows, and Eric Fassbender. Our consistent writing dates and your wise feedback kept me focused and inspired, as did discussions with graduate students Brad Bynum, Cole Peck, Geoff Scott, and Brian Wright. Brian Eno and Moby's ambient music calmed my anarchic mind for writing. Brett Van Hoesen and Julianne Lindberg deserve special thanks for forming the School of the Arts Research Group, a wonderful place to test out ideas. Thanks to Scott Smale for listening to my ramblings with an open mind and ear, and for loving to dance. Duke Day and Mike Richardson also deserve love and thanks, dear friends who always let me crash at their place in the most expensive city in the country, and who are always up for a laugh.

Historian J. D. Doyle has been unbelievably generous with his time and support; he's one of my heroes, and an inspiration for any scholar of our queer musical heritage. DJ and producer Josh Cheon is also a major force in the promotion of the legacy of queer popular and dance music, primarily through his Dark Entries record label. Thank you for your encouragement

X ACKNOWLEDGMENTS

and wisdom. Likewise, Joshua Gamson's friendship and guidance (not to mention the sharing of his personal archive) have been a constant gift to this project. With his biography of Sylvester he proved that it was possible to capture in writing the essence of San Francisco's magic and its influence on its unique artists. Thank you, too, musicologists, dance historians, and other friends throughout the world who have helped and guided me, especially Byron Adams, Christina Baade, Philip Brett, Jennifer Doctor, Robert Fink, Aaron Hill, Nate Hodges, Loren Kajikawa, James Kennaway, Val Martinez, Susan McClary, Mitchell Morris, Josh Reed, Cecilia Sun, and my colleagues in disco Hunter Charlton and Jaap Kooijman.

My greatest thanks must go to all the amazing people who shared their experiences with me, incredible stories of friendship, dancing, and musicking. Thank you to Mark Abramson, Ken Alan, Marianna Beachdell, Blackberri, Barry Blum, Joe Bomback, Steven Ames Brown, John Carollo, Brian Chin, Keefe Chow, Karl Davis, Dana Daye, Steve Fabus, Joan Faulkner, Lisa Fredenthal-Lee, Richard Guile, Katie Guthorn, Mike Gymnaites, John Hedges, Gregory Higgins, Linda Imperial, Audrey Joseph, Bobby Kent, Ernest Kohl, Jim Komarek, Kurt Lawson, Rhani Lee, Robert Lee, Gene Leone, John Levy, Sharon McKnight, Carla Ann Nicholson, Dan Nicoletta, Chris Njirich, Matthew McQueen, Jim Piechota, Benji Rubenstein, Jennifer Collier Salisbury, Randall Schiller, Chrysler Sheldon, Chico Starr, Ian Anthony Stephens, Peter Struve, Marsha Stern, Jon Sugar, Jeanie Tracy, Maurice Tani, Lester Temple, Horace Jack Tolson, Bobby Viteritti, Dennis Wadlington, and Joe Yeary. I especially want to thank David Diebold for capturing the memories and experiences of so many artists and clubgoers in his essential *Tribal Rites*.

Jim Hopkins's ongoing work with the San Francisco Disco Preservation Society has enabled those of us who weren't lucky enough to have been there to experience the music through his incredible recovery project. Thank you, Jim, for your generous patience with my endless questions.

Thank you to my parents for their unending encouragement and support; I wish mom could be here to see this project completed. I miss her every day. The loss of Mike, too, has been a huge blow to us all, but Oscar, Natalie, Lizzie, Violet, Chris, Heather, and Max are as solid a family as I could hope for. And finally, to my husband, David, who has listened to a lot of disco over the last ten years and hasn't complained yet, I love you, and thank you!

Introduction

Setting Up the Sound

In September 2018, I recruited my husband and two friends from Reno to attend a Go Bang! party at San Francisco's historic bar the Stud. Not that they needed much encouragement. Our trips over the Sierra Nevada mountains, through the Donner Pass, to the City by the Bay for barhopping were cathartic and soul-affirming; weekends of dancing, drinking, socializing, staying at the notorious Beck's Motor Lodge, and usually starting and ending with Marcello's Pizza on Castro Street. We were happy to be examples of the kind of tourists the gay mecca was known for attracting. This particular party at the Stud was a celebration of Sylvester, the high-energy disco star who in the late 1970s had kicked off the "San Francisco sound" in dance music, and the night would be filled with not only Sylvester's tunes but also the songs heard in San Francisco's gay nightclubs like the I-Beam and Trocadero Transfer in the early 1980s, from local labels like Megatone and Moby Dick Records. The DJ collective Go Bang! has hosted parties since 2008, focusing primarily on music of our collective gay past. This group of queer DJs—Sergio Fedasz, Jimmy DePre, Prince Wolf, and the legendary Steve Fabus—frequently themes its evenings around influential gay musical figures, including Patrick Cowley, Sylvester, Hector Xtravaganza, Juanita More, and Jerry Bonham.

That night while dancing, singing, and sweating on the Stud's packed dance floor, I felt a kinship not only with those whose bodies moved next to mine but also with a community of the past; I imagined I felt the same things *they* felt as they moved *their* bodies to the same music forty years earlier. In that space we danced, and in dancing shared these imagined pasts; imaginary mostly because their stories have been lost, forgotten, or buried in the wreckage of decades of the AIDS epidemic. I felt that the music and the act of musicking embodied on the dance floor captured some almost ineffable essence of their experience, and I knew I wanted to try and tell their stories in a less liminal way. The act of writing history is an act of history making, a point never made clearer to me than in the construction of this narrative, of the

---

Menergy. Louis Niebur, Oxford University Press. © Oxford University Press 2022.
DOI: 10.1093/oso/9780197511077.003.0001

2 MENERGY

attempt to restore individuals to the history of music. My version, of course, betrays my own prejudices and interests in electronics, in gay men, and in the seedier side of gay life, but I have as a historian attempted to portray people as I believe they were: complex, nuanced agents in a musical environment that for the first time celebrated rather than denigrated them.

The history of the San Francisco sound is inevitably bound up in the history of the "Castro clone," that subculture of gay men that thrived in the hothouse environment of San Francisco in the 1970s until the rise of AIDS in the 1980s. Close-cropped hair, mustache, tight Levi 501s, white t-shirt underneath plaid flannel, leather jacket; the look was one of exaggerated white masculinity. The emergence of the clone type was gradual, but by the mid-1970s it dominated the public's perception of the gay community in the Castro. Clone historian Martin H. Levine described the clone community as "a somewhat closed community in the 1970s—a gay ghetto organized around a set of socially isolated friendship cliques and crowds, which coalesced around a series of meeting spots known as the circuit."[1] This network of bars, restaurants, and bathhouses was centered primarily around the Castro and included venues south of Market (SoMa), but it largely ignored the established gay spots on Polk Street, which held on to its preclone atmosphere, despite the presence of discos like Bojangles, N'Touch, and Buzzby's. It's not a subculture without fault, and many have justifiably critiqued it, both from without and within. David Goodstein, editor of the nationwide gay magazine *The Advocate*, defined the Castro of the late 1970s rather uncharitably as "essentially a refugee culture made up of gay men who, in a sense, are convalescing in the ghetto from all those damaging years in Podunk."[2] He described "the Castro Street group" as a "really *rough* culture. Their relationships are brief, they don't work but live off welfare, they hang out like teenagers, they drink too much, they take too many drugs, they fuck all day and night, they are scattered—and of course radical politically. They act like kids in a candy store."[3] While it's easy to dismiss Goodstein's assessment with a "yeah, and that's bad how?," his critical view was shared by many disillusioned gay men at the time.

It was also, for those people of color who interacted or participated in it, a mostly white and racist culture, although most white participants ironically remember the Castro of the 1970s as a utopian environment where all individuals were welcomed equally. In this I'm reminded of Sherrie Tucker's discussion of the dancers at the Hollywood Canteen in the 1940s, who similarly recalled the space in differing terms:

Some white former Canteen-goers talked about racial tensions but most narrated the dance floor as completely integrated, friendly, and uncontroversial. One after another insisted that it was a "wonderful" place where "everyone was together" and "there was no prejudice.". . . Canteen-goers of color more often narrated a segregated or at least partially segregated environment. When I asked Mel Bryant, an African-American veteran, about the extent to which the dance floor was integrated, he replied, "Don't you believe it." He added that it was "a different thing, a wonderful thing to have a place where soldiers could go, but it wasn't integrated in an equal way."[4]

Similarly, none of the white interviewees with whom I spoke remembered the dance clubs or local music subculture as racist. But without exception the people of color I spoke with recalled incident after incident of racist behavior, both institutionally and by individuals in the Castro. Like so many of my white informants, I've been able to ignore the clashes of intersectionality faced by gay men of color in the Castro, seeing only the utopian aspects of gay liberation. Likewise, as a book about a primarily male world, women are not featured heavily here. Quite a few women did, however, feature prominently in the scene, particularly straight-identified women, and I have tried to highlight their contributions to a subculture that didn't always treat women with the greatest respect. Gay men are not immune to the historic problems of racism and sexism endemic to the United States; rather, San Francisco gay life reflected the biases inherent in all American cultures where different power dynamics are in play. I hope I have not downplayed these biases in my narrative. I have tried to look at the ways in which, despite these intractable issues, gay men of color and women sometimes found their own liberation in the San Francisco sound and on the dance floors of the city's discos, and I mark that experience as mediated through prejudice or privilege when others have observed it as such.

Disco

Before the changes fought for in Stonewall's wake, same-sex dancing was one of the many offences that could get you locked up. "It was a time when just moving in time to the music was enough to get you called down by an angry, frightened bartender yelling *no dancing*," one bar-goer recalled in the mid-1970s: "Even when dancing was eventually allowed, it would be a

4 MENERGY

risky business . . . permissible only so long as there was *no touching*."[5] With the gradual loosening of antigay laws after the Stonewall uprising of 1969, dancing took on a significance that is hard to overstate.

Disco was the sound and style adopted as the dominant musical force in the newly legalized (if still frequently stigmatized) public meeting places of American and European gay communities in the early 1970s. As Alice Echols has shown so eloquently, disco music gave several groups a sense of agency, including women and African Americans.[6] For gay men of any class or ethnicity, disco also held out the promise of freedom, as a vehicle for expressing a communal identity through dancing. Described by one gay man in 1976 as a physical manifestation of his liberation, his gayness made manifest, the act of dancing in a gay bar exemplified a new kind of public declaration of sexuality.[7] For San Francisco author Donald Cameron Scot, dancing was a catharsis, a transcending practice that embodied his identity entirely:

> Soaring higher as computerized lights flash from panel to panel across the lighted floor, bodies bobbing, jerking, dancing to the upbeat tempo. Feeling more than hearing the music. Tripping. Art-deco patterns of musical instruments weave in and out of prominence to swiftly changing music. Busby Berkeley neon violins recede to large spots as trumpets take their places to silhouette Gladys Knight against a now secondary background orchestra, only to give way as other instruments float around the backdrop, circling to front center stage, then retiring graciously in a continuum of swirling, circular motion.[8]

In 1976, for example, disco was used as a way to bring together various factions of the gay liberation movement. That year, a prominent group of gay liberationists established a National Disco Tea Dance, where they proudly proclaimed that, "In cities and resorts from San Juan to Waikiki, the gay community will dance . . . and to the same music. . . . And, as the lights and music around the country flash on in harmony, that Sunday and each Sunday thereafter new cities will join the network and the music will play, and as our numbers grow, so too will our power, and all we have to do is dance."[9]

San Francisco was second only to New York City in the cultivation of this dancing culture, but the legacy of 1960s counterculture ideals and the relative homogeneity of the participants (increasingly white, college-educated, middle class) forged a unique, highly performative subculture far from the grit of the New York scene. The emergence of San Francisco's Castro neighborhood in the early 1970s as an international gay mecca symbolized this new open face for homosexuality throughout the world, albeit one that privileged whiteness and affluence over an earlier, more inclusive philosophical approach, represented by the older, countercultural, and multicultural gay enclave centered around the Polk Street bars. Disco was the sound of the Castro, a music that literally embodied gay liberation in the minds of dancers.

In the early years of disco in San Francisco, despite almost all disco music being produced outside the Bay Area, the creative act of mixing by local celebrity gay DJs turned each night of standard dance music into unique communal experiences in the disco palace. The City Disco and the Mind Shaft of the mid-1970s were the prototypes for the larger clubs, first Oil Can Harry's and Alfie's, and later the I-Beam, Dreamland, and the after-hours club Trocadero Transfer. The discos were often active in local gay politics and had a prominent place in the Freedom Day Parades of the mid-1970s and 1980s. John Hedges, DJ at the City Disco, for example, mixed a live disco set on a parade float in 1976 while dancers boogied down around him. A Los Angeles writer touring the gay nightclubs in 1976 remarked how San Francisco DJs seemed to thrive in the gay demimonde of the Castro and SoMa neighborhoods, constructing unified sets of music binding the dancers together. In his discussion of Hedges's replacement at the City Disco, he joyously described the journey:

> As the evening with Jon Randazzo progressed, we moved from a Barry White big band sound into an almost calypso band style and finally into some really heavy disco beats, all with no actual break in the music. Sometimes Jon would mix the same record three or four times and at one point mixed one record into another and then went back to the first record and the crowd on the floor never missed a beat.[10]

If the San Francisco scene as portrayed in my history seems insular, that's because it was. San Francisco remains a relatively tiny city, one whose population was more than ten times smaller than New York City's, but with an outsized influence. The small size of the Bay Area led to close relationships between San Francisco's gay clubs and musicians, which in turn encouraged an exciting amount of collaboration when they began producing their own music. John Hedges and fellow DJ Marty Blecman worked for Berkeley-based Fantasy Records; disco group Loverde began as a live act at the City Cabaret (a floor below the City Disco) before moving to the Castro's own

6   MENERGY

Moby Dick Records; Patrick Cowley was working as a lighting technician at the City Disco when he formally introduced himself to Sylvester, who with his backup singers Martha Wash and Izora Rhodes (known collectively first as "Two Tons o' Fun" then "The Weather Girls") performed there up to six times a week. These relationships depended on proximity and the safety of the hothouse environment in which they thrived.

Cowley casually knew Sylvester from their shared countercultural circle of friends; both had made the transition into the more hedonistic, individualistic world of the Castro, even if Cowley, as a white man, had gradually adopted the clone aesthetic to a greater extent. He played Sylvester some remixes of disco songs he had made. The singer was impressed, if a bit baffled, by the electronic textures Cowley had created, sounds that were still quite new in 1977. Sylvester, however, could envision a melding of his rock gospel style with Cowley's dark, druggy electronic sound and Cowley was hired to add synthesizer to two tracks on Sylvester's newest album, *Step II* (1978). Both "You Make Me Feel (Mighty Real)" and "Dance (Disco Heat)" from that record became massive mainstream hits at the height of disco's popularity. With electronics recorded manually on 8-track tape, using no MIDI or sequencers, both songs celebrate a nascent gay aesthetic both Cowley and Sylvester were intimately familiar with. Despite both songs topping the dance charts and breaking into the pop charts, Sylvester was very public about the gay aspects of his music. He and Cowley continued this sound on Sylvester's follow-up album, *Stars*, about which he explained at the time:

> There's a song called "I Need Someone to Love Tonight'" which is bordering on my blatant sex disco music . . . with a wailing syncopated lyric line. The tunes are ten to twelve minutes long. There's Patrick Cowley's incredible synthesizers, synthesized singing . . . It's completely out there, we're not gonna be safe at all. I don't like safety.[11]

Sylvester and Cowley's outspoken sexuality seemed extreme to some. Michael Finden, Sylvester's gay keyboard player, recalls that Cowley "was very into sexuality, almost to the point of being obnoxious . . . I guess everybody enjoys that first realization and enthusiasm and freedom, although maybe not to Patrick's degree. If you listen to the lyrics of many of his songs . . . I mean, it's all very sexual, fantasy stuff."[12] Sylvester remembers, "We often talked of doing these great gay records about hanging around in deep dark places doing these nasty, lewd, wonderful things!"[13]

Gay disco dancers in San Francisco received a boost in late 1977 with the opening of two massive new nightclubs in San Francisco, the I-Beam in the Haight-Ashbury neighborhood and the Trocadero Transfer located in the heart of SoMa's leather bar territory. These bars were designed to be temples to disco. Music, sexuality, dancing; all were equal priorities to the patrons and owners of these new clubs. The after-hours club Trocadero Transfer in particular encouraged the development of a heavily drugged, highly sexualized dancing culture. It initially served no alcohol, and on the weekend averaged 1,000 to 1,500 people on its 4,000-square-foot elevated wood dance floor. As one commentator noted at the time, "One aspect of the gay discos . . . is the constant odor of poppers. Primarily a gay drug, amyl nitrite has so established itself on the disco scene that many clubs actually sell the stuff."[14] As was normal for after-hours clubs, the music started around 11:00 p.m. and peaked around 4:00 or 5:00 a.m., winding down around 9:00 a.m. By 1978, in addition to dozens of bars and nightclubs, the vast majority of which played disco, there were eleven gay bathhouses, six of which had a nightly DJ. All but one played disco.[15]

The San Francisco Sound

Just as quickly as it had arrived in the mainstream, disco went out of fashion for the majority of Americans. By early 1980, most straight discos closed or changed formats, putting their DJs out of work. Record labels dropped their disco imprints, and artists who had cashed in on the craze went back to rock, or country, or easy listening, or whatever genres they had emerged from. Not that anyone at the I-Beam or Trocadero noticed, or in any of the other gay discos in America's big cities. As John Hedges recalled, "Everybody was saying it was the death of disco and yet nothing was dying. There was still a need for the music."[16] In San Francisco, disco was still big business. March 11, 1979, was declared Sylvester Day by mayor Diane Feinstein, and he won a Cable Car award (San Francisco's annual acknowledgment of outstanding LGBTQ performers, composers, arts groups, actors, playwrights, and athletes) in 1980 for his sold-out disco show at the War Memorial Opera House. A review from an out-of-towner from September 1980 shows that disco was very much alive and well: "Thank god San Francisco; nothing has changed! . . . The highlight of the weekend was Saturday night (all night!) at the Trocadero Transfer . . . I have not heard music like this anywhere in the

8 MENERGY

country . . . I do not even really like to dance but in the Troc—it is impossible to stop."[17]

It was a defining moment for dance music in San Francisco. Almost immediately, those disco artists with an investment in the core gay audience of dance music responded with renewed, defiant energy, filling the vacuum left when the mainstream labels abandoned disco. But now that members of the gay community itself were creating the music, they were able to instill it with even more of their lived experiences and fantasies. In 1981 Patrick Cowley and Marty Blecman founded Megatone Records and Trocadero DJ Craig Morey and DJ Bill Motley founded Moby Dick Records in the heart of the Castro. There, in a postdisco environment, disco's musical and thematic traits were embraced rather than discarded.

One of these traits is the chromatic rising bass line, where the bass drops to the submediant and rises back chromatically to the tonic. This technique was pioneered by funk bass player Larry Graham from Graham Central Station, especially in tracks like "Feel the Need" (1974), but it is present in countless disco hits such as the Trammps' "Disco Inferno," Paradise Express's "Dance," and Voyage's "America." Another prominent trademark of classic disco, the off-beat hi-hat, introduced by drummer Earl Young at Philadelphia International Records and first popularized in the tune "The Love I Lost" (1973) by Harold Melvin and the Blue Notes, found its way into innumerable disco songs. There was also a return to the unashamedly sexual lyrical content of earlier disco. In a disco context, this trait is best known from Donna Summer's "Love to Love You Baby," (1976) but is probably most explicit in Cerrone's "Love in C Minor" from the same year.

All three of these traits had been almost entirely abandoned by 1980 in mainstream dance music but are prominent features of the San Francisco sound. The new music was largely electronic, a result of both the shrinking market making the music's production quicker and cheaper and the desire to depict a complex futuristic fantasy world through technology, a rebranding of disco under the label "high energy" (eventually dubbed "Hi-NRG"). Dancing, drug use, and the sexual experience of the bars; all three were articulated as "letting off energy" within gay club culture at the time. Patrick Cowley's first dance project under his own name crystalized this into what is probably the defining track of the high-energy San Francisco sound, "Menergy," released in late 1980. A collaboration with Marty Blecman, the record came about largely because there was nothing quite gay enough for either of them in the dance market. Blecman recalled, "Patrick and I . . . decided

SETTING UP THE SOUND 9

to get together and make a disco record, which turned out to be 'Energy': a tribute to high-energy clubs and the whole scene. We got high one afternoon in the studio and I put an 'M' in front of 'Energy' and we laughed about it and wrote all of these gay lyrics and that's how 'Menergy' came about."[18]

A prominent rising chromatic bass opens the 1981 hit "Disco Kicks" by Moby Dick Records' Boys Town Gang. They were created by Moby Dick founder Bill Motley to be an even gayer West Coast Village People. Moby Dick's music, like Megatone's, quickly gained a reputation for producing relentlessly high-energy covers of girl-group and R&B songs, like "Can't Take My Eyes Off You," and "Ain't No Mountain High Enough." Lisa, an artist who also recorded with Moby Dick Records, emphasized the electronic aspect to an even greater extent in a series of international hits including "Jump Shout" (1982) and "Rocket to Your Heart" (1983), as did Loverde with "Die Hard Lover" (1982).

Paul Parker's "Right on Target" (1982) was another huge success for Megatone, written and produced by Cowley. Again embracing rather than rejecting disco's strongest characteristics, "Right on Target" adds Cowley's trademark synthesizers to the disco formula. This style, mixing disco and electronics, was in some ways similar to what Giorgio Moroder had done in 1977 with Donna Summer's "I Feel Love"; the difference in San Francisco was one of immediacy. Cowley used electronics in an aggressively sexual, beat-you-over-the-head way, to simulate a high-energy rush of sexual and drugged ecstasy, more impulsive than Eurodisco's breezy swooshes.[19]

With a string of international dance hits, these two record labels had no reason to doubt that their future was bright. But AIDS had been gradually eating away at the foundations of gay San Francisco, and soon the entire edifice would crumble. Within five years, AIDS would fundamentally alter the vibrant, unique culture that produced this music. Most of these independent labels' employees died in the first years of the epidemic. Many men stopped attending discos, fearful in those early days of the mysterious causes of the diseases initially afflicting mostly gay men. This change of priorities in the lives of the ill and dying meant that the musical developments of the San Francisco sound would be picked up and expanded on by musicians in Europe, particularly in Britain and Italy, where infection rates didn't peak until several years later.

If not for the death of so many participants, the music of San Francisco would undoubtedly be more familiar to contemporary listeners and dancers, and this project of reconstruction attempts to restore these lost figures to

10 MENERGY

their rightful place in the legacy of twentieth-century popular music. Despite this largely forgotten history, their influence can still be heard in contemporary pop and dance music, mostly filtered through the lens of the British artists who succeeded them. In the United Kingdom, the slightly delayed arrival of HIV, and a public more sympathetic to electronic sounds in popular music, meant that the British interpretation of the San Francisco sound was able to achieve a much greater level of mainstream success than the deliberately more niche gay postdisco sound was granted in its home country. These San Francisco artists' music reflected a new way of life, a culture of sexual liberation, an idealized world in miniature where, despite very real challenges from the outside, LGBTQ people built a community out of whole cloth. Over the five years of its existence as a distinct musical phenomenon, San Francisco's high-energy music channeled the spirit of gay liberation through a shared dance-floor experience. This is the story of the music that for some gay men holds as if in amber the essence of that liberation.

1

Disco, the Castro, and Gay Liberation

Any starting point in the history of the San Francisco sound will seem, to some extent, arbitrary. Should a history begin with the unique counterculture centered around the Haight-Ashbury neighborhood in the 1960s, which influenced nearly all the players in the dance music scene a decade later? Or should it start even further back, with the political musings and sexual freedom of the bohemians of the North Beach area in the 1950s, which made clubs like the Black Cat so essential to this story? Or maybe with the influx of gay and lesbian soldiers to the Bay Area during World War II, as Allan Bérube's essential study *Coming Out Under Fire* demonstrated?[1] Or even perhaps as far back as the repeal of prohibition in 1933, which as Nan Alamilla Boyd has shown saw an exponential growth in queer establishments throughout the city, although "the public emergence of queer and transgender clubs can be measured in part by the civic outcry it generated."[2]

All of these would be potentially important starting places. However, unlike George Chauncey's groundbreaking study of gay New York in the first half of the twentieth century, in which he deliberately "pays more attention to the tactics by which gay men appropriated public spaces not identified as gay," this history relies on the first legally, publicly identified gay spaces and the role music played in them.[3] While rarely identified as "political" spaces, the discos and bars of the 1970s were among the first public places where many celebrated their status as out gay men without the earlier civic outcry. These were populations aware of their rights and perfectly willing to fight for them (they were also among the first generation that didn't have to fight if they didn't want to because of the work done by others before them). And the music that arose from those spaces was different because of this. I am not claiming one hegemonic subculture uniting the lives of all men who engaged in homosexual acts during those years (which indeed, if Kinsey's figures from those years are to be trusted, would include half of the male population). Rather, I am trying to come to terms with the way music was used by a specific subset of homosexually identified men who largely accepted the term "gay" for themselves and those willing to associate with them within

Menergy. Louis Niebur, Oxford University Press. © Oxford University Press 2022.
DOI: 10.1093/oso/9780197511077.003.0002

the confines of a "gay bar" or "gay disco," which was mutually agreed by the participants as such.

Therefore, it seems only right to begin this story with the rise of the gay discotheque in the wake of the Stonewall uprising of June 1969. In this chapter, I outline the parallel emergence of disco in the early 1970s as a gay cultural/musical phenomenon and a new gay male clone identity, with San Francisco's Castro neighborhood at its epicenter—what Randy Shilts called "the nation's chief liberated zone."[4] With roots in a combination of up-tempo rhythm and blues, soul, gospel, and rock, disco as a musical genre initially encompassed any music that had a strong groove and complex polyrhythms, essentially any music that encouraged dancers to feel compelled by the beat.[5] The recordings of Philadelphia International Records and its imitators dominated the early 1970s dance floors of New York's nascent gay discotheques, centering on a confluence of Black vocal styles, extended instrumental breaks, and Earl Young's trademark four-on-the-floor, off-beat-hi-hat drumming style. However, very often recordings that achieved great success on the dance floor and with DJs received almost no radio airplay and had little currency in mainstream popular culture.

But as gay bars and nightclubs in America's larger cities began replacing dated jukeboxes with live spinners, DJs in San Francisco's Mind Shaft (1973–1977), the Rendezvous (ca. 1962–1976), Oil Can Harry's (1976–1980), and the City Disco (1973–1980) found that they had the power to generate substantial interest in artists who had almost no presence on the radio. By 1975, disco had come to dominate the music scene in urban gay venues throughout the United States, and the influence wielded by these and other clubs' DJs lent them a celebrity status in the community. The sound, as manifested in San Francisco, ultimately derived its aesthetic from that city's unique configuration of places and people. Early gay DJs John Hedges and Marty Blecman at the Mind Shaft and the City Disco paved the way for legendary high energy DJs Bobby Viteritti at the Trocadero Transfer (1977–1996) and Steve Fabus at the I-Beam (1977–1994).

Eventually, many of these musicians would branch out into music production, extending their influence outside of the bay, with Megatone Records, Moby Dick Records, and other labels achieving worldwide success with San Francisco artists such as Sylvester, Patrick Cowley, Paul Parker, Lisa, Loverde, and Jolo, creating the world's first gay-owned, gay-produced music for a dancing audience. One of the most important of these early figures was John Hedges, who like many other Bay Area DJs was a transplant who came

DISCO, THE CASTRO, AND GAY LIBERATION   13

to San Francisco to be gay and found himself almost immediately involved in the burgeoning disco scene.

Johnny "Disco" Hedges

John Hedges had been into electronics and the technical side of music since childhood. In high school in Elyria, Ohio, in the late 1960s, he had built his own radio transmitter in his parents' garage where he broadcast a pirate radio station. The garage became like a clubhouse for friends from high school like Martin (known as Marty) Blecman, where they would goof off, get high, and talk music. After high school, Hedges started a music booking agency, J&J Attractions, with friend Jerry Gildemeister, hiring bands for local clubs in Cleveland, Detroit, and throughout Pennsylvania. The agency happened to book a rock band with Marty Blecman, and the two rekindled their close friendship (although neither knew the other was gay at the time). Hedges recalls meeting his future partner, Gerry McBride, at a local gay bar, Dante's Inferno, in 1971. Neither of them was out at the time, or even really aware of their sexuality:

> That gay bar called my agency to book a band so I booked in the best band we had. And I didn't know what a gay bar was. I didn't know what "gay" meant. I thought it was a happy bar. And when the band arrived there, we knew what was going on then. And later in the evening, Gerry arrived, and unfortunately for him, he was in the closet. He was friends with all the band members. So I kinda outed him. One of the band members introduced me to him and we hit it off right away.[6]

In the deeply closeted Midwest of 1971, serious long-term gay relationships just weren't something you heard about, but for Hedges and McBride, things clicked over potato chips:

> We went on to do rock concerts at the racetracks, and we'd do Sunday at "beautiful downtown," whatever speedway, and have big semi flatbed trucks. We'd pull them in and put the bands on them with all the equipment and stuff and people would come out and sit in the field or dance around to rock and roll, like little mini concerts outdoors. One of my sponsors of the event was Pringles Potato Chips, and they gave us a whole bunch of them

14   MENERGY

to give out to the kids in the audience. So we did, and I saw Jerry there, and I gave him some and I think he was tripping on acid. And I get back to the office and there's 35 minutes of him ranting and raving on how he wants to get together and I always thought it was cute.

The next day Hedges moved out of his apartment and in with Gerry. The relationship changed everything, giving them both newfound confidence and ambition, and over time Elyria started to feel too small; they felt trapped. McBride taught school in Kent, Ohio, but during a teachers' strike in 1973 he found himself cooling his heels, helping part time with Hedges's booking business. But that too was slow, and tension between Hedges and his business partner made the job less fun than it had been at first. Hedges made Gildemeister an offer to buy out the company. Gildemeister accepted, and Gerry and Johnny loaded up Gerry's Mustang and Johnny's Plymouth and headed to San Francisco. Theirs was a common story. Activist Peter Fisher had published his influential book *The Gay Mystique* a year earlier, which noted that gay people living in rural areas or in smaller cities "may never know that the gay world exists unless they happen to stumble on it, and even so their gay world is more likely to consist of a popular men's room than thirty or forty gay bars. They will find it infinitely more difficult to meet other homosexuals than anyone living in the city . . . Many conclude that the only solution is to leave home and move to the city."[7]

Although by 1973 the heyday of the 1960s counterculture had given way somewhat, cheap real estate and an affordable cost of living made San Francisco a good place for a young gay couple. Johnny and Gerry's first apartment, at 506 14th Street, placed them right in the center of the Castro neighborhood, right off Market. Hedges got a job fixing Baxton copy machines while McBride taught; both of them enjoyed the nightlife, which was unlike anything they had seen in Ohio. Although the Castro had yet to become the center of the gay scene, there were still several bars and cruising areas. Hedges recalls,

I took the car once we were settled and said "I'm gonna just drive around town to see what's going on." And I stumbled on Castro Street. I didn't know that was there. We didn't know anything about gay life, we just knew it was gay-friendly. And I got out, walked around, and the first place I walked in, this place called the Toad Hall [1971–1978] at 2:30 in the afternoon, it was packed, in the daytime. Holy crap, all these good-looking guys, like a kid in the candy store![8]

Just months before Hedges moved to San Francisco, Bob Damron had opened the Mind Shaft disco at 2140 Market (right around the corner from Hedges's flat). Dancing had been allowed on Sundays at the Rendezvous on the outskirts of the Polk Street district (also known as "Polk Gulch" or "Polkstrasse" by its habitués) at 567 Sutter since the owners won a legal case against the city, but the Mind Shaft in the Castro was central to the formation of that neighborhood as a new gay district (see figure 1.1).[9] Hedges was keen to get back into music, and approached the Mind Shaft's owner, Pat McAdams, about hiring him as a DJ. McAdams told him they weren't hiring, but if someone called in sick he'd let him know. "Well, somebody got sick," Hedges remembers. "I didn't have anything. I didn't bring all my records from Ohio. But I got it all together and borrowed this bit and that and made it through."[10] To come up with a more permanent solution to the record problem, Hedges made a deal with the bar owner, who gave him a monthly allowance to purchase records from Gramophone Records, the Castro's best dance music store, and he was soon working five nights a week, filling the club. The Mind Shaft had a huge gazebo in the middle of the building with lights on the top. "You had to step up into the gazebo to dance. And my little DJ booth was way up in the right-hand corner with a little hole, a square hole so I can see out."[11]

Marty Blecman

Marty Blecman, John Hedges's high school friend, had gone to college in Ohio after graduation. As a child, he had taken piano lessons and studied music theory in high school. While at the University of Ohio, he taught piano lessons, continued studying theory, and played keyboards in various dance rock bands.[12] But two things were to change his worldview. First, he recalls, "Rock 'n Roll was pushed aside after I contracted disco fever, an incurable obsession."[13] Perhaps more fundamentally, the introspection required of being a psychology major led to the realization that he was gay; he knew he needed the freedom of the West Coast. After a year's false start in Los Angeles working for Revlon Cosmetics, Blecman moved back to Ohio to run his father's grocery store. He soon tried the West Coast again, this time

Figure 1.1 Ad for Mind Shaft, from *Bay Area Reporter*, August 19, 1976. Reproduced with permission.

San Francisco, and moved in with Hedges and McBride, who by this time had acquired another housemate, budding gay comedian Danny Williams.[14] Hedges recalled, "He [Blecman] tracked me down in San Francisco and in a general discussion I said, 'Are you gay?,' and he goes, 'How did you know?' The rest is history."[15]

In the fall of 1975 Hedges left the Mind Shaft when the North Beach venue Cabaret reopened under new ownership as the City, and he got Blecman a job there doing lights on the main cabaret stage. The City's huge second-floor disco had an elevated DJ booth in the shape of an enormous 1950s jukebox, complete with state-of-the-art lighting and sound. It was here that Hedges, wearing his trademark cowboy hat and referred to by most people in the scene as Johnny "Disco" Hedges since he began writing a regular disco column in the weekly *Kalendar* newspaper, forged a signature sound based on tight mixing of soulful vocals and intense percussion. His reputation at the City grew to such an extent that he won the first San Francisco DJ of the Year award from *Billboard* magazine in 1976. At the time, the City, with its ground-floor cabaret and upstairs disco, was San Francisco's largest gay venue for sophisticated live entertainment, a format owner Tom Sanford had tested first in Marin County on a much smaller scale at his venue, the Woods.[16] Sanford, who at one time also owned the Castro bar Toad Hall, had a prickly attitude toward disco, DJs, and the music industry in general, with a hefty ego to boot. There were certain artists he would not allow DJs to play, he felt that DJs played the music too loud ("I have a feeling they are all partly deaf anyway, by choice"), and he had little time for the annual *Billboard* Disco Forum: "I don't think it's beneficial for anyone to go. You would think that after five tries, *Billboard* would have it together."[17] It was undoubtedly this attitude that led Sanford to refuse to give Hedges time off to attend the *Billboard* awards ceremony in New York.

Hedges realized that while he was considered a hero to many gay dancers, the reality of disco's unstoppable expansion into the mainstream meant that growing numbers of straight clubgoers had a different set of priorities than his underground fans. The shift at the City toward a straighter crowd, who preferred popular radio hits, frustrated Hedges because he felt unable to explore the sounds that had originally established his reputation. Sanford's powerplay over the *Billboard* award was the final straw, and when Hedges was approached by rival club Oil Can Harry's in the Polk neighborhood, he leapt at the chance to go where he would be returning to a gay crowd and management that was interested in creating a disco with its own identity.

18 MENERGY

Hedges had recently visited 12 West in New York, where he saw legendary DJ Jim Burgess spin using two variable-speed turntables connected by a mixer. Hedges was desperate to try it himself, and he convinced Oil Can Harry's to install new Technics turntables and a booth enclosed in glass.

Loverde

While disco dancing as a club format was growing exponentially in the mid-1970s, live entertainment venues still maintained a link to the traditions of a recent gay past. When Marty Blecman began working at the City, the ground floor's cabaret saw most of the major artists on the national cabaret scene pass through, including Charles Pierce, Gotham, Eartha Kitt, and prominent local acts like Sylvester, usually featuring an up-and-coming Bay Area group as his opener. One of the most popular of these local bands was Loverde. Made up of three singers (Frank Loverde, Linda Imperial, and Peggy Gibbons) and an ever-changing five-piece band, Loverde started as a conventional cabaret act, singing covers of old favorites, such as girl group songs, greatest hits of the 1950s, and show tunes. But within the crowded world of live cabaret in San Francisco, Loverde stood out for two reasons: Lead singer Frank Loverde had smoldering good looks and his two backup singers projected just the right amount of camp self-awareness for the City's primarily gay audience.

Frank Loverde was born in Los Angeles in 1947, but while still a teenager made his way to New York. There he DJed at chichi club Opus, run by his friend, Nino DePaulo, and at Yellowfingers on the Upper East Side, the club credited by some as ushering in the 1960s French-influenced discotheque craze.[18] When DePaulo moved from New York to St. Louis to take over the management of Chavala, the "hottest nightclub in town," set up by wealthy entrepreneur Harold Koplar, owner of the high-end Chase Park Plaza hotel, Frank came with him as the new club's resident DJ.[19]

Linda Imperial worked at Chavala as a go-go dancer while still a senior in high school (although her title, she remembers with a smirk, was "dance interpreter"). Wearing a leotard and a Spanish hat, she projected a sensuous silhouette on each wall; her figure made her lack of dance experience irrelevant. Or so she thought. One night she came up to Loverde, who had just put a catchy James Brown tune on, and asked him, "Can't you play anything I can dance to?" Needless to say, his initial reaction was not positive. Still, her infectious high spirits and love of music and singing drew them together, ultimately creating a powerful friendship.

This was cemented when Linda started dating Frank's best friend, Ricardo (who she eventually married). After several months of singing together for fun, they decided to form a performing group, naming themselves "Loverde." When Linda finished high school, the three of them packed their bags and moved to Los Angeles, helped again by DePaulo, who by this time was managing a small restaurant, the Green Café, near Melrose and San Vicente. Loverde gained experience in small clubs, with Frank on guitar and Linda singing. Before long, Linda's sister Anne joined them on vocals. They made some good connections and good friends, including Danny Strayhorn, nephew of jazz musician Billy Strayhorn, who was working as a choreographer on NBC's *Flip Wilson Show*.

Eventually, after a few years, a failed marriage, and a brutal mugging, which despite putting three of her assailants in the hospital left Imperial with a jaw broken in three places and a mouth wired shut for months, Danny Strayhorn convinced them that their destiny lay in San Francisco. So in 1973, Frank, Linda, and Danny moved to a rundown flat in the Haight-Ashbury district (Anne returned to St. Louis). Frank and Linda recruited a new permanent singer, Peggy Gibbons, and added occasional supplemental singers. This new Loverde began performing on the cabaret circuit in the Bay Area, with Strayhorn acting as their manager.

As well as playing supporting gigs for Sylvester at the Elephant Walk (1975–1988) in the Castro and the City Cabaret, they survived by accepting anything that came their way, including debutante parties, weddings, and birthdays. These first professional San Francisco gigs got off to a bumpy start, when an initial review praised Frank's "smooth, resonant voice . . . charming personality and exceptional good looks," but felt the singer, "under the direction of Dan Strayhorn . . . is continually in competition with three backup girl singers, a too-loud five-piece rock combo, unvarying arrangements that begin to sound like variations on one theme and an act geared more to a hard-sell black disco singer than a vocally smooth rock stylist."[20] The odd juxtaposition for this reviewer of "black disco" and "rock stylist" (i.e., white rock), however, captured part of the appeal for their largely white cabaret audience. Few actual male Black artists were "allowed" in the gay cabaret scene, and Loverde provided a safe entre for slumming straight and more conservative gay audiences.

20 MENERGY

Before long Loverde became a popular fixture in the gay arts scene, garnering positive reviews in the press. One notice observed that "The crowd loved them! . . . The women need a bit of tightening up when it comes to appearing before such an audience as found in the Castro, but the man, honey-baby, he was a hit from the moment he opened his mouth and smiled."[21] Their reputation only grew after Strayhorn got them an extended contract opening for Dionne Warwick in Las Vegas and in Reno/Tahoe for Harrah's casino. Upon their return to San Francisco in 1977, the mainstream press for the first time acknowledged the importance of this "gay" group, with a glowing review in the *San Francisco Chronicle* and a mention in *Billboard* calling them a "very hip act."[22] They remained behind-the-scenes players in the burgeoning disco scene until the early 1980s, when they began an influential post-disco career, forming a central part of the San Francisco sound.

Disco's Increasing Importance in Gay San Francisco Life

Change was found all over San Francisco's three primary gay neighborhoods (the Castro, Polk Street, and South of Market [SoMa]), as disco's popularity continued to grow in the mid-1970s. SoMa maintained its connection to San Francisco's gay bathhouse and leather community, with the historic Fe-Be's (1966–1986), the Brig (1979–1980), the Stud (1966–2020), and dozens of others, but also saw several discos open in the mid- and late 1970s, including the long-running Endup (1973–present) at 401 6th Street, Arena (1979–1985), and Ambush (1973–1986).

Polk Street

The Polk neighborhood, which by the mid-1960s eclipsed North Beach as the center of gay nightlife, catered to a relatively diverse gay clientele, despite numerous attempts at gentrification. Situated near the marginalized Tenderloin neighborhood, which in 1966 had seen an uprising by young queens, transgender sex workers, and hustlers at Compton's Cafeteria, Polk Gulch historically featured a mix of venues, from live folk music at the Palms (1976–1978), drag shows at the nearby Gilded Cage (1961–1969), and dive bars like the New Bell Saloon (1951–1988). Nevertheless, gay businesses in the Polk neighborhood energetically threw themselves into the disco fray.

DISCO, THE CASTRO, AND GAY LIBERATION   21

Oil Can Harry's opened in September 1976 at 709 Larkin, where Bojangles was previously located (ca. 1970–1976). As early as 1972, Bojangles (initially advertised as "San Francisco's first Gay Black nightclub"[23]) had offered dancing to "taped sounds and psychedelic lights," but Los Angeles's Oil Can Harry's, which advertised itself as LA's oldest disco, spared no expense in the opening of its San Francisco branch over Labor Day weekend.[24] It was such a success that within six months, the owners, Dan Turner and Bob Charot, invested in a major expansion. They enlarged the dance floor (the largest in the city at the time) and installed a raised back bar twenty feet above the dance floor, a computer-controlled lighting system, and a new sound system.[25] Several grand chandeliers and floor-to-ceiling mirrors completed the significant improvements, further demonstrating the "classing up" of disco as a genre and of the disco itself as a sophisticated venue.[26] One onlooker to the line of more than one thousand patrons waiting to get into the grand reopening noted with pride the "decorum" of the crowd, which in the Polk neighborhood was certainly code for the overwhelming whiteness of the patrons and a demonstration of how, as in the Castro, disco was seen as a gentrifying influence on so-called undesirable areas.[27]

Buzzby's (1974–1986), at 1436 Polk Street, installed a new sound system in July 1976 for their Saturday- and Sunday-night DJ, Christine Matuchek, one of the few women DJs on the gay disco scene. And in July 1977 they enhanced the dancing area for her with a space-age metal dance floor.[28] The N'Touch (1974–1982), at 1548 Polk Street, was getting into the act too, opening a new disco with "the newest most exciting light show in the world today."[29] In the gay press, praise was heaped on the N'Touch's Luscious Lorelei, who, with the renovations, had "really done a trip."[30]

The Castro and the Emergence of the Castro Clone

Despite Polk Street's attempts to stay up-to-date, however, attention was quickly shifting to the formerly straight Eureka Valley, now rebranded as the Castro neighborhood. In the summer of 1971 alone, four gay bars were added to the three already there, and the flamboyant Castro Street Fair, first held in 1974, signaled the changing demographic.[31] The new residents of the Castro, like Polk Street, were never a monolithic cultural block, but rather contained a complex mix of working class "art fags," older "assimilationist" men and women in the professional classes, and remnants of the

22 MENERGY

counterculture, including the "genderfuck" drag scene as embodied by the Cockettes' splinter group Angels of Light, Scrumbly Koldwyn, Kreema Ritz, and to some extent singer Sylvester. But by far the largest population of gay men in the Castro came to be known as "Castro clones." One typical Castro clone bar, The Balcony (1977-1983) (or "The Bal ony" as the sign usually read, leading to many silly jokes) was described at the time as the place "where Castro Street meets Folsom Street, where the t-shirt-clad 'All American Boys' rub elbows with the heavy leather crowd, where motorcycles line the curb along with Karmann-Ghias, where taxi cabs jerk to a stop to load and unload cars full of dancing 'hot' men on their way to and from the local boogie palaces."[32] Novelist (and erstwhile clone) Andrew Holleran efficiently defined the hypermasculine look of the subculture as "a male homosexual in his twenties or thirties . . . who . . . travelled in packs with other clones, had short dark hair, a short dark moustache, and wore levis, work shoes, plaid shirt, and bomber jacket over a hooded sweatshirt. The jeans were faded and sometimes frayed in strategic places. Dark glasses were aviator-style and occasionally mirrored."[33] The emergence of the clone type was gradual, but by the mid-1970s it dominated the public's perception of the gay community in the Castro, largely ignoring the established gay spots on Polk Street, which held onto its preclone atmosphere, despite the presence of discos like Bojangles, N'Touch, and Buzzby's.

The transformation of the Castro is remarkable for its speed. Peter Groubert arrived in the Castro in 1969 and observed,

> It was a quiet little neighborhood. There were some other gay bars right in the neighborhood but they were different. The Pendulum [1970–2005] had a black clientele. There was a bar called the Mistake [ca. 1968–1976] down on 18th just past Noe. . . . A bar called Toad Hall opened up supposedly for long-hairs. . . . They changed from bright lights and flashing psychedelia to much more toned down earthy kind of things with the mushrooms and gnomes.[34]

But within five years, that counterculture vibe had gone. "Machismo was no longer fashionable, it was ubiquitous," recalls Randy Shilts. "Few hippies walked the streets any more; the hair was kept closely cropped a la Korean War era . . . The dress was decidedly butch, as if God had dropped these men naked and commanded them to wear only straight-legged levis, plaid Pendleton shirts, and leather coats over hooded sweatshirts."[35] Toad Hall got a dance license in 1977 (after an earlier failed attempt) and installed a dance floor and a new light and sound system in time for their big Halloween reopening. One commentator observed about Toad Hall's remodel that "the time is ripe for Castro Street to have a dance alternative. Considering all the sexual energy that's evident, it's good to know that there's a place to work it out (or work up to it)."[36] December also saw the opening of Moby Dick's (1977–present) in the Castro, which, while not a disco, featured a huge 240-gallon saltwater aquarium behind the bar.[37] "I moved to Florida in the winter of '74–'75," ex-Cockette Kreema Ritz remembers, "and when I returned, the second half of the decade had begun—grocery stores had turned into bars and bathhouses. Then I noticed all these men with mustaches, and I thought, where are all these people coming from?"[38]

The clone identity emerged in New York City and San Francisco at roughly the same time, and quickly spread to other large cities in the United States and Europe, and could be broken down, according to Martin P. Levine, into "the 4 D's": disco, drugs, dish, and dick. One contemporary description of a night out seems to articulate all these elements: "As the night passes and gets crazier, alcohol and drugs take command and the odor of poppers permeates the air . . . It's where San Francisco's gay 'night people' bid farewell to the new day as they swagger home from over-nights at the baths and the late, late dance clubs. Disco music pierces the morning. Poppers get passed around almost carelessly, and the gropers grope their hearts out."[39] Levine experienced clone life as a profound reaction against earlier modes of homosexual sociability, which he articulates as based on three characteristics: passing, minstrelization, and capitulation. For him, "the gay world of the sixties functioned as a deviant subculture. This symbolic world constituted a relatively 'impoverished cultural unit'. . . primarily designed to facilitate social and sexual contacts and the management of stigma."[40] Both passing (presenting yourself as indistinguishable from your heterosexual counterpart) and capitulation (the acceptance of mainstream society's approbation of homosexuality, manifesting itself as self-loathing and shame) are emblematic of a time when gay people had little say in the construction of their own gay identity. Minstrelization, as described by Levine, was exemplified in gay circles through camp, an exaggerated femininity that parodied mainstream culture's image of homosexuality. In the 1960s, camp was the primary gay mode of protesting stigma, but fundamentally retained the dominant society's image of gayness as shameful, parodic, and inauthentic. This made camp the target of early gay liberationists, many of whom read it as reactionary.

24 MENERGY

The clone look however, with its stereotyped hypermasculine appearance, was created "in part as a new kind of camp . . . and in part as a vigorous assertion of a newfound, and passionately embraced successful masculinity."[41] This assertion wasn't without its contradictions, however, as it derived its power from an acceptance of mainstream society's privileging of a rigid definition of masculinity, giving gay men much-needed self-confidence by "expressing a more valued identity."[42] Gay men's susceptibility to this is convincingly described by C. A. Tripp as "the symbolic possession of those attributes of a partner which, when added to one's own, fill out the illusion of completeness."[43] Or, more bluntly, in the words of Brandon Judell, "by mixing your juices with someone attired in a flannel shirt, carrying a drill, or clad in a leather jacket, their manliness is rubbing off on you and in you."[44]

The Four D's: Disco

For some gay men, the disco phenomenon prompted soul-searching. In 1978, national gay magazine *The Alternate*, after observing that the gay disco is a "unique seventies environment for the gay person, an activity that becomes part of our lifestyle," posed the following questions:

> Beyond the general "why do we go there?" there are other questions. Within the gay person there's a reason for disco madness. Does the disco serve a positive function in our community? Are discos merely an outlet? Are we looking for something that's never gonna come along? Why is it such a big deal to talk to someone or ask somebody to dance? . . . Does disco fever support alcoholism and drug abuse?[45]

Bruce Voeller, gay activist and director of the National Gay Task Force, understood the central role gay people played in the popularization of disco music, writing in 1976 that "the gay population has a continuing important influence on the creative arts in this country, especially visible in the field of popular music; and, in particular, in the disco phenomenon, gay tastes in music are being picked up by the rest of the community."[46] It's telling that disco music was perceived as a universal gay phenomenon, rather than a specifically Black one within the gay community, and that the production of the music itself wasn't the important thing, but rather the act of dancing to it in distinct gay venues. This represents continuity with a preliberation idea of the gay bar as refuge, as safe space. Discos are just gay bars made public, made extrovert, or, as Wayne Sage wrote in 1976, "discos are gay bars gone happy . . . as gayness has become more socially acceptable, gay entertainment has come out of the closet and into the public's eye where it is enjoyed more by the gays themselves and by the straights who accept them."[47]

At the heart of gay people's appreciation for disco was a connection felt, an identification with, "the beat." Danae, a DJ at the New York disco Flamingo, remembered the time "someone came up to me, all excited and said, 'You were fucking me with your music! Do me a favor, fuck me again with your music.' I took it as a great compliment."[48] This personification of the beat as polyvalent sexual partner, nurturing mother, symbol of individual strength, and communal power, confronted contemporary activists as they tried to understand disco's appeal. Richard Dearborn, pondering the place of the gay liberation movement in the larger realm of civil rights, felt that, "It is their beat. The gay civil rights movement has eclipsed both the black and women's civil rights causes. We are the ones on the move and we boogie down the street during our gay day parades to disco, the most upbeat, happy, and positive musical idiom to come along since the '50s. . . . There is a driving need on the part of gay people to openly express these feelings, and they are doing so on the dance floor of discos from coast to coast to coast."[49]

Dearborn's implicit assumption that the ethnicity of the gay dancer doesn't matter denies the intersectionality of many gay participants but accurately observes the united use of African American music in nearly all gay male dance spaces in the first half of the 1970s. And it wasn't only the music itself that drew upon Black sources in the minds of contemporaries. The "gay boogie," as it was described in Patricia Nell Warren's influential novel *The Front Runner* in 1974, was a melding of the age-old racist assumption of Black uninhibited libido with a new, macho gay energy: "The gay who is a good dancer can turn even the foxtrot into an uninhibited celebration of male sexuality. Billy and Vince . . . were dancing like blacks. They were loose, cool, with all the foot-stomping and finger snapping that goes with it. Their shoulders and torsos barely moved. All the action was in the hip-jerking, the crotch-gyrating, the buttock-twitching and the thigh-weaving."[50]

Walter Hughes, writing in the 1990s, reaffirmed the visceral quality of the beat and its centrality in the construction of gay male desire: "Disco foregrounds the beat, makes it consistent, simple, repetitive. . . . Disco has the power to recreate the self because the beat embodies desire . . . It is said that one 'feels' the throbbing beat inside one's body, rather than merely

26   MENERGY

hearing it."[51] Endup dancer and Castro clone Dan Vojir described this physicality in his memoirs: "Disco music . . . has a pounding, driving force that evokes both my sensuality and my ego. . . . The urge to strain the body's limits seemed to pour out of me, just like the sweat. The sweat. I remember it all too vividly. It engulfed me, sheets of it running down my chest, my back, my legs . . . Maybe in that state of dripping exhaustion one seems more sensual, more alive."[52]

Vojir is hinting at an essential truth here about the nature of dancing to disco for gay men of his generation. Dancing evokes sensuality, while at the same time offers a cathartic experience of "realness," a state of being that expresses a fundamental reality about one's identity usually kept hidden or sublimated. Disco gave gay men (and anyone else with the need to let loose) permission to show themselves, for at least the length of a song.

The Four D's: Drugs

Robin Tichane's memories of his initiation into Castro life in 1974 positions drugs as central to clone culture: "I just plunged right in. Hot guys everywhere, the Castro Clone. I had my lumberjack shirt, it was the mustache. . . . My gay identity was emerging. I think everybody in the '70s did their black beauties, their what was then called MDA which is now called Ecstasy . . . From 5:30 when I got up until about 6:30, that was work, and then I would go out several nights a week, meeting a lot of people."[53]

Two types of drugs were widely used: First, psychedelic drugs (which had become largely passé in straight culture) were a legacy of the counterculture, but found a second home in the hyperstimulating world of the gay disco. Second, late-night partying encouraged the use of amphetamines and other kinds of "up" drugs as the only way to keep going all night. In June 1977, DJ Marty Blecman described his experience of New York gay discos and his loving account affirms the symbiotic relationship between disco and drugs: "New York DJs do have their act together and give the crowds 'a trip' of musical blending, overlays and special effects. Audience participation is at a frenzy with people whooping, stomping, screaming, and basically letting loose some high energy dancing! Most of the clubs open about midnight and start to really cook about one or two a.m. . . . It seems drugs are the high and alcohol the background. Picture a thousand people stoned out on Vitamin Q

[Quaaludes], poppers, pot, dust [PCP], and anything else that will keep them screaming until the sun comes up."[54]

In San Francisco, different bars and their music inspired the use of different drugs. For bargoer Benji Rubenstein, the Stud in SoMa was "Quaalude heaven."[55] He remembers, "I used to love them. My nickname in San Francisco was 'Ro'; they used to call me Ro." Rorer was the pharmaceutical company that produced Quaaludes, Rorer 714.[56] A night at the high-energy after-hours bar Trocadero Transfer, however, was fueled by methamphetamines and cocaine. At the I-Beam in the Haight district, dancer Emmet recalled taking MDA and magic mushrooms. He told a reporter at the time that "the whole dance floor stopped to watch him and his partner. They were letting off this energy; they were energizing the whole disco."[57]

Poppers were stimulants that had been ubiquitous on gay dance floors since the 1960s. Alkyl nitrites are a family of vasodilators (blood vessel expanders) used since the nineteenth century for heart patients and those suffering from cyanide overdose. Originally, the drug was dispensed in glass ampules that would be broken ("popped") and placed under the nose, but by the 1960s it was most often sold in small brown bottles that could be unscrewed on the dance floor and sniffed. The effect on the user was, according to a contemporary account in the gay press, "to lower their inhibitions, produce an attack of ravenous lust, or create a temporary suspension of their sense of identity."[58] Many serious disco-goers had metal popper inhalers that hung on a chain around their necks while dancing. Inside, cotton absorbed the liquid, and the dancer could unscrew the cap and sniff to get a quick rush. Although amyl nitrite was the original "popper," in 1969 the US Food and Drug Administration switched its classification to "prescription only," making it much more difficult to get. Poppers manufacturers, such as "Rush" out of San Francisco, switched to other kinds of alkyl nitrites that gave similar effects, such as butyl nitrite and isopropyl nitrite, but without some of the potential side effects. One user recalled amyl nitrite's risks compared to later formulations, particularly how "you'd get burns on your nose if you spilt it. Those were serious; these here are far tamer."[59]

Like the disco craze itself, the mainstream was late to the poppers game. In 1978, *Time* magazine ran a scarifying profile of the drug, which they called "the newest cheap kick for increasing numbers of people."[60] Far from being new, poppers were, for a generation of gay men, as integral to the dancing experience as the music itself.

28 MENERGY

The Four D's: Dish, Dick

Richard Dearborn's encomium of clone cruising encapsulates the joys of the pursuit: "At any bar or disco, everyone watches and everyone gets watched. Those watching are being watched while someone else is watching them watch. 'Who's Watching the Watcher?' Patti Labelle asks . . . It happens every night. Though it can be intimidating, it is fun to rise to the occasion. So when you get that look, feel free to give it right back because, after all, we are the mirror images of each other. Who said it wasn't any fun sleeping with yourself?"[61]

The act of cruising is inherently social, a celebration of sexual freedom that Alex Espinoza, in his study of the activity, calls "unabashedly gay and revolutionary."[62] Despite the macho posturing associated with clone culture, the central act of "dishing," or the campy collective act of gossiping with friends (who one may or may not know outside of the bar scene) went hand in hand with cruising. But cruising has historically been one of the central functions of the gay bar, certainly not something invented by the clone. Inside any gay bar, as sociologist Martin Hoffman observed,

> The patrons who are sitting at the bar itself usually face away from the bar and look toward the other people in the room and toward the door. When a new patron walks in, he receives a good deal of scrutiny, and people engaged in conversation with each other just naturally assume that their interlocutors will turn away from them to watch each new entering patron. All this, is, of course, part of the pervasive looking and cruising which goes on in the bar.[63]

The purpose of dishing in a gay bar evolved over time; initially, gossiping with bar friends, other gay men who were "in the life," served an essential networking function. Bar friends could dish the latest places to go, exchange gossip about fellow bargoers, and offer advice about jobs or places to live. Sociologist Evelyn Hooker's perception of gay men's ability to almost magically convey information with just a glance now reads as hilarious:

> If one watches very carefully, and knows what to watch for in a "gay" bar, one observes that some individuals are apparently communicating with each other without exchanging words, but simply by exchanging glances— but not the kind of quick glance which ordinarily occurs between men. It is

DISCO, THE CASTRO, AND GAY LIBERATION   29

said by homosexuals that if another catches and holds the glance, one need know nothing more about him to know that he is one of them.[64]

But as Hooker observed about the function of dish in the 1950s and 1960s, "They are also, paradoxically enough, security operations."[65] In a time when raids and arrest were common, dishing allowed men to share information about dangerous hustlers, informers, and suspected vice officers. Even as gay establishments became less stigmatized, one aspect of dishing remained; as an opportunity to, in Donald Webster Cory's words from 1951, "Let down their hair, to have a slow beer as they talk, joke, gossip, and gesticulate," and repeated in Hooker's language, sixteen years later, to, " 'let down their hair'— that is take off their protective masks, use their in-group language, discuss intimate details of their sexual lives, and 'camp.' "[66]

Despite cruising's reputation as a solitary activity, in the Castro in the 1970s, where for the first time in history cruising could be done in the open, it became a spectator sport. Tichane recalled how in the Castro, "Every night was a madhouse. Every night at two o'clock. This was for several years, the end of '72, '73, '74, '75, '76, '77. Two o'clock, Castro Street basically closed. Traffic couldn't pass. Hundreds of people from the bars out in the street."[67] Twenty-four-hour bathhouses also offered a continuation of the hunt after hours, albeit one for which the art of the chase was largely unnecessary. Even here, dish could be an important element of the culture. As George Heymont reminisced in 1983, "To this day I have fond memories of eavesdropping on a heated debate over the art of [Austrian soprano] Leonie Rysanek which took place in a darkened orgy room at the Folsom Street Barracks [1972–1976]."[68]

For some in the Castro, despite all the negativity surrounding the term, the label "clone" was embraced as a campy in-group identifier. In August 1978, for example, someone proudly put a "Welcome to the Clone Village" sign on Cliff's Variety Store.[69] But clones didn't exist entirely without conflict within the gay community, most vocally between the more politically active gays and those who were perceived to be just there to party. One of the most prominent distinctions between these two classes, and it seemed like you either fell onto one side or the other, was between punk and disco. In December 1977, the music reviewer for San Francisco gay political magazine *The Alternate* gave the *Saturday Night Fever* soundtrack one star while giving the Sex Pistols' newest effort four.[70] An antidisco columnist in the *Bay Area Reporter* lampooned clones when he noted that,

30   MENERGY

You'll be delighted to learn about another new euphemism given to those dudes who fight the battle of the little brown bottles at the Trocadero Transfer on weekend nights only to be called the "Troc-La-Dites" when they invade the 6am bars on Sat and Sun Mornings . . . likewise the disco queens who have the irresistible urge to swish those silver fans around at the I-Beam and the Troc are being called "Gay-sha Boys"—serious consideration is being given to ban those silver fans because one lady patron got a serious eye injury from an over-enthusiastic fanny, er, uh, fanner.[71]

The "Four D's" were a distillation of many elements already present in gay bar culture. But in the 1970s, gay men were given the freedom to participate in a subculture that was "about" gayness, one that was immediately identifiable among themselves, but, perhaps more important, recognizable to the outside world without shame.

2

Liberation for Some

The Continued Expansion of Gay San Francisco in the Late 1970s

Throughout the 1970s, gay people poured into San Francisco. As DJ Steve Fabus recalls, "So many people were coming here from everywhere and it was like a calling or something . . . People don't realize how much San Francisco was Mecca at that time."[1] Against the backdrop of this cathartic and liberating pilgrimage, concern was growing both within and without over the perceived racism and classism of the new San Francisco transplants. The example of long-established working-class communities being priced out of their own neighborhoods by middle- and upper-class newcomers is the classic model of gentrification, and on the surface this was what occurred in the Castro; the replacement of a racially diverse, largely heterosexual working-class population by a largely white gay middle and professional class one, and much of the tension arose because of the cultural distance between these two communities. The Italian American families of the Castro and the traditionally African American population of the Western Addition found themselves not only priced out of their neighborhoods but also confronted with a growing demographic they often resented as working against their interests.

The gay communities, for their part, struggled throughout the decade to achieve some measure of political power, and it was this conflict that can be read in Dan White's assassination of Harvey Milk and Mayor George Moscone in 1978 as a brutal lashing out against these cultural changes.[2] This chapter explores the more problematic aspects of clone culture against the continued growth of that scene's power. For some, the creation of new dance palaces and the emergence of a new phenomenon, the "megaparty," was the ultimate manifestation of sexual liberation through music and dancing. For others, it was the embodiment of all that was materialistic, shallow, and exclusionary about San Francisco's clone culture.

Menergy. Louis Niebur, Oxford University Press. © Oxford University Press 2022.
DOI: 10.1093/oso/9780197511077.003.0003

32 MENERGY

Gentrification and Racism in Clone Culture

Idaree Westbrook, program chair of the San Francisco Black Leadership Forum, wrote in a memo in early 1979 that, "Gays buy apartment buildings in the Western Addition, fix them up, and raise the rents so high that poor people cannot stay in neighborhoods they have grown up in. It's nice to fix apartments up. But you Gays don't give them to families, you give them to other Gays."[3] The Forum commissioned a report that brought up several issues related to relations between gays and Blacks in San Francisco. First, gay white men were exercising white privilege by taking out loans that were frequently denied to Black residents. Second, the Forum felt that "when the movement of Gays into previously Black neighborhoods is accompanied by a rhetoric . . . which equates the oppression of Blacks with the suppression of homosexuality, racial insult is added to white male arrogance."[4] The work to prevent Proposition 6 (which would have prompted the firing of gay teachers) from becoming law should have heightened the political consciousness of gay men, but for the most part gay men compartmentalized their struggle as separate from other minority groups.

Finally, the committee felt that gays were "being used as the leading edge of a quiet redevelopment plan geared toward driving non-white and poor out of increasingly white and wealthy San Francisco."[5] The city's gay Board of Permit Appeals president David Scott argued in defense of gays, who he said were "investing" rather than "speculating," since "investment is adding improvements and thus genuine value." He believed straight couples were fleeing the city's high crime and poor schools, while gays were "willing to take risks straight couples are not."[6]

For many gay Black men, the growth of the Castro Village as a gay center saw an unwelcome return to precounterculture segregation, and the kind of class-based culture absent from gay Polk Street. Musician Blackberri recalls his frustration over what he calls the "cliqueishness" of the Castro. "That's why I hung out in the Tenderloin and at the Polk Gulch, because it was more integrated, and you had the street scene. You couldn't afford to go drinking in bars, it was too expensive, the clubs had dress codes."[7] For gay Black patrons of the Castro, particularly those participating in clone culture, their intersectionality made life especially complex.

Gay Black clone Kurt Lawson grew up in Sacramento, where he learned to DJ. By his early twenties he was out and a friendship with fellow gay DJ Lester Temple got him a job spinning at the city's largest gay club, the Hawaiian

Hut in West Sacramento. The club had a DJ booth in a diesel semi cab and a lighted dance floor (in the years before *Saturday Night Fever* made that famous). On the weekends, he would meet up with several friends after the bars closed at 2:00 a.m. and either drive or take the Greyhound the ninety minutes to San Francisco. After getting a locker at the bus station and doing a quick costume change, the first stop was the Castro for a bit of cruising, then they would head over to the Trocadero Transfer to dance until closing, usually around 9:00 a.m., at which point they would continue dancing at the Endup until noon and stop in at a bar for a cocktail before driving home and collapsing.

For men of color, clone culture was just as rigidly enforced. "There's a whole different wardrobe for Castro," Lawson recalls. "You always had to take extra clothes with you and extra shoes. I'd wear my boots, my Levi's of course, and a shirt to match. Sunglasses, of course, and a hat for afterwards. I wouldn't be the only one. Most of the Greyhound buses would be 80% full of faggots."[8] But race was always an issue in the clone bars of San Francisco. Certain clubs, such as Badlands (1975–2020), were understood to be "notoriously racist places."[9] "That was real touchy," he remembers. "Back when I first started going out, I would have to have a white person with me to get into any of the bars. That's how it was, three pieces of ID. Until they got to know you. And I made that a quest to get to know everyone so I wouldn't have to go through that."[10]

Chrysler Sheldon remembers when fellow Black gay DJ Timmy Rivers was spinning at the Mind Shaft and needed a substitute for the night. He approached manager Pat McAdams about filling in and was told "two n****** will never play at the Mind Shaft."[11] "Club owners were afraid their club would 'go Black' if they had a Black disc jockey," Sheldon explains. "They built Oil Can Harry's with white lights and said Black people could not go there. You had to show three pieces of picture ID. It was a white gay club."[12]

In July 1977, the Mind Shaft in the Castro briefly closed and emerged a few weeks later renamed Alfie's (1977–1983).[13] Despite a successful reopening bash hosted by drag artist Pearl Heart, there were some issues with breaking in new DJs.[14] Nevertheless, Alfie's soon packed the dance floor and was even more popular than before, but it reflected the gentrification of the Castro. One commentator noticed the new crowd was markedly more white: "All I'm wondering about is where all our black brothers are now going to dance."[15] Lawson remembers, "You had to be with your white friend to get into Alfie's.

34   MENERGY

It was hard to get in there, for a Black man ... That's why they had Black clubs back then like the Pendulum."[16]

Eventually, Lawson began working at the Pendulum and was one of the only Black DJs at the club. In fact, despite the presence of dozens of gay clubs, he, Rivers, Chrysler, Don Miley, Chico Starr, and Roc Sands were practically the only DJs of color in gay San Francisco nightlife in the 1970s and 1980s. Ironically, Lawson's music at the Pendulum explored more "white" high-energy music than the traditional R&B the club had been known for: "When I first started working there, it was totally Black. It was 2% white, the rest Black, and by the time I left there it was half and half. My music brought in a totally different crowd, because every once in a while I'd throw on a country and western, like a popular one that everyone knows. I got heat for it, but I did it anyway. I'm the one who played the high energy stuff, and weird stuff. I'd put on a ballet in a heartbeat."[17] To Chrysler Sheldon, SoMa and the leather crowd on Folsom Street was always more welcoming to Black men than the other crowds, especially the Castro clones.

The I-Beam and Trocadero Transfer

Despite being the center of clone culture, it's perhaps surprising that the Castro didn't contain a single large discotheque. As a sign of the neighborhood's increasing gentrification, even considering the omnipresence of cruise bars and smaller venues for dancing, throughout the second half of the 1970s the Castro Planning Commission consistently refused permission to open any larger venues.[18] In late 1977, two clubs would open outside of the Castro that redefined what a disco could be, prioritizing for the first time the experience of dancers over simply providing a cruising space. The Trocadero Transfer, an after-hours club in SoMa, and the I-Beam in the Haight-Ashbury district quickly developed a following for their DJs and the unique family atmosphere they created, despite being outside the Castro.

William "Rod" Roderick helped design Alfie's sound system in the Castro and was recruited to work on both the I-Beam and the Trocadero Transfer. The clubs' sound and lighting systems massively raised the bar in a town that took dancing and disco music very seriously. In the winter of 1977 he told a local gay rag that:

The sound system there [the Trocadero Transfer] and I-Beam is going to cause other people to upgrade their systems. If you stand on the dance floor, it vibrates through your feet, right up to your crotch. If you don't start dancing, you're going to get a hard-on.... With the I-Beam, owners are discovering that people are willing to pay to go to a nice place. Going back into the history of gay bars in San Francisco they used to be very insecure. You were lucky if you had some toilet somebody opened for you. It might have been raided at any moment, and that was the end of it, and so they were really careful. With the opening of The City, and Dale Bentley doing the Club Baths, that major investment is safe and makes money.[19]

The I-Beam shook up the status quo with its location in the Haight-Ashbury District. At 1748 Haight Street, in an old Masonic Hall, the club sat right in the heart of what had been the counterculture less than ten years earlier. Since those days, however, the neighborhood had fallen into disrepair, and if the sidewalks were no longer filled with junkies to the extent they had been in the early 1970s, the area hadn't yet received the attention of gentrifiers. But by the fall of 1977, there were seven gay bars in the Haight, prompting some to wonder if it wasn't on track to become the new Castro.[20]

Businessman Bob Wharton and astrophysicist Sanford Kellman invested in an impressive sound system for the I-Beam's 2,200-square-foot dance floor, including Crown amplifiers and three Technics variable-speed turntables, but the real attraction was the custom lighting. Kellman tapped into his interest in all things celestial and had slide projections of stars, planets, galaxies, and other space-related photographs reflected by strobes, floor chaser, and spotlights throughout the club.[21] Despite this, the I-Beam almost wasn't allowed to open at all. After testing the waters with an invitation-only party in the space, the owners received so many noise complaints the city forced them to invest in costly noise reduction insulation in the old building before it was allowed to open. "They found out that it was little more than a huge resounding box in the middle of this residential neighborhood!" recalled Roderick.[22]

Kellman wasn't entirely new to the gay bar scene; in addition to being a regular club fixture, he and colleague Mel Ford ran Perceptive Audio Productions, a small company that made music tapes for local gay bars. His taste served him well on these tapes, often eclectically mixing genres and eras. For example, on a tape from March 1977 for the Bolt (1976–1979),

36 MENERGY

he combined Vangelis's space music with classic Philly soul and contemporary disco and rock.[23] He brought this eclecticism to the I-Beam, which throughout its long life passed through many forms. It was both a disco and a live music venue, where acts fused disco, dance music, punk, new wave, country and western, and any other genre you can imagine, but always with an air of inclusivity, honoring its origins as a gay disco.

It was a large space with a front area for pinball and pool (notorious for its heavy cruising) that led to the immense dance floor. At first the I-Beam was open seven nights a week.[24] Michael Garrett was the initial DJ when the club opened in November 1977, but soon Kellman brought Timmy Rivers onboard for the Wednesday, Thursday, and Saturday crowds, and Steve Fabus for the Sunday tea dances. This trio of DJs created the "I-Beam Sound," notorious for working dancers into a sweaty frenzy. In this they were helped by Kellman's savvy gimmick of turning up the heat as high as possible to encourage people to take their shirts off, and his habit of handing out Sunday Tea Dance passes to the sexiest men on Castro Street, ensuring a crowd. "The I-Beam was a good space and I always enjoyed myself there," remembers clubgoer and DJ Michael Whitehead. "It just seemed constantly jam packed with good-looking men and just swelteringly hot."[25]

Bathhouses as After-Hours Clubs

Unlike many cities, San Francisco severely restricted the operation of after-hour nightclubs. Until the Trocadero Transfer was granted its after-hours license, only the Shed (1971–1977), at the end of the Castro on Market, was able to stay open after 2:00 a.m.[26] But if you wanted to keep the party going, as DJ Steve Fabus explained, "the bathhouses were the only places before the Trocadero, and even before the Shed had its afterhours."[27] Rod Roderick vented to the press in the mid-1970s how "you can run a disco only four hours a night. Until that time is expanded, it's going to limit the amount of capital that can be expended."[28] This left the bathhouse market open to fill that gap, and while they didn't often have live entertainment like New York's legendary Continental Baths, about half of the gay bathhouses in San Francisco had their own DJ, including the Liberty (1978–1985), Club (1954–1978), and Sutro Baths (1975–1983).[29] By the late 1970s many of these had impressive sound systems as well. For example, Club San Francisco (1978–1985) blasted

20,000 watts of power over forty-two speakers on three separate floors.[30] Fabus fondly remembers that after the regular bars would close,

> People would go to the baths and not just for sex but also just to kinda hang out and party . . . The DJ booth would be near the front desk area, which looked like a classic bathhouse. In the front, you'd walk in the lobby area, and then even in those fetish clubs, most of them had a little snack area, a lounge area as you walked in, and people would hang out there and have parties, but you could feel the vibe. There were two turntables there, and a mixer.[31]

While the baths held a certain attraction for their clientele, dancing wasn't exactly a central concern. "Even with the dance floor and an excellent system, the effect of the sound will be unlike the effect felt in a disco," industry insider David Markham noted in 1978.[32] "The nature of the business, and the broad varieties of activities possible at any given moment, force the music to be more adaptable to a greater variety of actions." This sentiment was echoed by Sutro Baths DJ Maria Sanchez: "You shouldn't overpower them with a message ("dance" is one word to avoid repeating in your segues). If they wanted to dance, they would have gone to a disco. Keep in mind that you're playing to an audience that is varied . . . I don't keep them on the dancefloor but I want to keep them entertained!"[33] Eventually, the city yielded to powerful business interests, and, only a few weeks after the I-Beam's opening in the Haight, allowed for the opening of San Francisco's first after-hours dance club, where the focus for the first time was on all-night dancing.

Trocadero Transfer

Dick Collier's Trocadero Transfer opened on December 14, 1977, at 520 4th Street at Bryant, South of Market. With funding from his father in Maryland and local investors, Collier renovated the former KQED television studio to create a disco palace with a 4,000-square-foot dance floor, the largest in Northern California. "He wanted the Trocadero to be fashioned after 12 West in New York. So the look, feel and layout was very similar, and the Graebar [sound] system would be the same," recalled Steve Fabus.[34] But when the Trocadero had its grand opening, the attendance was disappointing, and

38 MENERGY

there was uncertainty about Collier's ability to get the city to approve his permanent after-hours request. With a $75 annual membership fee (which got you a reduced $5 admission on the weekend, $4 on weekdays) or $15 weekend nonmember entrance fee, the after-hours club was a leap of faith for eager partygoers, and few were initially prepared to take the risk.

Collier had been denied his license originally because of objections raised by the San Francisco Police Department. After long discussions with the Board of Permit Appeals, and with the support of gay board member David Scott, in early 1978 Collier convinced them to overrule this objection with a unanimous vote of 5 to 0 approving the license.[35] As a sign of his serious intentions for the club (and a mark of the importance of disco to the gay community), Collier touted the $230,000 he and his investors had put into the club, bringing in Barry Lederer to install the Graebar sound system from New York. Echoing Roderick, Collier praised the Trocadero's sound as "the finest disco sound system in the US," with Technics 1500 variable-speed turntables, a Bozac mixer, Kenwood 9100 preamps, and ten Phase Linear amps delivering 12,000 watts to 240 speakers housed in eight custom towers placed throughout the club. He bragged to *Billboard* magazine about the bass resonators in the floor, "so you can dance 12 hours and never hurt your legs."[36] Compare this to Stu Goldberg, the owner of popular bisexual disco Dance Your Ass Off, who boasted at the same time of his recent renovation that "I did my whole disco for $40,000."[37]

Collier marketed the Trocadero Transfer as an exclusive club where dancing was the draw. "Finally a place to dance," ran the advertisement in the weeks leading up to the grand opening. "Really dance. For hours. Sound . . . You've never heard anything like it. Lights. A real fantasy. San Francisco, you've had it coming. Now it's yours."[38] Although the Trocadero's "golden age" wouldn't really begin until the arrival of Miami DJ Bobby Viteritti in 1979, local resident DJ Gary Tighe slowly developed a following over the course of the first year, which translated into a loyal membership willing to pay the hefty membership fee.

On Easter Sunday, at the Trocadero's first White Party, March 26, 1978, Sylvester sang his newest hit, "You Make me Feel (Mighty Real)" before a packed house, and the management handed out membership cards. By April, the Trocadero had closed its doors to the public and became exclusively a members-only "private club." In August, the Trocadero was advertising with a new triangle logo as the "Ultimate Experience in Sound, Light, Space."[39] Tighe became famous (infamous?) for his themed DJ sets based on a lyric or word, such as "shame" or "fans." "I would play sets of love, and sets of fire," Tighe remembered.[40] "I even had bumblebee sets. I had a whole set of music that was bug music!" That first year, Tighe played a mix of American soul-based disco such as Carol Douglas, First Choice, and the Jacksons, and electronic European disco, including Giorgio Moroder, Cerrone, and Beautiful Bend. Perhaps most surprisingly, DJ Lester Temple remembers how Tighe was responsible for making Gloria Gaynor's "I Will Survive" a West Coast hit, when "he got all of us San Francisco *Billboard* reporting DJs together, and since we all liked it, we charted it number one. It flew to number one on the West Coast in two weeks."[41]

Unlike the cruise bars, the discos' emphasis on music and dancing allowed a number of women and various ethnic and sexual subcultures to occupy prominent social positions. Trocadero regular Gini Spiersch recalled how the Trocadero Transfer "was a place to get together with people and get high and spend 10 hours tripping."[42] Singers Linda Imperial, Jo-Carol Block, and Lisa Fredenthal-Lee, dancers and Russian émigrés George and Vera, and arc light operator Carla Ann Nicholson were frequent and popular clubgoers. Once the Trocadero Transfer got going, different areas around the club became like small villages: "When you first walk in the club as you turn the corner around from the coat check area, you had the international corner, which was a combination of the Pacific rim type people. They were Hawaiian, Chinese, Japanese, and then there were some of the Mexican or Latin persuasion," Frank Teramani explained.[43] Nicholson remembered "twirly corners, where everyone was twirly dancing."[44] Jim Komarek also explained: "As you go around the room, there's the arc stand by the restrooms, and there was the mirror, which was Bear Country . . . Towards the downstairs bar, that corner was the studly sort of leather, Levi's, muscle, gym crowd. All the body builders, and the fan queens."[45]

A Typical Night Out

It's worth taking time to explore a night out in San Francisco at the height of the first disco craze. The *San Francisco Chronicle*'s magazine, *California Living*, ran a profile of the city's gay nightlife in the summer of 1979, focusing on one gay clubgoer, "Emmitt."[46] Emmitt was a Black clone, giving his account a fascinating perspective into the racialized nature of clone culture. Emmitt describes his roommate George as a "gay social pariah" because "he's

40 MENERGY

a white person who likes black people."[47] After a frustrating interaction with a man at the Endup, Emmitt observed,

> He's cruised me and backed off, because he had a thing about going to bed with blacks. There are people in this bar right now who I haven't had sex with, who I will have sex with in a month from now, for the simple fact they got the hots, and I like them, too, but they got to get over what they were brought up with. A lot of them realize it's stupid to have prejudice against minorities when they're a minority themselves.[48]

Emmitt's participation in clone culture was contingent on his compartmentalizing the racism he encountered from some white bargoers, a response of self-preservation that was typical of people of color in that scene. Beginning Thursday night, twenty-one-year-old Emmitt would start at the I-Beam, where it was leather night: wearing leather got you in free. However, the I-Beam wasn't usually about how you dressed. He opined: "At the I-Beam, it's about emphasizing your body; at Trocadero it's about emphasizing your clothes."[49] The I-Beam Sunday afternoon tea dances had the best bodies on show in San Francisco, where, "you'll see them all in tennis shoes, Levi's, and a shirt tucked in the back pocket."[50] The main attraction of the I-Beam for Emmitt on Thursdays, however, was DJ Timmy Rivers, who he called the best DJ in Northern California. After smoking some pot, Emmitt would dance until closing. Friday nights the drug of choice was MDA. Nicholson remembered, "we used to say it stood for 'Must Dance All night.' And the next day it stood for 'Mustn't Do it Again,' because you were totally wrecked the next day."[51]

Friday evening for Emmitt started with some cruising in the Castro, hitting on other clones, particularly young-looking military types, before going into Toad Hall. After a while, Emmitt moved on to the Stud on Folsom to cruise some more before heading to the Endup to dance until the closing of the bars at 2:00 a.m. He arrived back to Castro Street as the bars let out, where the cruising and dishing continued until dawn.

On Saturdays, Emmitt's night began with LSD, which kicked in as he arrived at Alfie's around 10:30. Soon he headed to the I-Beam, where he danced until midnight. Then he went to Trocadero Transfer. For Emmitt and many other clones, drugs and disco were an intertwined conduit for his dancing catharsis: "I could hold on and say I'm controlling this high, but in reality I'm just letting it flow through me. That way I get on the dance floor and I get all my energy out of it. It's the only reason I take acid, like tonight Tim (the disc jockey) will leave you so you're totally wrung out at the end, you're stomping and kicking. Did you hear them yelling at the rooftops, the dancers? You'll never find that in a straight disco."[52] After dancing until dawn, Emmitt went home, meditated, ate some cereal, and went to the Sunday tea dance at the I-Beam. Emmitt's weekend was not unusual for those in the clone life; for those who desired and could afford it, the commercial world of discos and bars provided a way for some gay men to experience a newly emerged liberated identity through music, sex, dancing, and drugs.

Megaparties

While dancing in San Francisco's commercial discos continued to be the primary way most gay men experienced the city's dancing scene, by the second half of the 1970s the megaparty emerged as a powerful and seemingly spontaneous expression of gay liberation. Essentially huge private parties held in the city's largest venues, the megaparty became a material articulation of a hedonistic fantasy for certain, primarily white middle-class gay men, as well as an important marker of social exclusion for those who couldn't afford the often hefty price of admission. Similar to the "private club" model of the Trocadero Transfer and other newer discotheques, a megaparty, as does its modern equivalent the circuit party, attained its social cache as much through who *wouldn't* be there as who would.

While the gay megaparty concept didn't originate in San Francisco (as with disco itself, that honor goes to New York City), San Francisco's distinctive iteration can trace its beginnings to the huge parties for invited guests thrown by the wealthy Rod Roderick in the early 1970s. But his events were just a more extravagant example of the kinds of house parties that emerged out of the first large gay subcultures in America's cities in the early 20th century. Throughout the first half of the twentieth century, gay men and women were moving to urban areas where they could be with like-minded people in ever-increasing numbers, and yet public expression of same-sex sexuality was still dangerous. Michael Bronski notes that since the 1920s, and with the gradual population shift from rural areas to urban centers, "venues such as cafes, bars, clubs, and theatres, as well as events such as semipublic parties, dances, art shows, and literary readings, built and preserved a sense of sexual community."[53] Throughout the century, these private networks existed to

42 MENERGY

provide gay people with the only outlet outside of the bar scene to gather. As late as 1973, gay activist Peter Fisher would write,

> Some gay people frequent the bars only until they have developed a circle of friends and then meet most of their sex partners at private parties. Depending on the people involved, these parties range from sedate gatherings for cocktails and dinner to well-organized orgies. Entrance to the party circuit is often hard to gain, especially among the gay jet set. The wealthiest and most prominent homosexuals tend to look down their noses at the average gay as unsophisticated and uninteresting.[54]

While house parties weren't scrutinized to the same degree as bars and nightclubs, the security they seemed to offer was certainly exaggerated. Frank Thompson recalled how a party he held at his own apartment in the early 1940s was raided by the police, who arrested several men caught dancing together.[55] And during a raid on a house party in Philadelphia in 1958 thrown by the artist Emlen Etting, police Captain Frank Rizzo reportedly told Etting, "Unless you and your goddamn pansy friends get back in the house, quiet down and shut up, I will put you all in the paddy wagon and throw you in with the drunks for the night."[56] Still, as George Chauncey observes,

> Because gay men found their behavior highly regulated in most commercial institutions by managers concerned about police surveillance, they flocked to parties, where they could dance, joke in a campy way, and be affectionate without fear. To men who traveled in both the straight and gay worlds of the 1930s and 1940s, apartment parties seemed to be both more common and more significant events in the gay world than the straight. . . . Parties, whether held in palatial penthouses or tiny tenement flats, constituted safe spaces in which a distinctive gay culture was forged.[57]

The godparent of all gay megaparties was Harlem's Hamilton Lodge Ball, Held annually in the Hamilton Lodge No. 710 of the Grand United Order of the Odd Fellows since 1869, the event had had a visible gay presence since at least the 1920s, when it became known as the "Faggot's Ball," with some claiming the event always had a significant queer element.[58] African Americans formed the largest group of attendees, with a sizable mix of white and Asian participants as well; the dance was noted for its extravagant drag costumes and performances. The language used in the press of the 1920s and

LIBERATION FOR SOME 43

1930s to describe these massive parties resembles the descriptive portraits painted of the later San Francisco megaparties:

> To one of the largest gatherings that has ever graced this hall came the all-conquering Hamilton Lodge, resplendent in all the panoply of pomp and splendor, to give to Harlemites who stood in wide-eyed astonishment at this lavish display a treat that shall never be forgotten. The usual grand march eclipsed in splendor all heretofore given by them, and women screamed full-throated ovation as the bizarre and the seeming impossible paraded for their approval.[59]

For the 1970s parties, those who threw them weren't obliged to invite anyone they didn't want, and most of the big house parties were "A-Gay" affairs, where money, good looks or a good body, or social prominence afforded admittance. Rod Roderick hosted a party, for example, in 1977, called "Boiler Room," where Steve Fabus was the DJ. Fabus recalls: "South of Market, certain guys would give parties, and there were guys that became party givers and producers of, basically, the underground of its day. If they actually moved the party into a pier space like with the Creative Power Foundation, they sold tickets to it. Some people say it was the very beginnings of what was known as the circuit party."[60]

Halloween week in 1977 saw two big disco events at the Galleria Design Center, an expansive venue near SoMa that had opened in 1974. While the dance floor proper wasn't huge, it served as the atrium to an enormous four-story open area. Each floor above the ground floor had a balcony with a view of the dance floor. Dancing took place on all levels, with a live stage at one end of the ground floor. The Bay Area Disco DJ Association held the first event, a big party on October 22 called "Galleria Disco Goes New York, New York," at which John Hedges was the main DJ with support from Timmy Rivers from Bones (1976–1979), Mike Garrett from Alfie's, and Jon Randazzo from the City Disco, all coordinated by Don Miley, the booking agent at the City. The second event was the Society for Individual Rights's annual costume party, with gay live band Buena Vista performing followed by disco dancing all night.

The first iconic party that most people remember, however, was Michael Maletta's Night Flight, held on New Year's Eve in 1977. Maletta, a New York transplant to San Francisco, brought with him memories of huge gay parties and Fire Island extravaganzas and thought the utopic visions those parties

44 MENERGY

evoked would resonate with the gay population of San Francisco. Among many middle-class gay men, traveling back and forth between coasts was a sign of their aspirational culture, as were the parties there. "So, I was here [San Francisco] in '76 and I'd see all my old friends from New York," recalled Robin Tichane:

> People were flying back and forth . . . It was a real community floating from NY to LA to SF. Disco parties were starting to be put together. You could buy a share for $30 . . . I was excited to be a part of such a creative community-based endeavor. I had different friends who would handle different sub-specialties. I remember one man he was named Michael Maletta. Michael was a haircutter I knew from New York who came out almost at the exact same time as I did. He started a lot of the ideas behind the parties . . . The message was, instead of it being in the margins, moving to the mainstream community.[61]

Maletta "test drove" the market after being in San Francisco a year, throwing a party for the opening of his own hair salon for a relatively small and select group of five hundred, mostly Castro clones. He remembered, "If I could get this many people together in one place, and they're all having a good time, why couldn't I do it for more people, two thousand, three thousand maybe?"[62] To sponsor his new venture, Maletta contacted friends in the arts, many of whom had been to his earlier, smaller party; local businesses; and Rod Roderick, who had been holding huge and successful parties at his home. Maletta rented the Gay Community Center on Grove Street the night before New Year's Eve and filled it with white drapes, croupier-manned gambling tables, and performers and entertainers, including a robot. An orgy area filled the back half of the center, with tires, wrestling mats, and grand piano cases.[63] Roderick recalled, "At first we invited the hottest men in town and naturally word got around what was happening and we had to print more tickets. We ended up having 3000 people there."[64]

It was important to Maletta that tickets for the majority of partygoers were free, so he asked forty friends to donate $250 each to subsidize the event. Proceeds from on-site gambling tables and coat check went to the Gay Community Center, which was also remodeled for the event. "We built staircases and put in bathrooms and did a lot of painting. The most important thing perhaps, was that we made thousands of gays aware that the place existed for their use."[65] The invitations, featuring a drawing of Pegasus by

Edward Parente, enticed dancers to submit themselves to "a journey into the realm of fantasy." Maletta's attitude was essential to the event's success, declaring "I wanted to give a party for no reason other than the party itself. To provide people with an evening of dancing and entertainment unlike anything they had ever experienced before. I'd been to a lot of parties, but I'd never been to one like we were planning."[66] He was right; while there were some aspects a veteran of the New York party scene might recognize, many elements captured the unique character of San Francisco, such as the quarter mile of Christo mylar fence panels draped around three floors of the venue, reclaimed for the party by Sonoma farmers. As friend John Cailleau remembers of Maletta's visionary quality, "Officially, Michael was a barber and had a shop on upper Market. He did short haircuts of men who wore Levis and T-shirts . . . When he had you in his chair he could impart a lot of enlightenment and philosophy of creative activity . . . He acted kind of as spiritual leader, a guru in his role as barber."[67]

For Maletta, disco music was essential; the sound had the power to unify a crowd, and was treated equally extravagantly, with Sound Genesis bringing $17,000 worth of sound equipment for the night. New York DJ Vincent Carleo was entrusted with the task, and, as one commentator remembered,

> Relentlessly, song after song, the music took them higher and higher, until the air was charged, sparking with a contagious energy that embraced everyone, manipulating their feet, their bodies, their minds until they had no choice but to dance their asses off . . . Hundreds of hot men alternately boogied, drank, rapped, gambled and engaged in other esoteric activities from 9pm until DAWN. It was a party to end ALL parties and FREE.[68]

After the enormous success of Night Flight, Maletta and crew began planning the next megaparty. Stars, held on Pier 19 on May 27, 1978, was the most extravagant event yet. When sending away for a ticket, partygoers were required to submit a passport photo that was incorporated into their $30 ticket. They were also encouraged to submit a 35-millimeter slide "of yourself looking and feeling like a star."[69] As party habitué Mark Abramson's boyfriend Armando Arroyo, the event's caterer, wrote in his diary at the time: "They will project the pictures onto the walls around the dance floor, and everyone will be a star that night. They're trying to out-do *NIGHT FLIGHT*."[70]

For the third megaparty, Abracadabra, held after the June 1978 Gay Day parade, Maletta enlisted the help of pioneering gay adult film director

46 MENERGY

Wakefield Poole. Poole and five other San Francisco filmmakers stood in different spots along the parade route and filmed the celebrations. Poole described the excitement of the event:

> I had the film picked up by motorcycle at each locale and rushed to be processed . . . We had scaffolding built in the orchestra pit to hold six projectors and the cameramen. It rose up on elevators, as the screens, which were hanging over the dancefloor, descended—an immense undertaking. Less than an hour after the parade, the audience was watching the entire event from six different points of view, simultaneously projected by the filmmakers themselves. This was all raw footage, and we were all seeing it for the first time together. It was amazing.[71]

Over four thousand people attended that event, inspiring party promoters David Bandy and business partner Gary Roverana to organize their own megaparty, to be held at the Galleria Design Center during the weekend of the Castro Street Fair in late August 1978. The *Bay Area Reporter* plugged the event: "Those fledgling entrepreneurs . . . are staging 'a Salute to the Men of SF' at the Galleria, a splendiferous disco party with live performances by the one and only Sylvester and also Loverde and Sean Salgado. San Francisco's DJ of the Year, Marty Blecman will do the music."[72] The timing was perfect, as Sylvester's "You Make Me Feel (Mighty Real)" was currently at the top of the disco charts, making him a true celebrity guest.

With the huge success of the Salute the Men of SF party, Bandy and Roverana formed a company, Conceptual Entertainment, which would go on to dominate the megaparty scene for several years in San Francisco. Writer John Cailleau recalled them with a wistfulness and nostalgia that betrayed their significance to him and his friends at the time:

> There were times at the Body Center which was the first gay gym in the city, when people would say, "Are you going to the party?" And everybody knew what you were talking about. There was only one party worth mentioning and that was one of the mega-parties that was produced with that energy from Michael Maletta and the two guys at Creative Conceptual Entertainment who are long long gone.[73]

It is hard to overstate the centrality of these parties to clone culture, or to the passion and enthusiasm its participants felt toward them and their shared music. With Maletta's Night Flight party, all of the essential pieces were in place for the megaparties to come: tickets distributed from local gay discos, bars, bathhouses, and bookstores, as well as special invitations given to prominent men, important local DJs, special guest performers, games, and the sense that it was an exclusive party for a gay elite, one that had special permission to continue until dawn.

3

Sylvester's Fantasy Comes True

Fantasy Records

Initially, despite San Francisco's position as a center of the gay disco phenomenon, the music played in the city always came from other places. But in the second half of the 1970s Bay Area producers started creating their own music. At first, it drew from the sounds of American Black disco heard elsewhere, but by 1978 local studios were making dance music that incorporated the distinctive culture of the Bay. Soon, the rest of America would hear what made the city so special, starting with the outrageous, out androgynous rock singer Sylvester through the Berkeley-based Fantasy Records. This chapter describes Sylvester's rise to national prominence and the sacrifices he made along the way; compromises to his personality, his sexuality, and the realization that what worked in San Francisco was a harder sell to the rest of the country. Ultimately, those compromises would lead to his conviction that only by expressing his "realness" would he (and the millions who listened and danced to his music) find happiness.

A million miles from the Castro, both philosophically and, depending on Bay Bridge traffic, figuratively, Fantasy began life in the 1940s as a jazz label. By the late 1960s, principle owner and president Saul Zaentz was spearheading an effort to branch out into new genres, including spoken word recordings by Lenny Bruce and a reading of Allan Ginsburg's *Howl*. By the early 1970s, their jazz output had been surpassed by rock. Fantasy's biggest commercial success came from Creedence Clearwater Revival and all its associated acts, such as the Blue Ridge Rangers, Tom Fogerty (brother of John Fogerty), and various members' solo projects. Zaentz was also keen at the time to enter the film market, and after the unprofitable but well-reviewed *Payday* (1972) had a hit with *One Flew over the Cuckoo's Nest* (1975), at the time the eighth-largest-grossing film ever.[1] The popularity of this film and of Creedence Clearwater Revival enabled the label to sign more left-field artists, such as R&B musicians Johnny "Guitar" Watson and Stax Records' Staple

Menergy. Louis Niebur, Oxford University Press. © Oxford University Press 2022.
DOI: 10.1093/oso/9780197511077.003.0004

SYLVESTER'S FANTASY COMES TRUE   49

Singers. As their roster of R&B acts increased, so too did their association with funk and disco.

Nowhere is this demonstrated more clearly than with the Blackbyrds. Their 1974 Fantasy debut album *Flying Start* is jazz-inflected R&B, mixing up-tempo dance songs like "I Need You" and "Walking in Rhythm" with smooth midtempo instrumentals such as "The Baby" and "Love Is Love," and jazz funk, down-and-dirty songs like "Spaced Out" and "Blackbyrds Theme." When "Walking in Rhythm" was released as a single in 1975, it became a surprise hit, particularly on the dance floors of America's nascent discos. The Blackbyrds began tailoring their material for dancing more specifically, and their next dance single, "Happy Music," was released in that same year as Fantasy's first "Special Disco Mix" 12-inch single (the 12-inch single, a format tailored to club DJs, had only debuted as a commercial product a few months earlier).

Thus, Fantasy records almost accidentally slipped into the world of disco. Their half-hearted commitment to dance music is demonstrated by the small number of disco records they produced in the early years and the lack of promotion they gave to what little product they did release. In addition to the Blackbyrds, the funk outfit Spiders Webb had "Special 12-inch Disco Mixes" of their double-A-side release "I Don't Know What's on Your Mind" and "Reggae Bump" in 1976. The most important disco act acquired by Fantasy in the mid-1970s, though, was Side Effect, a Los Angeles band who scored a hit as the backing group for Arthur Adams's "Reggae Disco" before having a hit of their own with "Always There," a cover of a Ronnie Laws 1975 instrumental. Opening their second Fantasy album, *What You Need* (1976) with that track, Side Effect's arranger Paul B. Allen III stuck closely to Laws's arrangement, including a prominent clavinet part, adding distinctive breaks and a searing vocal part for future gospel superstar Helen Lowe. Fantasy issued DJ-only 12-inch copies of "Always There" in addition to the standard single 7-inch edit.

The hiring of Hank Cosby, a Motown veteran with years of experience, as director of marketing led to a distribution deal between Fantasy and Philadelphia-based WMOT ("We Men of Talent") Records releasing their Philly-soul disco output from artists such as Fat Larry's Band, Philly Cream, and Slick.[2] But Fantasy's dance music fortunes were about to really take off with a new partnership.

Harvey Fuqua had been a founding member of the Moonglows, a successful doo-wop group with a string of hits in the mid-1950s, including

"Sincerely." In the 1960s, he moved into production and songwriting, working for the Motown juggernaut and introducing Marvin Gaye to the label. By the early 1970s, he was producing funk and R&B acts for RCA Records, and by the middle of the decade he had moved to the Bay Area to start his own small label, Honey Records. He released a few singles by various funk, disco, and R&B acts, such as Hell Storm, who he brought with him from RCA, and local artists Grove Street Band, José Hernandez, and Grand Theft, but he hadn't had much success outside of San Francisco. He recalled, "I look a little vacation in Oakland and Berkeley and went around the clubs. The talent wasn't anything great but I thought, oh well, back to square one, back to the artist development thing again. So I found an old Safeway market and converted it into a studio and rehearsal rooms and got these three guys to help me set up an Artists Development center for the five acts I found in Berkeley."[3]

In 1977 Fuqua negotiated an arrangement with Fantasy Records to use their facilities and distribution network to produce two albums by any artist of his choosing. Fuqua's partner Nancy Pitts, who he had met during the RCA years, was scouting local clubs on the lookout for talent. Singer Martha Wash told Pitts she had been singing backup with fellow gospel singer Izora Rhodes for the notorious Sylvester. Pitts' attendance at one of their shows was a key moment in the fortunes of San Francisco disco.

Sylvester

Sylvester was a well-known figure in San Francisco counterculture circles, having been a member of the revolutionary hippy performance art group the Cockettes in the early 1970s. When that collective splintered after their disastrous New York debut, Sylvester with his Hot Band released a couple of singles and two albums for local San Francisco record label Blue Thumb. He performed with this group (renamed periodically as the lineup changed; sometimes "Forecast" and occasionally just "Sylvester"), primarily playing on his Bay Area turf with a few modest West Coast tours.

Despite his relatively high profile as a former Cockette, Sylvester had a difficult time breaking out of the local cabaret and club scene. He sang in a piercing falsetto and was usually costumed in flashy female attire, evoking the blues women of the 1920s. He was too openly gay for straight society, even in wide-open San Francisco, and while his combination of old-style blues, Janis-Joplinesque counterculture wailing, and contemporary rock fit right in at the eclectic Stud and Elephant Walk bars, many of the more traditional venues in the city were skeptical of his ability to draw a crowd. This was reflected in the mixed reviews and low sales of his two Blue Thumb albums.

On one level, Sylvester liked keeping his audiences confused, saying in 1974, "I think a lot of people enjoy my show because they don't understand it . . . I want to do all these things to bring a new culture to the Black world of entertainment so that we can get above 'Superfly' movies and stuff like that."[4] But fans who understood his act adored him. In 1974, after the release of his second Blue Thumb album, *Bizarre*, Sylvester defined his underground appeal:

> The thing that makes it work is the band plays rock music, but the way I sing, coming from a gospel background . . . something goes on that's not straight and rigid, but flowing with emotion because of the way I sing, which comes from being black and brought up in the church and singing the way we do . . . It's not a fad . . . My whole trip is very real . . . I can be a man if I want to, or I can be a very beautiful woman. See it's being able to do these things well, 'cause anything you can do well people will accept, if it ain't tacky and bad and in bad taste.[5]

But by August 1976, at the instigation of new manager Brent Thomson, he was marketing his gigs at the Palms Café (1976–1978) with a masculine publicity photo and wearing a three-piece suit onstage, downplaying the gender fluidity that had made his name up to that point.[6] Thomson also got rid of the amateur drag queen backup singers he had been using, convincing him that, "Nobody is giving out recording contracts to drag queens. Besides, touring will be a lot easier without all those wig boxes."[7] Sylvester auditioned new backup singers with Thomson and guitarist James "Tip" Wirrick, but was "growing weary from seeing these little tiny birdlike girls come in and doo-bop around. Then Martha came in. I took one look at her and *knew* she could sing."[8] Gospel singer Martha Wash had been working as a secretary when a friend told her to audition for Sylvester. Gospel had been part of Wash's life since she was two years old, she remembers: "I got a lot of support from everyone. Church people are good about that. If they think you just *hum* good, they'll put you up on chairs and tables and encourage you."[9]

She had toured Europe with her high school choir, and, later performed with gospel group Gideon and Power among other local choirs, including

52 MENERGY

the group NOW (News of the World). Wash auditioned for Sylvester and remembers how he was impressed as much by her size as her voice: "You're just the person I've been looking for. Can you find another singer as large as you are who can sing as well?," he asked her. "I said 'Yes,' and called Izora that night," Wash recalls. "He thought it would be a change of pace since most background singers were super-skinny."[10] Izora Rhodes, mother of seven, had been singing in NOW with Wash, but had known her since "she was a snotty-nosed brat running around church singing her behind off."[11] Like Wash, Rhodes was a big woman, bigger even, and also like Wash, she came from a gospel background, but had also studied classical voice at the San Francisco Conservatory. She was teaching voice and piano and working jobs as a nurse's aide and bartender to make ends meet when she received Wash's call. Her audition for Sylvester consisted of an impromptu rehearsal in the back of his Volkswagen bug, as the three of them drove across the Golden Gate Bridge on the way to a rehearsal in San Rafael. Sylvester's biographer Joshua Gamson described how, "singing to the radio and then finding their parts in a couple of gospel tunes," the group dynamic materialized, as "Martha and Izora would just fall in on either side of Sylvester's falsetto lead, Martha's soprano riding on top of his, Izora's alto rolling in just under."[12]

Rhodes remembers how they came up with their backup singer moniker: "I wanted something catchy. When you see Two Tons o' Fun, you can't help but wonder who they are. If we're going to be fat, we may as well use it to our advantage."[13] With a newly constituted Hot Band, complete with hefty glamorous backup singers, Sylvester was considered enough of a draw to open a new cocktail lounge, Andromeda (1977–1979), on March 5, 1977, alongside San Francisco drag legend José Sarria and Beach Blanket Babylon performer Glynda Glayzer.[14]

Gamson expertly recounted the story of Sylvester's "discovery" by Nancy Pitts and Harvey Fuqua in his biography *The Fabulous Sylvester*.[15] Suffice it to say, Sylvester would give free concerts at the Palms Café on Sundays, using the shows as a place to workshop new material and arrangements with his band. Pitts attended one of these shows and was overwhelmed by Sylvester's talent. Sylvester later reminisced,

> She liked the show and told me she'd been looking for an act like mine. Then I met Harvey Fuqua. They came to the next show I did at Elephant Walk and were completely blown away. . . . They came back and said I could have

this, this, and this, and I started working on the album literally before the contracts were signed. That's how much faith they had in me.[16]

Fuqua also recalled the impression Sylvester made on him at the time: "I said WOW! - that's it. Whatever we're doing, close it down as soon as possible. I wanna work specifically on this man here. . . . Of course, all my other artists were saying 'hey man, what's going on?' but I just had to explain to them; they didn't have anything special, Sylvester is dyn-o-mite."[17] Fuqua selected Sylvester as the first artist to record under his arrangement with Fantasy Records, and they set to work right away on the singer's eponymous debut for a mainstream label.

Sylvester

In spring 1977, Sylvester and his band—Sandyjack Reiner, Tip Wirrick, Dan Reich, John Dunstan, and David Frazier—recorded at Fantasy studios. Fuqua added more conventional brass and strings to their compositions and the Tons provided backup. As he had done with his earlier Hot Band, Sylvester workshopped the songs in live shows at the Old Waldorf, incorporating Leslie Drayton's brass arrangements and enhanced five-piece percussion into the collection of songs for the new album.[18] Some were old favorites, several were newly written by Sylvester, and two were cowritten with guitarist Wirrick.

While overall the self-titled album succeeds artistically, it suffers from an identity crisis. For all the criticism of Sylvester's Blue Thumb albums, they captured Sylvester's unique blend of rock and blues. The addition of Harvey Fuqua's R&B influence occasionally muddies the water; not necessarily in individual songs, but in the eclectic genre-hopping of the album in general. The first side starts with a frenetic, gospel-fueled version of the Ashford and Simpson hit "Over and Over." Sylvester had first heard the duo perform the song on *Soul Train*, and he and coarranger/guitarist Wirrick sped up the original's tempo from a mellow 118 beats per minute (BPM) to an initial 130 BPM.[19] The track opens with a slightly dated-sounding Philly intro, all strings and brass, Hammond organ syncopated in the background. In fact, it shares with the Harold Melvin and the Blue Notes track "The Love I Lost" drummer Earl Young's trick of reserving the driving off-beat hi-hat for the chorus, with a much more straightforward backbeat for the verses. Sylvester's

54 MENERGY

drummer Sandyjack Reiner continuously hints at a disco beat, withholding it through Wirrick's rock guitar solo.

At the three-minute mark, however, the song goes full disco, speeding the tempo up to a manic 137 BPM, thinning out the texture, and introducing a gospel choir improvising, clapping, and wailing while Sylvester repeats "find yourself a friend" again and again. More than half of the song's 7:05-minute running time is given over to this extemporaneous testifying, and with the increase in tempo, the stage is set for a full-on disco album. But that's not what we get. Instead, the second track is a midtempo ballad, complete with dueling flutes, as Sylvester laments, "I Tried to Forget You." The Tons liven things up on this traditional middle of the road (MOR) track with their soulful vocals, but by the time the saxophone enters for an extended, jazzy solo, any potential disco audience has fled the scene.

Next up, "Changes" reintroduces an upbeat disco groove and introduces David Frazier's Latin percussion. But Wirrick's electric guitar solo provides continuity with Sylvester's rock background, and the lack of a break ensures that the song never heats things up too much. Closing out the first side, "Tipsong" is another midtempo MOR track, with flugelhorn introduction.

Things get off to a more exciting start on the B-side. "Down, Down, Down" makes no attempt to hide its disco aspirations. Building a polyrhythm up from an initial four-on-the-floor bass drum and syncopated clavinet, horns and piano punch the off beats, and by the time Sylvester enters, telling us that "we're just gonna get on down," the strings have filled out the texture, creating a lush but propulsive groove. An incongruous saxophone solo takes the place of a dance break, however, and the eleventh-hour introduction of the Tons, clapping and wailing, does little to restore the momentum lost by the solo.

The most successful of the ballads is "Love Grows Up Slow," primarily because it allows Sylvester's voice to shine. It doesn't suffer from its straightforward Tin Pan Alley form or the Ton's backseat position. Here Wirrick's guitar solo adds to the overall melancholy mood, drawing upon a Robert Fripp–style detached, icy sound. The humorous, campy follow-up, "I Been Down," works well on its own, but suffers again by its placement on the album. Sylvester sits this one out, giving the Tons a chance to shine. They each get a verse, and then join forces for the final minutes. Alternating between speaking and singing, they commiserate over their failed relationships, taking turns reassuring each other. This song comes closest to capturing the essence of their appeal to Sylvester, a link to both the classic blues women of the past and a connection to his Black roots. According to his friend Yvette

Flunder, "Martha and Izora, and that kind of black, that's what I call basic black. Cornbread and black-eyed peas. That's the kind of black folks that he liked being around."[20] Sylvester's album ends with an inconsequential self-penned song, "Never Too Late," that captures some of the blues rock style of the Blue Thumb recordings, classed up with the Tons and some good brass solos.

Sexuality Problems

Despite an attempt by Fuqua and Fantasy to "straighten" out some of the campier aspects of Sylvester's persona, the singer pushed against it. A perennial outsider, Sylvester had fought hard to carve a place for himself as a rare Black man within the increasingly white, middle-class culture of the Castro ghetto. As a flamboyant androgynous gay man, he confronted head-on the macho clone monolith that had rejected drag and effeminacy as a legitimate expression of homosexuality in the 1970s. He wasn't keen to also give up his gayness now that he had the spotlight. Sylvester made his public position clear, in the gay press at least: "All my songs are associated with being gay. I've never been straight. When I sing a song, I sing the lyrics as they were written. I don't change the pronouns."[21] This sentiment was fine when Sylvester was his own boss. Now, however, he was under contract to Honey/Fantasy, and his album was a mainstream commercial product.

Problems started with the cover. The front photo featured the singer in a man's collarless dark shirt, unbuttoned nearly to his navel, three delicate silver chains around his neck. He is sitting up straight, looking directly into the camera with immaculately plucked and shaped eyebrows, and shiny glossed lips. His close-cropped hair does little to gender this androgynous-looking creature. The back cover is no more helpful, as Sylvester appears in full drag, complete with turban, draping caftan, bangles, and massive earrings. Rather than the messy hippy of his Hot Band years, here is a new polished look; the photo drips with glamour and maturity, and in fact captures the elegance of the album, free from the rock histrionics of his earlier work, replaced by an R&B queen of the caliber of Patti LaBelle or Diana Ross. But when several southern record stores complained, Fantasy panicked and commissioned a hasty reshoot. The replacement cover presents a suited Sylvester holding a single red rose. Gone is drag, and the only concession to his androgyny is a hint of lip gloss.

56 MENERGY

His past presented something of a problem for Fantasy as well. In the initial publicity materials for the album, issued in June 1977, much was made of his rise as "the gay black singer who rose to fame and international notoriety as the star of the Cockettes, the madly outrageous homosexual musical review ... The Cockettes quickly became the darlings of the liberated-by-acid crowd, and, of course, the gay community."[22] Two months later Fantasy revised his publicity materials, and the same passage now introduced Sylvester as "the black singer who rose to fame and international notoriety as the star of the musical review that opened in San Francisco on New Year's Eve, 1970," omitting the rest of the material about the Cockettes.[23] Among the elements also removed for this revised biography was his description as "an original glitter queen in a city that would send Anita Bryant up the wall," and a full four paragraphs describing his coming out to his grandmother, his appearances with and subsequent outgrowing of the Cockettes, and finally how he, "working as a woman under the name Ruby Blue, played for almost two years at the Rickshaw Lounge."

Keen to take the attention away from Sylvester's flamboyant reputation, the initial biography notes that "he does not perform in drag anymore and although obviously very feminine, he's a guy who is totally devoted to music." In the second version, this is completely omitted. In an attempt to again deflect attention away from his "reputation," Sylvester is originally quoted as saying, "People were more interested in my personal sexual orientation and my costumes than they were in my music. Sure I'm gay, and I'm outrageous about it ... But I don't tell gay jokes and I don't sing gay songs. So what if I'm outrageous? What about the music?" In the sterilized version released two months later, this is simply reduced to, "People were more interested in my costumes than they were in my music."

In the individual profiles of the straight Hot Band members, each of them emphasizes in a different way how Sylvester's musicianship helped them overcome their "natural discomfort" with his overt homosexuality. Among the press, however, Sylvester was already a known quantity. Vince Aletti, critic for *Record World*, was impressed enough to recommend the album, understanding that given the singer's "stunning performances with the outrageous Cockettes in San Francisco .... [Sylvester] has always been one of the more extraordinary performers on the fringes of disco."[24]

"Over and Over" was released as a single in July 1977 and was a moderate dance hit. Fantasy wasted no time in producing a promotional 12-inch disco version remixed by the Mind Shaft's DJ Wes Bradley, and the song proved to have legs. It appeared on several national DJs' top 10 lists for months and stayed on *Billboard*'s National Disco Top Action charts until early winter. Fantasy's biggest disco success since the Blackbyrds proved Harvey Fuqua and Nancy Pitts right, and they rushed to take advantage of Sylvester's dance-floor arrival, rereleasing the album with the 12-inch mix of "Over and Over" replacing the single version on the record.

But for all its success, the album wasn't exactly forward looking. For some it was too camp, others not camp enough, not quite disco, not quite funk, not really gospel or rock, but a watered-down combination of the four styles that nevertheless capitalized on Sylvester's unique voice (described by one critic during the Cockettes years as "a cross-bred permutation of Little Richard and Blossom Dearie") and the outré stylings of the Tons to produce an overall satisfying listening experience.[25] *Rolling Stone,* in a feature celebrating the release of albums by two Black gay artists at the same time (the other being Tony Washington's band the Dynamic Superior's record *Give and Take*) lamented the loss of personality Sylvester seems to have undergone. "At times Sylvester succeeds too well in dampening his eccentricities; there's a blandness to several of his compositions here. Also, his rather thin voice tends to get overpowered by some of Fuqua's arrangements or by the two powerful backup singers."[26] Vince Aletti hoped that the new "Over and Over" mix, "which has a lot more clarity and punch than the LP track," would give the single a boost, but a look at the other songs on the dance charts during July shows how unremarkable the album's style was.[27] The summer of 1977 was a pivotal one for the disco genre, which saw many of the old R&B traits that had characterized the genre since the introduction of Philly soul in the early 1970s becoming passé, replaced by a new cadre of artists from Europe who put an emphasis on electronic sounds, science fiction–influenced topics, and an overall tone that was campier—and much less Black.[28]

New Sounds in Disco

The song that epitomized the changes occurring in disco in the summer of 1977 more than any other was Donna Summer and Giorgio Moroder's "I Feel Love." The final track on the eccentric concept album *I Remember Yesterday,* "I Feel Love" comes across, after the album's nostalgic trip through musical genres of the past, as a glimpse into the future of music. Entirely electronic with the exception of Summer's vocals, the song has a robotic pounding

58 MENERGY

regularity mitigated by both the swirling synthesizer strings and Summer's sensual singing. Never has a more apt prediction of dance music's trajectory been penned, with its "inhuman" coldness and European precision a direct predecessor to the techno music of the 1980s and 1990s. The song essentially invents the electronic dance music genre from scratch.

Disco's new obsession with science fiction could be heard that summer in Kebekelektrik's "Magic Fly." A collaboration between Montreal producer Pat Deserio and session musician Gino Soccio, the song had already topped the disco charts in its original form by the French group Space, who released their album *Magic Fly* in April 1977. Less overtly electronic than "I Feel Love," Space's album combined synthesizer and traditional instruments to an extent unusual in earlier dance music, capitalizing on the current *Star Wars* craze sweeping the world. *Magic Fly* emphasized those aspects of electronic music impossible to reproduce on traditional instruments, such as rapid arpeggiation (made popular on the RMI Harmonic Synthesizer, and even easier to realize on the Jupiter 4 by 1978). In some ways, Space's album is old-fashioned; it flows one song into the next, less like a dance record and more in the tradition of a rock concept album. The song "Magic Fly" is closest to reproducing the Kraftwerk-style robotic and mechanical aesthetic also present in "I Feel Love," and was unsurprisingly the most popular song on the album, rising to the top of several dance music critics' best-of lists for 1977.[29] Kebekelektric's cover doubles down on its disco aspects, reinforcing the synthesized bassline, and filling out the lush synth string lines. The record proudly declares on its back cover: "This album was recorded entirely with synthesizers."

Finally, Fantasy's fear of an "out" Sylvester was probably less valid than it was perceived to be by mid-1977. While it's true that in certain markets a gay musician faced unique challenges, within the world of pop music, things were changing. "San Francisco (You've Got Me)/Hollywood/Fire Island," the first release by Jacques Morali's studio project Village People entered the national dance charts at the end of July 1977 and stayed there until the end of November, peaking at the top of many DJs' top 10 lists throughout that time. "San Francisco" opens with a celebratory list of the gay locales that were quickly becoming famous as clone havens: "Folsom Street, on the way to Polk and Castro . . . Leather, leather, Levi's and keys on the left now, alright . . . Disco, music that sets you on fire." These lyrics capture the mystique that had come to define San Francisco for gay people around the world. In Mark Abramson's diary of his life in the city, he wrote shortly after his arrival that:

I see so many sexy men in the Castro. Where do they come from? California state law says that the bars have to close from two am to six am. During those four hours, the neighborhood is especially wild, but men also spill out of the bars and onto the sidewalks all day long, even on weekdays. I am amazed at the sheer energy out here. Every day more young men arrive, and they are always cruising. I read in the *Chronicle* that on average, a thousand gay men are moving to San Francisco every week. That's over fifty thousand potential sex partners a year! I'll never get through them all.[30]

Unlike older Philly soul, with its swung rhythms derived from R&B, Village People's much more regular, almost robotic four-on-the-floor captures the fashionable obsession with strict clonelike, "masculine," rhythms. "An upfront gay album is clearly an idea whose time has come," wrote critic Vince Aletti in a rave review for *Record World* that was redolent with language affirming this new obsession with butch masculinity in the gay community, "especially for the disco market, and Village People's title cut, in spite of its simplistic lyrics, is bold and forceful enough to become an anthem for the strong new thrust of the gay movement."[31]

Sylvester's first album for Fantasy doesn't really reflect any of these trends that were emerging in San Francisco's gay disco scene. A review of the top San Francisco DJs and their clubs in 1977 gives a prescient insight into the future of dance music. A surviving two-hour set from August by DJ Michael Lee at San Francisco's Bones begins with the introductory track on Space's debut album, followed by Meco's "Star Wars," and incorporates old-fashioned Philly disco to a much less extent than even a year earlier. This, despite his reputation as a white DJ who was known for playing primarily R&B. For Michael Garrett at the I-Beam, the Village People's "San Francisco/Hollywood" was still at the end of the year the most danceable record for his audience, who "preferred a strong rock beat."[32] John Hedges at Oil Can Harry's expressed his crowd's love of "strings and high female vocals."[33] While holding up Donna Summer's *Once Upon a Time* double album as the hottest, he also praises the Alec R. Costandinos's (aka "Love and Kisses") Euro hit "I Found Love." For his part, Marty Blecman at the City Disco loved the science fiction aspects of Cerrone's "Supernature," especially how he "incorporates the use of synthesizers and crisp vocals to create a mood of the supernatural. Evidently, animal mutations are rebelling against humans who polluted their earth."[34] Blecman also praises both THP Orchestra's "Two Hot for Love" and Love and Kisses' new album, which he calls "an excellent album to kick back and listen to. Almost like the Pink Floyd days except this one gets to your feet as well as your head."[35]

Blecman's connection between this new European and electronic sound, science fiction, and the psychedelic was a common way for this generation of DJs to understand these new sounds. Much in the same way early electronic sound in film was used to show the uncanny or psychologically disturbed mindset, this first wave of electronic dance music connected with an audience in search of the uncanny and the futuristic; gay hippies had become clone futurists. Andrew Holleran observed this shift in clone culture, remembering the confluence of:

> short haircuts, moustaches, High Tech, and Disco: it seems remarkable, looking back, that these occurred simultaneously. But now and then you went home with a man with short black hair and a black moustache who lived in a loft furnished with industrial carpeting who hung up his Air Force flight jacket before turning on a light which illuminated a vase of gladioluses, a drawer in which he searched for his grass, his Crisco, his bottle of poppers: and you saw that it was all of a piece.[36]

How did gay tastes change so rapidly? The next chapter explores the context of the Castro and how its hothouse environment led to the creation of its own unique aesthetic.

4

The First Wave of the San Francisco Sound

The San Francisco sound emerged in 1978 from the influence of four gay San Franciscans: Marty Blecman, Patrick Cowley, John Hedges, and Sylvester. But the sound was equally the manifestation of the Castro world they inhabited. These four men encompassed the range of gay Castro life perfectly. Blecman and Hedges moved into music production and remixing from their successful careers as DJs, and therefore were at the center of the local dance music scene. Cowley was an electronic musician, producer, and composer who, through his life as a Castro clone, channeled his experiences and desires into his own music. Sylvester captured the public's imagination as a singer whose intersectional experiences as a gay Black rock counterculture-musician-turned-disco-artist symbolized most visibly the new postliberation gay movement.

The San Francisco sound was characterized by fast tempos, a paring down of texture with a focus on simple basslines, often eighth-note repeated octaves, powerful four-on-the-floor kick drums, expansive instrumental breaks tied to the reduced importance of verses and vocal lines in general, and the addition of electronic, space-age sound effects and synthesizer melodies. While Blecman and Hedges (alongside other DJs in the city, including Gary Tighe, Michael Lee, Tim Rivers, Rob Kimbel, and Christine Matuchek) initially pursued these sounds on the dance floor primarily through European import records, by 1978 musicians like Cowley and Sylvester began incorporating these ideas in their own music. In this chapter, I outline how Cowley and Sylvester cultivated a new sound in San Francisco, and how Berkeley's Fantasy Records was the first place to introduce the Bay Area sound to the rest of the world.

Patrick Cowley

Patrick Cowley was born in Buffalo, New York, in 1950, the second oldest of Kenneth and Ellen Cowley's five children. He grew up a musical child in

Menergy. Louis Niebur, Oxford University Press. © Oxford University Press 2022.
DOI: 10.1093/oso/9780197511077.003.0005

62 MENERGY

Rochester, and by the time he graduated high school he could play the guitar (wrong way round, left-handed, like his hero Jimi Hendrix) and poke his way around a piano and was an accomplished drummer in a rock band. After a brief time at Niagara College and the University of Rochester studying English, in 1971 he moved to San Francisco to attend San Francisco City College, telling his father as he left Upstate New York, "I'll never be able to get the music I want here."[1]

Almost immediately Cowley met Professor Jerry Mueller, who founded the Electronic Music Lab at City College in 1972. Mueller's wife Madeleine was head of City College's music department and team-taught class piano with her husband, where the two of them formed a nurturing community for City music students. The electronic music class met in the Mueller's basement until City College provided them with a room, or rather several small "telephone booth sized rooms, each equipped with a quirky, English-made VCS3 'Putney' synthesizer and a reel-to-reel tape recorder," as classmate Maurice Tani recalled.[2] That first semester only three students enrolled in Mueller's course in electronic music (Cowley, Arthur Adcock, and Jerry Judnick). They were soon joined by Tani the second semester, who had also been learning piano from Madeleine Mueller. Cowley, Tani, and Adcock became close friends, playing in various rock bands and experimenting with electronic music together. Cowley's job as the Electronic Music Lab monitor gave him unlimited access to the studio's equipment, which within a few years had grown to include an ARP 2600 modular synthesizer, an E-Mu system, and a custom Serge kit. Mueller recalled one day coming into the studio, out of which he heard "A Whiter Shade of Pale": "I assumed Patrick was playing a tape, but it turned out he'd synthesized the whole thing! Not an easy thing to do!"[3]

Meanwhile, Adcock had begun equipping a studio of his own in his apartment, where he invited Cowley and Tani to collaborate. Among the equipment he purchased was a semipro TASCAM 3340 quarter-inch four-track recorder, making multitrack recording possible for the first time, and a sturdy ElectroComp 101 synthesizer. While the ElectroComp was marketed primarily to universities, it proved a reliable instrument, staying in tune where the much more temperamental EMS and MiniMoog synthesizers struggled to hold a pitch. As Tani remembers, "The beauty of the ElectroComp was it was extremely stable . . . They were a company back east in New England somewhere, and somehow Arthur [Adcock] had found these guys and bought

THE FIRST WAVE OF THE SAN FRANCISCO SOUND 63

a bunch of their gear."[4] Together, the trio wrote and performed their own music, often combining the new electronic sounds with traditional rock instruments. That first year's class ended with a student concert where they premiered Cowley's piece "Crickets," with Tani on bass, the composer on synthesizer and guitar, and Adcock operating several synthesizers at once. The piece was performed, remembers Tani,

> using every synthesizer in the lab, all of Art's gear and every other unit we could lay our hands on. "Crickets" was Pat's first long form musical piece combining melody with all the wild electronic sounds and was the grand finale of an evening of short blip and squeak taped student pieces. It took half a dozen students to set up and control all the sounds required during the performance . . . All the gear was set up in front of the stage, orchestra pit-style with the rear curtain closed. I was at the front of the band, the only player standing with everyone else seated behind synthesizers, madly pulling patch cords and twisting knobs.[5]

Adcock and Cowley formed a very close working relationship in these early years, collaborating on many projects. Adcock knew how all the equipment worked after studying the manuals and spending hours testing out the equipment's various capabilities. Cowley worked in a more intuitive way, happily stumbling across sounds, or relying on Adcock's knowledge to help create the noises he was after. "Between the two of them," Tani observed, "Pat made Art's material much more musical and Art brought Pat technical possibilities he wouldn't have come up with on his own."[6]

Short Circuit Productions and Other Early Collaborations

In 1973, the three friends created a company, Short Circuit Productions, to provide local businesses with electronic jingles.[7] This came about because Tani's friend Marti Baer and her roommate Conni Gordon worked at KFRC, one of the biggest Top 40 radio stations on the West Coast at the time, controlling when ads were placed. Their connections there and with advertisers meant they were able to introduce the composers to DJs and companies who needed stingers for their airtime. "'Bang! It's the news,' that kind of stuff," Tani explains:

You could buy these kind of stinger packages from these various companies around the country that were quite expensive, but they were sort of generic . . . And the producers, the music director, and the disc jockeys that are at KFRC knew us personally. We could make stuff for them that was specific to them, that nobody else had . . . I think if we were to have made that into a real successful sort of thing, we should have had somebody who was a little more business-oriented than we were. We liked the idea of doing this kind of work because it was a way to apply what we were already doing to something that could make some money, but we didn't really have the business acumen to go out and sell this thing on a broader scale than we already were. And honestly, at that time, the world that we lived in didn't value money all that much, and so we didn't really have the drive to try and make this thing into something that we could make a bunch of money off of. An opportunity would come along and we would do it and then our attention would go off elsewhere into doing other art stuff.[8]

In addition to his work with Short Circuit and City College, Cowley was heavily involved in the gay counterculture. He lived at various times with ex-Cockette Scrumbly Koldwyn, the avant-garde artist Jorge Socarrás, and future erotic film star Candida Royalle, where his proximity to these theatrical figures offered opportunities to write and perform music. One of the first was with Warped Floors, a post-Cockette performance collective featuring Koldwyn, Socarrás, and probably Bobby Starr on their first production, *Rickets: A Portrait of the Counterculture*, in 1974. For this, Cowley wrote a freestanding overture using the equipment in the music lab, primarily the ARP synthesizer. The ARP also features heavily in "Don't Ask," written in summer 1974, which takes advantage of that instrument's ability to slide smoothly between pitches, albeit monophonically. Basically a slow drone piece in 3/4 with a repeated synth pulse on the eighth note, the inclusion of two electric guitars, one with wah-wah pedal, lends a funky quality to an otherwise progressive rock–inspired piece.

This funk element was explored further in several songs written in 1975, including "Cat's Eye," "Pigfoot," "5oz of Funk," "Uhura," and "He's Like You." "Pigfoot" was probably the closest Cowley got to proper funk. Featuring real drums with a strong backbeat, rhythm guitar, and a funky synth bassline reminiscent of Herbie Hancock, the synthesizer solos anticipate his later extended disco breaks. Despite the title, "5oz of Funk" is more indebted to progressive rock with its mixed meter and extemporaneous quality. A meandering fuzzy

THE FIRST WAVE OF THE SAN FRANCISCO SOUND   65

synth melody evokes a kind of funk without ever committing itself entirely to the groove. "He's Like You" features a drum set, cowbell, and a repeated synthesizer bass line. The expansive and atmospheric "Cat's Eye" uniquely features piano, snare, and toms, and a complex combination of synthesizers. "Uhura," a moody, abstract synthesizer piece, owes more than a little to Louis and Bebe Barron's "Electronic Tonalities" created for the 1956 film *Forbidden Planet*. Cowley includes a heavily echoed electric guitar melody toward the end, but still the piece is as close as he would get to the dreamy, science fiction language of Tomita or Jean-Michel Jarre in these early years.

That same year, Cowley worked with vocalist and actress Candida Royalle (aka Candice Vadala) on a set of experimental sound pieces for use in the theatrical productions of the Angels of Light and Warped Floors.[9] "Candida Cosmica" features amorphous vocal improvisations by Royalle treated with electronic echo and reverb by Cowley. "Elementals" uses sampled movie quotes (taken from the 1971 British horror film *Blood on Satan's Claw*) with electronic noises freely added, in a sound reminiscent of John Cage's *Williams Mix*. At the very end of "Elementals" parts of "Candida Cosmica" return. Finally, "Shimmering," as abstract as "Candida Cosmica" but with a few synthesizer melodies thrown in at random, completes this experimental collection of atmospheres. The eclectic nature of Cowley's electronic music before 1977 shows perfectly how his influences—funk, hard rock, psychedelia, Indian Classical music, European electronic music—all rather cleverly, if aimlessly, wound their way through his projects. His emersion and participation in clone culture, however, would eventually provide a focal point for his energy. Cowley's unification of a bathhouse ethos, overt gay sexuality and sensuality, and obsession with electronic music was to come in the form of the new sounds of disco.

Michele, "Disco Dance"

In 1977 Cowley created his first disco remix, an extended version of Michele's "Disco Dance," a track from the artist's album *Magic Love*. Ambitiously, he sent it to her producer, Pierre Jaubert, who chose to release it as the A-side of the song's 12-inch single on West End Records, despite its rather awkward transitions and much lower sound quality (having been dubbed from his semipro tape recorder). Cowley extended the already long 8:42 album track to a trance-inducing 13:40 by looping a breakbeat instrumental minute (from 2:14–3:20 in the original) several times and layering his own synthesizer playing on top. Additions included a propulsive synthesized backbeat, phased birdlike chirping sounds, and spacey synthesizer melodies and countermelodies, including a bluesy two-minute solo (10:36–11:47).

But most strikingly, unlike other disco breaks of the time, Cowley seems less interested in building up polyrhythmic elements modularly, such as those by John Davis and the Monster Orchestra in tracks like "I Can't Stop" (1976) and Giorgio Moroder in his influential "Love to Love You Baby" remix (1976), to increase tension and give the track a sense of forward motion. Instead, Cowley is content to allow the texture to remain static, with sounds entering and leaving at will absent any sense of forward motion—teleology at a standstill. True to his counterculture and progressive rock roots, Cowley's mix lives in the individual moment, in the two-bar phrase, repeated until he decides to stop. Like other drone works of the pop counterculture, such as Titanic's "Sultana" (1970), Cowley's first commercially released piece of music is a perfect snapshot of a mind swimming with multiple influences all combined for the first time in service to the dance floor. "Disco Dance" foreshadows Cowley's preoccupations with dance, hedonism, science fiction, and non-Western cultures.

"I Feel Love"

For his next project, completed in September 1977, he worked with commercial copies of Donna Summer and Giorgio Moroder's electronic masterpiece "I Feel Love" to produce his own remix. He had recently recorded his own instrumental arrangement of the new tune using a combination of electronics and traditional drums and incorporated some of the experiments from that project into his new remix of the original recording. A month later, he felt confident enough after his success with West End Records to send it to Casablanca Records to see if they were interested in releasing it, to which he received a humbling "no."[10] Despite the revolutionary nature of Summer and Moroder's "I Feel Love," the Casablanca original 12-inch 1977 remix was nothing special. The anonymous Casablanca editor extended the song from its six-minute single to 8:15 by simply repeating the last 2:15 of the original (the break and the third verse).

Cowley took a much more innovative approach. His goal was to create a mix that would recreate the feeling of both the bathhouse and the dance

THE FIRST WAVE OF THE SAN FRANCISCO SOUND   67

floor, the dark, seedy, sweaty, single-minded masculine energy that defined these gay spaces for him. His mix opens with Summer's original for the first three minutes. But at the end of the second chorus he introduces new polyrhythmic elements into the front of the mix. Against the regularity of Moroder's propulsive bass drum and smooth synthesizers, Cowley's own electronic sounds, more abrasive and percussive, punctuate the texture in syncopated low-frequency waves. These sawtooth pulses are given an electronic echo, allowing them to reverberate throughout the background, but always emphasizing the downbeat. The pattern is repeated for an astounding seventy-seven measures, or three full minutes of hypnotic instrumental rhythm, individual modular elements entering and leaving like building blocks of sexual tension. The spell is so complete that when Summer's voice returns at the six-minute mark, it comes as a shock as dancers are brought back down to earth in the presence of the human again.

Verse three and a chorus are quickly dispatched and Cowley's modules return, this time with the addition of an even more aggressive synthesizer line emulating an electric guitar. In fact, this distorted "guitar" solo resembles nothing as much as Jimi Hendrix's legendary psychedelic improvisatory style. Maurice Tani remembers how Cowley would run his Gibson guitar through the studio's ARP 2600 or ElectroComp synthesizers, and then run that signal through a low-frequency oscillator-controlled filter, "so it was just constantly opening up."[11] The ARP 2600 had a built-in preamp, and "if you turned it all the way up, it generated this heavy distortion. It wasn't designed to do this but we were just overriding it."[12] When overlaid on top of Moroder's cyclical drone pattern, the effect is an intensification of the simmering energy. Your skin becomes electric, the hairs on your arm standing on end like they're charged with static electricity, and you respond as if experiencing an erotic reimagining of Terry Riley's *Rainbow in Curved Air*. A percussion solo and dive-bombing sound effects resembling falling meteors cue the return of Summer's vocals once again for a repetition of verse two and a chorus.

At 11:40, it's Cowley's turn again. For his third and final interlude, he takes his dancers to the top of the frequency range with treble tweets, electronic bird sounds deployed in the way that future acid house tracks would use the Roland TB-303, to fill in the gaps between the beat. Eschewing melodies, Cowley uses the repeated syncopated twittering patterns to complicate the polyrhythmic texture even further, filling out the environment of the dance floor with an all-encompassing beat, so that at the level of the individual the entire body is filled with an integrated and interlocked repetition or drone. And at the communal level, the dance floor is equally interlocked in a primal thrusting, pounding carnal Carnatic trance. Individual and communal, the remix is an embodiment in sound of both the liberation and pleasurable prison house of newfound gay freedom. As his remix concludes after sixteen minutes, with the return of Summer's voice and the original ending, Cowley has presented his dancers with a new kind of dance music. For the first time, the voice of gay liberation intended purely for the liberated had been manifested sonically. His pride in the remix practically jumps off the pages of his diary as he records sending it off to Casablanca, and he knew he was at a crossroads:

> A sudden and even awesome stroke of good energy comes to me via the MUSIC. I wait for the next step with baited breath. What'll it be? A new turn in my life toward rewarded creativity? Casablanca Records possesses the extended, augmented version of "I Feel Love" and I await their judgment. Nevertheless an important shift of perspective has taken place. I now realize my talents are valuable and are fast approaching a level of maturity sufficient to pay the rent. I'm ready for it. Ready to dive into the business of music and come up with my share of the large life, The Extended, Augmented Version![13]

Sylvester and Patrick Cowley Meet

Sylvester's second Fantasy album, *Step II*, came out in the summer of 1978, and while there remained a distinctive difference between the disco and R&B material, the overall quality was much higher. Now disco was the star, filling the A-side with the charged, energized atmosphere of the Castro. And even on the B-side the mix of Sylvester's blues, rock, and gospel background works *with* Fuqua's R&B impulses. But this change was hard won, with most of the effort in finding a new sound falling onto Sylvester's shoulders. He had attended the annual *Billboard* New York Disco Forum by himself in June 1978 to familiarize himself with the latest trends and fashions in disco music. He recalled that he "sat way back, just listening. Then I went back in the studio and applied everything I had seen and heard, arrangements, music, sound attitudes. I have everything it takes to be a disco star—personality, charisma, special powers, and a voice that works for disco."[14]

THE FIRST WAVE OF THE SAN FRANCISCO SOUND   69

Some of the changes were due to a personnel shakeup: Bob Kingson played on bass now instead of John Dunstan, and Randy Merritt played drums. While James Wirrick remained as Sylvester's guitarist and songwriting collaborator, the most profound difference in sound came from the replacement of Dan Reich on keyboards with Michael C. Finden. "I actually got Michael that job," recalls Linda Imperial, who in between gigs with Loverde had been singing in an East Oakland band, Spectrum. "Michael was the only gay guy in this band. So when we would tour, you know, they're all East Oakland African-Americans, so Michael and I became roommates. And it was great, we had so much fun. And I looked at him and I said, 'Honey, you are in the wrong band.' So, I told Sylvester about Michael."[15] Finden was primarily a jazz pianist, as well as a jazz vocalist, having sung in various jazz ensembles in the Bay Area. This sensibility moved Sylvester's sound further from the R&B style of the first album and closer to a polished kind of funk.

But even with all these changes, the songs on the album went through several versions before Sylvester was happy with the sound. As before, Sylvester tested his material live around town, and he realized that something wasn't right, it wasn't coming together the way he had hoped. The sound was still too close to what he had done on his first Fantasy album. During one of these performances, while Marty Blecman DJed upstairs at the City Disco, downstairs in the cabaret Patrick Cowley worked as a lighting technician for Sylvester. Despite the City's increasing straightness, it was still one of the premiere dance palaces and live gay venues in the Bay, and while Cowley's lighting position didn't provide him with an outlet for his music, it put him in contact with those who could. This opportunity for Cowley would provide Sylvester with the distinctive element missing from his new sound: the synthesizer. Frank Loverde (who often opened for Sylvester) recalled that,

> Patrick was our lighting technician at The City Disco and we had no idea at all that he was doing music, he kind of kept it under his hat for a long time. After he had worked with us for many shows he asked if we'd like to come down and do backups on some songs he'd been working on. We went down to his studio one day and as it turned out he had all this wonderful music. We did "Kickin' In" which was never released, "Love Me Hot" which was never released and many others.[16]

Sylvester's live run-throughs of his *Step II* material at the City in late May 1978 were the perfect opportunity for Cowley to introduce himself and share

70   MENERGY

his remix of "I Feel Love" with the local celebrity.[17] For Sylvester, this remix showed him that Cowley was the magic ingredient his half-finished new album needed. Abandoning the already recorded backing track for the new song "You Make Me Feel (Mighty Real)," Sylvester gave Cowley free reign to incorporate his electronics, both as science fiction sound effect and hard-driving propulsive rhythm into that song, as well as the other disco track on the A-side of the album, "Dance (Disco Heat)." Despite Sylvester's mistaken belief that Cowley "only had this one little machine, and his first synthesizer," he said at the time,

> This is the direction that I wanted to head into. I was very frustrated and bored with the way I was sounding. Very bored. And I didn't want this album to sound anything like the last album—I wanted a total new concept and a total new feeling about the music. And I was prepared to go to New York and go wherever I had to go—Europe, if necessary—to get the sound that I wanted. And just weeks before I was ready to leave and go scouting for people, I found the very person I was looking for—Patrick Cowley—had been here all the time, had worked at the City as a spotlight man. He invited me over to hear some of his music, and I totally flipped out, 'cause it was what I was looking for; I saved a lot of money and a lot of time. I worked with Patrick personally, and he became a very good friend of mine . . . And the funny thing is, he'd never done any professional recording before.[18]

Cowley was added to the live band, and the revamped live shows received a positive response, confirming Sylvester's initial faith in this new direction. The *San Francisco Sentinel* observed of one evening's performance:

> Patrick Cowley, conducting a synthesizer programmed to add orchestral textures and dramatic sound colorations . . . assists in the interplay of images by undercutting the smooth, good-natured sweetness of some tunes with eerie, piercing synthesonic missiles that explode from below every time the songs threaten to reach the self-destructive heights of vainglorious religiosity. But when you get right down to it, this is truly glorious music, rushing, soaring and high-spirited. Congratulations, Sylvester![19]

Cowley's contribution immediately changed the character of the album, with side one comprising deep, electronic disco and side two a more familiar

R&B-based disco sound. Sylvester said at the time, "The music's all totally different—we recorded the B-side in LA with LA musicians and LA arrangers and concert-masters, and we did the disco stuff here. And then we put all the synthesizer recording on here. This sound is really what's going on right now. It involves lots of synthesized music—very Munich Machine, almost bordering on the Casablanca Records sound—and the music is mellower on one side and heavy, heavy disco on the other side."[20]

The album opens with "You Make Me Feel (Mighty Real)," and one of disco's most memorable two-bar hooks. After a brief introduction that sets up the four-on-the-floor rhythm, a synthesizer sweeps upward with a dramatic "whoosh," landing on electronic bass octaves on F, establishing the bright major key for a measure before dropping to the iv on a B♭m7 for two beats, rising up a fourth to E♭ for two beats and resolving satisfyingly on F to start the pattern again (see example 4.1). This simple act of resolution, of tension and release, in two bars, repeated four times, especially given the rhythmic activity that accompanies it, resembles the circularity of Cowley's "I Feel Love" remix, the satisfying static quality that made it so successful. Doubling Cowley's bass eighth-note octaves is a traditional electric bass, with electronic twittering on the sixteenth note. Handclaps reinforce the backbeat, with help from a mechanical off-beat hi-hat between each beat.

Cowley's "galloping" bassline would become a trademark for him, and it can be heard in a near identical form in a remix he made at the same time for Pierre Jaubert's latest production, Brenda Mitchell's "Body Party." In its string arrangement and vocal style, Jaubert is merely repeating what he had (effectively) done on his and Cowley's first collaboration, Michelle's "Disco Dance," but Cowley had evolved from the earlier, abstract, almost psychedelic improvisational style to a much more focused, bass-driven high energy

Example 4.1 "You Make Me Feel (Mighty Real)" two-bar repeated phrase.

72 MENERGY

space disco sound, and this octave, bouncing, swooping texture is transposed effortlessly onto Sylvester's track.

Filling out the background of "Mighty Real" are an electric guitar, electric piano, and synthesized strings, giving the texture warmth and a feeling of up-tempo joy. After these initial moments of synthesized bliss, the entrance of Sylvester's voice begins the first verse, which quickly directs us downward, as the bass descends, avoiding E for the more plangent E♭ to D. It's like a splash of cold water, a shock of reality that grounds the verse in the human, the mundane of the relative minor as Sylvester relates the act of cruising on the dance floor. The harmony of the verse repeatedly moves downward, establishing itself on the D minor tonic every second measure four times, reinforced by the C♯ of the A+7 chord each time it moves down. The intensity of the minor mode evokes the erotic shabbiness of the bar backroom, the bathhouse's subversive sleaziness. But all this earthiness sets up the ecstatic move to the chorus, "You make me feel mighty real." Dramatically shifting back to F major for the chorus, the B♭ acts like a plagal cadence, the "amen" cadence, as we fly to heaven, reinforced by the repetition of the electronic swoop upwards.[21] The song draws on two primary metaphors in Western culture, as discussed by linguists George Lakoff and Mark Johnson, "More is Up" and "Happy is Up."[22] In much the same way that nineteenth-century German composers would move to the ♭6 to signify transcendence, Sylvester takes the dancer out of the banal and into the territory of the transcendent. The second verse drops the dancer back into the relative minor, and away from the dance floor and into the bedroom. The unusual absence of his backup singers Izora Rhodes and Martha Wash reinforces the erotic intimacy of the moment. Again, the chorus swoops us back to the stratosphere for an experience of "realness." From this moment on (1:19) the song never returns to the gloominess of the minor verse territory; it remains in the F major realm of the real for the rest of its 6:35 duration, primarily through Cowley's mechanistic instrumental texture with Sylvester interpolating cries of "I feel real" reverberating throughout.

The combination of Sylvester's gender-bending vocals and the sensual coldness of Cowley's synthesizers reconfigures the concept of "realness" into a celebration of self-actualization, at once erotic and anonymously impersonal. The "you" addressed in the lyrics can be read as the gay community, or anyone participating in the act of cruising, and ultimately gay sex itself, as a manifestation of gay liberation. Gay sex and gay dancing are two sides of the same coin; the sweaty, passionate dance-floor simulation is as real as the sex

THE FIRST WAVE OF THE SAN FRANCISCO SOUND   73

act itself, both had been illegal until fairly recently, and both were still stigmatized by mainstream America. Sylvester sings out loud what the Castro clone had been thinking and doing for the past several years in the security of San Francisco.

"Dance (Disco Heat)" opens at the same tempo, with a driving off-beat hi-hat and electric bass playing octaves. Over this, Sylvester asks the Tons, "Got a match? It's a fabulous club, look at all the fabulous people. Wanna dance?" "I'd love to," Martha replies. "Let's party a little bit," Sylvester continues, and Wash and Rhodes sing the first and only verse. Although it starts on a bright B♭ major, the verse quickly moves down to the relative minor (as in the earlier song), setting up the revelatory transition to the major for the majority of its 5:58 length. Nearly all of the song is given over to an extended instrumental break, surrendering to its own invocation, repeated over and over, to "dance." Side A of *Step II* concludes with a cool-down "Epilogue," a slow version of "Mighty Real," this time performed with the backup singers in a gospel style, reinforced by a church piano. The voices of Sylvester and the Tons affirm the "realness" of the past twelve minutes in glorious sacred style, taking the dancer and listener to church.

The B-side of the album opens with the aggressive disco/funk track "Grateful." Sylvester's unapologetically flamboyant vocals and soaring strings continue the prideful sound of the A-side. The song shares with "Dance (Disco Heat)" a focus on the groove, and the repetitious riff reinforcing the almost chant-like shout of the word "Grateful." This is followed by the ballad "I Took My Strength from You." The flutes from the first album make their return, now with the inclusion of a Spanish guitar and gospel organ. In the second verse the Tons take over the vocals, and for the rest of the song Sylvester interjects over their delicate high singing.

For the next song, "Was It Something That I Said," a funky girl group-style song, the Tons open with a play on the "mystery" of Sylvester's sexuality, speaking the lines,

> "Child, have you heard the latest?"
> "Uh-oh, what's going on now?"
> "About Sylvester breaking up,"
> "Uh-uh, he done broke with, um . . ."
> "Girl, it's a mess."
> "Uh oh, you better tell me about this one,"
> "Honey, he tell you better than I can."

"Sylvester, tell me about this, please honey."

"Girls, I'm in the dark just like you, I really don't know what happened, I got this letter, and I ran to the telephone, picked it up and dialed the number and it was disconnected with no referral."

Sylvester then sings and speaks the rest of the song in his baritone range for the first time on record rather than his trademark falsetto, and the listener discovers that Sylvester possesses a lower voice closer to the warmth of Lou Rawls than a gritty Teddy Pendergrass, giving the song an air of calm sensuality despite the campy spoken elements. Closing out the album, the ballad "Just You and Me Forever" joins guests Eric Robinson on piano with Motown legends James Jamerson on bass and James Gadson on drums.

When it came time to design the album cover, Sylvester took the lead, with an unapologetic focus on glamour and elegance. Assisted by future Oscar-winning designer Dennis Gassner (then working in the art department at Fantasy), and photographer Phil Bray, Sylvester's idea was to show a martini glass halfway, but not entirely, tipped over by a wayward, glitter-encrusted woman's bare foot, while a man's foot, dressed in a sophisticated loafer, remains firmly planted on the pink-and-black tile floor. "Everything was especially made," Sylvester proudly told the press. "The shoes are Ralph Lauren and the tile floor was just made for the shooting. The crystal glass is an heirloom from Dennis' family, and that's Nancy's [Pitts] foot. We used a thin wire to actually tip the glass over, and we ended up breaking four of Dennis' glasses before we got it right!"[23] On the back cover, a photo taken at a live presentation of the album's songs at the Trocadero Transfer showed Sylvester in a gold lamé caftan, dripping with heavy African-inspired jewelry and painted nails and face. The Tons, flanking him, appear in sequined black-and-blue choir robes, while smoke swirls around all three. "We rented the building and had the fog machines and lighting and we sang to our disco mixes," Sylvester remembered.[24] Unlike his first album, there seems to have been no scandal about Sylvester's androgynous look, and for the moment, at least publicly, Fantasy seems to have overcome its reservations about an "out" Sylvester. Nat Freedland, director of artist relations at Fantasy, declared of disco in spring 1979, "The music is a symbolic call for gays to come out of the closet and dance with each other."[25]

"You Make Me Feel (Mighty Real)" entered the *Record World* dance charts (a collection of DJs' top 10 lists from across the country) in July 1978.[26]

THE FIRST WAVE OF THE SAN FRANCISCO SOUND   75

Reviews, and there were many, were practically unanimous in their praise, with critics finding in Sylvester's anthems a variety of empowering and motivating messages. Most also singled out Patrick Cowley's synthesizer contribution as the perfect complement to Sylvester's unique, very human, style. The critic for the *New York Daily News* found the interplay between Sylvester, the Tons, and Cowley's synthesizer "charged" with an energy reminiscent of Little Richard.[27] Robert Christgau of the *Village Voice* felt that while Sylvester's earlier work never quite worked, here he "finally captured the true 'femaleness' of a woman's voice, rather than the male falsetto."[28] *Cash Box*'s reviewer called *Step II* a "soaring, throbbing disco/R&B album," and observed that "Sylvester's smooth, high-pitched voice is at the heart of *Step II*'s winning formula, but equally valuable is the innovative synthesizer textures from Pat Cowley and Leslie D's sophisticated horn and string arrangements."[29] The gay press, which usually pilloried disco, made an exception for *Step II* and Sylvester, as in Brian Chin's review in *Gaysweek*, where he praises the insightful blend of futuristic science fiction and gay liberation: "A strobelike synthesizer dominates the cut, but, unlike the cold, mechanized feel of Giorgio Moroder's and Kraftwerk's tracks, a small band . . . keeps this cut at a very human, very emotional boiling point. Spacey synthesizer beeps and Sylvester's understated performance counter the surging rhythm track, creating the most extraordinary tension."[30]

In the wake of the album's success, Fantasy rushed Sylvester and his band (including Cowley) on a hastily organized international tour. In the United Kingdom, Simon Frith at *Melody Maker* said it was the "best show I've seen in ages."[31] Despite calling Sylvester a "plump Tina Turner," he acknowledged the singer's unabashed ability to channel the energy of his largely gay audience, admiring how he "set up ripples of sexual tension (I found myself envious of the collective pleasure of Sylvester's 'boys') without making waves of sexual exclusion."[32]

"Dance (Disco Heat) / You Make Me Feel (Mighty Real)" stayed at the number 1 position on the *Billboard* dance charts for six weeks, from August 19 to September 30, and remained in the Dance Top 40 for the next six months. More remarkably, the song had crossover appeal, appearing on both *Billboard*'s R&B and the Hot 100 charts for months, and *Step II* appearing on the Top Albums charts, peaking the week of October 28, 1978, at 28.

The overwhelming success of *Step II* hid a fundamental conflict between Sylvester and producer Fuqua, however. The singer couldn't deny the skill

76 MENERGY

with which his producer organized and shaped the final album. He never publicly dismissed the tempering influence Fuqua had, stating that,

He is a technical, experienced ear in the music industry. I am mad. Crazed. He balances Patrick and I out . . . If it were left to us we would be doing absolutely mad, crazy things in the studio that would probably be very successful. But the system has to be a certain amount of tameness and a certain amount of safety, and he bends with us very much. He's the safety, the balance. We don't hear a lot of the things he hears because he's the more seasoned listener.[33]

But privately, Sylvester was generally unhappy that he was not allowed to pursue his more adventurous ideas, beginning with the remixed versions of the album's two singles. He and Cowley edited them themselves, expanding, as Cowley had done with Donna Summer and Michele, the original material and incorporating more of his trademark synthesizer effects. Totally enthused by their new hybrid sound of propulsive cutting-edge electronics and gospel-infused realness, Sylvester bragged that "we programmed a total new sound and package" for the remixes.[34] Despite their effort, Fantasy rejected their mixes and released two quickly edited, conventionally extended version of the singles instead. Sylvester and Cowley were furious.

Fuqua's more conservative approach is representative of the larger attitude of Fantasy Records in general. As a relatively small label, they just weren't capable of or interested in paying for the kinds of large-scale aggressive marketing campaigns the major labels were known for when releasing mainstream disco products. In an article for the *San Francisco Bay Guardian*, Sylvester complained, "I don't feel personally that they have the resources. They do an excellent job with what they have. I can't complain at all. They treat me fabulously . . . But you see, I don't want to compete with the middle-of-the-road disco people, who have only one or two hits. I want to compete with the stars . . . If you're going to compete in that league, you cannot be safe."[35]

For Sylvester, disco was the music that finally felt authentic to him, that enabled him and Cowley to express their feelings of an authentic liberated gay self, specifically a musical representation of the Castro culture. He explained his connection to the Bay:

San Francisco is my favorite city. I'm happy and comfortable there. . . . A lot of artists I know don't like to be classified as disco artists but I don't mind because it has been good to me. It opened the door for me to be able to express myself musically in a way in which I feel very comfortable . . . I do love disco music very much. . . . Had I not been gay myself, I would not have had the support of the gay community. But, since I AM, the community respects me for being successful––and for being upfront about my sexuality. They can relate to me so it has its merits there.[36]

More specifically, Sylvester was claiming this new sound for San Francisco, a sound he had heard in the discos and at megaparties. Sylvester felt he was uniquely positioned to spread that sound to the rest of the world:

I would like my music to become the new wave of music coming out of San Francisco. There's been no-one innovative enough to come out with something different and say "I am from San Francisco," THIS is what the music's about in San Francisco and not going to New York to record and not going to Los Angeles to record and not going to Europe to record. And that's what we've done and proven that there IS a definite sound and people ARE into things coming out of the city without having to go all over the world.[37]

He was certainly successful at demonstrating the strength of the San Francisco dance music scene, a production industry that while small was growing with each hit. As the next chapter shows, things were just getting started. Blecman and Hedges built off the momentum Sylvester and Cowley had generated to make their once-provincial scene resonate with dancers around the world. If none of the music was to top the astronomical mainstream commercial success of *Step II*, it still proved to the residents of the Castro that their culture was something worth dancing about.

5

Blecman and Hedges

A Tumultuous Year

The success of *Step II* in the summer and fall of 1978 is just one part of a remarkable period in San Francisco's history and gay legacy. It might have been a coincidence, but Sylvester's success as the first out and proud musician to have a disco hit occurred right as singer and Florida orange juice spokesperson Anita Bryant's Save Our Children campaign failed in California through Proposition 6 on November 7, 1978. For more than a year leading up to elections, San Francisco's gay community had taken the lead in the statewide effort to defeat the homophobic proposition that sought to remove openly gay teachers (and those who supported them) from California schools, through a series of fundraisers, mailings, and a boycott of Florida orange juice. For example, in May 1977, Oil Can Harry's held a benefit for the Dade County Coalition, with Jane Fonda, Sheriff Richard Hongisto, and supervisor candidates Rick Stokes, Barry King, and Harvey Milk that raised almost $3,000.[1] The bar advertised that it would "continue to fight Anita Bryant and her bigoted forces" by donating half of the revenue from John Hedges's Sunday Tea Dance to "whatever city or locale she is trying to force her prejudices upon. We Shall Overcome."[2]

The joy of that election victory for the gay community was short-lived, however. On November 18 Jim Jones led a mass suicide of 918 of his followers in Jonestown, Guyana. His Peoples Temple was headquartered in San Francisco and was seen as one of the few "churches" that not only tolerated gays and lesbians but openly advocated for them. "Everyone is gay," Jones had once said, and progressive Mayor George Moscone and openly gay City Supervisor Harvey Milk had been supporters of Jones. The final tragedy occurred less than a month after the Jonestown massacre: On November 27 both Mayor Moscone and Supervisor Milk were assassinated by fellow City Supervisor Dan White.

Against this chaotic backdrop, Marty Blecman and John Hedges were establishing themselves at the center of the nascent San Francisco sound.

Menergy. Louis Niebur, Oxford University Press. © Oxford University Press 2022.
DOI: 10.1093/oso/9780197511077.003.0006

First through their DJing, then as remix artists at Fantasy, and finally through their own original productions, Blecman and Hedges shifted the course of disco through their sparse but intense arrangements, incorporation of electronic sounds, and hedonistic ethos. This chapter charts their progress through the late 1970s; while Sylvester and Cowley continued to explore their space-age sound, Blecman and Hedges worked behind the scenes to steer disco further away from its Philly origins and toward a high-energy style that would serve the culture well when disco, seemingly overnight, was dropped by mainstream America.

Bay Area Disco Deejay Association (BADDA)

Laying the groundwork for the San Francisco sound, local DJs like Hedges and City Disco Music Director Jon Randazzo drew upon their experience forging connections with dance music labels to establish the Bay Area Disco Deejay Association (BADDA). In 1974, legendary operator of New York's Loft private club David Mancuso and DJs Steve D'Aquisto and Paul Casell had created the first disco record pool (the New York Record Pool), providing a model for the creation of similar organizations in San Francisco, Los Angeles, and other major cities. Hedges and Randazzo had been frustrated by the lack of a central location for the distribution of the growing number of dance records released each month. In 1976, they invited twenty-three of the Bay Area's most prominent DJs to lunch at the P.S. (1976–1978) on Polk Street, where they laid out their vision of an organization that would serve as a link between record promoters and DJs.[3] The DJs present were overwhelmingly excited about the idea, and elected Hedges as president, Randazzo as vice president, Don Miley as treasurer, and Roc Sands as secretary, with Marty Blecman on the Board of Directors. Randazzo offered the name BADDA and Timmy Rivers designed a stylish logo for the group. Within a few months, they had fifty members and an office in the Fox Plaza on Market Street. Record company reps started sending BADDA five to seven recordings a week for the DJs to sample, but that number quickly grew, as did the number of companies participating. By 1977, the nonprofit pool had expanded to include around seventy DJs, who were given free records in exchange for completed informational feedback sheets.[4]

For DJ Chrysler Sheldon, Hedges and his cocreation of BADDA was the initial reason San Francisco became such an important dance music center: "I

80   MENERGY

owe that man my life. Because the way he conducted the business of making music, we got a lot of respect from club owners. We got to demand regular salaries, good salaries, and he brought a patina of perfect professionalism to our profession."[5] As the disco phenomenon began to take hold outside the gay ghettos of urban centers, executives started taking dance music more seriously and noticing the promotional impact a prominent nightclub DJ could have. For example, Atlantic Records presented Hedges with a gold record for promoting their premiere disco artist Chic's song "Dance, Dance, Dance."[6] For Black DJs like Chrysler, membership in BADDA also provided access to clubs where the overt racism of club owners would otherwise have made things more difficult. He remembers how "Oil Can Harry's made a special dispensation to allow me and Timmy [Rivers] and Don Miley, as members of BADDA, to come to the opening of Oil Can Harry's, because we were Black."[7]

By 1977, Hedges was spinning at Oil Can Harry's. At the City Disco, Marty Blecman made the leap from lighting man to DJ, sharing turntable duties with Randazzo, and cultivating a dark, electronic sound. In February 1977, Blecman wrote of Grace Jones's promotional appearance at the City, "Making her entrance on motorcycle, her beautiful body-men slowly unwrap the hooded slender cat as the crowd goes into a frenzy over every move she makes."[8] Her newest album, *Portfolio*, was a compilation of earlier hits like 1976's "Sorry," a rerecorded version of "I Need a Man," and new songs such as a disco-fied "La Vie en Rose," currently rising in the dance charts. It fully captured the campy yet intense energy embraced by the San Francisco crowd and savvily exploited by promoters and DJs like Hedges and Blecman. But such events were becoming rarities at the City, and eventually Blecman, as had Hedges before him, tired of the club's ever-straightening crowd. By 1978 he had moved to Alfie's (formerly Mind Shaft) in the Castro, where he became program director. And in late 1977, after a request from a bar in Oregon, Blecman and Hedges decided to collaborate on a "Disco Technique" course and manual, teaching prospective DJs the tricks of the trade.[9]

In the summer of 1978, both Hedges and Blecman also began working for Fantasy as "disco consultants." Blecman's winning the *Billboard* 1978 San Francisco DJ of the Year Award (in addition to Hedges's win two years earlier) certainly helped them get into the music production business because Harvey Fuqua sought them out. As Hedges remembers, Fuqua

came in and asked me if I would come over to his studio and listen to a couple tracks and tell him what I thought of them, and to maybe help mix which I had never done. The news of me working at the City helped me get into the recording industry, so I was helping, doing work with the engineers and mixing Sylvester records with Marty . . . We also worked as their publicity people for the discos to promote the records around the country and so you get to know everybody. It was pretty much, "We have a record. Can you take a look at it and give us a disco mix?" and we'd do it.[10]

Paradise Express

It makes sense that Fuqua would call upon these two veterans of the DJ booth, and of San Francisco's gay disco culture, to consult at Fantasy. Paradise Express, Fantasy's attempt to replicate the success of Sylvester for themselves, was among the first projects Blecman and Hedges worked on. (Harvey Fuqua was the mastermind behind Sylvester at his independent label Honey Records; Fantasy was just the distributor and producer.) Fantasy had recently hired Phil Jones as director of marketing (a new position) based on his twelve years of experience at Motown, and he was keen to personally enter the disco market. Jones chose to coproduce Paradise Express with renowned Motown producer and songwriter Henry (Hank) Cosby. Fantasy was also eager to add more pop music to its jazz-heavy roster of artists; the label hadn't had a Top 40 hit since the Blackbyrds' "Walking in Rhythm" in 1975.

Publicly, Fantasy insisted they weren't worried, and Vice President Orrin Keepnews told a reporter in 1978 that it was "nice to have a solid underpinning of a catalog of jazz so that while you are out there making your guesses about possible hits, you are not in a situation where, God forbid, if you guess wrong, you will starve yourself to death."[11] But to mitigate their precarious position, Fantasy acquired the Stax Records' back catalog in 1977, and in 1978 added twenty-four new pop artists to their roster. Cosby was hired as A&R director for Black artists specifically because he had helped drive Stevie Wonder to the top of the charts in the early 1970s. Consequently, Cosby and Jones had the savvy and experience to choose their first disco act carefully.

Paradise Express was hardly the product of musical newbies. The brainchild of long-struggling musicians Herb Jimmerson and his vocalist wife Vi Ann, Paradise Express was the latest iteration of a career the two had built in nightclubs and bars across the United States. They met in 1969 when working in different lounge acts in Phoenix, Arizona, and put together a touring band, the End Result. Throughout the mid-1970s, they played all over the country,

82 MENERGY

but in 1974, they and the band moved to Placentia in Orange County, California, where they found modest success as the house band for various hotels and restaurants, including the Airporter in Santa Ana, the Jolly Roger Inn in Anaheim, the Hong Kong Bar in the Century Plaza Hotel, and the new Hotel Bonaventure in downtown Los Angeles.[12] Primarily a Top 40 cover band with some originals thrown in, the End Result was noted for its ability to mimic anything from the latest sounds to nostalgic classics. When disco came on the scene, Herb Jimmerson felt it was a perfect fit for them: "We were ready to start playing it right away. Disco quickly became a main part of our live show. It's much more interesting music to perform than the top 40 songs that used to be expected in the kind of intimate dance lounges where we played."[13]

Herb and Vi Ann were just right for Phil Jones's plan to create an in-house disco band, and he signed them to Fantasy as Paradise Express, confidently offering a two-album contract and $50,000. They recorded the first album using session musicians drawn from San Francisco's best dance music groups, such as Sylvester's percussionist David Frazier, and Two Tons o' Fun, joined by frequent Sylvester collaborator Sharon Hymes on backup. Hedges remembers, "Basically, he [Phil Jones] wanted to use our musicians and to create and sign a couple of songwriters, and Paradise Express was one of them."[14]

Their first release, a double A-side 12-inch of Paul Jabara's "Dance" backed with a discofied "Poinciana," reached number 17 on the *Billboard* dance charts. The subsequent album was also warmly received, as this review in *Billboard* attests:

> "Reverend Lee" is a gospel flavored rocker. Starting off with a mild tempo, the song gradually builds to a rousing crescendo with a drum break nicely placed to add spice. "Star in my Life" is simple in musical structure in that no elaborate orchestration is needed in making this a disco pleaser. The lead vocalist carries the melody with her refreshing voice . . . Producers Henry Crosby and Phil Jones with arranger Herb Jimmerson have offered DJs good material for club action.[15]

As a sign of just how mainstream disco had become (even disco from a small label like Fantasy), "Dance" received a huge boost on January 20, 1979, when Minnesota Vikings running back Chuck Foreman gave a disco dance exhibition on the NBC pre-Superbowl show using Paradise Express's music.[16] And yet, as the reviewer noted, their style departed from earlier mainstream disco in its stripped-down austerity. Just as Sylvester's first two albums increasingly focused on the beat, paring down the thick textures and jazz-based harmonies of earlier disco to their elemental core, Paradise Express's first single in particular removes everything that could distract from the forward motion of the beat.

A comparison to Jabara's original shows just how radically Jimmerson changed the song in his arrangement. Jabara's poppy, "rock 'n' roll" backbeat is replaced by a more insistent four-on-the-floor drum, the pulse accentuated by a sixteen-beat clavinova rhythm. Jabara's campy, nostalgic "Shimmy Shimmy Ko Ko Bop" lyrics are removed, and only lines that directly reference dancing and sexuality are retained. "Blame it on the heat of the beat" is replaced by a more specific "Blame it on the disco beat." The theatrical line "Rosemary's angel dust will make you dance" is removed. The extroverted drama of the original, clearly intended to be listened to, has been replaced by an introversion, a focus on the body and the self, just as clearly meant to be danced to. But as on Sylvester's albums, the bombastic tackiness of earlier disco is replaced by a fusion of gospel and electronic music. The presence of the Two Tons improvising and testifying behind Vi Ann's more restrained, steely performance lifts songs like "Reverend Lee" and "Dance" to a place of transcendence, and Patrick Cowley's (uncredited) electronic swooshes and sweeps keep us there.

Hedges had mixed feelings about including him, feeling it was a step too far: "We put Patrick Cowley on there and it was just too much of a rip-off."[17] But reviewers (and dancers) seemed to appreciate the homage. One critic said of "Dance": "Extremely infectious with strong dance rhythms throughout and this is gonna make a lot of people get up and boogie. The bass lines are *very* effective and the presence of the Two Tons of Fun on the track as backup vocals, provide the distinct Sylvester feel to this outing. It's blatant—but it works—and I guess that's the name of the game.[18]

It was those specifically San Francisco contributions, Cowley's relatively understated sounds, and the Tons, that raised Paradise Express above other disco artists of the late 1970s, as the field was rapidly filling up with overproduced, ill-advised cash-ins. While Paradise Express may have started this way, the end product was an important fusion of many of the elements that defined the San Francisco sound. "Dance" and "Poinciana" coexisted with Sylvester's "You Make Me Feel (Mighty Real)" on the dance charts in the early part of 1979, alongside other new Blecman and Hedges projects. Fantasy's

84 MENERGY

attempt to rehabilitate its image within the pop music world was working. One *Billboard* reporter observed at the time that "in the last year, Fantasy has really started to come around. They've hired a new man from Motown named Phil Jones. They're hipper, more aggressive and have a new beefed up marketing staff. The new Sylvester record is an example of how hip they're becoming."[19]

One of the most unexpected Blecman and Hedges projects was a disco version of the *Lord of the Rings* theme. As Hedges recalls: "Saul Zaentz, who owns Fantasy, was a movie producer and he produced that movie, *Lord of the Rings*. And so there's a soundtrack, and Marty and I ran into him in the elevator and asked if we could hear the theme and put it to a disco song and he said 'go for it!' So we did."[20] The 12-inch single was released under the name the Aragorn Ballroom Orcestra (a double pun on "orc" and the Aragon Ballroom in Chicago). Fantasy's willingness to take a risk on this project is another example of the label's attempt to learn from past mistakes. Despite the huge success of Zaentz's *One Flew Over the Cuckoo's Nest*, that film's soundtrack had failed to make a dent in the charts. They were determined not to let that happen again. Gretchen Horton, publicity director, was keen to use the success of *Saturday Night Fever* as a model: "They had the marketing of that project *down*. At one time, the Bee Gees had four of the five songs in the *Billboard* pop chart. It really was all computerized . . . And they had those songs in your head, before that movie ever came out."[21] The "Lord of the Rings" dance 12-inch was positively reviewed in *Billboard*, with Barry Lederer singling out Blecman and Hedges's disco mix, with its "elaborate orchestrations, driving brass, and electronic usages . . . intermixed with a drum break and deep voices which chants in an unknown tribal language."[22]

Fever

But it was Blecman's connections back in Elyria, Ohio, that led to their biggest early commercial and artistic success, Fever. Saxophonist Dale Reed and his friend, keyboardist Joseph "Joe" Bomback, had been playing together in progressive jazz and jazz fusion groups, performing in bands for the past six years with Gentle Giant, Weather Report, Peter Frampton, Al Jarreau, and others. Joe knew Marty Blecman from high school in Elyria and from working in his father's grocery store, and they were still in touch despite Blecman's move to San Francisco. Blecman called him one day and suggested that he and Reed make a disco record. He told Joe, "if you guys wanna do some dance stuff, do something and send it to me and I'll see what I can do."[23] Dale recruited his cousin Dennis Wadlington to play bass. Wadlington was known to them primarily because he would come hear them perform in their various bands, and Reed knew he was, despite scraping by in Ohio as a rock musician in a covers band, an excellent player. Wadlington had been playing five nights a week with the group COCO (Cleveland Ohio Comes On) but felt that things were coming to a natural end with that group. Together, the three of them studied the dance music currently on the charts, including Chic and Sylvester, who Dale and Joe knew from their trips west to visit Marty and John. Eventually they settled on an old Four Tops song, "Standing in the Shadows of Love," which they felt had potential for a rhythmically dynamic disco song, especially its driving bass line.

Despite the many live music venues in Cleveland, there were few recording studios there at the time, so their options were limited. They hastily assembled a pickup band (which they called "Oasis" for the day), recruited Gladys M. Richardson and her cousin Dianne Jacksom as backup singers (who despite still being in high school had already sung in several of Wadlington's groups), and hired local drummer Danny Reese to sing lead vocals. The rough, funky sound of their recording resulted from the basic environment they were working in as much as an unfamiliarity with the disco genre. The gritty quality of Wadlington's 1956 Fender Precision bass came from its direct output from an old Ampeg bass amp with no treatment or processing. "The first thing was we isolated the bassline," recalls Bomback.[24] The first forty seconds or so establishes a strong four-on-the-floor beat with the powerful bass riff reinforced by both a synthesizer and piano. Other than some Latin percussion, this pared-down quality is maintained throughout the whole song. In contrast to the full sound of Philly soul, with its lush strings and brass, Fever's song simplified and honed the various polyrhythmic elements to the bare essentials, giving it a San Francisco edge.

Much of this quality in the final release, however, was down to Blecman and Hedges, who reworked the material extensively. "Marty's brother Vic was getting married . . . and he said, 'I'm going to be back for this wedding,'" remembers Bomback, "and I said, 'well please stay with us, I have a surprise for you.'"[25] After the wedding Joe took Marty to the studio where they were wrapping up some final elements of the recording. Blecman was impressed with what they had accomplished, especially as this was their first disco effort. A few weeks later back at Fantasy, when Blecman received the Fever

86   MENERGY

tape, he and Hedges set about remixing the various elements with Phil Kaffel, the studio's engineer. The most drastic alteration they made was to get rid of the lead vocal entirely. With that gone, they pared the song down even more, focusing on the percussion breaks, making them the center of the recording. Bomback admits that "we had extended solos, too much of our jazz fusion in it."[26] When Blecman and Hedges were done, the 12-inch release was a stripped down, bass-heavy disco floor filler. The song quickly rose up the dance charts, taking Fantasy and Fever by surprise.

Their excitement was tempered with fear as they discovered established disco artist Deborah Washington had coincidentally released a version of the same song a few months before theirs. Hedges remembers his reaction when he realized what had happened:

> We had a heart attack when we heard about her record coming out. She had big promoters behind it. And I remember, we had to go to a DJ convention in Phoenix, and I was there to promote that record. Well, I met the promoter for that other record. He was drunk or whatever, but he grabbed my records, my promos out of my hand and threw them on the bathroom floor and said "piece of shit!," it was terrible. But I got him back. I wish we had cell phones back then. I caught him in the restroom having sex with a transvestite. Would have been great.[27]

They need not have feared. While Washington's single was good, it was old-fashioned, with her breathy, Diana Ross vocals and brass-and-string arrangement reminiscent of Carol Douglas's hits of several years earlier. Her single started strong, appearing on several DJs' disco charts in September and the *Billboard* dance chart throughout fall and the beginning of winter. But while the always contrary Trocadero Transfer DJ Gary Tighe reported the out-of-towner's record as one of his top 10 dance records of the week on October 28, 1978, most DJs preferred Fever's version. The single stayed on the dance chart from the week of October 28 to well into the new year, surpassing Washington's the week of December 2.[28] *American Gay Life* called Fever's version "a hot tip on the disco scene" and "red hot, pulsating and irresistible."[29] The success of the single inspired the two producers to form a company, Blecman and Hedges Productions, on the advice of Chic promoter Marc Kreiner. "We are planning to handle everything from publishing to promotion," they declared shortly after the founding of the company, a promise that would ultimately be fulfilled.[30]

Over Christmas, Conceptual Entertainment (the name David Bandy and Gary Roverana gave to their megaparty organizing business) threw their latest Galleria megaparty—"Let It Snow"—with Marty Blecman as DJ and Pattie Brooks as special live guest. And as winter turned to spring in 1979, Fever began working on a full album.[31] With the dance-floor success of "Standing in the Shadows of Love," Fantasy had offered them their standard two-record deal, with Dale Reed producing alongside Blecman and Hedges. "Watch for a great new LP by Fever," *Baseline* (BADDA's music magazine) reported in April. "The LP, which is non-stop on side one and two, three cuts to each side, features the incredible vocals of Clydine Jackson, with backups by Maxine and Julie Waters . . . This exciting new LP should be a sure hit on your dance floor."[32]

Sylvester at the Opera House and *Stars*

At the same time, Sylvester was preparing his third Honey/Fantasy album, a more extensive collaboration with Patrick Cowley. *Stars* would feature only four songs, but each one was an expansive mix stretched out for the dance floor, the most elaborate example yet of the San Francisco sound, combining Fuqua's traditional string and brass sound with Cowley's futuristic synthesizer on three of the four tracks. Sylvester and Fantasy wasted no time in getting the first single into the charts, releasing a disco cover of the 1963 Ben E. King hit "I (Who Have Nothing)," probably more famous in gay circles for Shirley Bassey and Tom Jones's versions. The orchestral arrangements for "I (Who Have Nothing)" were recorded at Island Studios in London. Background vocals on the first two tracks, "Stars" and "Body Strong," were done without the characteristic timbre of the Tons. Instead, Pat Hodges, Denita James, and Jessica Smith sang backup. The three singers had never quite found lasting success as solo artists and were collectively known as Hodges, James, and Smith, a nightclub act created by Motown producer William "Mickey" Stevenson in the early 1970s. The press previewed *Stars* in November 1978, with one reviewer reflecting the ambivalence toward electronic sounds felt by Fuqua. Emphasizing the traditional orchestral aspects of the project and downplaying the extensive synthesizer elements, the reviewer teased that the songs "call for heavy orchestrations and the classically trained San Francisco string sections are more orientated to slow bowing. Disco requires a brisker style and in Los Angeles there are specially selected

88   MENERGY

and groomed disco orchestras whose musicals are snappy and crisp on changes."[33] Sylvester himself initially downplayed the strong synthesizer presence heard in three of the four songs on the record, highlighting the more traditional sound of the single:

> I always loved the song by Ben E King and so it was my idea to record it. . . . it is similar to the hits I've had—but yet it is completely different. It is more orchestrated—Don Ray did the arrangement, by the way. All together it covers more than 13 minutes and there are lots of Latin percussion breaks. The other three songs are original—there is "Body Strong" a sort of muscle-disco song! Then there is "Stars" and a sensuous song that is called "I Need Someone to Love Tonight." All except for "I Need Someone" are out and out disco—and you could dance to "I Need Someone" but it's a more hypnotic record. The songs were written by me, Michael Finden and Patrick Cowley—my pianist and synthesizer player. The whole thing is so fabulous, that's all I can add.[34]

It's a brilliant dance album and shows Sylvester, Cowley, Fuqua, and Blecman and Hedges at the top of their game. Side one opens with the Cowley-penned title track, "Stars," named after Michael Maletta's megaparty that heard its premiere on Pier 19, where "over 4000 people attended the celebration which was planned to turn people's fantasy into reality."[35] As Sylvester was receiving his *Billboard* awards in March for Best Heavy Disco Single (for "Dance [Disco Heat]") and Best Male Disco Singer, "I (Who Have Nothing)" entered the dance charts. Reviews were glowing for both the song and the album. *Billboard*'s Barry Lederer wrote, "As usual, the song is full of hooks, smooth vocal harmonies and well-crafted production. The artists' performance is filled with high-voltage energy and should prove a good follow-up to his 'Disco Heat' success."[36] Despite Fuqua's reservations about the increasing presence of electronic sounds in dance music, this was precisely what most reviewers found praiseworthy about the album (alongside Sylvester's distinctive persona). Lee Horning, for example, wrote that "Sylvester now has a style all his own, and is copied on most new disco singles. Credit should be given to arranger writer and keyboard player, Patrick Cowley, for without his style and excellent synthesizer this sound wouldn't have come about."[37] *Billboard* likewise praised the seamless integration of traditional and electronic elements on the album: "A strong synthesizer introduction is followed by the uplifting quality of the artist's voice with fine background arrangements and orchestration. The pulsating beat is built up with electronic effects and nonstop momentum."[38]

The most original song on the album is the finale, "I Need Somebody to Love Tonight," a lethargic, fully electronic sleaze track written years earlier by Cowley as an instrumental. With Sylvester's slinky vocals and Cowley's loping synthesizer melodies, the song is a vivid depiction of the act of cruising. It is also prefigures Cowley's later solo work; like most of his Megatone songs, he uses the synthesizer to capture both the casualness and intensity of San Francisco bar and bathhouse culture, its minor mode darkness and intensity slightly disarmed by the slow shuffle rhythm.

Just as the album was rising in the dance charts, Sylvester had another dream fulfilled. On March 11, 1979, he performed a solo show at the San Francisco War Memorial Opera House, at which Harvey Milk's openly gay successor Harry Britt presented him with the keys to the city, on the order of Mayor Dianne Feinstein, declaring it "Sylvester Day."[39] For a city still in mourning over the assassination of Mayor Moscone and Supervisor Milk, Sylvester seemed uniquely equipped to provide the kind of "church" service the community needed. *Billboard* observed at the time that, "There is something magical about Sylvester. His transition from the Cockettes of San Francisco years ago to his recent appearance at the city's opera house has made him a disco star of merit."[40] Over 3,000 people dressed for the occasion, whether in tuxedos and formal dresses or assless chaps and feather boas. Sylvester later remarked that "I suppose everyone's dream fantasy for living your life the way you want it is to go to the opera."[41] Nancy Pitts at Honey Productions bragged at the time, "the Opera House people backed away at first, but with the good reviews we had piled up and 100% backing from Fantasy, we made it happen. We were so determined that in the end that made the difference."[42] The sold-out show was produced by megaparty producers David Bandy and Gary Roverana of Conceptual Entertainment, and featured an eight-piece band, enhanced with a twenty-piece orchestra featuring musicians from the San Francisco Symphony contracted by cellist Terry Adams. The heft of the Tons was supplemented by the addition of two singers, Jeanie Tracy and Sharon Hymes.

Jeanie Tracy

Tracy had opened shows for Sylvester a few times before, but they were still getting to know each other when she was invited to sing at the Opera

House. Eventually, Tracy's relationship with Sylvester would turn into a lasting friendship, one of the most important in both their lives. She grew up in Fresno, and while working in a nightclub with her own group, playing keyboard and singing, she met Rodger Collins, who invited her to join his band in the Bay Area. By the early 1970s, she was working as the resident vocalist with Jimmy Mamou at the Brass Rail in Sunnyvale. "They had topless dancers, which I had never seen before, coming from a little farming town. . . They had a huge stage, and the band was absolutely wonderful," she recalls.[43] She ended up staying there two-and-a-half years before moving on to clubs in North Beach, and the Galaxy where she sang with Rick Stevens from Tower of Power. In 1975, she recorded an R&B single on Marvin Holmes's Brown Door Records written and produced by Bob Stewart.

A few years later, when she was singing at the Fox in Oakland, Harvey Fuqua came in with a radio DJ. The DJ had recommended Tracy to him, "Because I guess Harvey said he was just looking for other artists to manage and record . . . And so he talked to me and he sat down at the piano to see what my range was. And so I started going in, answering phones, that kind of thing, and writing songs."[44] And on one of those days, while answering phones, Sylvester walked in. "I thought it was just a big woman," she recalled to Sylvester's biographer.[45] They hit it off right away; Sylvester knew that Tracy could read music and had been writing and arranging songs in a gospel style for Tina Freeman's Voices of Harmony, so when he was looking for backup support in the same gospel style as the Tons, she was the perfect choice.

At the Opera House concert, Sylvester explicitly brought that feeling of church during the evening's finale of "Dance (Disco Heat)" and "You Make Me Feel (Mighty Real)." Tempos had been rising throughout the night, peaking at a frantic 144 BPM, and the crowd had been driven to ecstasy. Eric Robinson's gospel piano solo pushed the spirit even higher, and when Jeanie, Izora, and Martha started wailing at the top of their lungs, and the clapping shifted from a simple backbeat to eight beats a measure, Sylvester realized things were different. "I don't know what happened but the whole thing changed and we had service," Sylvester said later.[46] "You may not understand this," Sylvester cried out into the audience, "but tonight *is* Sunday night, you know it is. And that's why we carryin' on like we know, 'cause tonight is Sunday night. Sounds good to me."

Martha Wash knew something special was happening on that stage, something essential for the city's healing, bridging whatever gap that existed between gospel and disco: "While we were singing, listening to the roar of those people and their approval, it's like a spirit when you connect. Everybody's thinking along the same lines and it's explosive. They're feeding us, we're feeding them. We have this eruption of kindred souls."[47] That night at the Opera House, Sylvester and disco music provided the kind of release and collective catharsis people often seek through religion. Wash recalls that "after the show was over we were told that we would never be able to appear at the Opera House again because the two balconies, the people were moving so much you could actually feel the balconies shifting. There was so much energy there that it almost felt like a slight earthquake."[48]

Tracy's relationship to church was more ambivalent. "I went so much as a kid growing up that I swore that I wasn't going to go," she says. While she regrets missing out on a period of gospel songs, "The reasons of me not attending church was because it was just shoved down our throats all the time. And not only that, the church that I went to was very strict, with no lipstick, no pants, no this, no that. Everything was a sin. So I didn't really believe and I rebelled against it. Take away my hair and my make-up, my pants, my dance? I can't dance? Are you kidding me?"[49] Shortly after the Opera House success, Tracy joined Sylvester's band full time, and when Fantasy decided to add two new songs to the live double album of the concert, she contributed backup vocals alongside the Tons. She took her career seriously and knew that she would be joining a well-established musical family. "When I came there, I had to find my place because the girls already had set the tone. Trust me on that. They had already set the tone," Tracy remembers. "I had to find . . . my niche, and it wasn't hard to do that because the girls were friends of mine as well. And they're the ones that encouraged Sylvester to hire me too. Martha encouraged Sylvester to hire me, and so did Izora. And I was told this by Harvey, 'If the girls weren't friends of yours, you'd have a hard time.' So they weren't going to let just anybody come in there."[50]

While "I (Who Have Nothing)" was still high in the charts, Fantasy sent the whole band touring the country in support of the upcoming live album. Alan Mambar, disco promotion head at Fantasy, arranged for the promotional release of two new songs, "Can't Stop Dancing" and "In My Fantasy" mixed by Blecman and Hedges, which were gushed over by most critics and DJs. For *Billboard*, the songs' success was a foregone conclusion: "Needless to say, reaction to these cuts is more than favorable in keeping with Sylvester's preeminence as one of the top male disco stars"[51] (see figure 5.1). In the United Kingdom, *New Musical Express* called the new release "definitely a

Figure 5.1 Sylvester publicity photo. Photo courtesy of Photofeatures International. Reproduced with permission.

poke in the eye for anyone like me who thought old Jesse was about to become the Slade of disco."[52]

Fever's Album

Meanwhile, Fantasy was preparing the release of the second Paradise Express album, which was again positively reviewed.[53] "Smooth and flowing" was how *Billboard* described the record. Herb Jimmerson's production was full of "rich arrangements that sparkle with harps and violins skillfully blended with electronic keyboards for a scintillating and spacey feeling," provided by Jimmerson and an again-uncredited Patrick Cowley.[54] Their synthesizer playing emphasized both the erotic and science fiction feel of the album, particularly on a cover of Martha and the Vandellas' "Nowhere to Run," which the reviewer praised as a "combination of a futuristic and sexy flavor with only the lyrics reminding one of this oldie."[55]

Fantasy was also getting ready to release the first 12-inch singles from Fever's full-length album. The band had been working on demos back in Cleveland, fine-tuning their approach and consulting with Blecman and Hedges. Dale Reed and Mike Bomback went out to San Francisco in early 1979, staying at Hedges's place, to research what was happening in the gay club scene there. Bomback remembers,

> "Shadows of Love" was just kind of actually starting to lose its steam a little bit. And when we got there Marty wasn't working but John was at Oil Can Harry's so we ended up going to Oil Can to see John. [DJ and "disco consultant" on the album] Lester Temple was introducing us to people and all that. And then we would take our rough mixes to other DJs and ask "what do you think? Where are we? How do we stand here?" And as we were doing it, we lived at the discos and we listened to the songs and we saw what got people off. What do they hear that makes people run to the floor to dance?[56]

From the beginning, they wanted two sides that played nonstop, with one an early night 118 BPM and the other for peak time at 132 BPM. Bomback programmed all the main synthesizer parts. For the rest of the band, they were at a loss. Bassist Dennis Wadlington remembers, "We knew a couple of the guys in Sylvester's band, Patrick Cowley and Tip Wirrick. But we didn't really know a host of musicians when we got to California, so we brought our guys that we knew from Ohio. And we brought one of the hottest drummers in the Cleveland area."[57]

They also contacted Pat Gleeson, a synthesizer and keyboard player they had met when he would pass through Cleveland while touring with Herbie Hancock. Gleeson had contributed Moog synthesizer on Hancock albums in the early 1970s, and Mercury Records had also released two albums of electronic arrangements by Gleeson, Holst's *The Planets* and music from *Star Wars*, both performed on the massive Emu Systems modular synthesizer. Gleeson and his wife owned their own studio in the Bay Area, Different

94 MENERGY

Fur Studios, which he used for his contributions to Fever's record. "Let's see if Pat could program some really whack shit," Bomback remembers thinking.[58] They told him to use his imagination, and probably his best addition was a massive, slow synthesizer rising tone cluster that forms the heart of the opening track on the B-side, "Pump It Up." When Gleeson was finished, coproducer Marty Blecman still felt like it needed more electronics, and recommended Patrick Cowley. Bassist Wadlington remembers, "Patrick [Cowley] we brought in for all the sparkle and special effects kind of stuff sounds, because that was his forte."[59] More substantially, Blecman was looking for Cowley's trademark "gallop" on some of the songs, so they found a couple of places where they could drop that in. "That was also one of the things that was suggested to us by a lot of the DJs too," Bomback recalls.[60] Cowley worked with Fever for only two days, because he was headed out on tour with Sylvester. Bomback remembers bumping into him at 18th and Castro right before he left, "And it was so funny, he said, 'I'm going to be in Europe for two months with Sylvester. I got to get laid before I go!'"[61]

For vocals, the band auditioned thirty or forty background singers, and no one seemed right, until they remembered the Waters Sisters. Herb Jimmerson had recently worked with them on his Paradise Express album, and when Blecman and Hedges brought Jimmerson in to arrange the vocals for Fever, it brought additional continuity to these Fantasy projects. But the Waters were in demand: In one weekend, they recorded backup for Donna Summer's *Bad Girls* album, flew up to San Francisco and sang the entire Fever album, and flew back, telling the band, "if we fly back tonight, we might be able to do another one before we go home tonight."[62] When the band admitted they didn't have anyone for lead vocals yet, the Waters suggested Clydene Jackson. "Cause we didn't want a male vocal on it, we definitely wanted a female vocal," Bomback recalls. "So Maxine and Julie said, 'Well, we know this young lady.' And she came in and first note she hit, we were like, 'You got it, girl. Go for it.'"[63]

The songs were all recorded individually straight through, without complicated splicing (with exception of the postproduction synthesizer parts and percussion), and Blecman and Hedges edited the songs together in a nonstop mix on each side. The first single, "Beat of the Night/Pump It Up," was released in early summer, and entered the dance charts in mid-September. As positive word grew, with *Billboard* calling the release "especially notable," it rose in the charts, and by November it reached the number one position, the first Fantasy artist to do so since Sylvester's Honey Records hits the previous year.[64]

It's ironic that just as the San Francisco Sound was gaining in traction, disco was about to "die" for the rest of the country. When Chicago rock DJ Steve Dahl held his "Disco Demolition" promotion on July 12, 1979, declaring the death of disco, Castro clones were too busy dancing to notice. They, and all the other queer people in the city, had built their own Mecca, with its own community, style, literature, and now their own dance music. They were not about to give it up without a fight.

6

Disco's Dead/Not Dead

For most of America, disco died in 1979. Triggered by the infamous "Disco Demolition" night at Comiskey Park in Chicago on July 12, 1979, at which a near riot accompanied the exploding of a crate of disco records, a backlash made the word "disco" an overnight punchline. Major labels dropped disco artists and producers, and mainstream musicians who had jumped on the bandwagon just as quickly threw themselves off. Ostensibly reacting against the perceived omnipresence and overcommercialization of the genre, many participants at the demolition were in truth reacting to the replacement on radio of straight white male rockers with a whole panoply of newly empowered groups, including gay men, people of color, and women.[1] Just as profound had been the changes behind the scenes; for the first time in history, people of color, women, and gays held positions of influence and power up and down in the recording industry. As gay record producer Mel Cheren observed of disco at the time, "It was like musical monopoly, and gay people ran the bank."[2]

Gay men, however, continued to dance, and in the gay enclave of the Castro district in San Francisco, enterprising gay DJs, record producers, and musicians started their own small dance music record labels to make up for the lack of new, danceable tracks. These independent labels did more than copy what the larger industry had been doing, however. Instead, the upstart companies built on the musical experiments their roster of local musicians and producers had been exploring over the last several years, developing a distinctive style of their own. Known as "high energy" (later spelled "Hi-NRG"), the music reveled in electronics, fast tempos, disco and DJ culture, and, above all, gay liberation as it had emerged over the previous decade in the Castro neighborhood.

It isn't necessary here to explore why or how mainstream music journalists mostly responded with an apathetic shrug when white young people trashed the field of Comiskey Park. But there was also a surprising lack of dismay from the gay music press as well, even in San Francisco where the more politically active members of the community had never warmed to disco. The

Menergy. Louis Niebur, Oxford University Press. © Oxford University Press 2022.
DOI: 10.1093/oso/9780197511077.003.0007

DISCO'S DEAD/NOT DEAD   97

Disco Demolition debacle was thus a more nuanced event than merely "straight racist misogynist homophobes cancel disco." Many gay rock fans welcomed the death of disco and hastened the emergence of a new underground form of the music. They hated precisely those same elements of disco that many in the straight audience reacted against; perceived inauthenticity through the use of often nameless studio musicians, banal lyrics, a focus on hedonistic sexuality, overly polished orchestrations that reveled in the blatant commercialism of ideas of "luxury," and the "mindless" repetition articulated most clearly though the never-changing pounding four-on-the-floor kick drum. Against this, punk emerged as a new, "authentic" form of DIY musicmaking that didn't need a studio's apparatus, and as a music that expressed rebellion through an "antiglamour" and ugliness many perceived as a more accurate representation of young people's lives, gay or straight. As disco gained popularity in the mainstream, the gay press had almost uniformly embraced punk, post-punk, and new wave styles as more representative of their interests. Dance music in gay clubs didn't remain static in the early 1980s, however. It absorbed this critique to a greater and greater extent by incorporating aspects of rock, punk, and new wave into the music's style while retaining the proud legacy of disco at its core. The "Disco Sucks" movement caused changes that were already occurring in dance music to accelerate, and in San Francisco the arrival of DJs like Bobby Viteritti allowed for the evolution of the San Francisco sound, wholly electronic and more energetic than disco had ever been.

Red Hanky Party and the Politics of Solidarity

The period 1979–1980 saw the biggest expansion of disco and dance music in gay culture in the city to date, despite the decline in other markets; and it became bolder than ever. The national profile of the city as a gay party center was strengthened when, at the Seventh Annual *Billboard* Disco Awards, Conceptual Entertainment won Top Disco Concert Promoters in the US, and Bobby Viteritti tied with the Saint's DJ Roy Thode for best National DJ (see figure 6.1).[3]

The quality of life for many gay people improved after the Stonewall uprising of 1969. But for many others the struggle for equality was still very real. As gay people grew more confident and more visible in American culture, relations with "traditional" society became fraught and more tense. In May

98   MENERGY

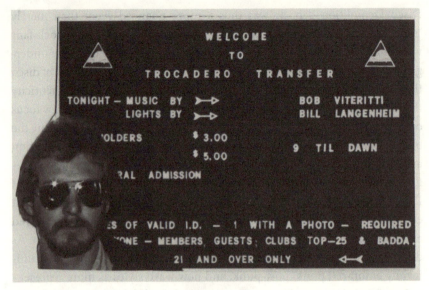

Figure 6.1 Trocadero Transfer ad celebrating Bobby Viteritti's win at the national *Billboard* awards, from *Bay Area Reporter*, February 28, 1979. Reproduced with permission.

1979, 150 gay people were beaten in Hadley, Massachusetts, when a straight crowd who didn't want a gay night at their local disco took it upon themselves to clear out the undesirables.[4] That same month, ex-cop Dan White, the assassin of Mayor George Moscone and Supervisor Harvey Milk, received a sentence of voluntary manslaughter rather than first-degree murder. What followed was more than three hours of protesting and rioting at City Hall by San Francisco's gay community, now known as the White Night riots. In 1984, friend of Harvey Milk and activist Cleve Jones recalled, "The rage in people's faces—I saw people I'd known for years, and they were so *furious*. That to me was the scariest thing. All these people I'd known from the neighborhood, boys from the corner, these people I'd ridden the bus with, just out there, screaming for blood."[5] In retribution, later that same night, dozens of police officers raided the Elephant Walk at Castro and 18th Street (the bar at which Sylvester had performed so often in the mid-1970s), beating many of the patrons and shouting "dirty cocksuckers" and "sick faggots" before moving out onto the streets where they continued beating people for two hours.[6]

DISCO'S DEAD/NOT DEAD   99

Only two weeks earlier, an incident between the police and patrons of a megaparty had demonstrated the tension in the air. After the success of the first "High Time" Red Hanky Disco Dance Party at the Gay Community Center at 330 Grove, sponsored by the SoMa bathhouse Handball Express (975 Harrison, 1979–1982), a second was held at the same place on Friday, April 20, 1979, with Steve Fabus DJing.[7] In the aftermath of Moscone's assassination, Dianne Feinstein had been appointed mayor, and the perception among many in the gay community was that she was less tolerant than her predecessor. "She wasn't antigay, of course," Fabus remembers. "For one thing, she had to represent the gays. But her idea about the bathhouses, she made it difficult for the bathhouses at that time to get licenses ... She would make remarks like, 'I wish you guys wouldn't walk around in your chaps and with your ass hanging out.'"[8] When Moscone was mayor, he went out of his way to be friendly to his Castro and SoMa constituents, going to leather and drag parties, and would join Harvey Milk at discos and even occasionally go on his own. Feinstein wasn't like that. Fabus recalls the night of the second Red Hanky Party:

We were partying and partying, and it was like 3:00 in the morning and full. I mean, it's like, guys were in leather or they're half naked or totally naked on the dance floor. And sex going on all over the place. So, it's 3:00 am and then all of a sudden a bunch of cops come up to the DJ booth and they said, "Turn it off. This party's over." After our freedom that we had with Moscone and Milk during that period, it just seemed weird. I actually didn't turn it off right away ... So then the cops just filled the DJ booth. There were cops all around me, and so I turned it down. Well, I turned it down suddenly actually, bam! And then I got on the microphone. I said, "the cops are here and they're shutting the party down." And I said, "I guess since George Moscone and Harvey Milk aren't here anymore, and since Feinstein is in office, things aren't quite the same, are they?" And then the people were angry. They were ready to riot down there. And so the cop said, "Alright, we should arrest this guy, we should take him out of here, where's the handcuffs?" And Rod Roderick was standing right there in the booth, and he said, "No, don't do that, don't do that." And Rod came up to me and said, "Steven, Steve, Steve. The media is here now, too. If you don't just shut it down and shut up, you're gonna be arrested." He calmed me down and then I was thinking, "Well, yeah. I'll be arrested," and at the same time I don't think they really wanted to arrest me. I mean, people could see into the DJ booth, so they could see and they were angry. They were shouting. But [the police] also thought there was a possibility that maybe there'd be a huge riot or something.[9]

Whenever gay people and straight culture interact, there is a careful negotiation that occurs. For gay people used to finally getting their own way, used to having their rights respected, and celebrating their sexual freedom, there was no way they were going to go back to the way things were before, hiding in the shadows.

Disco Adapts

In 1980, most straight discos closed down or changed formats. The *Los Angeles Times* reported on the sorry state of the mainstream disco in April, quoting Gene La Pietra, gay co-owner of the popular Latin nightclub Circus Disco: "The gays are our big support. Discos that have a big gay clientele are much better off. They have a better future."[10] Steve Forbes, at Studio One disco, concurred: "The drop in disco attendance is due to the straights dropping out. When they don't hear disco music or hear about discos as much on the radio or TV or don't read about it as much anymore, they assume the disco thing isn't trendy anymore. So they lose interest."[11] Clubgoer and lighting technician Chris Njirich thinks that ultimately the "death" of disco was a good thing for club music. "It had a neat effect." he says, "because once the Disco Sucks thing happened it made gay people band together for disco even more than they had before. It was our music. It was more energetic. It had more soul . . . So it was even more special. Instead of playing pop music or radio disco, it became uniquely its own music."[12]

Gay discos, bathhouses, and megaparties in the 1980s were bigger and better than ever, spurred on and altered by the influence of punk, post-punk, and new wave. Some in the gay press, however, didn't hear the changes right away. Jerry de Gracia, critic for the *Bay Area Reporter* in 1981, expressed his frustration at the existence of discos: "It's as if the majority of gays came out with the discos, found nirvana, and are going to carry 'I Feel Love' and 'Love Hangover' through middle age with them oblivious to the fact that the rest of the world is still growing."[13] The mainstream music press also heard intransigence in the survival of the gay disco (here not very subtly referred to as a "special interest group"):

DISCO'S DEAD/NOT DEAD   101

The major problem in transition of the sound are posed by those purists of the industry who are either unwilling or unable to adjust to change ... These special interest groups may decide to adopt a stone walling attitude in the hope of staying the wheels of change. If this attitude prevails, it could well result in a schism within disco's ranks . . . The purists, with the group of loyal supporters could well move the conventional disco format back underground where it had been nurtured for years before bursting on to the national entertainment scene.[14]

They were, of course, correct in that disco did indeed move back underground. But, while gay DJs sometimes did cling onto what New York Saint DJ Robbie Leslie called "the romantic period of disco,"[15] the disco sound *had* moved on, and DJs were playing a wider variety of music in their sets. Jim Farber traced the changes to early 1978, claiming Divine's show "The Neon Woman" at New York's Hurrah disco heralded the new "disco rock" genre, with that club starting a rock disco night soon afterward.[16] The mainstream press starting paying attention to the shift to rock in clubs as early as 1979, when *Billboard* profiled the phenomenon.[17] As the *Los Angeles Times* noticed, "The music isn't dead but it has changed. It's been slowed down, blended with rock and other genres and redubbed dance music. Probably the biggest change in discos is the music. It's not just those long, rhythm and blues oriented, 130 beats per minute numbers anymore. Anywhere from 10%–40%—depending on the club—is new wave or rock."[18]

Even in the local San Francisco gay press, it was admitted that "in New York and San Francisco the first bars to start playing rock music, new wave, reggae, and old Motown hits as an alternative to disco were gay bars."[19] The change was felt all over gay America, where, for example, Lee James of *Cruise Atlanta* noted "New Wave Music is rolling in at a rapid rate, drowning Donna and Barbra forever (Enough is enough, already girls!). Old favorites are rocking in again with new sounds. Bette Midler turns rock star and looks pretty goddamn good doing it."[20] DJ Chrysler remembers that when he began managing the disc jockeys at Castro Station in 1980, "No one really wanted to play just disco. They wanted to play Talking Heads, Ian Dury and the Blockheads, Tom Tom Club. There was a lot of music that wasn't formula, or formula in a way that wasn't disco. There was a lot of music being made, and rhythm is not only native to a certain genre but is native to a lot of genres."[21] In 1983, Marty Blecman considered the role gay clubs played in the popularization of a mainstream dance-rock aesthetic: "As in New York and Paris, the progressive

102 MENERGY

dance-rock basically is broken first in San Francisco's gay clubs. I think it's because gays go out all the time. They get tired of hearing the Human League seven days a week, and they stop dancing to it a lot faster than a normal crowd would. To be programming in the gay community, you have to be on top of what's new."[22] Jon Randazzo observed in early 1980 that while "80% of its members still program traditional disco fare," the choices had become more eclectic: "The gay clubs will program more progressive cuts, more LP cuts, and experiment with blending different cuts. Some jocks will play these real obscure cuts and try and be innovative."[23] As Tim Lawrence observed of the New York dance scene in 1980: "Mutation, convergence, and freedom were about to define the night."[24]

Dance Your Ass Off (1977–1979), which had been billed as San Francisco's only "bisexual disco," altered its format to rock and changed its name to X in late 1979. Management was taken over by Jeff Pollock who also owned the sixty-seat Old Waldorf rock club. When Pollock declared X the city's first "rock disco," rock DJ Howie Klein protested "the Stud had pioneered its wildly successful Monday nights over a year ago," to which Pollock replied in an interview, "We'll put in the word hetero then."[25] That same winter, signaling another massive shift in San Francisco musical life, the City Disco removed the downstairs live cabaret part of the club and turned it into "The Back DOR," [dance-oriented rock] with rock DJ Phil Pople.[26] Oil Can Harry's started a "New Wave A-Go-Go" on Tuesdays and Thursdays with gay rock DJs Larry LaRue and Alan Robinson.[27] The I-Beam, which had always had some live music, began a regular series of Monday night live concerts of new wave acts, including Duran Duran and Siouxsie and the Banshees. These changes went mostly unappreciated by the gay press. Jerry de Gracia, for example, still believed that, at the same time he praised the I-Beam, "the status quo will not face the fact that we as a group are changing and that possibly drag queens and Sharon McNight are nothing more than beached whales and certainly not the wave of the future."[28]

Metro Madness

The battle between the musically "progressive" and the "backward-looking" disco fans in the Castro came to a hilarious and chaotic head at the Metro Madness Party, celebrating the opening of the Metro Muni Castro stop on May 31, 1980. Sylvester headlined the event in an elegant red sequined jacket, which was held at the Van Ness station because it had a central loading platform to act as a stage. Shuttles transported revelers from the Castro station, past Church, where mannequins had been installed to look like people waiting for trains, to the Van Ness station. Stationary trains had been placed along both sides, to prevent people from falling onto the tracks. The train doors were left open, with about half lit up for revelers to sit and relax after dancing and the other half left dark, for more intimate activities.[29] Music was also provided by Howie Klein and *Billboard's* Best New Wave DJ award-winner Larry LaRue. Music critic Adam Block proudly noted,

> Some of the stylishly myopic fled in panic, but most of the crowd rose rousingly to the occasion. Afterwards, DJ Howie Klein was raving that DOR (that's Dance Oriented Rock) is just closet-disco and the true enemy. Klein claimed he won't attempt to please a same-gender crowd again. The Stud's Larry LaRue was threatening to kill "eligible Gay bachelor" Randy Shilts for charging the DJs booth screaming hysterically that people were leaving in droves. Shilts, who has been trumpeting his credentials as a gay rocker in the last few months, put on a thoroughly baffling display that had quite a few folks in stitches.[30]

Block issued a correction in his next column, saying that it wasn't Randy Shilts but "normally mild-mannered" Randy *Schiller*, sound man for I-Beam and many of the clubs South of Market, who had made Larry LaRue so upset, and that Klein called to assure the newspaper that he has never sworn off same-sex crowds. For Schiller, the problem wasn't the music itself; he was an avowed rock fan.[31] Rather, the party organizers had used Conceptual Entertainment's coveted mailing list of megaparty disco devotees, who had little time for rock and new wave's electric guitars. Ken Maley, Muni party planner, remembers the situation as "the battle of dying disco and rising New Wave."[32] Klein explained in an editorial, however, that the crowd included only "15% disco-bunnies who I would have gladly seen pogoed onto the subway tracks," but that the rest of the crowd reaffirmed his faith in gay men's musical tastes. The reporter ironically concluded by hoping that "the next great sexologist will poll people's musical taste to find if there is a correlation between gender-preference and the lust for disco, which Mr. Klein has been so unkind as to class with congenital idiocy as a social problem requiring radical solutions."[33]

104 MENERGY

More seriously, the disco–rock division had split the Bay Area DJs as well, predictably around lines of sexuality. Even disco celebrities Marty Blecman and John Hedges gave lip service to the new trend, telling *Billboard* in late 1979 that mixing and producing the new dance rock was not all that different from disco: "Essentially it is still a case of bringing out the beat, only with rock mixes there is more emphasis on the guitar rhythm."[34] But in February 1980, the straight contingent of the Bay Area Disco Deejay Association (BADDA) staged a coup and took over, with Nick Lygizos succeeding Jon Randazzo as president. As a result, most of the gay founding members split from the group to form a new pool, T.O.P. 25 (short for "The Original Pool"), including Blecman and Hedges, George Ferren from Toad Hall, Timmy Rivers and Lester Temple at Music Hall (1980–1991), Tommy Ridgeway and Ken Alexander at Oil Can Harry's, Michael Garrett and Steve Fabus at the I-Beam, Vince Carleo and Kevin Burke from Dreamland 1980–1982), and Tommy Williams from Alfie's, among several others.[35]

Randazzo denied that it was simply a defection of the gay DJs, but a refocusing on professional spinners: "We want only DJs who spin at top progressive clubs within the city; not at commercial clubs from out in the suburbs. We don't want DJs who spin at discos that are in the back rooms of Ramada Inns. And we have some straight members in the pool. It doesn't matter if they members are gay, straight, black, blue or green."[36] But regardless of Randazzo's public statements, as soon as T.O.P. 25 formed, BADDA consolidated their new rock intentions by merging with the Western Association of Rock DJs, marking the significant division between gay and straight as essentially a split between disco and rock. Ultimately, T.O.P. 25 was successful in promoting gay records and even branched out into concert events. Ferren and business partner David Miller produced sold-out performances at Dreamland, Trocadero Transfer, and Music Hall, and two important shows at the Endup: "Menergy," in November 1981 with the Patrick Cowley Singers, and "Celebration," in December 1981 starring Sylvester.

Bobby Viteritti

In 1979, San Francisco was given a boost by the arrival of Bobby Viteritti, a Miami DJ with a growing national profile who transformed the Trocadero Transfer from a disco club to a temple of high-energy dance music, the spiritual home of the San Francisco sound of the 1980s. DJ Casey Jones remembers, "As far as mixing goes Bobby Viteritti was very instrumental in creating an awareness of what became known as the 'San Francisco Style.'"[37] Viteritti is credited for his deep dives into electronic music to an extent not heard before in San Francisco. The trend had been building since Donna Summer's "I Feel Love" in 1977 of course, but part of the evolution of disco's sound away from R&B and Black-identified traits had increasingly included spacy sounds, faster tempos, and stronger beats, which *Billboard* noted in March 1979, observing "the increasing reliance on synthesized sounds to provide disco dance tunes. Most of the music has come from Europe, particularly Germany, where groups like Kraftwerk, noted as avant-garde rockers, scored a surprise hit with its 'Trans Europe Express.'"[38]

Viteritti made his name at Fort Lauderdale's Marlin Beach Hotel, where in 1977 and 1978 he had won *Billboard*'s Regional DJ Award. Originally from Massapequa, New York, he started his career in 1973 in Florida at Keith's Cruise Room in Hallandale when he was twenty years old. His parents had a condo in Hollywood, Florida, and they agreed to let him stay there if he fixed it up and furnished the place. Keith's had recently replaced its jukebox with a DJ booth and two turntables and was looking for a hip young DJ to replace their disappointing initial hire. Viteritti brought to his audition two copies of "Rock the Boat" by the Hues Corporation, "Little Bit of Love" by Brenda and the Tabulations, and "Just One Look" by Doris Troy. Despite the lack of pitch controls on the QRK turntables, he remembers "banging 'em in and out showing off like a big shot, you know. Showing them I could mix."[39] He got the job, making $75 a week for four nights. He had honed his technique as a teenager, observing the work of Fire Island DJs Roy Thode and Tom Moulton: "I used to love the way Roy played. The way he would slip cue and overlay and how he used technology."[40] At home in his bedroom he would imitate their style, and when the technology hadn't caught up with the latest trends in mixing, he built his own: "I kind of designed my own mixer . . . I had a toggle switch for cuing and I was able to actually do mixes back in 1971–72."[41]

His first night at Keith's was a memorable one, for both good and bad reasons. Viteritti recalls transitioning between "Who Is He and What Is He to You" by Creative Source and O. C. Smith's version of "La La Peace Song," slowing down one of the records with his fingernail to beat match between them. "They're not looking at a jukebox anymore, they were all looking at me in the face and saying, 'What is he doing up there? Listen, he's got 'em both going together.' Meanwhile, my fingernail is burning and I got the

106   MENERGY

motherfucker in there! My fingernail fell off about three days later, but it was worth it."[42]

He worked for a time as principle resident DJ at John Castelli's Tangerine, where he met future Saint spinner Robbie Leslie. By the time they had both made the move to the Poop Deck at the gay Marlin Beach Hotel, Viteritti had perfected the techniques that would make him famous. He recalls how he would start by "pick[ing] a spot in the record—an instrumental piece—and fuck with them, their heads. They know it, but they think they know it . . . You start it from the break or sometimes at the end of the record . . . People were always confused, and I would go in and out and sometimes *I* wouldn't know what it all was about."[43] Leslie remembers doing the lights for Viteritti during those early years: "What followed were hysterical, unforgettable nights and Tea Dances, and always flawless, imaginative, sometimes even daring record blending and true showmanship."[44]

One example from those years at the Poop Deck will serve as a demonstration of his legendary technique. In a set that survives from May 1, 1977, he changes from Space's "Tango in Space" to Donna Summer's "I Feel Love," which had just been officially released that day. Working with two copies of the Summer record, he starts the song at the first verse, but just as the chorus is about to enter, he returns to the middle of a verse, avoiding the blissful chorus, postponing its resolution. He continues teasing the dancers like this, returning to earlier places in the verses several times, for two minutes before climaxing with a chorus. He allows the song to reach an instrumental break and another chorus, but just as the song reaches the final long instrumental section, he phases two copies of the record so they are exactly one beat apart, and on every beat he moves the fader back and forth, creating an artificial stasis that counteracts the built-in stereo panning in the production. One is left with a feeling of disorientation, with the pulsating effect of a drone combined with synthesized sensuality. Unlike Patrick Cowley's remix, there is no countercultural psychedelic aspect, just pure futuristic sound. He seamlessly takes the dancers back to more familiar ground by fading into Summer's "Spring Affair" before returning to the hypermodern with Giorgio Moroder's equally new "From Here to Eternity." The rest of the tape continues the roller-coaster ride for another three hours of complex mixing and editing.[45]

With his *Billboard* awards, he had become a local celebrity in Miami, but was lonely and looking for new challenges. He was also frustrated by the media attention the city's gay clubs were receiving in light of antigay crusader Anita Bryant's Dade County "Save Our Children" campaign. And he was sick

DISCO'S DEAD/NOT DEAD   107

of having to accommodate the frequent drag shows that would interrupt his gigs. But it took meeting a good man to motivate him to take the plunge and leave Miami. One night, a sexy tourist, Dennis Croteau, a bartender from Holyoke, Massachusetts, caught his eye.[46] "I liked him because his arms were real nice and natural . . . we clicked and we had sex, and then we talked a lot about disco," Viteritti remembers after their meeting. "I don't know, we just kind of took a liking. I showed him around. Maybe I was lonely, I don't know. 'Why don't you move down here? Let's move in together,' I asked him."[47] Bobby secretly drove up to Holyoke to help Croteau move back to Florida with him:

> I saw him out of the corner of my eye. He's loading up. And I snuck behind the stairwell, he didn't know. But when he opened the door, he was carrying out something to load. I had my 8-track deck on the floor just by the elevator, and I was playing "How Deep Is Your Love," by the BeeGees. That's our song. And he looked around and he says, "Where's that music coming from?" and I go, "Surprise!" So I drove back with him from Holyoke to Miami, to Fort Lauderdale, and he moved in.[48]

After seeing pictures of the Trocadero Transfer and other West Coast bars in the gay entertainment magazine *After Dark*, Viteritti gave Trocadero owner Dick Collier a call. The Trocadero's current DJ Gary Tighe was popular, but Collier didn't completely shut Viteritti down. Bobby and Dennis took a risk and got a three-month vacation from work in Miami to take a trip to Los Angeles and San Francisco to check out the clubs, driving in his new Cutlass (complete with power moon roof). Through his experience as Florida's premiere DJ, Viteritti knew Scott Forbes, owner of Los Angeles's biggest gay discotheque, Studio One, and they made his home their first stop. By sheer coincidence, Collier happened to be visiting Forbes as well, and a proper introduction was made. Collier asked him if he had any tapes, but Viteritti had only brought eight-tracks, a format that wasn't as popular on the West Coast, so he had no way to demonstrate his skill. "It just happens we have the Black Party coming up," Collier told him. "Me and the DJ Gary Tighe, we're not getting along. He's on some ego trip or whatever and I want you to play the Black Party."[49]

Bobby and Dennis drove up to San Francisco to check the club out, which blew them both away. "Wow, what a club!" he enthused. "Look at this, it looks like 12 West but it's bigger . . . The acoustics are fabulous. It's the best sound

108 MENERGY

system I ever heard, I think, in any disco."[50] Trocadero and New York's 12 West shared an ultra-high-end sound system by Graebar Productions, with their trademark "coffin" speakers and massive tweeter array. Remembering his first night, he says, "I don't think they had ever heard overlays and mixes like that on the West Coast before. Music there was totally different."[51] His nerves were calmed by one mix in particular: "I played 'Shame' by Evelyn King and the way it just came in so smooth . . . I had a whole list of records I was going to play on the night because I had rehearsed and was nervous. But I ripped it up and just screamed, 'Come on girls, let's party!'"[52] That first gig would leave a huge impression with the crowd, but was exhausting for the DJ: "I never played such a long shift. I started playing at 11 pm and went till about 8 and I kept on telling my lover Dennis, 'go down to the car and get me more records.' The crowd really liked me; they liked me, but they didn't like me, because they were all Gary Tighe fans."[53] Sutro Baths DJ Maria Sanchez noted his arrival in her column in the *Bay Area Disco Report*, but was careful to put the "blame" onto Collier rather than the disc jockey for Tighe's eventual dismissal: "Veteran DJ Bob Viteritti has relocated to our SCENEic City and is doin' it at TROC thurs, fri, sat . . . Love to Gary Tighe, who is loved and missed by many at Troc. Good breaks for G, but bad timing on the Troc side. . . . seems MGT/owner didn't believe he was big enough star?"[54]

Billy Langenheim

Because of loyalty to Tighe, it took Viteritti about six months to really ingratiate himself with the Trocadero dancers, and a large part of his eventual success was the contribution of his lighting man, Billy Langenheim. On a trip to Los Angeles, Viteritti saw Langenheim working at Studio One, and loved his work. Viteritti introduced himself and suggested Billy join him in San Francisco. Langenheim had been looking for a way out of Los Angeles, so the offer came at exactly the right time. Viteritti put him up in his flat and made sure he got a good salary, and the combination was a success. Before Langenheim, he remembers,

> I had so many bad nights because the DJ before me didn't like me. Nobody liked me. I would tell the lightman before Billy came on board, "Blackout." He looked at me and gave me the eye and said, "Listen, you play your records and I will do the lights . . ." We had no communication, lots of animosity

DISCO'S DEAD/NOT DEAD   109

and during those breaks in the songs he would turn on practically all the house lights. Strobes going a million miles an hour. Everything's lit up and everyone's dancing waiting for the beat to kick in—fully lit—on purpose. I don't know whether he did it on purpose or not or if he was just stupid. He had no feeling for music![55]

But he and Langenheim quickly developed a rapport, which enabled them to create certain effects that required close collaboration. One of their most memorable tricks would occur right around dawn:

> We had eight skylights [at the Trocadero]. And during the night the sun would slowly come in and the music was starting to get more and more morning. And next thing you know everyone realized "Holy Shit! We hardly see the lights anymore, we just see the sun in here." And then I do an encore and Billy would have his walkie-talkies and he had eight people on the roof and he said, "Now!" and they pulled tarps over all the skylights and people down there would get popped in their eyes of flashes and the whole place would turn absolutely black . . . He'd blackout and then I'd start "Relight My Fire" or something like that start climbing up again, you know; we were doing round two now.[56]

One of Langenheim's biggest material contributions was the Trocadero's mirror ball collection. Until Langenheim acquired the balls, the club had a much simpler central lighting arrangement: "It was like those lights that used to go on silver Christmas trees, where the light sat on the floor and there would be a round thing with gels on them," "Lighting Bear" Chris Njirich recalls.[57] "They had those all the way around this thing that were aimed at the dancers, so they were moving around with different colors, and the whole thing was moving around, sort of like the mirror balls."[58] Langenheim went to a Rolling Stones concert in the East Bay, and they had a huge mirror ball cluster on their set. "Like most straight people, they don't pay attention to mirror balls or light," Njirich jokingly observes, "and when they were leaving to go back to wherever they were going, I guess Billy put a bid in on that mirror ball cluster and the apparatus that ran the whole thing, 'cause it was really ingenious how it was done. And he bought it and he took it back to Trocadero and hooked it up."[59]

"Billy Langenheim was a really big influence on me," Viteritti acknowledges. "I could have never gotten to where I am at right now if it weren't for

Billy. Never. I was the first person to realize the importance of a lightman, and I even told him you would get same billing as I for special parties. 'Music by Bobby Viteritti and lights by Billy Langenheim.' He really liked that" (see figure 6.2).[60] By the summer of 1979, Viteritti and Langenheim had turned the Trocadero into not only San Francisco's premiere after-hours nightclub but also one of the most important clubs on the West Coast. Over the summer, KTSF TV and SMC TV broadcast a monthly "Trocadero Transfer Music Special" featuring Bobby Viteritti.[61]

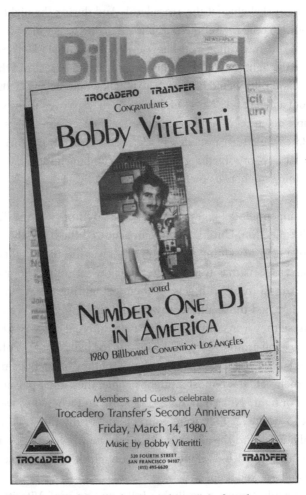

Figure 6.2 Doorman Joel inside the Trocadero Transfer. Photo courtesy of Carla Ann Nicholson. Reproduced with permission.

DISCO'S DEAD/NOT DEAD 111

Dreamland

The opening of new gay clubs in big US cities had almost nothing to do with the life and death of disco, but rather a celebration of a queer life where relatively affluent gay men and their friends were able to share the same privilege as their straight counterparts with the sexual freedom they had earned. Some larger clubs in the Bay didn't survive long because, unlike New York City, San Francisco didn't have the sheer numbers necessary to keep the expensive dance palaces open. There was never going to be enough Bay Area "A-Gays" to support an exclusive environment like New York's Saint. But attempts were certainly made. On May 31, 1979, Studio West, brainchild of club impresario Frank Cashman, opened in San Francisco as "a new dimension in Discoteque on the Embarcadero."[62] The members-only club had the new Gay Freedom Day Marching Band and Twirling Corp perform for the massive crowd lined up outside the club, which was located in a beautiful historic Victorian building. With a staff of close to forty and employing a top list of DJs spinning for two dance floors, the club garnered largely positive reviews that praised the excellent sound system, and although, "according to some 'discoholics' the dance floor could have been a bit larger . . . the music was first-rate."[63]

The press raved that "Cashman's crew did a splendid job of renovating a musty old warehouse and the bar itself keeps some 10 bartenders slinging the booze without let-up. . . . Studio West should do well. It's slightly smaller than Trocadero Transfer but bigger than the other discos in town."[64] It also featured a mezzanine from which you could look down onto the dancers below. That same year another new disco, Music Hall, opened in an old movie theater on Larkin. Built in 1961, the theater had morphed from showing art house movies to gay porn before this latest incarnation as a disco. Like most gay discos, it offered membership (six months for $100), although $20 would get you in the door without being a member. But, in a sign of the times, from the beginning it marketed itself as a dance club that specialized in new wave and disco rock, and accommodated events like "Black Dawn," a leather event sponsored by SoMa party promoters Folsom Fantasies. "Expect to see a sea of black leather, boots, chains and humpy dudes" plugged the *Bay Area Reporter* in May 1980.[65]

But when Dreamland opened on February 8, 1980, at 715 Harrison, it was without a doubt the most ambitious launch of the postdisco era. Designed by Peter Fisk, and with Peter Sparr's $80,000 Graebar sound system (with eight

112   MENERGY

coffin speakers, unlike the Trocadero's four), this new 9,000-square-foot club sported a 2,000-square-foot dance floor, a light show designed by Roy Shapiro worth $175,000, and, like Studio West, a second floor that looked down on the dance floor. Owner Michael Maier relocated New York DJ Kevin Burke to be a part of the initial three-man DJ team alongside Vincent Carleo and Larry Rossiello.[66] It was basically an after-hours club, open from 10:00 p.m. to 6:00 a.m., had live shows at 2:00 performed on what the *Bay Area Reporter* called a "Busby Berkley–type stage."[67] Ken Crivello remembers that the "stage . . . was unbelievable. It was a huge spiral structure which just came around and opened onto the dance-floor like a giant, white seashell."[68]

Maier justified the expense and extravagance of the club, telling *Billboard*,

> Disco died with John Travolta. Prior to that it was mostly underground—gay, black, or Latin. Very few middle-class whites knew about it until *Saturday Night Fever* . . . However, that entire segment of society on which it was founded is still there and still wants to dance to individually selected music . . . You can't preprogram for a crowd because you never know what the crowd will get off on. It can't be run by a manager who just looks at the bar and the door. You have to be sensitive to the people. That's what Dreamland is built on.[69]

As a high-end after-hours club, Dreamland could be seen as direct competition for the Trocadero Transfer, but, in the beginning at least, clubgoers felt the two were fundamentally different. "Dreamland was what we used to call a 'professional club," DJ and Loverde manager Don Miley remembers. "It drew the same type of crowd that Flamingo in New York did . . . a very handsome, proper, professional crowd."[70] In its first year, it had success hosting Sylvester's birthday party, fundraisers for the 1981 Gay Day parade, for politician Willie Brown, and a huge bash for the magazine *Drummer*.[71] "Dreamland attracted a different kind of gay male," Gini Spiersch, who worked at both Trocadero and Dreamland, explains, "ones into standing and posing a lot and never really perspiring. At Troc it was totally opposite, more like 'let's take our drugs, take off our t-shirts and get sweaty together until morning.'"[72] Not that drugs were the exclusive purview of the Trocadero, as Chris Njirich clarifies: "Dreamland was pretty boys in white tank tops and shorts: the muscle A-crowd . . . Dreamland was definitely the cocaine club and attitude club. It was a great club, don't get me wrong, but it didn't have that friendliness and you wouldn't fit in as easily."[73]

DISCO'S DEAD/NOT DEAD   113

Part of the problem for many people was the brightness of the club. When Njirich says "Dreamland was white. Trocadero was black," he isn't just referring to the race of the clientele.[74] Dreamland was painted a stark white throughout. Spiersch remembers that "They had a marvelous sound system and a lot of space but it just never was quite what the Trocadero was. The main reason for this was that the place was painted white inside, so even with the same music and the same drugs you could never really get to those dark little places; those spacey, trippy places where Bobby liked to go with his music sometimes."[75] Viteritti hated the brightness so much he "offered to paint the club himself."[76] The atmosphere didn't alienate everyone, however. Black singer Shawn Benson loved Dreamland, and always felt at home: "They played good music there and the hottest people went there . . . That same crowd went to the Music Hall . . . Those two were the best. In a lot of ways they were better than the Trocadero."[77]

Bobby Viteritti disagreed. According to him, "All the leather people and butch guys that didn't know how to dance—they just wanted to be with the scene and that macho music were there. Trocadero played all that light strings and they were more serious and they had better ears."[78] Despite this feeling, ten months after Dreamland opened, Viteritti managed to be lured away from his Trocadero home to the new club. In November 1980, he got a business manager who negotiated with the Dreamland bosses and secured $1,000 a night and $1 per person above 561 (compared to the $18,000 a year he made at Trocadero).[79] Spiersch speculates that "he had left Trocadero Transfer for several reasons including (I'm sure) the amount of money he had come to demand at the time. That really hurt Trocadero for a while because there was a huge contingency that just followed Bobby right over to Dreamland."[80] But Viteritti insists he didn't make the move for purely financial reasons. At the Trocadero, he had been frustrated for a while, and he realized,

> I wasn't tapping my feet anymore, and I was getting very afraid of that because every week I would go back home and remix something else because I couldn't stand putting it on the turntable anymore. It came to the point where I would tell Billy my lightman that I can't hear this one more time. I felt as though I had nothing else up my sleeve. I had no more tricks . . . There was no new music out there and I felt I was letting the crowd down. I would be damned if I had to sneak out the back door of Trocadero—the highlight of my whole life—and lower my head. It got to the point I wanted to get

114   MENERGY

Patrick Cowley on stage with his keyboard to play along with the music live.[81]

The change was important enough for *Billboard* to announce the move and Viteritti's replacements, LA's Studio One DJs Craig Morey and Mike Lewis.[82] Viteritti also insisted on bringing Langenheim with him, and one of Langenheim's first actions was to install a new lighting system that allowed the control of the club's lights with a keyboard. Chris Njirich, who with partner Bob Giudice also did lights at Dreamland, remembers, "You would play the keyboard and Bob could play a piano. So once you knew what keys were what colors, and where they were in the room, and how it was shaped and what you were trying to achieve and say, you could play that keyboard just like a piano, and it was beautiful!"[83]

Perhaps predictably, the local gay press predicted Dreamland's failure from the beginning: "I do think that it is ironic that a massive new gay disco opened just down the street from Trocadero last week." One client remarked, "Honey, it's fabulous. It's just two years too late."[84] But Dreamland *did* play more than disco. In the first year it started a successful country and western night. And shortly after Viteritti arrived, manager Roy Shapiro told the press that Dreamland was "making a transition from disco to nightclub."[85] That same month, a restaurant catering sideline was begun. They also had a no-competition policy with I-Beam (they had live acts on Mondays, with rock dancing on Tuesdays and Wednesdays while Dreamland booked live acts for Wednesdays).

But ultimately, critics of the club were correct, and a bit less than two years after its grand opening, Dreamland shuttered its doors. When the Saint opened in New York in 1980, it seemed to demonstrate that big new discos for affluent gay white men could work. But it was simply unrealistic to expect a city the size of San Francisco to support more than one major gay after-hours venue. With Dreamland's building and lighting rental costs more than $10,000 a month and lighting operators and DJs another $2,000 per week, the club just didn't work out financially.[86] They also didn't pay their federal and state employee taxes for three quarters in 1980, resulting in a lien of $120,000 against the business. While Dreamland did pay their taxes the first quarter of 1981, and although they averaged 300 attendees on Fridays, 700 on Saturdays, and 200 on Sundays, it just wasn't enough to make the club profitable.

When Viteritti left the Trocadero Transfer for Dreamland, one of the reasons he cited was that "there was no new music out there and I felt I was letting the crowd down."[87] The lack of new music was real, and, as Tim Lawrence notes in relation to the opening of the Saint in New York in 1980, "In urban centers such as New York and San Francisco public clubs and private parties continued to attract significant numbers of dancers, and this vibrant network provided independent record companies with a core market that was focused, enthusiastic and hungry for innovation."[88] With the lack of new music from the major labels, "DJs turned with renewed interest to the release schedules of New York's and San Francisco's independent sector, as well as . . . import recordings."[89] This new wave of music, however, came too late to save Dreamland, which closed October 4, 1981, just as Megatone and Moby Dick Records were starting up. The next chapter explores how these labels were created in the wake of the shortfall of dance records.

7

The San Francisco Sound Thrives

Dance music's continued popularity after the "death of disco" spurred a second wave of records in San Francisco, encouraged by the arrival of a new group of gay DJs escaping the blandness of Los Angeles for the Castro's enticements. Bill Motley led the way with his high-energy medleys of Motown hits, initially just remixes of the originals, but soon with fully arranged remakes in the form of his creation, Boys Town Gang. Encouraged by packed dance palaces and megaparties, the success Sylvester's backup singers Two Tons o' Fun achieved with their first solo outing, and Motley's string of dance hits, Loverde and Patrick Cowley also decided to step out from behind the curtain to produce their own music. By the end of 1980, Fusion Records and Moby Dick Records had become San Francisco's first gay-owned, gay-run dance music labels, producing worldwide hits rivaling in commercial success anything corporate record labels could offer and paving the way for Megatone Records. This chapter relates how the small, isolated city by the bay came to dominate the world of dance music through a combination of good timing, solid networks of distribution, savvy marketing, and, most of all, really great tunes artfully produced.

Two Tons o' Fun Go Solo

With Sylvester still floating high on the charts in late 1979, Fantasy signed his backup singers Two Tons o' Fun to a two-album deal, to be produced by Harvey Fuqua from his Fantasy Honey Records division, which up to this point had only released Sylvester records. It was, in many ways, a logical move for Martha Wash and Izora Rhodes (now Armstead), and the production on their first, self-titled album overflowed with Sylvester veterans, both in front of and behind the microphone, including backup singers Jeanie Tracy and Eric Robinson, percussionist David Frazier, bassist Bob Kingson, guitarist Greg Crockett, and longtime Sylvester collaborator James Wirrick. Patrick Cowley was notably absent, but Wirrick (who by this time was

Menergy. Louis Niebur, Oxford University Press. © Oxford University Press 2022.
DOI: 10.1093/oso/9780197511077.003.0008

sharing a studio space with Cowley at 8th and Minna) did his best to emulate his trademark synthesizer gallop and sound effects. Cowley eventually contributed a remix of the debut single, "I Got the Feeling," for DJ-only remix service Disconet.[1] Sylvester was publicly supportive of their ambition, and he provided a dedication on the back cover of the album: "God has given you both such great voices and talent. I'm very grateful to you both for sharing them with me. I love you both so very much and wish you the best 'cause I know you can do it."[2] But privately he was hurt, and he turned to Jeanie Tracy even more for support. Years later, he complained that "the girls . . . left when someone told them they were too fabulous to be working with me. We have, however, all remained friends through the years and that's what really matters."[3]

Alternating between five straightforward disco songs and three more contemporary downtempo R&B tunes, *Two Tons O' Fun* is the sonic successor to *Step II*, with Fuqua's signature brass and strings supplemented by electronics. Without a doubt, "I Got the Feeling" stands out as the album's high point, an essential San Francisco high-energy song. Originally written by Frank Loverde, Wirrick, and Don Miley for Loverde to perform, Harvey Fuqua heard the demo recording produced by Jeffrey E. Cohen and asked if he could have it for the Tons. In early March 1980, album cuts "Do You Wanna Boogie, Hunh?," "I Got the Feeling," and "One-Sided Love Affair" all entered the *Billboard* dance charts, alongside Sylvester's still-top-10 "Can't Stop Dancing" and Paradise Express's "Let's Fly." By the middle of April, the Tons were featured on *Billboard*'s front page, with "I Got the Feeling" now charting on the "Disco Action" charts in fifteen cities. The song ultimately rose to the national number 2 spot in the final two weeks of May. Wash and Armstead promoted the album across the country. Perhaps the quirkiest event was Maneuvers at the I-Beam in February 1982, where they launched Sanford Kellman's new leather and uniform night at the club. Armstead was in full camouflage with a canteen as jewelry around her neck, and Wash was in black leather, complete with fetish cap. —"Company Two Tons" showed they hadn't lost their sense of humor as they performed to a packed house of leathermen (see figure 7.1).[4]

They had proven they were not just Sylvester's sidekicks but successful performers in their own right. While they continued to sing backup for him over the next decade, by the time they were signed to Warner Brothers under a new name, the Weather Girls, they were among the most successful musicians to emerge out of the San Francisco dance music scene.

118 MENERGY

Figure 7.1 I-Beam's Maneuvers party with special guests "Company Two Tons," from *Bay Area Reporter*, February 25, 1980. Reproduced with permission.

Los Angeles

An influx of Los Angeles musicians to San Francisco in early 1980 provided an injection of a different energy and aesthetic to the evolving San Francisco sound. Probably the best example of this was the founding of Moby Dick Records by Bill Motley, Stan Morriss, and Victor Swedosh. Swedosh was born in Chicago but had been adopted as a baby by the wealthy New York Swedosh family, who had made their money with a type of nylon pantyhose

THE SAN FRANCISCO SOUND THRIVES   119

during World War II.[5] After receiving an undergraduate degree from the University of Wisconsin, he, like so many gay men in the early 1970s, made his way to San Francisco for the sexual freedom it offered. After studying in the MBA program at the University of California at Berkeley, he settled in the Castro and in 1977 Swedosh became part owner of the Moby Dick bar at 573 Castro Street. Swedosh's sexual interests had always tended toward "bears" (a term for larger, usually hairy gay men that was only just beginning to gain currency in that decade). On one of his many trips to Los Angeles, Swedosh met local DJ Bill Motley at Griff's, a popular bear bar, and the two began dating. Despite his unfashionable bearish physique, Motley was at the center of Los Angeles's gay clone scene, working at Hollywood's Circus Disco alongside DJ "Trip" Ringwald and lightman Stan Morriss, with good friends and fellow DJs Craig Morey and Michael Lewis down the street at the massive Studio One disco in West Hollywood. Lewis had recently won *Billboard*'s Los Angeles area DJ of the Year and the Southern California Disco DJ Association's DJ of the Year awards, and like Blecman and Hedges in San Francisco was keen to dip his toes into the production and remix arena.

Lewis's first project was a complete reworking of the 3:26 minute track "Party Boys" by Foxy for T. K. Records. He expanded the track to 10:30, adding a long break filled with background chatter of himself, Morey, Ringwald, and Motley. Despite the heavy reverb and distortion, it's possible to make out someone asking "Where's Craig?" and "Where's Tripper?" and another voice replies, "They're back downstairs." When Lewis sold the remix to DJ service Disconet, they ran a contest for DJs to see if anyone could figure out what the hell they were saying:

> If you check out this program's feedback card, you'll find a spot to enter Disconet's "What *are* they saying during the fabulous Foxy remix" contest. . . . The winner wins a trip to Miami where he or she will personally meet Ish [Foxy's lead singer] and go for a ride in his Jeep. Ish may even tell you what the lyrics to the song are! The winner will also meet TK/Dash President Henry Stone, who may or may not let you pull on his bushy white beard.[6]

The original version of the song entered *Billboard*'s Disco Top 100 the week of February 16, 1980, where it languished in the bottom half of the chart until the Disconet remix boosted the track in May, shooting up to a high of 24th place by the week of June 7 (understandably jumping into 6th place in Los Angeles's local chart). T. K. Records released Lewis's mix on the song's 12-inch single in July, which helped the track stay on the charts until October, nine months in total, a remarkable achievement for Lewis's debut. It was a hit at the Trocadero Transfer, where Bobby Viteritti usually included it in his Saturday night sets, and John Hedges was still playing the song a year later at Badlands, where on January 21, 1981, he mixed it between Kano's "I'm Ready" and Queen's "Another One Bites the Dust." Craig Morey, meanwhile, knew Trocadero DJ Viteritti, and was headhunted by him to be the opening DJ before Viteritti's shift began for the night. When Viteritti left the Trocadero for Dreamland in early 1980, Morey was hired to be one of his replacements.

Bill Motley also had ambitions to move from DJing to the production side of the music business, and in December 1979 produced his first mix for Disconet in a collaboration with Ringwald, a nine-minute medley of songs by the Supremes. The two added percussion, replacing the original Funk Brothers Benny Benjamin and Richard Allen's drum track with a prominent disco four-on-the-floor kick drum and high-hat. Excerpting six songs, the two DJs constructed a track that builds in intensity primarily by holding off the Earl Young–inspired off-beat high-hat until the 2:30 mark, and gradually raising the tempo from a relatively mellow 120 BPM to a frenetic 135 by the end of the medley. While an unapologetic "greatest hits" medley, it never feels like a simple sequence of songs placed one after the other. Instead, it demonstrates Motley and Ringwald's skill at constructing a miniature DJ set that takes dancers on a journey, a well-crafted suite that works independently. It was so well crafted, in fact, that Motown released their own version of the remix in 1980, copying without credit practically every edit and effect, releasing it a few months after Disconet's version. The Motown version lived on *Billboard*'s Disco Top 100 from March 15 through the end of June that year.

Their second project for Disconet was a medley of "Bitchin' '50s" songs. Opening with the slow introduction to Neil Sedaka's 1975 rerecording of "Breaking Up Is Hard to Do" (in an arrangement by Richard Carpenter), the song abruptly switches to the original 1962 version with an added disco four-on-the-floor bass drum. After a few bars, a new electric bass enters as well, and the medley seamlessly blends eight hits for seven-and-a-half minutes of nostalgia with a modern twist. As with the Supremes medley, the song builds in intensity, reserving and postponing the driving off-beat hi-hat until five minutes in, as the chorus to the Four Seasons' "Sherry" arrives. *Billboard* praised the medley, an unusual accolade not often given to a "greatest hits" compilation track, as "distinguished and well-balanced" where "the right tunes have been chosen, and the production has been kept slick, tight and listenable."[7]

One final medley was completed for Disconet, made during the chaotic period of relocation to San Francisco by the Los Angeles crew, this time by Motley alone. His "Original Elvis Medley" collected nine of the King's biggest hits together, with added bass and drums, starting at a reasonable 124 before building to an ecstatic 202 BPM. He front-loaded the rhythmically trickiest songs, including "Good Luck Charm," and "All Shook Up," helping out DJs by starting with a few bars of an isolated four-on-the-floor.

Motley's fixation with medleys was not unique in the late 1970s and early 1980s. The gay liberation movement had matured in a few short years, to create for many gay men its own musical and dancing history, canon, and, despite the oppressive nature of the past for so many, its own nostalgia. Even before AIDS, the kind of nostalgia evoked by Motley and Ringwald's medleys was central to the dancing lives of gay men in urban centers. "Reinterpreted for the '80s" was a common phrase used by high-energy artists who were remixing and remaking hits of the 1950s and 1960s in a new electronic vein, which nevertheless invoked the spirit and memory of the originals. "Nostalgia arises when the desire for homecoming is simultaneously coupled with a recognition of its impossibility," Michael D. Dwyer explains.[8] Despite the emotional scars and trauma many gay people carried with them from their teenage years, and the overall oppressive nature of the 1950s, Dwyer suggests that, "When Fifties music re-emerges in the radio, records, and film soundtracks of the 1980s, it still operates as an alternative to sterility and homogeneity."[9]

Michael Pickering and Emily Keightley observed that nostalgia can be "seen as not only a search for ontological security in the past, but also a means of taking one's bearings for the road ahead in the uncertainties of the present."[10] In other words, these "reinterpretations" of music of the 1950s and 1960s are meant in some way to redress the past, to remake them for the 1980s containing all that was pleasurable about them and replacing that which was horrible, reclaiming them for a gay dancing audience. Despite their pastness, these old songs carried real hope for the gay crowds that danced to them. "Nostalgic longing, in other words, can be used in efforts to remake the present, or at least to imagine corrective alternatives to it," Dwyer offers, through what Grossberg describes as "a politics of fun that is defined by its rejection of

122 MENERGY

boredom and its celebration of movement, change, energy ... lived out in and inscribed upon the body."[11]

Moby Dick Records and Boys Town Gang

By the time Motley, Ringwald, Morey, Lewis, and Morriss had at least partially relocated to San Francisco by the end of 1980 (Ringwald, for example, kept his residency at Hollywood's Circus Disco), Motley, Morriss, and Moby Dick's Swedosh had decided to create a record label of their own, with Ringwald, Morey, and Lewis on hand to help and additional financial help from Will Smith. The new label, to be called, logically enough, Moby Dick Records, was conceived as filling a void in the massive gay disco market, which was suffering from a lack of product with the closing of so many major labels' disco departments. It would do this in two ways. First, the label planned to release US versions of current but expensive and hard-to-find European dance records that, through their use of electronic instruments and fast tempos, matched the energy of the San Francisco high-energy sound (though not necessarily the gay ethos). Second, Moby Dick Records would release music of its own, made by mostly homegrown San Francisco and Los Angeles talent.

For his first original production, Bill Motley came up with the name Boys Town Gang as a West Coast version of the Village People, and musically didn't look too far from his own wheelhouse with a medley of two 1970 Diana Ross songs written by Motown's Ashford and Simpson, "Remember Me" and "Ain't No Mountain High Enough." Motley wrote the basic arrangement and drew upon the skills of old friend Denver Smith to arrange the string and brass sections. Between 1975 and 1977, Motley and Ringwald had cut their teeth as the house DJs at the Red Onion chain of Mexican restaurants in Los Angeles, traveling between branches and spinning records for dancers in between sets by the house band, Popeye. The band had started in San Diego in 1973, and quickly gained a reputation as a reliable Top 40 dance band, winning their audition with Red Onion in 1975 as well. Popeye was well versed in classic disco, and Smith incorporated modern electronic elements to update their sound.

Popeye guitarist Mike Gymnaites recalls about Motley and Ringwald, "I didn't know that any of these guys were gay, but they went up there to participate in the whole music scene up there [in San Francisco]. And then

THE SAN FRANCISCO SOUND THRIVES   123

I remember they called somebody in the band, I think Rudy [guitarist Mike Guess's nickname] or Denver, who they were friends with and said, 'Hey we got this project.' "[12] Motley explained that he essentially wanted to make extended versions of the original two songs, as he had done for Disconet, but because of copyright issues it would cost too much. So, he arranged the two songs as a medley, then had the musicians record, layer by layer, over the original songs, adding more of a disco, four-on-the-floor feel. "And then one by one," Gymnaites remembers Motley telling them, "we'll filter out the rest of the tracks, the guitar and stuff, and you'll come in and do some guitar tracks."[13] Salty Dog Studio owner and engineer David Cole laid down the instrumental tracks over several days, and Motley had Gymnaites, Smith, percussionist Louie Rick, and keyboard player Ted Andreadis come back to the studio to record backup vocals shortly afterward.

One problem remained: Swedosh (who was acting as "executive producer") and Motley still hadn't found a lead singer that fit their project. They wanted someone whose voice combined old-fashioned soul (re: Black) and '80s rock (re: white), but after auditioning dozens of men and women, they were still unhappy with their options. Smith suggested they try an old friend of Popeye's, club singer Cynthia Manley. Manley grew up in Oklahoma as a musical child, performing in church from the age of three. When she was fourteen her family moved to Sacramento, California. After graduating high school in the early 1970s, Manley became a fixture on the Sacramento cabaret scene, performing four shows a night, five and six nights a week in various clubs around town, and touring the West (it was during one gig in Stateline, Idaho, that she met the members of Popeye). After seven years of this transient existence, she moved south to Los Angeles, where she continued her successful career. When Motley and Swedosh heard Manley, they were impressed by her ability to channel both the soul style of Motown and more current rock sensibilities dominating the Top 40 charts of the early 1980s. Manley acknowledges this hybrid nature of her voice: "I considered myself a pop singer, but I was raised on James Brown, Aretha, Chaka, Marvin Gaye . . . I had that raspy sound because I worked all the time. I loved Janis Joplin and her stage persona."[14] Boys Town Gang had found its singer.

Clocking in at nearly fourteen minutes, the medley, with its strings, brass, backup vocals, and gospel piano, emulates without slavishly adhering to a classic Motown sound. True to the burgeoning San Francisco sound, as heard in Fever, Paradise Express, and Sylvester, there is a surprising amount of open space on the recording, filled with a basic kick drum and piano, or simple

124　MENERGY

instrumental sections, giving dancers space to inhabit the song with their own energy, in between singing along with the familiar choruses.[15] This extended, open format was perfectly suited to the dance floor, and Motley tested the waters with a DJ-only release from Disconet before its official commercial release. Disconet announced the song's arrival with typical hyperbole:

> Well, it had to happen . . . Bill has produced his first record from scratch, and has created a very nice medley arrangement . . . There is a wonderful charm about Bill's medley. It combines the energy that is California with the R&B/Motown sound which the Supremes' original versions . . . had. One tape and one acetate leaked out a few weeks ago, and the talk of San Francisco and Los Angeles still centers largely on that Motley production. When you play it for your crowd, you'll see what we mean . . . The songs have it, Cynthia's vocals have it, and Bill's production has it. And those background vocals are a breath of fresh air today—remember how the guys with top hats and canes would sing backgrounds in the old Fred Astaire movies?—they're back.[16]

Cruisin' the Streets

By May 1981, Motley and Swedosh issued "Remember Me/Ain't No Mountain High Enough" as the first release on Moby Dick Records as one side of a two-song LP, *Cruisin' the Streets*. If the Motown medley was pure nostalgia, the "other A Side" (as the record calls it), "Cruisin' the Streets," drops the listener smack dab in the middle of the Castro Village, 1981. Beginning where Village People's 1977 gay anthem "San Francisco" left off, with its references to "Folsom street on the way to Polk and Castro," "Cruisin' the Streets" is even more upfront about what goes on there. In a verse, Manley directs potential cruisers to Folsom and Castro, where "you might find a big ol' boy, nine inches or more." Popeye plays a simple, pared down two-chord repeated pattern without a melody, emphasizing the pounding four-on-the-floor beat. Gone, too, are the polished backup singers of the medley, replaced by Motley and his friend Chuck Spero robotically chanting "cruisin' the streets" at the end of each line of verse.

The highlight of the song is a five-minute "street scene" in lieu of a break. Recorded in Stan Morriss's Hollywood bathroom, Manley, Ringwald, Morey, Motley and several other friends play the part of Castro cruisers out on the prowl. The scene opens with two clones dishing with each other, one telling the other, "Tell me all about it, Miss Thing." As they pass, two other men start cruising each other, but it ends with a dismissive, "I didn't think *anybody* was really into *that*!" Manley's character, a "hooker who's always hanging around here," asks another guy walking by, "Have you seen a friend of mine? He's dressed a lot like you. Same plaid shirt, Levi's, leather jacket, kinda kinky looking?" She eventually finds him, cruising a guy, "Got a cigarette?" he asks the man. "I've never seen you here before. You're a hot man." With the preliminaries out of the way, we hear the moans and slurps of more explicit activities. "Ooh, you guys mind if I watch? It really turns me on to watch two hot studs," Manley's character interrupts. Things progress, until they are interrupted by two police officers. "What do you think we should do to 'em?," one asks the other. "I know just what to do to 'em," he replies, in typically campy banter. As they all start moaning and carrying on, the band comes back in for a final set of choruses. "I remember laughing a lot when we recorded it," Manley recalls.[17] Although the scene was scripted, Manley remembers telling Motley to say "stuff that big sausage in me" at the end, assuming they would edit it out, which of course they didn't.[18]

The phenomenon of the sexually explicit gay disco song had precedent, but never in quite the same way as in the Boys Town Gang's "Cruisin' the Streets." The obvious origin of the genre was Donna Summer's 1975 megahit "Love to Love You Baby," with its reputed "marathon of 22 orgasms."[19] Cerrone followed hot on its heels with "Love in C Minor" in 1976 and the even more explicit "Cerrone's Paradise" in 1977. Patrick Adams's brainchild Musique specialized in "disco porn," with hits like "In the Bush" and "Love Massage," with its outrageous lyrics including "spread your warm juices on my back and neck" and "Baby, squirt your lotions, fill me with your love emotions." Other than some fabulously erotic album covers—including Macho's sweaty men on their self-titled first album and Rod McKuen's peculiar vanity project Slide's album *Easy In*, with a fold-out photo of an arm ending in a fist over a can of Crisco (relabeled "Disco")—until "Cruisin' the Streets," disco, perhaps surprisingly, had not produced anything as explicit for a gay audience. Mickey's 7, a short-lived glam-rock band featuring Mickey Brewster, recorded an album of explicit gay rock songs in 1975, including "Stroke My Spoke" and "Uranus (Space Butt Hole)," which vanished as soon as it was released. Back on Folsom Street, the spring of 1981 also saw the release of the punk album "Sleeze Attack" by the anonymous Canya Phuckem (consisting of local musicians, including keyboard

126 MENERGY

player Sunshine), which sold primarily in leather establishments like the Ramrod, Mr. S. Leather, the Trench, and the Cave, and featured "in-group" songs such as "Castroids bs. Smarkets" and "This Guy's the Limit."[20] This, too, failed to make a splash.

The double-header of "Remember Me/Ain't No Mountain High Enough" and "Cruisin' the Streets" represented two sides of the same Castro clone dance-floor coin; pure but campy nostalgia and down-and-dirty sexuality. Motley's pride in his, and Moby Dick's, first record is clear from the 12-inch's runout (that portion of the vinyl after the song has ended, where messages are often scratched), which reads "Cynthia, we love you!," "Thanks, Victor, for giving me a chance!," "To Trip, Craig and Mike: you made it happen!," and "Mr. Thing, to you Honey! Oh LAWD!" This 12-inch entered the *Billboard* dance chart on May 23 and rose to a peak position of number 5 by early July. Motley and Swedosh quickly revised and released a special blue-vinyl "DJ Version," which also caught the attention of club spinners. *Billboard* reviewed the release as "a breath of fresh air": "Both tunes sustain the melodic flow of the originals but take on the R&B sound that is popular today. Lush strings provide a beautiful background for Manley's sparkling vocals that are given an assist by a harmonious male backup. The transition between the tunes is smooth as well as the overall production."[21]

Making Boys Town Gang, the Band

Striking while the iron was hot, Motley contacted Manley about recording a few more songs, but she wasn't interested in continuing with the group. She had signed up as a session musician for the first record, but if she was going to be officially part of Boys Town Gang she wanted to negotiate better terms of compensation. She didn't want to be known as a disco diva; she wanted a pop career. "I never signed a contract with Moby Dick because they offered me a shit deal," she remembers.[22] She was, however, able to capitalize on the success of the songs: "About three months [after recording] I got a call from a booking agent, telling me . . . he wanted to book me at the Pipeline in Boston for $10,000, just to sing that medley. I said 'absolutely!,' and off I went!"[23] Although she has great memories of her experience with Moby Dick, she ultimately had to fight to get adequately compensated. "I was paid $300 for the audition (because they were recording it) but I didn't get a piece of all the units I sold until . . . Steven Brown, their lawyer, signed all royalties from

THE SAN FRANCISCO SOUND THRIVES   127

Moby Dick over to me, saying, 'There would be no label if you hadn't been out there performing.' "[24]

With no lead singer, Motley contacted Jackson Moore, a Los Angeles–based vocalist, and recruited a collection of four additional backup singers (Robin Charin, Don Wood, Keith Stewart, and Tommy Morley) to perform at a Conceptual Entertainment megaparty at the Galleria for the Gay Day Tea Dance in June, kickstarting a series of gigs for the group around the country.[25] This configuration only survived a few months before another shakeup occurred, finally settling on the glamorous African American Moore flanked by two white clone backup singers, Tommy Morley and newcomer Bruce Carlton, complete with black leather vests and thick mustaches (figure 7.2). "The other girl [Charin] was really more of an actress than a singer, and the other guys had different things to do and didn't really like life on the road," Carlton explains.[26] "I had my own band back in high school and was the lead singer, so I was capable (and luckily available) . . . I was actually brought in due (in large part) to my physical similarities to the other male singer, in coloring and stature."[27] These three singers went back to the studio to record Boys Town Gang's second single in summer 1981, a cover of Little Sister's 1970 dance-floor hit "You're the One." As on the first record, members of Popeye and a few other session musicians in the Los Angeles area essentially copied the bones of Little Sister's recording, replacing Sly Stone's gospel-style organ with a more percussive piano, speeding up the tempo, adding a four-on-the-floor kick drum, and smoothing out and replacing the funkier edge of the original with a polish and precision more reflective of the Castro's high-energy scene. In fact, the only substantial changes were the addition of a third verse and a short rap at the beginning, both serving to extend the song's length.

Motley wanted Moby Dick Records to reflect the spirit of clone culture through the high-energy aesthetic of places like the Trocadero Transfer and Dreamland. To DJ Bobby Viteritti, Motley was doing more than just reflecting that spirit; he was literally reproducing a night at one of his clubs. Shortly after his move to Dreamland, Viteritti recalls, "One night I played 'You're the One' by Little Sister, it was a 45 [rpm]. And they loved that song. Somebody asked me to play it again. Next thing I know, they had it copied, they did a copy of 'You're the One.' "[28] Longtime South of Market DJ Chrysler also felt that Moby Dick was emulating the sound of the bars, but that the effect was a parody of their trademark energy. "Moby Dick happened because it was trying to build off of Trocadero, plain and simple . . . I loved Craig

Figure 7.2 Boys Town Gang (*left to right*: Tom Morley, Jackson Moore, Bruce Carlton). Photo courtesy of Photofeatures International. Reproduced with permission.

Morey, Tripper was actually a good DJ, but after Bobby left Troc it just became a cartoon, and that was part of the cartoon music."[29]

For the B-side, they recorded a cover of a song that Viteritti had also been playing at Dreamland, "Disco Kicks." It was a three-year-old track that had been remixed by Randy Sills as the flipside to his disco arrangement of the *Mork and Mindy* theme on Ariola Records. Although Ariola closed its disco division in 1980 and the song had never had an official release on its own, acetates had been circulating among DJs ever since.[30] "So you only heard it at Trocadero because I had it," Viteritti explains. "And they [Moby Dick's producers] heard it so much at Trocadero, they said 'I love this song, what's the name of it?' And they made their own version of 'Disco Kicks.'"[31] Moby Dick only just scooped Sills's version, which did finally see the light of day on JDC Records a month after Boys Town Gang's release.

The single immediately entered the *Billboard* dance charts, sharing space with "Remember Me," still in the top 20. "You're the One/Disco Kicks" peaked at number 6 in October 1981, receiving positive reviews:

> Moby Dick Records has found the right combination in redoing classic songs of the past with its remake of "You're the One." . . . West Coast DJs who previewed the record found that the original melody and powerful drive of this former hit by Little Sister has been maintained. When slowed down the tune becomes perfect for late night dancing. The flipside is "Disco Kicks" and is a treat with tracks that sizzle from beginning to end. Bongo and percussion instrumentation provide a hot break. DJs will no longer have to rely only on imports for high energy as "Disco Kicks" certainly fills the bill.[32]

Moby Dick's Gold Standard

In addition to their own output, Moby Dick also consolidated their influence in the high-energy market by establishing a distribution network with dance records from abroad. Since disco's mainstream crash in 1979, a number of small independent companies had begun filling the role that in disco's heyday had been managed by the major labels.[33] In particular, Disconet co-founder Mike Wilkinson's Importe/12 Records had achieved remarkable success reissuing European and Canadian records, as well as smaller projects by US artists who had been unable to find deals with larger labels. Unlike these other labels, however, Moby Dick's reissues, released under the subheading "Gold Standard," would contain their own remixes, often labeled a "Moby Mix," as well as the original version. Their choices reflected the distinctive Moby Dick blend of 1950s- and 1960s-style Black dance music with modern Eurodisco electronics.

Included in Moby Dick's first Gold Standard batch in 1981 was Carol Jiani's "Hit 'N Run Lover," originally released on Canadian label Matra and

130 MENERGY

produced by the prolific team of Joe La Greca and Denis Le Page. Of all the dance music made outside of the United States, these Montreal artists probably came aesthetically closest to the San Francisco sound, a high-energy combination of electronics, sexually suggestive lyrics, and unapologetic disco roots. Moby Dick's "Moby Mix Version" was a collective effort between Motley, Morey, Lewis, and Ringwald with additional synthesizer by Denver Smith and bass by Mike Guess. They also released Jiani's "Mercy" backed with "The Woman in Me," which *Billboard* described as having "musical stylings similar to the Supremes and Mary Wells . . . [which] give the dancer a definite feel of the '60s but with a 1980s pulse."[34] While La Greca and Le Page were relative newcomers to the dance charts, having topped the charts first with Kat Mandu's "The Break" in 1979 and scoring a significant hit with Lime's "Your Love" (a band consisting of Denis and Denyse Le Page), "Mercy" had been cowritten by disco royalty in the person of Pete Bellotte. Longtime collaborator of Giorgio Moroder and Donna Summer, Bellotte had, among countless other projects, coauthored and co-produced the seminal "I Feel Love" in 1977.

German singer/producer Peter Griffin's "Step by Step" was the title track of his 1981 full-length album on Electrola Records, whose 12-inch import single was already popular throughout gay discos. For Moby Dick's release, the song was expanded to nearly nine minutes of pounding electronic disco. Likewise, Moby Dick extended two songs, "His Name Is Charlie" and the Moroder-esque instrumental "Laser" by Laser (German producer Wolfgang Hermes), who had released an album under that moniker and a 12-inch single containing his own remixes of the two songs in 1979. In early 1982, Moby Dick Records released a special DJ LP featuring their best Gold Standard remixes, including most of the abovementioned tracks. The *Castro Times* proudly announced the DJ-only release as representing the best of contemporary dance music, of which "San Francisco has the pleasure of listening first."[35] Their reviewer singles out "Step by Step" as the highlight, predicting correctly that "you'll be hearing it for many months down the road, as the rest of the country awakens and tunes in."[36]

8th and Minna

The worldwide success of Moby Dick, the Tons debut, and Sylvester's *Step II* and *Stars* albums were a confirmation to many in San Francisco that what they were doing would be of interest to the rest of the world. This gave a larger scope to several projects that up to that point had been essentially local. One of these was a small Bay Area vocal jazz group Acapella Gold, with Sylvester veteran Michael Finden alongside several other singers including Jo-Carol Block, Lauren Carter, and Carol McMacken. Another was a shift in cabaret stalwart Loverde's (Frank Loverde, Linda Imperial, and Peggy Gibbons) output to more overtly danceable material.

But Sylvester's success also brought inevitable clashes. Several of the musicians associated with Sylvester, including Patrick Cowley, Finden, and James "Tip" Wirrick, believed they were being shortchanged by Harvey Fuqua's Honey Productions and sued, ultimately settling out of court for an undisclosed amount of cash and their publishing rights.[37] This, alongside Fuqua's desire for Sylvester to move in "a different direction" (read: less gay and less electronic) led Cowley to part ways with Sylvester (amicably) and Honey and Fantasy Records (less so), and gave him the opportunity to pursue his own music. For his part, Sylvester used mainly new musicians on his final two albums for Fantasy, *Sell My Soul* (1980) and *Too Hot to Sleep* (1981).

Wirrick and Cowley used the money to establish a small studio at 8th and Minna, sharing the space with two of Cowley's old City College friends, bassist Maurice Tani and synthesizer wizard Art Adcock. "It was just a vacant storefront in a 2-story brick building with a commercial laundry next door," Tani remembers:

> It was ideal for us. The downstairs was large enough for us to divide in two with a massive double wall and a 10" thick, sliding, soundproof pocket door. Pat and Tip took the front half and traded days. Art and I took the rear. We rented out the three spaces upstairs to help cover the rent. One of the first tenants was Nicholas Graham who started Joe Boxer as a necktie company up there. The other two were used as rehearsal rooms. The laundry next door never complained about the loud music because their operation was so loud and the large sliding door at the back was at street level on Minna, making loading gear in and out for gigging a breeze. Pat loved that we were a block and a half off of all the action on Folsom.[38]

"Iko Iko"

One of Cowley's first projects after separating from Sylvester was a collaboration with Loverde on a new dance version of the classic girl group song "Iko Iko." Loverde had been performing a version in their live show for years, but

132 MENERGY

through David Rubinson at the Automatt recording studio, they hooked up with A&R man Jeffrey E. Cohen. Cohen was also a respected producer, songwriter, and arranger. In addition to Herbie Hancock's *VSOP* album, he had produced Patti LaBelle's first solo album (which included Sylvester favorite "You Are My Friend") in 1977. Cohen had also produced Loverde, Wirrick, and Morey's "I Got the Feeling" on Two Tons o' Fun's debut album.

Listed as a co-production between Cohen and "Megatron" (a pseudonym for Cowley), the "Iko Iko" 12-inch single is a not-entirely-successful blending of problematic "West Indian"–accented vocals by the white and African American musicians involved and Cowley's trademark electronics. Cohen and Cowley make no attempt to integrate the two styles. The song moves back and forth between "patois dance party" and "electronic disco freakout," each distinctly separate from the other. Praise for the recording came from I-Beam DJ Timmy Rivers in the *Baseline Bay Area Disco Report*, (which given its publication date of February 1979 suggests the song had been in the works for some time): "There is also in the making, by a San Francisco based group—LOVERDE—using San Francisco talent (Pat Cowley—synthesizer for Sylvester with Tip Wirrick, Bob Kingson, Michael Fendon [sic]—guitar, bass and keyboards for Sylvester) a TOO HOT DEMO (?), if I must say so myself—four cuts are killers!!!"[39] When the song eventually saw the light of day in June 1981, *Billboard*'s review was less enthusiastic: "Although the approach is different and features an interesting instrumental section laden with saloon piano, Les Paul guitar, chanting pagan maidens, and Kraftwerk synthesizer effects, there is a lot missing, increased tempo, decreased length and added drive is warranted. The flipside 'San Francisco Serenade' is an alluring disco tune with bouncy perky tracks with which the group, Loverde, seems more at ease."[40] Indeed, the B-side is much more typical of the kind of cabaret song Loverde would have performed as part of their live act. "Serenade" was arranged by Frank Loverde and Michael Finden (as the more substantial close harmony singing betrays) and produced with Cohen by Loverde's new manager, DJ Don Miley.

Regardless, the single was a moderate hit when it was released on New York–based Prism Records, one of the largest surviving independent dance music labels. It rose to number 18 on the *Billboard* dance charts by August 1981 and introduced Cowley to Cohen, a relationship that would benefit them both over the next few years. Cohen offered Cowley free or reduced-rate time at the Automatt recording studio in exchange for his contributing synthesizer elements to various other productions made there.[41]

THE SAN FRANCISCO SOUND THRIVES 133

Fusion Records and Bobby Kent

In addition to his work for Cohen, Cowley had kept himself busy performing synthesizer on various dance tracks, including a third collaboration with Pierre Jaubert on Beckie Bell's "Super Queen," enlisting the help of Art Adcock. When his old friend Jorge Socarrás returned to San Francisco after several years away, they decided to prepare the album's-length worth of material they had worked on earlier in the decade. Recording under the name Catholic, the material was stylistically closest to Socarrás's post-punk band Indoor Life, and in 1980 he asked Cowley to produce their debut four-track EP, to which Cowley also contributed synthesizer. Meanwhile, Cowley had also been working on his own high-energy dance music that combined his love of futuristic sounds with the visceral gay world of the Castro. Working with Marty Blecman, Cowley began putting together a set of songs, taking advantage of his deal with Cohen and the owner of the Automatt, David Rubinson.

The biggest hurdle Cowley faced was finding a label willing to take a chance on his first solo project. As Blecman remembered, "We shopped it around and no one would put it out . . . it was too disco, too gay, too high-energy."[42] When they approached tiny San Francisco–based Fusion Records, the timing was perfect. Cowley's was exactly the kind of music they were looking for: gay, local, and dance. The label, after all, had been started essentially as a labor of disco love between white gospel musician Bobby Kent and ex-boyfriend, now best friend Billy Stracke, and as a showcase for the remixing skills of DJ Bobby Viteritti.

Bobby Kent played keyboards and directed the choir at Glide Memorial United Methodist Church in the Tenderloin, under the pastorship of the Reverend Cecil Williams. Glide was famous for Williams's passionate advocacy of gay rights. The church helped with the formation of the Council on Religion and Homosexuality in 1964 and had been performing same-sex weddings since the 1960s. Before joining Glide in 1970, Kent had learned gospel music from his preacher grandmother in Redwood City and had been the lead singer in the rock group Rushin' River.[43] Throughout the 1970s, he continued to combine his spiritual and rock music-making, at Glide, in his group the Gospel Pearls, as a solo rock artist and organist, and briefly as keyboard player in Sylvester's "Hot Band," where the singer once famously observed, "You're pure church, honey."[44] The Glide services were like a "morning night club,"

134 MENERGY

Kent remembers, with the two Sunday services having a light show, choir, and a large rock band called "Together."[45] After a performance one day in 1976, churchgoer Bill Lane approached Kent and explained that he was a record producer and wanted to release an album of Kent's music. Kent assembled a pickup band and choir of the best voices and players he had and Lane released *Glide Memorial's Bobby Kent* on Olympia Records later that year, a collection of original songs and new arrangements of tunes done in Kent's exuberant fusion of rock and gospel.

During a tour of the Glide choir to the University of Nebraska in Omaha, Kent met Billy Stracke, who had traveled with the choir to take tickets at their performance and had family connections in Stuart, Nebraska, a tiny town about 200 miles from Omaha. It turned out that they both lived in the same building at Cole and Haight, Janice Joplin's old house, known as the "Crystal Palace," but they had never bumped into each other. A whirlwind romance led them to move in together, but it quickly became clear they were better friends than lovers, and eventually Stracke became Kent's de facto manager. Stracke arranged for Kent and his band to perform in two Gay Freedom Day celebrations, and in 1980 asked him if he'd be interested in recording a dance album. Kent was skeptical but curious, and Stracke recruited Bobby Viteritti to mix the songs. Stracke drew from his land holdings in Stuart and recruited his cousin Alan Smith and Toni James to help fund the project, forming Fusion Records.

Stracke reassured Kent that he would be in control of the project: "I didn't know if I wanted to do it," Kent remembers, "but Billy said, 'Bobby, you be you. You get out there and you take the songs that we decided to do and you do them in your style, and you have the full reign.'"[46] Fusion initially released a 12-inch EP containing the record's most danceable tracks edited by Viteritti, and sent Kent out touring with the material. Always savvy about marketing, Stracke was determined for the record to make a splash. "We used to go to discos and go up to the DJ booth and lay out a line of coke and say, 'would you play the album?,' and they would," Kent laughingly remembers.[47] The album, called *Juice*, had an attention-grabbing cover (voted "Rock's Beefiest Graphic" by *In Touch* magazine), which was inspired by a shirtless dancer Stracke saw in a New York disco: a muscular man, wearing only an orange lei, squeezes an orange onto his chest, juice dripping down his body. All this marketing worked, and the album got a nice plug in *Billboard* in early 1981: "Fusion is a new label emanating from San Francisco. It has hit the right mark with its first release . . . The tracks are driving and are overlaid

THE SAN FRANCISCO SOUND THRIVES   135

with various electronic effects. Kent's vocals are initially whining but can be appreciated on a second listen."[48] For Viteritti's part, he had been expanding his reach over the last two years, most importantly by also entering the commercial DJ mixing realm, and his remix of Magnifique's eponymous single and fellow Miamian Ray Martinez's "Lady of the Night" had both been recent minor hits. In addition to announcing his move from the Trocadero Transfer to Dreamland, in the same column *Billboard* singled out his contribution to the Fusion record, noting that "San Francisco DJ Bob Viteritti has done a fine job of editing the 12-incher as well as mixing 'Can We Still Be Friends' on the LP."[49]

"Menergy"

While Bobby Kent's *Juice* was only moderately successful, it gave the fledgling Fusion Records some credibility in the local dance market, and Cowley approached Stracke with his four-track fifteen-IPS tapes of his latest solo material, selling them to Fusion outright (a decision that would later come to haunt Cowley and Blecman). The tapes contained several songs, including "I Wanna Take You Home" and the first versions of "Menergy" and "Megatron Man," alongside a bunch of demo tracks. Cowley had recorded the material using synthesizers and a new Oberheim DMX drum machine he had purchased with money from his Sylvester heyday and legal settlement. The inspiration for "Menergy" came from a late night in with Blecman. After smoking a few joints, they listened to Cowley's new work. When he heard the demos for a track called "Energy," Blecman jokingly suggested tacking an "M" onto the front. After they had finished laughing, they realized how perfect that was.[50]

Vocals were provided by Cowley's friend Paul Parker, and four singers from the group Acapella Gold: Jo-Carol Block, Lauren Carter, Carol McMacken, and Michael Finden. The women knew each other from Lone Mountain College's vocal jazz group, and Acapella Gold formed out of that collaboration. They had been renting the rehearsal space right above Cowley's studio at Minna Street, and Block recalled their initial contact with Cowley: "One day Michael asked us if we wanted to sing on this little disco thing that his friend Patrick had written and we all said sure . . . We heard 'Menergy' and sang on it with Michael and basically thought, that was that."[51] Carter also recalled that "Patrick was also the first person to ever record Acapella Gold

136 MENERGY

for our demo tape. He really loved what we were doing in the group which was why he asked Michael to see if we would sing for him."[52]

Fusion released "Menergy" backed with "I Wanna Take You Home" in August 1981, and it immediately entered the *Billboard* dance charts. Barry Lederer's "Disco Mix" column described it as being in "a very Euro-disco style." He continued, "This disc is one of the more uplifting and energetic tunes around. The tempo quickens and intensifies as the record progresses."[53] This rather tepid review aside, the song was, without a doubt, a watershed moment in San Francisco dance music history, probably equal only to Sylvester's "You Make Me Feel (Mighty Real)." Its influence would be felt in dance music throughout the world. Disco had always, at least in part, been about sexuality, but one that was manifested largely through a heterosexual model. With the so-called death of disco in the mainstream and dance music's subsequent return to the gay clubs that had created the phenomenon, why shouldn't songs embrace the new clone culture that had arisen in cities like San Francisco? For the Village People, worldwide success had meant sacrificing the specificity of their earlier work for a generalized "inclusiveness." For Boys Town Gang, there was no longer a need for this kind of ambiguity; "Cruisin' the Streets" had initiated a new kind of San Francisco dance music, at once campy and hypermasculine, drawing from all four of Clone Culture's "D's." It's a culture perfectly exemplified by a flyer posted in the Mineshaft, a legendary "macho" New York bathhouse, which read: "The Mineshaft playrooms are for one purpose and it surely is not the place to gossip, discuss your European trip, or how well Joan Sutherland sang 'Carmen' at the Met. This you do in the Main Bar which is a social area."[54] Mainstream depictions of this world of bathhouses and leather bars had, of course, existed before, but always from a distinctly heterosexual perspective; that is, without any of the campy humor participants in that culture acknowledge. The leather scene was taken at face value by straight culture (as depicted in films like the unintentionally hilarious *Cruising* [1981] and intentionally stupid *Police Academy* [1984]), who looked on in horror at the bacchanalian excess that subculture celebrated.

The overt sexuality of "Menergy" begins with the beat, a relentless four-on-the-floor. Constant repetition of simple syncopated electronic patterns layered onto each other, and monotone, robotic chanting of the word "menergy" on the downbeat of every bar is calculated to send dancers into a trance. The song adds humanity in the form of the close harmony singing of Acapella Gold (soon to be renamed the Patrick Cowley Singers), responding with a rhapsodizing repetition of the word. A two-bar bass progression grounds the

THE SAN FRANCISCO SOUND THRIVES   137

song in C minor, dropping to G, B♭ and back to C, over and over, reaffirming the drone-like bass progression by constantly returning to the tonic. On top of this, an improvisatory solo electronic melody, guitar-like, moves in and out of the texture. Most of the song consists of this repetitious pattern, but there are three sections with "verses," such as "They boys in the backroom, laughin' it up, shootin' off energy" and "The boys in the bedroom, lovin' it up, shootin' off energy."

For the B-side, "I Wanna Take You Home," Cowley's off-beat synthesizer gives a galloping quality to the pulse. Live drumming by Cowley mixes with the utopic major-mode jazz harmonies of the singers. Sylvester remembered about Cowley, "Patrick was fun. He was funny and never too serious. At the time he was very into his Masculine Music trip. We often talked of doing these great gay records about hanging around in deep dark places doing these nasty, lewd, wonderful things!"[55] Finally, as a solo artist, Cowley was able to fulfill that dream, even registering his publishing copyright name as Masculine Music.

"Menergy" hit the number 1 spot on the dance charts on October 31, 1981. The success of the 12-inch surprised everyone, a woefully unprepared Fusion Records perhaps most of all. The records were in demand all over the world, and unlike the major labels, Billy Stracke didn't have an established distribution or international licensing setup. His lawyer Steven Ames Brown recalls,

> Billy walked in and said, "I have a hit record. It's on the charts, it just hit number one and I just got a call from a record company in the Netherlands and they wanna license the track and I don't know what to do and I have $100,000, can you help me?" And I said, "Yes, I can." And then I very quickly learned the international licensing business. Then I developed my first form which I use to this day. And then the first thing I did an hour later was start the international licensing of "Menergy," the original version of "Menergy." And I drafted a sales contract and Billy bought it from Patrick Cowley.[56]

Brown wasted no time, advertising in *Billboard* announcing the availability of the song for international exclusive territory licensing.[57] But Cowley already had his sights on starting his own record label. His solo success had proved him right; despite what the larger labels believed, there was a substantial market for gay-targeted high-energy electronic dance music. The fledgling Moby Dick Records was soaring on the charts with Boys Town Gang and their reissues of Eurodisco: why couldn't he do the same?

Fusion was not about to see their most successful (and, essentially, only) artist walk away without a fight, particularly as they still owned "Menergy," "I Wanna Take You Home," and several other unreleased tracks including "I Got a Line on You." They hired a dance music promotion company, the well-known Go Dance out of New York, for their Cowley product and rushed forward a full *Menergy* album of that material, putting a quarter-page ad in *Billboard* on November 28 in anticipation, announcing "The Patrick Cowley Album 'Menergy': Evolving from the #1 12" Disco Hit on the Billboard Chart, including the NEW SUPER HIT 'I Got a Line on You' and other Patrick Cowley Originals."[58] The album was prominently labeled "A Bob Viteritti Master Mix," and, indeed, Viteritti seems to have done much more than simply mix the record. Stracke instructed him to take Cowley's tapes and create some additional songs without any input from Cowley, as Viteritti recalls:

> They said, "We're gonna go to a recording studio in Russian River and it's a barn, and it used to be the old Beach Boys recording studio." . . . And I remember getting there and saying, "Where the fuck are we? It's like a farm." . . . And as soon as we went in there it was high tech, with the Beach Boys' mixing board, they made all their hits on that. And so we had the studio and we recorded one night. . . . "X-Factor" was something they came up with because they needed another track to make it an album. So they said, "Make something." So I got some of the tracks out of "Menergy" and "I Got a Line on You." I used them to make another song out of it. We took their voices out and changed it around and brought up the bass. [It's] another one where we just started doing it and never finished it or something. That's why it loops a lot.[59]

By the time Fusion was able to get the album out in early January 1982, they had been scooped by Cowley's initial release on his own new label, Megatone. While Fusion's *Menergy* remained on the chart until March, it was the last hit the label would have. Cowley would go on to the biggest year of his life. That it was also to be his last was something no one could have predicted.

8

New Heights

The years 1981 and 1982 were in many ways the most successful, most artistically fulfilling years of San Francisco's dance music scene. With the launch of Megatone Records, Patrick Cowley and Marty Blecman solidified their places at the center of the San Francisco sound, releasing hit after hit, relaunching Sylvester's career, and discovering a true star in singer Paul Parker. John Hedges returned to the production field with his first roster of solo artists and discovered his own Patrick Cowley, Barry Blum. Together they made a formidable songwriting and production team. The scene's apotheosis was probably the massive First Encounter megaparty at the new Moscone Convention Center, an event that magnified and epitomized the best (and, to some, the worst) aspects of San Francisco clone culture. This chapter describes the events that made 1981 and 1982 such monumental years for San Francisco music, musicians, and gay men. These years could, with hindsight, be seen as a Mardi Gras for a way of life that celebrated a new liberated identity; at the time, they merely represented a continuing, upward trajectory of progress that participants had no way of knowing was about to be irrevocably challenged.

Masculine Music for Macho Men

In his short life, Patrick Cowley wrote and recorded a huge amount of music (figure 8.1). "He really didn't have much of a social life, it was just music and the baths, music and the baths," Frank Loverde remembered.[1] So while Fusion Records was, in Cowley's mind, dragging its feet getting his record out, he wasn't just sitting around. In the eight months from when he dropped off the tapes to Fusion's Billy Stracke to the time the records were actually in record stores, he had produced enough new material for several albums. He was constantly looking for outlets for his material, when he wasn't cruising,

Menergy. Louis Niebur, Oxford University Press. © Oxford University Press 2022.
DOI: 10.1093/oso/9780197511077.003.0009

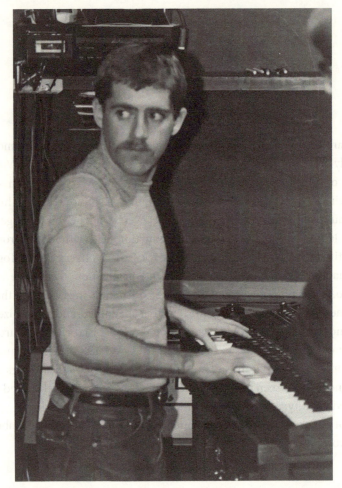

Figure 8.1 Patrick Cowley. Photo courtesy of Josh Cheon. Reproduced with permission.

that is. Collaborator Jorge Socarrás recalls how Cowley introduced him to the seedier side of the Castro:

> One day he unexpectedly presented me with a membership card to the Jaguar Bookstore in the Castro, insisting I was going there with him. Now I was no prude, but mine was a free-love type of promiscuity, and the adult bookstore's backroom sex club represented something quite different. Patrick practically marched me to the Jaguar and took great satisfaction in

NEW HEIGHTS   141

my ritual initiation. (I of course had the even greater satisfaction). At about the same time he also turned me on to the gay porn films of Wakefield Poole (*Boys in the Sand*), themselves informed by a quasi-mythical sense of ritual and initiation.[2]

So it's no surprise that one of Cowley's most personally rewarding projects was a collaboration with gay porn producer John Coletti.[3] They had met in the late 1970s through Sylvester, and when Coletti decided to reissue some of his old sixteen-millimeter silent porn loops in a series of collections through his company Fox Studios, he thought of Cowley as someone who might provide an appropriate soundtrack to the action. For the first, *School Daze* (1980), Cowley sent Coletti reels of music from his years in the electronic music lab at San Francisco City College. The collaboration was ideal: Cowley had originally conceived of much of that music as an ode to the emerging bathhouse culture, and now these tracks were actually accompanying the kinds of scenes he had envisioned. Lab partner and fellow musician Maurice Tani recalls how Cowley constructed his imaginary (now literal) soundtracks: "His first attempts were song-based—sort of odes to sex—but he soon moved to more extended atmospheric pieces. He might create a 7–10 minute, multi-layer percussion bed and I'd lay a bass line groove over it. From there he would add layer on top of layer of synths, guitars, voices (spoken or sung), piano, whatever."[4] For example, in the nearly fourteen-minute "Journey Home," Cowley gradually builds up the instrumentation (including didgeridoo by Charlie McMahon) over a harmonically static but rhythmically active drone. Coletti's next film, *Muscle Up* (1981), likewise contains mostly extended drone tracks from Cowley's college years. For his third collaboration however, *Afternooners* (1982), Cowley wrote new material, some of which were demos for later dance songs, including "Bore and Stroke," a trial run for *Mind Warp*'s "Goin' Home." But with the exception of an instrumental version of "Somebody to Love Tonight," included that same year on Sylvester's *Stars*, none of the tracks were ever commercially released independently of the soundtracks during Cowley's life.[5]

These songs were becoming more and more explicit in their evocation of San Francisco Castro clone and SoMa culture, and consequently less commercially viable, even in the open, gay dance music market. "Thief of Love" described the bathhouse experience, as Cowley recites his lyrics over a persistent, polyrhythmic beat: "In doorways, against walls, stalls. Rooms empty save for beds, or carpets, or couches. All night long the men walk

142 MENERGY

the narrow halls and dark rooms. Small, subtle, yet distinct compact ritual is performed again, and again." In the sultry "You Gotta Make It Loose," Cowley again intones a scenario in a dispassionate, detached way: "It's a small tool shed out back. When you step inside in the darkness you see maybe six men. One man is getting off, moaning as another on his knees sucks his cock. Next to them, a bearded man facing you and bent over is getting an even, energetic balling from a young man who moans 'yeah, yeah, yeah.'" "Kickin' In," a twelve-and-a-half minute pounding endurance test of high-energy dance music describes the rituals of sex and drugs as Loverde (Frank Loverde and Linda Imperial, with Timmy Rivers) sing, "When your heart starts to thumpin', you can feel it kickin' in . . . Then your body starts to movin', you can feel it slippin' in." Like his music for porn, none of these songs were released during Cowley's life, and were probably recorded more for the satisfaction of the artists than for any thoughts of commercial success.

This is how many of Cowley's collaborations happened, by drawing upon local Castro talent. Singer Paul Parker remembers, "One day I was walking down Castro Street and came upon Patrick Cowley sitting on a stoop . . . A friend of mine introduced us and he invited me to come to his studio to sing a demo, to see if we might work together."[6] Parker ultimately recorded many demos with him that weren't released, including "Love Me Hot" (which also included Frank Loverde's vocals) and "Pajama Party Massacre" with old friend Maurice Tani (which eventually became "Teen Planet" on his debut solo album).[7] Cowley's most influential collaborator, though, was Marty Blecman, whose instincts as a DJ helped guide Cowley back to the beat again and again.

One of the most complex collaborations was a 1980 project between Blecman, John Hedges, and Cowley. Hedges had been approached by Douglas Goldman (one of the heirs of both the Haas and the Levi Strauss families), who was interested in producing an original dance track based on popular "Western" melodies, such as "Wild, Wild West," "El Paso," and "Apache." "He said he had this idea to do this thing of TV songs and he would pay for it," Hedges remembers.[8] "He had a ton of money. So I go, 'Fine.' So we went in and recorded it with everybody I could get, even Patrick Cowley. And just everyone I could get, whoever laid tracks, the more the better."[9] Hedges and Blecman mixed various elements together, adding extended dance breaks, and for its first release created a version omitting nearly all of the cheesy Western themes. They sent it to Disconet, where it appeared as

"Ride It" next to Cowley's "I Feel Love" remix and Bobby Viteritti's mix of Ray Martinez's "Lady of the Night." Disconet's Wilkinson added the vocals of Poussez's Holly Oas and "Julie" (a pseudonym for singer Christine Wiltshire), chanting "Your 'pou-ssez' is hot!" and "Ride it!," as well as an additional vocal by Scottish funk singer Jesse Rae in an appearance toward the end that resembled Loleatta Holloway in "Relight My Fire."[10] It's a complete transformation, but Hedges and Wilkinson's "kitchen sink" approach never sounds cluttered, with each element given its turn in the front of the mix. Cowley's synthesizers are relatively restrained, but his distinctive gallop transforms the track into a high-energy feast.

Wilkinson liked the song so much he included it on the debut release from his new label Import 12, *Prime Cuts 1: The Double Dance Album.* The material saw a more faithful (and extended) release on Moby Dick Records in 1981, renamed "An American Dream (Medley)" and credited to "Hot Posse (featuring synthesizers by PATRICK COWLEY)." Here, the Western themes are presented as Douglas Goldman had intended, one after another, with the "Ride It" material between the tunes. This more literal version, as mixed by Bill Motley, Craig Morey, and Mike Lewis, features, as the artist credit would suggest, a much more pronounced contribution from Cowley, extending the song to a marathon 10:14.

Megatron Man

Since being let go from Fantasy with disco's crash in late 1979, Blecman and Hedges Productions remained as a blanket moniker for their related endeavors, but by 1981 they were collaborating less and less. They had both returned to DJing; Marty was working at Alfie's again at night, and John was at Badlands (where he stayed for eight years). Blecman also got more serious about his work with Cowley. Specifically, they began assembling a full solo Cowley album of dance material, with Blecman contributing a sense of shape and form, bringing the expertise he had earned over the years as a DJ, producer, and remixer. Equally important was his experience at Fantasy Records as a research and marketing consultant and record promoter. Blecman understood the business. "Marty has excellent ideas," Cowley explained in a contemporary interview, "Really commercial, but creative. He's also got a great feel for the business end of things, which I know nothing about. We work well together. Thus the partnership was born."[11]

144 MENERGY

Blecman's professional biography from the second half of 1981 suggests that they *were* hoping to release Cowley's album, *Megatron Man*, on Fusion Records, as well as an album of songs with Paul Parker, starting with the single "Too Much to Dream" (a cover of the 1960s psychedelic hit).[12] With their frustration with Fusion growing by the day, however, they considered accepting a deal from Moby Dick. Blecman remembers, "We were down to the last twenty-four hours before we had to give them [Moby Dick] an answer, when we met with Huntly Gordon who decided to back the company for us."[13] With Gordon's investment of $20,000, they were able to start their own label, Megatone Records, with *Megatron Man* as its first release. Their plan from the beginning was to issue not only Cowley's music but also that of other artists who matched San Francisco's high-energy aesthetic. As he explained later, in 1982, "Make no mistake about it, the music we're involved with is primarily aimed at clubs. If it crosses over to R&B radio, great, but the backbone of this label will always be dance music."[14] The label was run out of Blecman's flat, which was already a hub for local musicians and DJs. As Hedges remembers it, "you'd just go there around 11 o'clock and talk about music and what we're gonna do."[15]

Cowley's album was recorded at the Automatt, taking advantage of his deal with David Rubinson to exchange studio time for contributing synthesizer on various projects (see Chapter 7). "As it turned out, it took us about eighty hours but he still gave it all to us for free, so he [Rubinson] is really financially responsible for the production of the *Megatron Man* LP," Blecman noted.[16] Cowley's electronic "gallop" drives the motion forward through most tracks, pushing forward with relentless energy. None of the songs are less than 120 BPM, and the album shines with a blissful technological sheen throughout. Science fiction themes abound, but always in concert with invocations to dance and more erotic pursuits. It is no surprise that around this time Cowley registered his songs under the publishing name "Masculine Music," a label he would use for all his music licensing that campily reflected his brand of clone identity.

The first track, "Megatron Man," was the perfect follow-up to "Menergy" in that it reaffirmed the ethos of futuristic hedonism. Cowley had probably submitted a version of the song with his original tapes to Fusion, but for the Megatone album he completely rewrote the track with new instrumentation, including beefier synth textures, a stronger backbeat, enhanced stereo effects, a thicker vocoder sound, and the synthesized bass reinforced by Maurice Tani's electric bass. The song opens with a powerful four-on-the-floor kick drum and a strong backbeat. The polyrhythm is added to by a synthesized bass in octaves and phased electronic off-beat pulses. Finally, the pattern is completed with Tani's bass playing driving sixteenth-note "and a," creating the Cowley gallop.

Rich synthesizer chords play over this polyrhythm in a minor mode and, similar to Black Sabbath's 1970 hit "Iron Man," a monotone, vocoded voice intones the words "Megatron Man." Science fiction–sounding electronic blips rise in response to the words, and a more musical, but still vocoded, voice continues, harmonizing the words, "Megatron Man, Megatron Man, the world is waiting, Megatron Man." As new synthesizer riffs play over the relentless polyrhythmic pattern for the next nine minutes, the dancing body is transformed into the "Megatron Man." Without any additional lyrics, the body locks into the beat, and the electronics give the hint that, unlike the heavy metal Iron Man, this Megatron Man is a sensual android, a suspicion confirmed when toward the end of the song the vocoded voice begins improvising words in rhythm: "I love you, I love you, I love the way that you move. Bop-a-boom bop, etc." At that moment, the dancer and all the dancers around them *are* Megatron Men, the dance floor a passionate circuit board connecting them all.

This science fiction opener is followed by "Thank God for Music," a bright, upbeat ode that shifts the emphasis onto the singers. All vocals were arranged and sung by Carol McMackin, Jo-Carol Block, and Lauren Carter, dubbed the Patrick Cowley Singers, and their jazz harmonies are an essential ingredient to the success of the album as a whole. Cowley leaves plenty of room for them in his background synthesizer track, even abandoning the gallop when the singers enter, but continues a mysterious mythic atmosphere through the lyrics. "Thank God for Music" is the most traditional song on the album, with three verses, chorus, and a break. The track opens with a *Star Wars*-esque "Long ago and far away, the world was a silent place." Until, that is, music appears, setting people's spirits free and allowing them to express emotion "through rhythm and harmony." These simple, some might even say simplistic, words allow the vocalists to sing complex, shifting chords, unusual for the generally concise and immediate harmonic language of postdisco dance music. Rounding out the first side was "Menergy," the hit that had made Cowley's name as a solo artist.

Side B opens with "Get a Little," written by Block and Carter with Cowley. As one might expect, it emphasizes the close harmonies of the vocalists. Cowley combines Latin timbales and standard four-on-the-floor drums with heavy backbeat with buzzy, staccato sawtooth synth hits, doubling the singer's major seventh tonic chord at the beginning of each line. Even the verses, sung with a reduced two-voice harmony, are complex a cappella units. The break, rather than removing all elements and building up, as was standard practice in dance records, layers multiple vocal lines in a polyrhythmic mélange, with Cowley's ARP synth solo sliding up and down with the instrument's distinctive portamento.

The highlight of the B-side is "Lift Off." One by one, Cowley introduces the characteristic elements of his sound, starting with a bass drum pulse. Next, a synthesizer on the offbeat fills in where the disco hi-hat ordinarily sounds. After a synthesizer line outlines a rising minor minor seventh chord with added fourth, building suspense, Cowley drops into a bass gallop. Finally, a two-note riff on beats 3.5 and 4 complete the polyrhythm (see example 8.1).

The first verse opens with close harmony singing, this time with Paul Parker's voice adding to the already thick texture of the Patrick Cowley Singers, directing dancers to "take a trip to another dimension . . . far beyond all space and time." Climbing synthesizer effects lead into the chorus, which consists of a simple repetitive demand to "Lift Off!," and after another verse and chorus an effects-filled bridge enacts an actual rocket launch, complete with countdown from ten to lift-off. The effect is clearly meant to enhance a collective drug-induced euphoria, the "mind expansion" mentioned in the lyrics. As DJ Casey Jones remembers, "The whole scene in San Francisco at the time pretty much revolved around 'up' drugs . . . Patrick created a synthesized sound that would enhance a drug induced high."[17] Cowley is again using the language of science fiction to create a communal gay dance experience, one where drugs like LSD, Quaaludes, and even poppers find a dual use on the dance floor and in the bedroom, in both places a manifestation

Example 8.1 "Lift Off," Cowley gallop.

of the newfound liberation of gay sexuality. Cowley fittingly concludes the album with the B-side to "Menergy," "I Wanna Take You Home," which had had a successful life of its own on gay dance floors across the country, and for one final time reaffirms the connection between electronics and the act of cruising.

Problems with Fusion

Right as Fusion's "Menergy" hit the number one spot on the *Billboard* dance chart, Megatone's *Megatron Man* was released. In their review of the album, *Billboard* mentions every one of the new tracks, praising the "relentless electronic and synthesizer usage, with Cowley's vocoder-like vocals offset by female backup singers."[18] "Thank God for Music," "Liftoff," and "I Wanna Take You Home" were singled out as "high in quality, pulsating in momentum and polished in production."[19] The album was also praised in the gay press, both in the United States and abroad, but just as it began climbing the charts, Megatone was hit by an injunction from Fusion Records. Megatone's lawyer, Gerald Weiner, who had helped Cowley with his lawsuit against Honey Productions, had assured them it would be fine to include "Menergy" and "I Wanna Take You Home" on *Megatron Man*, as long as they recorded new versions of the songs. This legal argument didn't hold up, however.[20] Fusion's lawyer Steven Ames Brown remembers,

> I liked Patrick, [but] Patrick did something stupid, he listened to his lawyer who said that he didn't contractually agree to not re-record it. He rerecorded it and tried to walk off with the profits. And it never occurred to him that that would have rendered the Fusion sales contract essentially valueless. So I didn't sue on copyright, which I had no right to do, I sued under a contractual theory, which you always have a right to do. . . . The judge entered a temporary restraining order and the settlement was they had to pull the album. They had to reconfigure that album.[21]

All 10,000 units of *Megatron Man* had to be recalled, and new copies made with different songs replacing the illegally used tracks. Scrambling, Cowley and Blecman settled on two songs that showed a different side of Cowley's temperament. "Sea Hunt," an arrangement of the brassy, noirish theme tune to the 1960s television show, is, in Cowley's reimagining, perhaps more

148 MENERGY

evocative of another 1960s program, *Dark Shadows*, with a squiggly, uncanny theremin-like melody replacing the original's trumpets. Jo-Carol Block had originally suggested the tune to him: "I told Patrick one day that I thought it [Sea Hunt] would make a great song done over in some way and he said that he couldn't believe I'd said that, because his very first male fantasy figure had been Lloyd Bridges during his *Sea Hunt* days."[22] Even his sister, Madonna, remembers that growing up, "he had a mad crush on Lloyd Bridges."[23] "So we went in one night and did the song," Block recalls. "I played some keyboards and sang the siren's-call vocals."[24] According to Ian Anthony Brown, the choice of "Sea Hunt" was more directed at Fusion Records: "Steven Brown took an injunction out and had the record withdrawn. So, although he hadn't actually been paid anything for it, he had to take those tracks off the album and replace them, one of which was "Sea Hunt," which has a clue in what that's about. If you substitute the word 'Sea' for the letter 'C.'"[25]

In an interview from 1982, Cowley described a common reaction to *Megatron Man*: "When people hear that record, they refer to it as new wave, while I look at it as traditional disco. But people think of it as being current because it's very electronic."[26] Listeners making that designation were probably referring to "Teen Planet," the second replacement song. Totally unlike the others on the album, "Teen Planet" demonstrates Cowley's interest in the new wave and post-punk sound, one he had explored over the years with Jorge Soccarás, particularly with their *Catholic* project. While new wave has points of overlap with Cowley's San Francisco sound, including an obsession with science fiction and the use of electronics, the two genres have little else in common. With the changes forced upon the album, the acoustic drums, electric guitar, staccato vocal delivery, and short duration of "Teen Planet" unexpectedly allowed Cowley to highlight a different aspect of his futuristic vision.

For its own part, Fusion Records engaged in a bit of misleading tom-foolery when, later in 1982, they commissioned a remix of a version of "Megatron Man." It's unclear how Fusion came by what sounds like a demo version of the song, but they managed to find $15,000 to hire producer Joe Long to remix the track. Long, a gay veteran of the disco and R&B scene, had produced hits for Pat Hodges ("Fly By Night"), Liquid Gold ("My Baby's Baby"), Edwin Starr ("Twenty-Five Miles"), and prolific backup singer (and secret wife of Bob Dylan) Clydie King. At the height of the disco craze, he pioneered the "Joe Long Sound" on extended disco novelty records like the fourteen-minute "O Holy Night" and the equally epic "Hallelujah

2000" for Casablanca Records. Working from the Golden Age Recording Studio in Culver City, Long, fellow musician Jeryl Thompson, and editor Carl Lang began by playing over Cowley's original, adding elements such as a flanged drum track, new vocoder lines, and electric bass. Long would take the very green, and very straight, Thompson over to Studio One in West Hollywood, where they'd absorb the atmosphere (and astringent odor of poppers), afterward pouring back into the recording studio where, as Thompson recalls,

> I reproduced all of the sounds that Patrick had used. I had different instruments and I'm a pretty good programmer, so I was able to program the sounds so it sounded just like his sounds. You couldn't tell the difference. We used the Prophet-5, and we also used the Yamaha CS-80 and the CS-60. And we always kept the drums set up, and we kept the bass amp and basses plugged up, and we always had music ready 'cause at any moment we just wanted to capture a performance. And Joe and I came in and Carl was playing the track, and I just went in, I sat down, I started playing these drums. But we had a massive drum set set up and I just began to play, not the track, but play just some funky stuff and these big drum rolls like Billy Cobham from Mahavishnu Orchestra drum rolls.[27]

Just as they took Cowley's song as raw material and expanded on it, they similarly extrapolated on the lyrics, as Thompson remembers, "I was sitting there going, 'this is cool, but what happens to the Megatron after this song?' and so we decided to make a Megatron Woman, and then from that we'd be able to make a whole series of this Megatron thing. . . . I was straight. And so it just made sense and I'm like 'hey dude, if we did Megatron Woman, then we could turn this into Megatron Baby, and we can make a whole Megatron trilogy of songs.'" Together, they fashioned a heterosexual love story, where there "Once was a Megatron Land, where lived a Megatron Man, who needed a Megatron Woman. Where is this Megatron Woman who wants a Megatron man?" These words never made it onto the Fusion 12-inch single, but over the course of several weeks, Long, Thompson, and Lang recorded a series of increasingly loose interpretations of Cowley's original, finally settling on an eleven-minute A-side and a tight eight-minute "percussion instrumental" B-side. Fusion gives no artist credit, but sneakily puts songwriters Cowley and Blecman's names in large print below the title, implying they in fact were the performers.

150 MENERGY

Fusion's release never seriously challenged Cowley's Megatone version, but shortly after Cowley's death, Joe Long, without Thompson or Lang, took the Cowley "Megatron Woman" remixes to Salsoul Records. Long released a 12-inch single under the name Native Love (a name African American Thompson believes came from Long's unrequited love for him), "Megatrone Women," with only his name listed as composer. The misspelling is undoubtedly a transparent attempt to avoid a lawsuit, and almost as surely it was only because of Cowley's death that year that Long and Salsoul were able to get away with it.

The Patrick Cowley Singers

The brief interruption caused by reissuing *Megatron Man* did nothing to stem its rise, and over the first three months of 1982 Cowley saw both the Fusion and Megatone albums sharing space on the *Billboard* dance charts. *Megatron Man* peaked in March at the number 2 spot, where it stayed for four weeks before beginning a slow slide down. Blecman had been promoting Cowley's music ever since "Menergy" and "I Wanna Take You Home" in the summer of 1981. Jo-Carol Block remembers, "After that record came out on Fusion Records, Marty Blecman asked us if we'd like to make five hundred dollars singing at Alfie's. . . . Well, in the jazz group [Acapella Gold] we'd be lucky if we made five dollars a week (we actually spent more than we brought in), so naturally we thought it was a good idea."[28] Block, Lauren Carter, and Carol McMacken loved that first bar gig and the taste of gay club culture (Michael Finden declined performing live with the Patrick Cowley Singers, probably because he had just returned from a long tour with Sylvester and needed to rest). That initial Alfie's performance on June 20, part of a five-day celebration in honor of the club's fourth anniversary and Gay Pride Week, included the debut of "Menergy" and "I Wanna Take You Home," as well as new tracks from Cowley's solo work with Paul Parker. They joined the bill with fellow San Francisco artists Sylvester, Edwin Starr, and Cynthia Manley, and international disco stars Carol Douglas, the Love Twins (producer Alec Costandinos's latest project), Jessica Williams, Debbie Jacobs, and Belinda West.[29]

Through the summer and early fall they also continued performing with Acapella Gold, most significantly at a benefit for the Council on Entertainment, where a reviewer remarked that they "won more friends with their close harmony jazz and pop singing."[30] But by November, Block, Carter, and McMacken had broken off from the group and started performing only as the Patrick Cowley Singers, including a trip to Atlanta for a Christmas concert at popular nightclub Backstreet, but not without some fallout from their jazz world.[31] Carter recalled, "a lot of our friends . . . felt that we sold out or something, going into disco, but unless you become involved in it you can't really understand what the scene really is. It's a lot more exciting and fulfilling for us."[32] Block concurs, "Let me tell you, it's a helluva lot more exciting playing at the Saint in New York to a screaming crowd of thousands, than crooning at the Sea Witch in Ghirardelli Square to a group of quietly staring patrons."[33]

For a directionless woman who had been living off food stamps with her brother and his pregnant girlfriend in a rundown hippy flat on Bush Street, these performances focused Jo-Carol Block's energy into a successful singing career.[34] From Acapella Gold to the Patrick Cowley Singers, and eventually as the hit duo Jolo on Megatone Records, these performances honed Block's and Carter's artistry and stagecraft. They went on to become one of the biggest acts in the San Francisco dance music scene. In late 1981, the Patrick Cowley Singers were making small public appearances promoting Cowley's album, including an event for the Endup's eighth anniversary produced by the record pool T.O.P. 25. They performed at the "Search for Mr. Drummer" contest at the I-Beam, where audiences witnessed "a splashy dance routine . . . with [outgoing] Mr. Drummer Ray Perea cavorting onstage with the Patrick Cowley Singers."[35] At another event for the third anniversary of Studio West, they were advertised as "San Francisco's own three ladies who set the world afire with 'Menergy,' 'Liftoff,' 'Megatron Man,' 'Thank God for Music.' "[36] Disconet gave Cowley a boost by commissioning a remix of "Thank God for Music," which received a plug in Lederer's "Disco Mix" column in *Billboard*, which also singled out album track "Get a Little" as a hot choice on the nation's dance floors.[37]

Closer to home, Cowley's *Megatron Man* won a prestigious Cable Car award ("which honor outstanding achievement in the Gay community for a variety of events from sports to journalism") in one of two new categories created to acknowledge the rise of San Francisco dance music, "Outstanding Club Recording."[38] Sharing the nomination with Cowley in this competitive year were Sylvester (for his latest Fantasy album, *Too Hot to Sleep*), Two Tons o' Fun (for their second Fantasy album, *Backatcha*), Boys Town Gang ("Cruisin' the Streets"), Loverde ("Iko Iko," which Cowley had co-produced),

152 MENERGY

and Romeo Void ("It's a Condition").[39] The winner was voted on by the various local disc jockey pools.[40] For the February ceremony, Sylvester flew in from a tour of Florida and Boys Town Gang (with new singer Jackson Moore) came up from Los Angeles to perform live, alongside Meg Christian and other prominent lesbian and gay performers. This award confirmed Cowley's position as *the* defining player in the San Francisco sound.

First Encounter

On Saturday, January 16, 1982, Trocadero Transfer owner Dick Collier and business partner John Vukas threw the First Encounter megaparty, a massive event that, in hindsight, holds a significance no one could have predicted. It was by far the biggest event of the year. Even by the excessive standards of Bandy and Roverana's Conceptual Entertainment parties, this extravagant, decadent bash seemed truly bacchanalian, generating a gross income of over $100,000.[41] It was one of the first big events in the new Moscone Convention Center, to this day the largest convention space in the city.[42]

For weeks, First Encounter was plugged in the gay media, promising a "lavish, Broadway/Las Vegas spectacular with four super sound systems, thousands of lighting gimmicks, smoke machines, 35ft. spruce trees, [and] 20 search lights outside."[43] Michael Lewis and Craig Morey shared DJing duties for the evening, and at 3:00 a.m. live entertainment was integrated into the flow of the dance. Sylvester, complete with sixteen-piece orchestra, performed, as did Jeanie Tracy (premiering some of the new tracks from her own upcoming solo Fantasy album, *Me and You*), Boys Town Gang, and the Patrick Cowley Singers. In total, twelve hours of music was provided for the party. For the 11,000 revelers who attended, it was a truly polarizing event.

First, the negatives: The backup at the coat check caused major headaches for many people, some of whom waited over an hour to get through the line. Also, the bars were understaffed and unprepared for the sheer volume the gay attendees drank. Finally, many people complained that the live music interrupted the flow of the evening and their individual dancing trip. A more profound and subtle criticism was heard in the weeks after the event, however, from those who viewed these parties as the antithesis of "gay pride," and for whom the sheer scale of First Encounter disgusted them. One attendee of several who wrote letters to the *Bay Area Reporter* felt that "the Moscone affair remains far below the threshold of passion, far below the threshold of real celebration."[44] For him, the pursuit of significance has led to empty "quantity" over "quality": "More lights, more sound, and more hunky men. And lots of very expensive drugs," a "plastic scene with millions of boring flashing lights and distorted disco electronics."[45] I would be more inclined to respect the author's plea if he didn't then recommend drum circles as an alternative to the megaparty. A more thoughtful critique came from music critic Jerry de Gracia, who, as usual, was unable to contain his disdain for disco. After admitting he had never attended a Conceptual Entertainment Galleria party, he nevertheless decided to

> see what the disco dollies were up to these days. I'm afraid they're not up to much. The site of the party was impressive, as was the size of the crowd. But the music, except for the live entertainment, was technically perfect boredom. Listening to two and three year old disco hits is not my idea of a good time . . . His mixing of the old song "Magic Bird of Fire" was exceptional but he should be forced to eat Dan Hartman's "Relight My Fire" and regurgitate it on his turntable."[46]

De Gracia's critique is slightly disingenuous, however, since Lewis and Morey's sets were anything but old-fashioned. Over the course of the evening, they combined disco classics with the latest in high-energy dance music, including Ruby Wilson's "I Thought I Would Never Find Love," Presley Gomez's "The Letter," Lisa's "Jump Shout," and Hot Posse's "An American Dream." *Billboard* reported that the entire production was "dazzling, artistic, and creative."[47]

For Konstantin Berlandt, the sight of ex-hookup John Vukas's name in lights was enough for him to dish that "I imagined the auditorium was full with 10,000 of his former tricks, some of whom cheered him by name when he was presented by Sylvester with a plaque from the Board of Supervisors for services rendered."[48] It's hard to read as anything but sarcastic his eventual "praise" for the event. The intense silliness of a party of this magnitude seemed to draw from him a frustration that this was, apparently, the most substantial manifestation of liberation San Francisco gays could muster:

> This was the Columbia launching, the Declaration of Independence Party, the taking of our place in the center of the central city. It was our birthright and our born-again party all at once . . . Clones on the half-shell, their bodies pumped up for days, and plenty of average looking men as well,

154 MENERGY

some women, some straights, some drag queens and people of color. The prospect of holocaust in a twinkling of an eye was taken for granted as the beat continued from one song into the next, the transitions of the disc jockeys smoother than the architects of this glorified airport.[49]

Here he is drawing attention to both the uniformity of people and their difference. Dance theorist Danielle Goldman calls improvised dance "a practice of freedom" that requires an acknowledgment of the variation among dancers.[50] Ignoring these differences "diminishes one's understanding of the social potential of improvisation," and conversely, "assumptions of 'sameness' in dance experience blocks one's ability to appreciate the political power of dancers' interactions within constraints and therefore of 'the possibility for meaningful exchange.'"[51] It was exactly this potential for political power that gay City Supervisor (and Harvey Milk's replacement) Harry Britt was responding to in his glowing analysis after the event:

> Saturday night the spirit of San Francisco found its way to Moscone Center. As I stood on the stage and looked out on the vast room where thousands of people were dancing, I wished all the other elected officials in SF could have seen what I was seeing. The sheer number of Gay people was amazing— 11,000—filling a dance floor that stretched for hundreds of feet. The energy, the enthusiasm, the fun people were having, couldn't have failed to impress any visitor. First Encounter at the Moscone Center was an expression of a huge and growing community with a spirit that shows we can never be pushed back in the closet. That strength and spirit shows itself in many ways, but First Encounter showed one of the things that's most important about our community—we know how to have fun . . . It's a long and serious struggle, but there's nothing to prevent us from having a great time along the way. Our love and our joy are an important part of what we have to offer each other and ourselves.[52]

Britt experienced the event as a manifestation of communal "fun," understanding that these necessary expressions of "mindless" release contain within them the power to motivate change. Dance theorist Andrew H. Ward explains that "those groups for whom dance does play this role are definitionally marginal and almost always suspect," and this quintessential megaparty, despite its critics' misgivings, gave the participants the momentary feeling that they had some degree of individual autonomy.[53]

NEW HEIGHTS 155

Hot Tracks

As the San Francisco sound took over more and more space on gay dance floors across the world, one local DJ decided to build on the real estate by starting a new remix service specializing in high energy. Steve Algozino was another Los Angeles–based DJ who made his living shuttling back and forth between LA and the Bay Area. Having grown up in Chester, West Virginia, he attended Marshall University for two years, majoring in drama. Like so many gay men of his generation, however, he was lured by the West Coast, and by 1976 he was in San Francisco, learning his craft as a DJ at Buzzby's.[54] In his five years DJing, he had moved variously between LA's Gregg's Blue Dot Lounge and Man's Country, and San Francisco's Probe and the Trocadero Transfer. His professional remixing experience was limited; with fellow West Coast commuter Mike Lewis and engineer Bob Logan he had reworked the Jacksons' "Can You Feel It" in February 1981 for Disconet, splicing over 300 cuts and extending the song by two minutes. But few people in the industry had Algozino's enthusiasm for the high-energy sound, and he had grown frustrated by the lack of DJ-specific material in that style.

With his financial partner Ross Lopez, he started Hot Tracks on Thanksgiving Day 1982, reporting to the press that he felt motivated to create the service because of "a need for high energy danceable music, produced and mixed by innovative djs dissatisfied with much of the currently available products."[55] For a subscription fee of $140 a year, a qualified DJ would receive one record a month featuring special remixes of four or five songs "drawn from dance classics, never released or poorly promoted records with potential, imports, and new releases."[56] Initially, Algozino recruited fellow Los Angeles DJs (and Moby Dick Records contributors) Craig Morey and Mike Lewis, and San Francisco veteran DJ Rob Kimbel to contribute the majority of mixes, expanding his stable of remixers over the course of the first year, especially with the ambitious simultaneous releases from subsidiary services, Hot Rocks (specializing in rock and new wave remixes), Love Tracks (dance versions of love songs), and Hot Classics (rereleases and new mixes of older hits). Hot Tracks was immediately successful, and while only three Hot Rocks and one Love Tracks were ever issued, Hot Classics ran to 43 issues, and Hot Tracks itself continued until May 2009, becoming the longest-running remix service of all time. By the end of its first year, Algozino expanded the releases to include four sides a month and began widening the musical scope of their efforts. Gini Spiersch, who started working in a promotions

156   MENERGY

and public relations position for the company in late 1983, eventually created an even broader and more flexible framework for the company that enabled its longevity.

But in its first years, Hot Tracks' distinctive "remixing and additional synthesizers by" credit guaranteed a San Francisco high-energy dance experience. Algozino's initial offering in November 1982 reads like a masterclass in the San Francisco sound, starting with Lisa's "Jump Shout," then Night Force's "Dance," followed by Yoko Ono's "Walking on Thin Ice" and Carol Jiani's "Mercy." Night Force's "Dance" had appeared on Disconet's September 1981 edition, exactly as it had appeared in its original 1980 version from producers Bart Van de Laar from the Netherlands and Belgian Francis Goya. Algozino's version of "Dance" remains instrumental for more than half its six-minute duration and adds a sine wave that appears throughout like a space-age laser bolt. Lisa's song, which would again reinforce San Francisco's reputation as a center for high-energy dance music, is the first Hot Tracks' gauntlet, however, a game-changing song that reintroduced John Hedges to the top of the dance charts and introduced two new figures to that scene, Barry Blum aka Barry Beam, synthesizer wizard, and punk artist and soul diva Lisa.

Barry Beam and John Hedges

Seeing old friend Marty Blecman's success with Cowley, John Hedges was looking for his own San Francisco sound project. "They did that, and the critics loved it. It was groundbreaking. The sound of San Francisco. I was very wowed," Hedges recalls about Blecman and Cowley's work.[57] "I knew how to do all that stuff too, and I said 'you know, if I could find a synthesizer player . . . ,'" which he eventually did with synthesizer wizard Barry Blum (figure 8.2). Blum was a rare San Francisco native, born into a family of entertainers. His father had been a comedic vaudeville dancer and his mother a touring burlesque and tap dancer. His first love was rock and roll, however, and he taught himself the guitar by learning the Beatles' songs, eventually becoming infatuated with synthesizers as well. "Control voltage, I got involved with that early on," Blum acknowledges.[58] "The first time I saw a synthesizer player, he was in a synthesizer group in the city . . . I'd go over to his house and he would have his synthesizer going, a monophonic synth going, absolutely freaking loud. Back then, it just blew my mind. He had one of those modular

Figure 8.2 John Hedges and Barry (Beam) Blum.

things, he had all the wires going in and out of things and that was a really cool set up."[59]

By the late 1970s, he was playing guitar and keyboards in his own band, the Stingers, with a shifting crew of musicians, including two backup singers, Lynn Ray and Catherine Beckwith. As he got more involved in the San Francisco new wave scene, he invented an alter ego, Barry Beam: "I thought of Barry Beam as a clown project. It was sort of a clown from space thing."[60] As Beam he frequently performed solo, accompanied only by a four-track tape recorder and a trademark gooseneck microphone attached to his guitar, modulated by an array of pedals at his feet. He occasionally supplemented his solo show with backup singers Katie Guthorn and Marthetta Blakley, who doubled on keyboards. Guthorn remembers, "he would walk around with the guitar and singing into the mic that was attached to his guitar. And Marthetta and I, our keyboards, we looked like Thomas Dolby or something. She dressed like Randy Newman, so she was a little blonde in this tiny spacesuit, and I had a kilt and cowboy boots on."[61]

Beam was also producing local punk and new wave bands either in local studios or in his home in the Mission, where he had assembled a professional quality if slightly cobbled-together studio. Projects like the Symptoms' EP *Pictures for Girls* were recorded and mixed there.[62] Beam's song "Wacs in Slacks" was included on an influential album early in 1981, *Rising Stars of San Francisco*, which was released by War Bride Records and involved mostly local new wave artists, including Readymades, Holly Stanton, and a song by gay cabaret artist Timmy Spence, "Brand New Dance," which Beam also produced. Both "Wacs in Slacks" and "Brand New Dance" have significant

158 MENERGY

synthesizer parts and share a similar B-52s, retro rock 'n' roll groove, not entirely unlike Cowley's "Teen Planet."

The night John Hedges came to hear Barry Beam, the rest of the audience at the Sleeping Lady in Fairfax had failed to show, so Hedges was treated to a nearly private performance. "It was a kind of audition," Blum remembers.[63]

> In the middle of the show, I jumped off the stage and landed on the snake and broke the feed, and the show was over! Everything was going through that one feed. But he liked what he saw, and he asked me if I could do synthesizer work . . . John got me involved into the gay scene, and then we started working on our first record . . . I was the straight guy at the parties...
> . . . John needed a synthesizer guy and he found me. I think that was John's motivation, and we coproduced for the next five, six years."[64]

"Show Me Yours" and "Radio Head"

Their first collaboration was, naturally, a high-energy dance song, "Show Me Yours." With Ray and Beckwith singing along to Blum's synthesizer, the song used real drums, but was clearly indebted to Patrick Cowley's electronic work coming out at the same time. "To me, he [Cowley] was the grandfather of the whole deal, we worked similarly," Blum recalls.[65] In addition to the breathy, harmonized vocals so popular on Cowley's album, "We both had Prophet-5s . . . We used the same rigs, and we both used a lot of similar ways," Blum explains. "For example, the 8track TX in those days ran at 15 and 7.5 [inches per second]. If something was too fast for us and we needed the sound more robotic, we would play the part at 7.5 and then speed it up, so it had to play an octave lower and then double the speed . . . . 'Show Me Yours' was done that way."[66] Alongside Hot Posse's (Patrick Cowley) "Ride It," the song was released on *Prime Cuts 1: The Double Dance Album*. Hedges remembers how optimistic they felt with the success of "Show Me Yours": "They bought it for cash and we were in heaven. 'Oh wow, we made this and they paid us cash!' "[67]

The song was also released on Disconet, part of the same volume that contained Mike Lewis's mix of Tantra's "Top Shot." In *Billboard* at the time, in an interview for a positive review of "Show Me Yours," Hedges observed, "Disco is definitely on the upswing. I've been getting mixing and producing offers right and left, from labels as well as from groups . . . The question no longer is, 'does disco live?' The answer is apparent."[68] There were hardly any aspects of dance music culture that were not touched by the San Francisco sound at the time. As Disconet's *D. J. Notes* observed in July 1981, "As far as we can see, the leading area for electronic music in the U.S. is San Francisco. They are years ahead, with a growing following of electronic devotees."[69]

But with Blum, Hedges had the chance to spread his wings a bit, and their next collaboration was a new wave single followed up with a full album for Barry Beam and the Backup Band. "Radio Head" and the subsequent *Barry Beam* fit naturally on Fairfield Connecticut's Aim Records and was a college radio success. But because of Hedges's expertise, "Radio Head," in an extended 12-inch version, also found a home on dance floors across the country. "I have to really just credit John Hedges for settling me down . . . John sort of settled me down and pointed me in the direction of commercial music, which he was really good at," Blum acknowledges. "I was really very thankful to get involved in the gay scene through John's eyes. Because whenever we would release a record, he would take me out and we'd celebrate the record either going high in the charts or whatever. And so we go to the clubs and that would be the only time I would do any drugs."[70]

Lisa

After the success of "Show Me Yours," the two producers wanted to make an anthem for the high-energy gay clubs at the peak of their popularity. They wrote and produced "Jump Shout" as a tribute to the underground nightlife and culture, but the song needed a strong female vocal, someone who could express both soul and sass, but most of all the revved-up hyperactivity of the backing track. One evening Blum was performing with his band at an underground venue and heard Lisa Fredenthal: "I knew her from the underground punk scene . . . she had some pipes. She had really good, good sound and voice."[71]

Lisa Roberta Fredenthal-Lee came from an artistic Detroit family, and after a brief stint at the University of Michigan moved to San Francisco in 1976 to attend the San Francisco Art Institute, where she earned a bachelor's degree in fine arts with a concentration in painting. By the early 1980s, she was living in an art space on Valencia called "Tool and Die" (named after her father's job as a machinist) and self-publishing *Water Drinkers*, a monthly, small-format (4"x4") zine, in which, for a small fee, local artists could pay for a page to advertise images of their work. Her connection to the punk

160   MENERGY

scene led her to start performing, at first purely on the side. "My roommate heard me singing one night while I was doing the dishes," Fredenthal-Lee remembers. "He went crazy for he had never heard me sing. I was a visual artist in his eyes and that was it."[72] His punk band, the Nubs, had had a successful single in 1980, "Job," but with the arrival of Lisa, the group expanded their range, and it wasn't long before they shifted their sound to a blend of punk and R&B, performing on the weekends in the basement of the collective as a Motown review. Fredenthal-Lee explains, "Every weekend our alternative art space put on concerts in the basement while the upper levels were devoted to art and exhibits dealing with the visual arts."[73] Blum remembers the venue: "It was like one of those typical basements in houses that have poles. It was never meant to be a performance space; it was probably an illegal fire trap. They put the bands in there and I played down there at one point and she sang with her band, the Nubs."[74]

For Fredenthal-Lee, their approach was direct: "He and John [Hedges] asked me if I would be interested in working on a song they had written called 'Jump Shout.'" She had recorded vocals on several songs for another local punk band, the Invertebrates, but that had been her only studio experience as a vocalist. Fredenthal-Lee fondly recalls, "and at that point this was very exciting because I was basically starting to explore the idea of singing in a professional way . . . we recorded it in a few hours and that was that, I thought."[75]

Like "Show Me Yours," "Jump Shout" has a rough-and-ready quality. Recorded at Starlight Sound in Richmond, and produced without MIDI, the entire song had to be played live, with each synthesizer line recorded individually, giving it a slightly off-kilter, human feel. Octave synthesizer bass, a simple synth countermelody, a rhythm guitar, Lisa's vocals, and a harmonic structure that does no more than move between I-vi-IV-V-I, are all subservient to the driving 132 BPM percussion, unapologetically disco with its four-on-the-floor kick drum, backbeat snare, and hissing offbeat hi-hat. The music declares its high-energy qualities, reinforced by Lisa's vocals, in lyrics written out on Blum's kitchen table: "Tick tock goes the clock," wails Lisa, "Everyone is at the Troc." She goes on to namecheck all the prominent high-energy gay clubs in the country, including Studio One in Los Angeles, New York's the Saint, and of course San Francisco's Badlands and Dreamland. Everyone, she seems to be saying, is dancing to the same sound, brought together by the synthesized pulse of high energy.

As noted previously, the song made its initial appearance on the first issue of *Hot Tracks*, where they gushed, "John [Hedges] has come up with another hit with this uptempo song aimed primarily at the dancing crowd . . . Overall it is a fun song which is still up for grabs label-wise, but it shouldn't be long before it is released commercially."[76] They shopped the song around, and it found a natural home at Moby Dick Records. Hedges remembers, "Bill Motley, one of the owners, fell in love with the song, and he said, 'I'd love to give it a shot and remix it.'"[77] Hedges gave Motley the twenty-four-track master, "And when you make a record, you don't know when to say 'Stop': you just keep going. You go in there and take the best tracks and make a record, which he did."[78] Moby Dick released the song as a 12-inch, with the original on one side and Motley's "Moby Mix" on the other. *Billboard* praised Motley's mix, and the song in general, noting that "Lisa's vocals contain a sense of urgency and excitement, with fast-paced synthesizer tracks maintaining an irresistible and gutsy amount of vitality."[79]

Motley's remix is actually shorter than the original and pares the elements down to the essentials: a concentration on the beat and the repetitious drone of the bass pulse. The Cowley-esque rhythmic gallop of Blum's version is removed, the texture reduced to a simple octave bass, four-on-the-floor drums with strong backbeat, rhythm guitar, and synth melody. The long break in the middle is taken out, and the intensity of the entire song is increased as the momentum never has a chance to let up. Lisa's almost manic delivery, possibly sped up slightly, has an aggressive, petulant quality aligning it with other punk and post-punk singers of the time, such as Poly Styrene of X-Ray Spex and the Slits' Ari Up, and gives "Jump Shout" an utterly contemporary sound while maintaining its roots in disco.

Lisa's debut entered the *Billboard* dance chart on March 6, 1982, and quickly broke the top 10, where it sat alongside Patrick Cowley's "Megatron Man" for several weeks before peaking at number 7. The song ultimately stayed on the dance charts for four months but found its greatest success in Europe and in Mexico, where it went double platinum, selling over 120,000 copies. Fredenthal-Lee put her heart into promoting the single. Still new to the music game, she had looked to Beam and Hedges to guide her during the recording process, but now she was mostly on her own. While Moby Dick helped her acquire a booking agent, the Los Angeles-based Robb Cooper, most people at the small label were preoccupied with the forthcoming release of the second Boys Town Gang album, *Disc Charge*. After a successful debut of the song at the Endup (where Lisa performed "Jump Shout" twice, since it was the only song she had), Lisa was sent to sing at some New York clubs. She was, according to her boyfriend at the time, "basically abandoned by the

162 MENERGY

record company employee who had been sent to look after her."[80] Learning from that experience, when she got back, she took a much more proactive role in her career.

Right away, Moby Dick knew they had a good thing with the combination of Beam, Hedges, and Lisa, and were desperate for a follow-up. Hedges began negotiating an album deal, initially between him and Beam, with Lisa nothing more than a session musician. "As far as they were concerned, I was a voice for hire," she recalls.[81] "I was told I could be replaced at any time. There were many Lisa's out there." But after lobbying the producers, and with the support of label co-owner Stan Morriss, who had seen her perform live and was impressed by her individual style, she got herself included on the album contract alongside Beam and Hedges. This ultimately gave her a level of input on the record uncommon for many vocalists in the producer-driven dance music genre.

The first song recorded for the album was a cover of the old Sam and Dave hit "I Thank You." The Detroit native Lisa chose this particular song because of her love of the original, which allowed her to show a more soulful side of her voice, but most importantly, she needed a second song for her live shows. She contacted friends Peter and Mary Buffett, who owned and ran Independent Sound Studio, and quickly worked the song up. For a touring dance artist, one of the trickiest things was figuring out how to transfer the recorded ambience of high-energy dance music to a live stage performance. "Initially, I was just trying to figure out what persona I was supposed to project," she explains.[82] "What did a high-energy dance music person look like and how did one present oneself? Do they do flips on stage while they sing or what?"[83] As a visual artist, she put a lot of energy into designing her costumes and makeup, and with boyfriend (and eventual husband) Robert Lee, commissioned professional headshots. For the rest of the album, also recorded at Independent Sound, Blum arranged for the loan of an expensive LinnDrum machine from local musician Paul Parker, who was himself on the cusp of a major dance music career.

Paul Parker

By the time Megatone Records started, Daly City native Paul Parker had already developed a local reputation as a singer to watch. After three years at San Francisco State University and a brief stint in Governor Reagan's volunteer Ecology Corps for conscientious objectors, Parker began a singing career in earnest.[84] While only having about a year of voice training, he had built a solid fan base performing in local coffee shops for several years. He had known Cowley since August 1979, when he had been performing in a five-piece cover band in local clubs and occasionally singing backup for him on his demos.[85] "I started my singing career in a top forty band . . . where we did hotels, restaurants and juice houses; basically anywhere that we could sing. We did a lot of work for almost nothing but we had a great time," Parker recalls.[86]

In the early 1980s, Marty Blecman became Parker's de facto manager, helping to secure an independently released single, "Welcome to Freedom," a collaboration with San Francisco–based songwriter and journalist Jon Randall, who performed all the instruments. In a soft-rock style, "Welcome to Freedom" and its B-side "Nowhere to Fall" suited Parker's voice; smooth and warm, with an edge of aggressive passion. "Nowhere to Fall" recounts the singer's ambivalence about the end of an affair, while the heavier "Welcome to Freedom" tells the conflicted story of a man who traveled west but is finding it difficult to reconcile his newfound "freedom" with the lack of meaningful relationships in his new city. The bridge of the song shifts to a telephone call, spoken: "Hello mama . . . Is dad still mad at me? I know it was a shock, but I just had to stretch my wings."

The release was positively reviewed in the gay press, with Jerry de Gracia calling it "a sensitive, haunting single which subtly touches upon the gay experience in the seductive manner of such artists as the Moody Blues, Rick Wakeman, and Anthony Phillips."[87] De Gracia expressed the hope that, "The low-key approach to the gay experience through this type of music may be the key to getting our music and our viewpoint across to a wider audience."[88] While D. Lawless felt "Welcome to Freedom" was "too soapy," they loved "Nowhere to Fall," which to them "sounds a bit like The Stones' 'As Tears Go By,' only prettier, and with words and music that've burrowed their way into my stream."[89] The record was nominated for a Cable Car award in 1982 in the "Outstanding Community Contribution by a Recording Artist" category against such heavy hitters as Meg Christian, Holly Near, and Conan.

As Cowley and Blecman were first conceiving of Megatone Records, one of the original projects they envisioned, alongside Cowley's solo work, was an album of material highlighting Parker. He had sung backup on several tracks on *Megatron Man*, but Cowley had been working on a set of songs specifically for the singer. This new, more professional relationship between them

164 MENERGY

all instigated a shift, with Blecman giving up his managing responsibilities. "We realized it to be a conflict of interests," Parker remembers, and asked his new romantic partner, Ken Crivello, to manage him (which he still does to this day).[90] Still, his relationship with Cowley was a driving force in the project, and Parker recalled years later that "since Patrick and I were such good friends I never worried about being paid or anything like that."[91] It's clear that the first two songs to be released, "Right on Target" and a cover of the 1965 Seeds song "Pushin' Too Hard," are further explorations of Cowley's interest in the murkier side of clone culture. Despite being described, rather oddly, on its June 5, 1982, debut on the *Billboard* dance charts, as "influenced perhaps by the laid back music coming out of Montreal lately," both songs amp up the intensity of Cowley's album tracks.[92] By making the unusual move of including a sticker of the muscular, shirtless, and mustached artist on the generic Megatone Records 12-inch single jacket, the label aligned the record as the aural analog of the clone aesthetic.

"Right on Target" begins with an unapologetic disco beat, but with a particularly strong backbeat and syncopated, reverbed electronic cowbell in the foreground. The drums were taken from a tape loop Cowley made of the drum track from his Hot Posse song "Ride It," slowed down by about 10 percent. After eight bars of rhythm, Cowley deploys a minor mode, buzzy sawtooth synth bassline to establish the mysterious and cruisy mood, amplifying this by layering a second sawtooth countermelody on top of the first, four bars later. The polyrhythm is completed with a reinforcing four-on-the-floor cowbell, firmly and insistently drawing the dancing body to the floor. The phasing counterpoint of the dueling bass melodies give way to Parker's clear tenor as he erotically muses, "Baby, what's your secret? How do you know what you know?" The fantasy clone lover Parker embodies is as assertive as the beat; macho, aggressive, and inducing an almost involuntary impulse to submit to his power. As Parker sings, "If you're thinking I'll be loving you, you're right on target," Cowley abandons the camp of "Menergy" for the pure sexual fantasy of masculine clone desire.

The song's directness clearly spoke to clubgoers, and the song leapt up the dance chart, hitting the number 1 spot at the peak of summer, on July 31, 1982, giving Cowley his third hit of the year. While even greater success was still to come, Cowley was already desperately ill, and it would take a monumental effort to keep working. It was a fight to the death that many, including Cowley, would lose over the next few years. But for the moment, it was as if everything were possible, and nothing in the world could stop the momentum of the San Francisco juggernaut.

9

Trouble in Paradise

Michael Maletta, the megaparty pioneer, was the first person to die of an AIDS-related illness in the San Francisco dance music scene. But by the time of his death on August 4, 1982, at the age of thirty-nine, many had already been diagnosed with what was being dubbed the "gay cancer." Maletta's diagnosis of Kaposi's sarcoma (KS) in December 1981 came after more than a year of mysterious illnesses, but only a few months after the first announcements of the strange new ailments observed in several dozen gay men in New York, Los Angeles, and San Francisco.[1] Within three years, HIV/AIDS would ravage the San Francisco gay community to such an extent that nothing would ever be the same. It saw the mass extermination of musicians, producers, labels, clubs, and indeed the very patrons that kept such institutions alive.

As John Hedges succinctly put it, "Our customers were dying. Let alone our talent. The producers, the musicians, the singers, they're all dying. It was a very dark time."[2] In hindsight, the beginning of the end was the ironically titled "Previews" megaparty, celebrating Megatone's release of Patrick Cowley's second solo album, Paul Parker's Cowley-produced solo album, and the spectacular rebirth of Sylvester's career on Megatone. As Cowley observed of the dancing bodies on the floor of the Galleria from his wheelchair, only weeks before his death, "Those stupid queens, don't they know?"[3] It is worth tracing the history of the disease as it emerged, first in the medical community, then in the population most affected at the time, to understand the multiplicity of responses and attitudes toward the disease in the dance music community and to appreciate how clone culture and everything associated with it served as a scapegoat for a pathetic national response to the epidemic. It was a moment when, in the words of Nancy E. Stoller, "disbelief and horror spread through the white gay community as the realization that AIDS was a real and transmissible illness . . . meant the failure of systems they had believed in: modern medicine, individual success, white and male privilege, American privilege."[4]

Menergy. Louis Niebur, Oxford University Press. © Oxford University Press 2022.
DOI: 10.1093/oso/9780197511077.003.0010

166   MENERGY

The Arrival of AIDS

The hard-won sexual freedom so many gay people treasured in the years after Stonewall didn't come without a price in the 1970s. Sexually transmitted infections (STIs) among the sexually active San Francisco gay male population had exploded in the second half of the decade. But most, like syphilis, gonorrhea, and amebiasis, were relatively easy to treat and were seen as an acceptable risk, of no harm to anyone but the sufferer, and a small price to pay for the huge amount of liberated fun to be had in the acquisition. But not all emerging infections were so easy to get rid of. Hepatitis B in particular surged among urban gay men in the middle of the decade and was almost exclusive to that population. One study from 1978 showed that between 50 and 60 percent of homosexually active men at one time had had the virus in their system.[5] The condition was so prevalent among gay men that research into a vaccine was hampered by the difficulty researchers had finding candidates who had not already been exposed to the virus. According to Dr. Robert Bolan, a gay doctor working in San Francisco at the time, "Those were the storm clouds that were gathering on the horizon a good eight, nine years before the first clinical HIV case popped into the scene."[6] In 1979, overwhelmed by the surge in STIs in the city, Bolan began working on a pamphlet, "Guidelines and Recommendations for Healthful Gay Sexual Activity," publishing it three years later.[7] He recalls,

> When the guidelines were finished and ready for distribution in 1981. . . already the virus HIV had been incubating in the community for at least four years, and . . . we were about five years too late with this project . . . We believed our process was very carefully crafted, and our end product was going to be the beginning of this fabulous education campaign. But it was too late. When we all realized that, when the lightbulbs went on one by one, we all felt very bad.[8]

A number of doctors in the Bay Area later recalled seeing patients in 1979 with swollen glands, mostly sexually active gay men. Biopsies revealed that they had hyperactive lymph nodes, suggesting an immune overload, but the cause wasn't understood.[9] Dr. Donald Abrams remembers that in early 1981, "I noticed that a lot of . . . patients had swollen glands. And I said, 'Hey, how long have you had these swollen glands?' And they would say, 'Two or three years.' So that's when I said [to myself], 'I wonder if those people with swollen glands that I saw in 1979 are now these people?' "[10] Bolan was having a similar experience. When he opened his general practice in the late 1970s, it was with the intention of having a largely gay clientele, and he quickly observed "a lot of people in 1980 and '81 that had very peculiar illnesses that I couldn't explain—fevers and night sweats and lymph node enlargements and very bizarre neurological presentations."[11] He realized later that while some of his patients were manifesting symptoms, "the vast majority of my patients who were infected were still incubating, if you will. They were infected but clinically well."[12] As AIDS historian Victoria A. Harden observed, "Those suffering from its symptoms and their caregivers perceived AIDS in the most direct and painful way, but as a group, they had no way of understanding that what was happening within their bodies represented a new disease entity."[13]

When both Los Angeles and New York reported a number of mysterious cases among gay men, doctors in San Francisco made the connection right away. At a conference on June 26 and 27, 1981, entitled "Medical Aspects of Sexual Orientation," the largely gay Bay Area Physicians for Human Rights reported on a number of cases of KS and *Pneumocystis carinii pneumonitis* (PCP) among gay men in those three cities, and confirmed it in print a month later in the organization's newsletter.[14] The Centers for Disease Control and Prevention (CDC) issued their first notice of "Kaposi's Sarcoma and *Pneumocystis* Pneumonia Among Homosexual Men" on July 3, 1981, and reported twenty-six cases of KS and twenty-one diagnoses of PCP over the prior thirty months in Los Angeles, San Francisco, and New York City.[15] All were gay men with a mean average age of thirty-nine, and of the cases of KS, twenty-five of the twenty-six identified as white and one as Black. The dark lesions that were the visible aspect of KS quickly became the most recognizable aspect of the new ailments.

Immune Overload Theory

In the race to understand the causes of these malignancies, doctors looked closely at the lifestyles of the men affected, particularly those aspects of gay life that differed from their straight counterparts. From the very first CDC report, the diseases were tentatively linked to "some sexual and drug practices," noting that most of the patients had histories of multiple sexually transmitted diseases, including amebiasis and hepatitis.[16] These were reported consistently in the gay press, but the messages were often conflicting and confusing,

168 MENERGY

and some attempted to assuage the public's fear, noting, for example, that "although the relative incidence of the disease [KS] in America is extremely high, the absolute numbers are not. There is still only a 0.01 per cent risk for a particular individual."[17] In Bolan's first article on the subject in the *Bay Area Reporter*, entitled "New Bugs . . . No Alarm," he is clearly trying to mitigate feelings of panic: "This is not an epidemic spreading out of control—the number of cases is a very small percentage of the total gay population; there will probably be a rather rapid increase in the total number of reported cases for the next few weeks or so because as the word spreads . . . more cases already in existence will come to diagnosis."[18] Nevertheless, Bolan wondered aloud whether something about gay life was behind the illnesses:

> What factor or factors make Gay men more susceptible to these terrible things? . . . It is largely, but not exclusively, our sexual activities that set us apart from heterosexual people. No clear associations have emerged as yet between specific sexual activities or number of partners and any of these conditions. The use of various "pleasure chemicals," most notably poppers and ethyl chloride, is being considered as possibilities.[19]

One of the original hypotheses was the "immune overload" theory; that gay men were taxing their immune systems too much, leaving themselves vulnerable to immune suppression. "The immune system is simply overwhelmed by the barrage of diseases," said Dr. Alvin E. Friedman-Kien, who theorized that "immunity disfunction might activate potential tumor cells present in all individuals."[20] Right from the beginning, reports mentioned that many patients had been treated for viral or parasitic infections and had used amyl nitrate or LSD while having sex.[21] Bolan felt that the theory supported his observations over the last several years, later acknowledging, "I suppose that I probably found myself more receptive to the notion of immune overload because of my history with STD (sexually transmitted disease) work, and knowing what the burden of STDs in the gay community really was. I mean, I knew that for years."[22] The same was true of the heterosexual Abrams. His thinking at the time was that,

> Most of these patients were sexually active gay men with numerous sexually transmitted diseases and were using a number of the drugs that were popular in the community at the time. So we said, "Listen, we don't know why your glands are swollen, but you're living in the fast lane. Maybe you should

slow down and not have so many partners, not get so many sexually trans-mitted diseases, give your immune system a break and don't use so many recreational drugs, and maybe your lymph nodes will go away." . . . These patients were having too many sexual partners. If they were taking in semen from each different person, then that was foreign proteins that their body was responding to. They had histories of gonorrhea, hepatitis, herpes, everything else, so that was a stimulation, and then they were using all these drugs.[23]

Another theory was that perhaps "the new rage for taking antibiotics before a fling at the baths" was confusing the body's immune system, ac-cording to Thomas Nyland, clinic administrator at the Lesbian and Gay Community Services Center in Los Angeles.[24] Confusing matters further, nearly a year later, reports emerged that gay men were also developing other kinds of cancers, in addition to KS. It was reported that, "Four gays in San Francisco and one in Chicago were found to have diffuse undifferentiated non-Hodgkin's lymphoma . . . It is not always fatal, but is so rare that statistics that would show its mortality rate have not yet been compiled."[25]

Over a year into the epidemic, when it was finally given the name acquired immune deficiency syndrome (AIDS, or as it was initially occasionally re-ported, AID), the press was still reporting that "despite the growing body of informed speculation about such potential risk factors as frequent sexual encounters with many partners, whatever it is that causes AID remains unproved and unknown."[26] More than this, the Gay Men's Health Crisis of New York was reporting that, "Unsettling though it is, no evidence exists to incriminate any activity, drug, place of residence or any other factor con-clusively, in the outbreak facing us."[27] Despite some studies reporting that perhaps as many as "80 to 85 percent of gay men in some major cities may already be immune-deficient," some gay publications were stating that "there is not incontrovertible evidence to suggest that AID is overtly contagious."[28] In August 1982, however, Jean L. Marx wrote in the journal *Science* that, "al-though other explanations have not been ruled out, most investigators cur-rently think that the disease is caused by an infectious agent, possibly a new virus or a new variant of an existing virus."[29] Several researchers theorized that sperm could be the carrier of the new virus, and after at least two re-search centers discovered antibodies against sperm in patients' bloodstream, posited that perhaps, "exposure to sperm from many sources may con-tribute to the immunodeficiency of homosexual men" because "sperm are

170   MENERGY

immunosuppressive if they enter the blood stream."[30] Friedman-Kien qualified this theory, stating, "I don't think it is just the sperm; it may be a multiplicity of factors."[31]

The "Disco Disease" and Conservative Attitudes

One controversial idea that received a lot of support from researchers in the beginning was that poppers caused the illnesses. In the first mention of HIV-related illnesses in the *Bay Area Reporter* on July 2, 1981, the reporter singled out poppers from the beginning: "According to sources at Mt. Zion Hospital, it is impossible to say what role, if any, the use of poppers plays in the development of Pneumocystis pneumonia (i.e., 'Gay men's pneumonia')."[32] Abrams recalled how, "In May or June of 1980 . . . we saw this guy who was a youngish gay man and I started talking to him about habits. I said, "Well, do you use poppers?" . . . They guy said, "Yeah." And I said, "Well, how often do you use them?" He said, "Well, every day."[33] This was enough to convince Dr. Abrams that "clearly this guy has poisoned all of his alveolar macrophages . . . and that's why he has *Pneumocystis* pneumonia," he later recalled, with a hindsight that acknowledges his own hubris.[34] "I was very, I know everything, I'm just finishing my first year of my fellowship and I'm pretty glib about it. And that was my first patient with AIDS. I didn't even realize it."[35] But the poppers theory was persistent, especially since so little was known about what was precisely in a bottle of poppers. Bolan was shocked to discover that,

> The stuff was out there, being sold in bookstores and over the counter in gay sex shops and stuff like that, totally unregulated . . . The companies were very, very careful not to explicitly state what the function and the purpose of poppers were . . . . That really pissed me off, because here are these companies making money on this shit, and not owning up to the fact that it was used for a purpose other than for which it was advertised. It was just so patently ludicrous and obvious that if there was an iota of possibility that it could be linked with AIDS—and there was more than an iota of possibility—I was pissed off that the FDA wasn't doing anything about it.[36]

Nitrates, the key ingredient of poppers, are blood-vessel dilating drugs, and Bolan and others suspected that if used often enough the vasodilation would force blood out to the extremities, such as the bottom of the foot (where KS often initially manifested itself), and the root cause was being deposited there, ultimately developing into KS.[37] In early November 1981, Marcus Conant, chief of the newly established Kaposi's Sarcoma Clinic in San Francisco, gave a slide presentation on KS to the Stonewall Democrats, and was joined by Hank Wilson who also posited a possible link to poppers. A reporter from the presentation came away confused: "Even the simplest things are not established, like whether it's catching or whether it comes from some activity or some contact," they reported.[38] Nevertheless, Wilson "displayed one reprint after another of articles that question the safety of using some of these chemicals [poppers] . . . Hank indicated that activists might at least cause the manufacturer to put some kind of warning statement on the label, so that people might think about it before developing a strong habit."[39]

In December, in an editorial in the *New England Journal of Medicine*, Dr. David T. Durack theorized that, "So called 'recreational drugs' are one possibility . . . The leading candidates are the nitrites, which are now commonly inhaled to intensify orgasm."[40] His theory was that maybe the poppers exacerbated a persistent viral infection in men who were already genetically predisposed to develop KS.[41] Support was lent to this theory by Arthur Evans, who, perhaps putting the cart before the horse, extrapolated that because "nitrites have previously been proven to deform and destroy red blood cells. . . . If they have a similar effect on white blood cells, then the link is proven."[42]

One reason the popper theory caused such controversy was that they were seen by many as a material example of gay liberation and therefore an easy target for conservatives and religious zealots. People realized right away that the rising "moral majority" of the era could use aspects of urban gay men's lives as proof of the divine retribution being rained down on them. As one anonymous editorial explained in early 1982:

> Because unlike the legionnaire's disease or toxic shock syndrome, no one
> blamed veterans without battle experience or menstruating young women
> for their turpitude. We know how the moralists will come down on gays
> for *their* medical breakthrough. The issue will become a pulpit issue more
> so than disease control or medical journal issue. . . . And if poppers *are* the
> easy out, why don't we call it the Disco Disease as fliply as we label it the gay
> disease?[43]

172   MENERGY

AIDS and the Backlash against the Clone

By March 1983, although still without having found it, researchers felt confident enough that a virus must be at the root of these symptoms that the CDC issued a set of guidelines directed to gay men that warned against sex with too many partners or with people diagnosed with AIDS.[44] By the time the virus was discovered in the summer of 1984, public opinion about AIDS had been firmly set as a gay condition. Despite the fact that as early as January 1982 the "gay syndrome" had been identified in heterosexual people as well, the medical community continued to connect it to gay men, with both curiosity and a morbid fascination with the lives of these men. There was often more than a hint of judgment in their evaluation of them, especially since, as Dr. Arthur Ammann remembers, "many of us referred to it as the 'gay syndrome' because many people felt that it wouldn't be spread by any other means. And I think 'any other means' included heterosexual spread, casual contact, blood transfusion, and accidental inoculation."[45] Ultimately, in the words of Surgeon General C. Everett Coop, "AIDS pitted the politics of the 'gay revolution' of the seventies against the politics of the Reagan revolution of the eighties."[46] A year into the epidemic journalist Wayne April was afraid that although "not everyone who snorts poppers and disco to the wee hours is going to die of spots, Kaposi's sarcoma and pneumocystis pneumonia are probably going to do more damage to the image of gay people than they will ever do to their health."[47] Thomas Nyland believed that a slow medical response betrayed a moral judgment from the medical community. "If AIDS is God's punishment for homosexuality, why aren't lesbians getting it?," he countered.[48]

Gay men themselves were not immune to this reaction, and AIDS prompted an era of reevaluation about what it meant to be a liberated gay person. Unfortunately, much of this tapped into deep-seated and unresolved internalized homophobia and self-loathing. Nyland counseled some gay men who theorized that it was God's way of punishing them: "I was hearing some gay people saying 'My mother was right,' or 'My minister was right.'"[49] Marcus Conant, a founder of the San Francisco AIDS Foundation, observed that:

> So most gay men, at least in the early 1980s, were coming to an understanding of their sexuality, believe that it was wrong. They had to overcome that . . . You finally say, "I'm just not going to deal with this feeling that I am

TROUBLE IN PARADISE   173

some kind of evil, wicked person anymore." ... So what a lot of people do is they just say, "Screw it, I'm going to move to San Francisco." Suddenly, this man has AIDS, and he's now dying, and society's saying "It's your fault." All of that garbage that he's carried from his late teens comes roaring up: "Oh, my god, am I really this evil, wicked person? What have I done? Was Mother right after all? Is society really right that I deserve this?"[50]

This kind of guilt and self-loathing was rampant in gay centers at the beginning of the epidemic and resulted in a sea change in attitudes toward partying, drugs, and sex. One can hear the anguish in Stanley Ross Specht's heart as, after his diagnosis of KS, he wrote in a letter to the editor of the *Bay Area Reporter*:

> Why did *I* get it? I exercised, took vitamins, ate right, just like most everybody else I knew. I was also going to the baths twice a week, hitting poppers for sex and dancing ... I've been terribly promiscuous, only caring or loving my partners till I came. I'm not really a brute, but many of you know how it is. I just used them. By just using them, I was only using myself. ... I have managed to manifest within myself the effects of my actions. I know that I need only seek and I shall find my health again. I say to all my brothers, whatever your spiritual persuasion, to be mindful of your thoughts, for they can and will manifest themselves physically, as I am the visible truth.[51]

Despite, as Richard Lebonte expressed in 1982, "No one knows whether it can be caused by staying at home and reading a lot or going to the bars every night," a new "healthy living" lifestyle took over the Castro, and a backlash emerged against the Castro clone.[52] A new kind of health advertisement began appearing in gay publications. "Introducing HIM: Vitamins, Minerals and Herbs for the Sexually Active Male" one ad announced.[53] Containing a monthly supply of thirty packets of eight tablets each, HIM ("Health and Immunity for Men") promised to "maximize the immune system to fight infection" while "maintaining sexual vitality and potency," primarily through echinacea, saw palmetto, sarsaparilla, and "freeze-dried glandular prostate tissue."[54] Another man desperate for a cure looked to "the East" for help, sharing his findings in a letter to the editor:

> In hopes that medical practitioners, researchers, and sufferers from Kaposi sarcoma (the gay cancer?) will see this letter and be able to benefit

174   MENERGY

from . . . the health benefits of Shitake Mushrooms . . . I am not a medical researcher, but I am a believer in the incredible healing value of plants and herbs. I have several friends and acquaintances who have cured themselves of life-threatening illnesses through holistic medical, herbal and naturopathic practices. I urge "victims" of Kaposi's sarcoma to pursue inquiry as to the beneficial aspects of eating a few delicious purchasable mushrooms each day.[55]

It wasn't just gay men in San Francisco grasping at straws. As reported by Scott Anderson, editor of *The Advocate*, "In gay communities across the country, homosexual men are making modifications. Many men are getting out of the bar and bath scene."[56] In New York, the disease was being called "Saint's Disease," since so many of the first men to die were members of that exclusive high-energy nightclub.[57] The club and party world was being held responsible, as if the participants could have known what was about to happen. Critiques of the party scene were now reinforced by the plague, as Wayne April articulated:

Has gay liberation really been realized in the gay neighborhoods of our largest cities? Are the bathhouses and sex clubs, the poppers and MDA, and the assemblyline "tricks" and "lovers" really what being gay is all about? . . . There's something missing from the lives of many gay men. They're attempting to fill the void, but they're filling it with too much of the same thing.[58]

On December 16, 1982, after receiving a diagnosis of KS, Richard Herbaugh committed suicide by hanging himself in Golden Gate Park. His friend Arthur Evans wrote a letter blaming his suicide not on the diagnosis, but "the appalling quality of life in the current 'Gay Mecca.'"[59] According to Evans,

In the beginning we aimed to create a new society. But all we've done is make a cracked reflection of the worst abuses of the old. How did this happen? First because we've been indoctrinated with straight homophobia—many of us hate ourselves so much that we actually use sex and fantasy to punish both ourselves and each other for being gay. Second, because the gay business establishment deliberately fosters a compulsive objectifying lifestyle . . . and this has made them rich. The angel of death is here because we invited him. But some day the spirit of Stonewall will again arise. We will throw off the carcinogenic businesses that parasite on us. And we will learn the nurturing love that transcends the Siamese twins of self hate and patriarchal fantasy.[60]

While very few questioned the importance of the Castro as a "much needed ghetto of shared identity and sexual freedom amid the general anonymity and greater repression of the larger American landscape," Eric Hellman wondered if the prioritizing of sexual freedom as the primary goal of gay liberation resulted in a personally limiting and spiritually destructive culture, one where, "The fever of sexual exploitation is further aided by the current vogue for Clone fashion: a mustachioed and macho man is ready to service you at every street corner or bar stool."[61]

Not everyone thought a wholesale rejection of Castro clone culture was the best response to the current crisis. The kind of liberation clone life represented in the minds of so many men was articulated by the Reverend Rick Weatherly in a thoughtful, nuanced essay where he concluded,

> There is pain here and defeat, but it is the pain and defeat which results from trying and reaching and changing. In this place, perhaps uniquely, gay people are becoming a people. We are being who we want to be, acting like we want to act, dressing as suits us, looking like we want to look. Some see our "clone" look and see depressing uniformity. I see it and feel it is a part of our coming to be.[62]

And yet, the reality of Castro life after 1982 was hard to reconcile with this optimistic outlook. For many gay men in San Francisco, the choice whether to dance or not became political for the first time, applying the same aesthetic of beauty to death, in what Paul Lorch called a "Gay way of dying with style, with verve, with elan" that had before been dedicated to the art of living out our collective gay fantasies.[63] Even if you were still healthy, the decision to attend a disco or a megaparty became imbued with a gravity and significance absent in earlier years. As David L. Heranney wrote about his internal struggle:

> So, why am I hesitant about a little pampering in the "Summer Heat" with fabulous Linda Clifford? [The latest Conceptual Entertainment party] After all, it is Memorial Day Weekend, right? . . . Then I know: The present reality

176 MENERGY

is stronger. There are too many dead and dying right NOW. I see the pain and anguish, the sudden disruption of lives. All come with AIDS . . . And I want to help, but feel at a loss. I give out good energy. It's not enough. People keep dying. And that fact is so much a part of my conscious and unconscious hours that I am not disposed to celebrate "summer heat . . ." $20–$25 for another dance celebration? I pass, this time, and choose to give my money to those involved in the fight to save all our lives.[64]

Patrick Cowley: "Do Ya Wanna Funk"

When Michael Maletta, the Market Street barber turned megaparty founder, got sick in 1981, he was the first person most people knew with the mysterious cancer, KS. "When I asked a friend where he was 'cause I wanted to go see him, he said, 'You don't want to go see him,'" remembered John Cailleau.[65] "I guess at the time the wasting and the KS spots were so uncommon as to be horrifying. Now people just say, 'Oh, he's got KS,' but then it was more than we could handle 'cause we were immortal, never to have any infirmities." A benefit was held for Maletta on April 25, 1982, at Trax (a new bar at 1437 Haight, where the Question Mark had been), which enabled him to die at his own home, looked after by a hospice nurse. Many in the music industry, unless they were keen followers of the gay press, were probably unaware of the conditions starting to affect men in the Castro. Patrick Cowley had first shown symptoms while on tour with Sylvester in South America over a year earlier. "I just thought it was the food, but when he came home he was still sick and got progressively worse, never truly getting well again and they were treating him for parasites and just any other disease you could think of," Sylvester recalled.[66] Cowley was ultimately diagnosed with PCP in November 1981, "just as the album [*Megatron Man*] was hovering in the top ten in Billboard," remembers Marty Blecman.[67]

By January 1982, Cowley had taken a turn for the worse and spent several weeks in intensive care. His family even came out from Buffalo when it seemed like he might not make it through this latest bout of illness. Blecman told Sylvester how serious Cowley's condition was and asked him to tell Cowley how much he was needed, how they had to complete all the projects they had discussed over the years. Sylvester remembers that he "told him that we just had to do a record together, that everyone was waiting on a joint

TROUBLE IN PARADISE   177

project from us, and that he just had to try harder. I told him I wasn't going to have it anymore and to get his ass up so we could go to work!"[68]

For the past year, Sylvester had been in an ugly legal dispute with Fantasy Records, and until the terms of his contract with them were resolved he couldn't record anywhere else.[69] But just as the singer's contract ended, Cowley rallied. He was discharged from the hospital and went to live with Paul Parker and his partner Ken Krivello; Parker had to carry the frail, ninety-pound Cowley up all seventy-two steps to their apartment, and there they nursed him back to relative health.[70] He couldn't get around without a wheelchair, and his persistent illnesses had turned his once bright and hyperactive personality dark and cynical. But with the help of his friends (Sylvester in particular, who would drive Cowley from Parker and Krivello's place to the Automatt recording studio on his moped), he was able to complete their next collaboration, "Do Ya Wanna Funk."

When the two met to discuss what to record together, they each had a song prepared. Sylvester's was little more than a demo, with just a piano and drum part worked out. "Patrick's was a proper track . . . and much better!," recalled Sylvester.[71] Sylvester took the lyrics from his unused song, inspired by a Jeanie Tracy song from her debut Fantasy album released a year earlier on which Sylvester had sung backup. Despite his misgivings about her solo career, they were still close friends. (Sylvester had in fact recommended her to his longtime manager Tim McKenna.) In "I'm Your Jeanie," Tracy and Sylvester fill the last three-and-a-half minutes of the song by vamping on the phrases "let me funk with your emotions" and "I wanna funk." Sylvester loved this word play, and expanded it into "If you wanna funk, let me show you how. Do ya wanna funk with me?"

As Lauren Carter remembers, Cowley "would be in the studio laying on the couch and directing the engineer and just be really out of it, yet determined to finish that record."[72] Produced for under $500, "Do Ya Wanna Funk" would turn out to be one of the biggest commercial hits to come out of Megatone Records, largely through its placement on the soundtrack to the Eddie Murphy vehicle *Trading Places* and on one of Jane Fonda's bestselling workout videos, becoming one of the few Megatone songs to cross over onto the mainstream pop charts. "Do Ya Wanna Funk" closely follows the established Cowley formula with a strong four-on-the-floor kick drum, disco-era offbeat hi-hat, and a catchy synthesizer melody supporting Sylvester's gospel vocals. Cowley had a habit of choosing left-field but familiar tunes

178 MENERGY

for these supporting countermelodies, whether it was "The Streets of Cairo" for "Menergy" or the theme to *Sea Hunt*, or, in this song, a variation on the nineteenth-century "Oriental riff." While this blatant pentatonic stereotyping perhaps made some kind of sense when used in the recent hits like the Vapors' "Turning Japanese" or Amanda Lear's "Queen of Chinatown," here Cowley seems to use the melody simply because of its familiarity and sing-a-long-ability.[73]

That "Do Ya Wanna Funk" ended up as Cowley's biggest commercial hit just as he realized he was dying has more than a little tragedy about it. Released on the 4th of July, the song entered *Billboard*'s dance chart on July 24, 1982, and early reviews noted that Cowley "provides typically zippy backing to Sylvester's abandoned singing. Early signs are that the combination is again reaching a wide audience."[74] Another review boasts of its "gutsy bravado missing from dance music lately" and hopes that "Sylvester and Cowley will continue their partnership since 'Do Ya Wanna Funk' proves they are a slick and powerful musical team who can make chateaubriand out of meat and potatoes."[75] The song peaked at number 4 on the *Billboard* dance charts just in time for the release of Cowley's second solo album, which Sylvester dubbed his "conceptual science fiction dance album."[76]

Mind Warp

With the success of "Do Ya Wanna Funk," Cowley was inspired to dedicate what little energy he had to a final push to complete his next record. When set beside each other, his two solo albums sound like alternate sides of the same coin. The technology portrayed so optimistically on *Megatron Man* has turned cynical and brooding, as if Cowley hears in it a betrayal of the robotic macho ideology in which he had put so much faith. Right from *Mind Warp*'s first track, "Tech-No-Logical World," an ominous feeling pervades the album. Opening at a much slower tempo (which, not accidentally, reflects the slower tempo of dance music in general in the second half of 1982), a strong backbeat compliments the four-on-the-floor kick drum, and an eighth-note octave bass pans across the stereo channels, creating the Cowley gallop. But in the front of the mix, obscuring the electronic clarity of the familiar dance groove, sits a more aggressive, atonal and unsyncopated, mechanical series of random pitches in a raw sawtooth waveform. Clearly representing "technology," the random blips resemble the sounds of countless computers as seen in film and television, the sonic equivalent of a logical but inhuman "thinking machine." Rather than an offbeat hi-hat creating a polyrhythmic groove, as in traditional disco, here forward motion is created by a complete lack of syncopation; the driving predictability of events occurring on the beat moves the song ahead. When Paul Parker's tenor voice enters, it is warm and comforting rather than the aggressive, sexual attitude of "Right on Target" or "Shot in the Night." "All our needs fulfilled, all our passions killed. Tell me what will become of us," Parker sings alone, without backup. "You'll be meeting Doctor Terminus," concludes each verse, "But the flags of doom unfurled, on Tech-no-logical World."

This B♭ minor track fades out and gives way to a confident arpeggiated E-minor chord, racing up and down, a faster four-on-the-floor kick drum, and a phasing bass pulse on that pitch. The tritone segue between the two songs is remarkable, particularly since Cowley intentionally overlaps the two for a good twenty seconds. This second, instrumental track, "Invasion," really begins with the entry of a modal riff on E that falls down to the dominant. The only harmonic shift in the song is a modal move down to the flat-seven every sixteen bars for four beats. Track three, "They Came at Night," returns to the slower tempo of "Tech-No-Logical World," also in a minor key, and at first resembles some of the drone mood tracks he had written for his Fox Studios porn projects. This is the first song in Cowley's solo career that isn't high-energy dance music. It ends the first side on a sinister, down note, with the Patrick Cowley Singers harmonizing the lyrics: "They came at night and patiently they waited there to steal the seed . . . uh-oh, beware of darkness."

"Mind Warp" opens side two in D minor with a pulsating high-energy polyrhythm, complete with Latin percussion by Sylvester stalwart David Frazier. But the verses, delivered by a heavily vocoded robotic voice (credited as "the San Francisco Vocoder Choir" in the liner notes), quickly transform the energy into one of hallucinatory, manic paranoia: "I woke up in the middle of the night, a voice behind my eyes. It spoke to me in an ancient tongue I could not recognize . . . Chemical contractions in a vortex spinning round. Critical facilities, planets falling down." There is an irony behind the pleasure derived from the propulsive, driving beat, urging dancers on and on, while the song's lyrics propose a more malevolent, dervish-like mastermind controlling the dance floor. After a searing synthesizer solo, the song seamlessly segues into "Primitive Man," a purely percussive track with no pitch center, not dissimilar to Barrabas's legendary 1972 groove rock floor-filler "Wild Safari." Two choirs of voices, one male and one female, chant "ey ya, ey ya, ey ya" to each

180   MENERGY

other. It provided Cowley with a chance to include many of his friends on the album, including the entire Buffett clan from Independent Sound, John Hedges, DJ Michael Bailey, and others in the San Francisco dance music community. Hedges remembers the motivation behind the track:

> It was kind of a promotional gimmick for one track of the album. So, we brought in everybody we knew who could help us or something. And if they sang on a record, they would probably promote it for us. And we had, I think, a hundred people. So when you put that many people together, Patrick was leading us and keeping us in key, the group all got in sync and it worked. I think they got one passage really good. Once you get one "hook" of a song they can take it and move it where they want it.[77]

The final two tracks close out the album on a truly dystopian note. "Mutant Man" chugs along at a stultifying 55 BPM. Surreal and nightmarish, it tells an obscure story of a man in a postapocalyptic hellscape, the vocals again delivered by a heavily vocoded, dreamlike voice. Cowley, the Mutant Man himself, offers a small measure of relief in the final line, "Rhythm touching rhythm is the underlying force. When he hears the harmony, inside mutant man, he will understand." Finally, "Goin' Home" returns to a slow jam groove of 114 BPM, and in an ironic major mode attempts to reconcile his impending death with the transcendent life disco had shown him, both the pleasure and pain disco had brought to him: "Going home, leave your troubles far behind. Going home, far beyond all space and time." He is insistent on this point, directly referencing his first solo 12-inch with the lines, "Come on, I wanna take you home." It's purely down to Cowley's musical skill that the gesture doesn't appear overly maudlin or trite. Toward the end of the song, dissonant electronic effects invade the bright optimism of the words "goin' home," implying that the journey will not be painless or easy, and that the musical messengers were not entirely truthful about the peacefulness of death.

For the friends working with him on the album, "the 'death record' as we called it," Jo-Carol Block remembers, the experience was extremely upsetting.[78] Hedges knew Cowley was desperately ill: "He was going down, he was so frail . . . He was just a little guy anyway, just a little skinny kid."[79] Cowley again directed the artists from the Automatt couch, although the drugs controlling his pain made it difficult for him to express exactly what he wanted engineer Maureen Droney to do, and the musicians found it distressing to articulate Cowley's paranoia and disillusionment during the sessions. "We'd tell

Patrick that we just were not singing that stuff, but he'd put his foot down and tell us that it was just what he wanted to say," Block recalls.[80] "With Patrick," Sylvester explains, "knowing death was near, I feel it was his way of dealing with death. I believe it was his way of putting into words and music the termination of this part of his existence."[81]

Previews

In late 1982, the megaparty organizers Conceptual Entertainment split, with David Bandy retaining the name and partner Gary Roverana starting a new company, GZR Productions. Relations between the two had soured after an attempt to branch out into other areas earlier that year, most significantly into public relations and promotion for the New Body Center, a new dance studio/gym on Sutter Street. They had also taken on the responsibility of producing the closing ceremonies of the August 1982 Gay Games, as well as producing a series of live shows in the Russian River.[82] By April 1982, they had dropped out of the Gay Games ceremony (with Bandy ultimately producing both the opening and closing ceremonies alone), and by the end of April they had dissolved their partnership.[83] Roverana's first solo event as GZR Productions was the Previews party at the Galleria on October 9, 1982. The megaparty was advertised as a "Concert-dance celebration starring Megatone recording artists The Patrick Cowley Singers, Paul Parker and Sylvester," and was intended as a showcase for the high-energy music coming out of the local label (see figure 9.1). Randall Schiller, who had sided with Roverana in the Conceptual Entertainment "breakup," continued to provide sound for his events, assisting DJ Michael Garrett at the event.

In classic megaparty style, elaborate invitations were sent to Roverana's extensive but exclusive mailing list and included a flexi record narrated by Garrett promoting the party. His voice is treated with thick reverb as he entices invitees with excerpts from the artists' upcoming albums. Cowley's "Goin' Home," Parker's "Shot in the Night," and Sylvester's "Don't Stop" each play for forty seconds until Garrett concludes with the promise that, "These and other cuts will be premiered live in concert at Previews!" Parker appeared on the front cover of the *Bay Area Reporter* advertising the event two days before, and most clubs and boutiques around the Castro and South of Market sold tickets. While the party wasn't any different in character than any other Galleria megaparty, many of those who attended realized its significance in

Figure 9.1 Previews flyer. Courtesy of the San Francisco GLBT Historical Society. Reproduced with permission.

later years. "Although it wasn't necessarily a success in numbers of dollars, it was very special to me, perhaps because it was Patrick Cowley's last party," Roverana later told a reporter.[84] John Carollo, who was at the party, also recalls seeing Cowley there, "in the DJ booth; he was in a wheelchair. That was the last time I saw him."[85]

For Cowley, the event was bittersweet. He was at the peak of his career, his records were selling worldwide, and yet he understood that things in the Castro were about to change forever, even if he wasn't going to be around to see it. Sylvester hated this transformation in him: "What really destroyed me was how (at the end) he became so bitter. All of the plans we had made for future projects were getting so far out of reach for him."[86] And Michael Finden, the keyboardist he had worked with for so many years, was dismayed when "I told him how happy I was that his music was doing so well—because at that point everything he did just rocketed up the charts, and all he could say was 'What's the use of it?' I could tell he was in tears. It was very tough."[87]

Cowley's final weeks in the hospital were terrible, as they were for many people this early in the epidemic, when no one knew how the illnesses were transmitted. The hospital staff were afraid to touch him, afraid to feed him or bathe him. Linda Imperial was disgusted by this treatment, which she was to experience many times with countless friends over the next few years, "when you're in the hospital, how one is treated . . . at the most crucial time of their departure, how one was treated so inhumanely."[88] Friend Chris Njirich remembers those last few weeks: "Bob Guidice and I went in there and Bob gave him a bath. Bob was a paramedic and he said, 'You can't catch AIDS from touching these people.' So he shaved him and got him cleaned up, and got them to change his sheets so he didn't have to lay in his own filth and, it was a hard time."[89] For Ken Crivello, by late November, the end was a relief for Cowley: "When I finally went in to see Patrick, there was water welling up in his eyes, but he couldn't talk at that point. I told him that it was time to let go, that he'd been suffering too long (which he had). By the time I got home from his house, they called and said he was gone."[90]

Patrick Cowley died on November 12, 1982, a little over a month after the Previews party. Linda Imperial remembers Cowley's death as just the first of a seemingly endless stream of losses. "You just assume that they'll last for your life and all of a sudden everyone was gone, and it was really, really, really hard for me to deal with."[91] At his musical memorial on December 9th at the Metropolitan Community Church, a still-shell-shocked group of friends and family celebrated his life with tributes, memories, and promises to carry on the legacy he had created. Over the next year, before many of them too succumbed to the epidemic, they did just that.

10

Dancing with AIDS

Patrick Cowley's AIDS-related death in November 1982 heralded a new, transitional chapter in the story of San Francisco dance music. But it took a while for the dance community to realize the significance of that moment, partly because the parties continued unabated, and because Cowley left so many unfinished projects that would see the light of day over the course of the year. In fact, 1982 still contained much to celebrate in San Francisco's dance music world. Sylvester, relocated to his friend's label, Megatone, returned to the dance music so loved by his fans, and released a string of high-energy hits. Likewise, Paul Parker's album exceeded all expectations, confirming Megatone's place as a leader in dance music. Moby Dick Records also peaked in 1982, with Loverde scoring big, and established acts Lisa and Boys Town Gang topping the charts throughout the year. But the virus was quietly taking its toll, and by the end of the year competition in the form of British imitators began to overwhelm homegrown high-energy dance music, crowding the market, and the world's gay dance floors, with well-made songs in the style that until recently had been the exclusive province of San Francisco.

This chapter tells the story of how, despite an intensifying critique of clone culture and a dwindling of their ranks due to AIDS, many gay men in the Bay (and beyond) continued to look to dance music as a representation of their liberation. Within three years of its emergence in 1981, AIDS had the triple effect of wiping out the musicians, producers, and dancers from San Francisco (relocating the center of high-energy music production to the UK), reversing much of the progress that had been made in the realm of gay liberation through a widespread conservative shift in American politics, and triggering a shift in gay dance music from one of individual liberation experienced communally to a search for the negation of the individual for the security of the community. The San Francisco artists who made this music struggled to adjust to this new reality, uncertain whether to follow the earlier hedonistic model or the new paradigm of brotherhood. That both

Menergy. Louis Niebur, Oxford University Press. © Oxford University Press 2022.
DOI: 10.1093/oso/9780197511077.003.0011

DANCING WITH AIDS   185

approaches continued to yield successes throughout 1982 and 1983 shows that dancers were uncertain too.

Sylvester's Final Two Fantasy Albums

Sylvester's move to Megatone from Fantasy was a long time coming. His relationship had soured with both Fantasy and Honey Records, the subdivision owned by Nancy Pitts and Harvey Fuqua. Honey had continued to discourage Sylvester's openness about his sexuality, both in his personal life and musically. After disco fell out of fashion in 1979, they pushed him toward songs in a lower vocal register and emphasized a slower, jazzier sound with more butch acoustic instruments. While 1980s *Sell My Soul* was still essentially a disco record, the electronic sounds that had gained a foothold in gay dance music were practically absent. (Despite this, the single "I Need You/ Sell My Soul" peaked at number 6 for three weeks on the *Billboard* dance charts: Sylvester, even old-fashioned disco Sylvester, still sold records.) The 1981 release *Too Hot to Sleep* continued the move away from contemporary dance culture, with the majority of tracks in a slow R&B style with an orchestration that included saxophone, vibraphone, Fender-Rhodes keyboard, and traditional jazz-style drumming. Some of it is convincing, especially the "Quiet Storm" duet "Here Is My Love" with Jeanie Tracy, but this new Sylvester generally sounds unsure of himself.

While Sylvester welcomed the diversity of musical styles Fantasy allowed him (he always hated being pigeonholed as a "disco singer"), that variety came at the price of his own honesty. He also had some difficulty with the crossover from disco to R&B, a style that, to him, had little to do with his rock and gospel influences. In late 1979, Fantasy had chosen to release the slow ballad "You Are My Friend," taken directly from the live Opera House concert, as a single instead of the dance track "In My Fantasy," which was his preference. This was the label's first play in their attempt to move his image away from disco.[1] Initially, he seemed excited to be breaking with dance music for *Sell My Soul*, at least in public, raving to a reporter at the time, "I'm going to include more Rock & Roll and more New Wave kind of material. Ohhhhhh . . . like Joe Cocker did, maybe."[2] While some reviewers missed the Sylvester of old, with Guy Trebay longing for the singer that "sang like a street girl—sassy, hot, skirt hiked-up, paying it no mind," and feeling his natural baritone "wobbly and unbelievable," most mainstream critics loved

186 MENERGY

the new "legitimate" sound, giving *Too Hot to Sleep* the strongest unqualified reviews of his career.[3] At the time, the artist expressed his pleasure over all the attention: "I know it's good—and I can't deny that the vocals are excellent, the tracks are good, the production is good and even the cover is excellent."[4] But within a year he admitted to a reporter, "I think the music scene is very confused these days . . . It's hard to move onto new ground if you're not prepared."[5] He later confessed that he had no control over the recording sessions for *Sell My Soul* and *Too Hot to Sleep*, and considered them "incomplete."[6] He also lamented that on his last Fantasy album, he wasn't allowed to include any dance songs: "However, I will include more dance music in later albums . . . There were songs that I wanted to do that were never included."[7]

Ultimately, the conflict was not about musical style, or vocal range, or electronics, or dancing, but rather that Sylvester presented an unacceptable image for the Fantasy brand. Sylvester resented the way they shaped his image to conform to a more "acceptable" masculine image; he knew that they had "*always* wanted to make me straight: a Teddy Phillygrass or a Luther Vandross."[8] When Phil Jones, vice president of promotion and marketing for Fantasy, saw the photos Sylvester had suggested for the cover of *Sell My Soul*, featuring the artist surrounded by bursting champagne bottles, foam oozing off his face, he nearly died. "We're not going to put that out," he decreed, "it's suicide."[9] It was all down to Fantasy's belief that black radio stations wouldn't play records by an openly gay artist. They would get albums sent back, as Fantasy publicist Terry Hinte remembered: "They weren't playing the guy's records, because he's too outrageous, too outrageously gay. At the time it really felt like if we did what he wanted to do, he'd just be dismissed."[10] But while Sylvester was occasionally willing to dress up in boy drag in the interest of mainstream accessibility, he was confident his openness didn't need to be a problem. He told a reporter in 1980 that being gay had been "a plus for me. As long as you don't come out under false pretenses . . . that destroys you. But if you come out being whatever you are, for real, then you don't fool people."[11] Things came to a head during the production of *Too Hot to Sleep*, as Sylvester engaged in what biographer Joshua Gamson called a "minor act of gender terrorism."[12] Sylvester loved telling the story of the day he walked into Fantasy for a recording session:

> I went into the studio, into the lobby of the record company, wearing a purple negligee from the all-male production of *Mame* and a blonde wig. The president of the company came down and said, "I'm spending all this

DANCING WITH AIDS   187

money to change your image! What are you doing?" I said, "*You're* changing my image . . . *I'm* not." I walked into the studio with rhinestone earrings flying and just being a queen all the time, in open defiance of it all, bringing porno magazines to the studio with boys carrying on and stuff like that. I completely outraged them until they put me on suspension.[13]

All I Need

By the time he recorded "Do Ya Wanna Funk" with Patrick Cowley, his suspension had been lifted, his contract had expired, and he was free to do as he pleased. The timing was perfect, as Marty Blecman had recently contacted old friend and business partner John Hedges to co-produce some new material by James Wirrick for Megatone Records. The songs they wrote had originally been intended for Gwen Jonae, a performer known primarily as part of the Paul Sabu–produced studio act Sister Power. However, when she insisted on a $5,000 gown for the album cover, something the tiny record label couldn't possibly afford, they were back to square one. One night at the I-Beam, Hedges and Blecman bumped into Sylvester, and they explained the situation to him. His recent positive experience with Megatone must have been on his mind when they suggested he take a look at the songs. He was a natural fit for the label, and if further collaborations with Cowley weren't possible, working on his label was the next best thing. He was even convinced to invest some money into the fledgling label. His first Megatone album, *All I Need*, would contain "Do Ya Wanna Funk," as well as Wirrick's new songs.

The new, "real," Sylvester announced himself with *All I Need*'s cover, with androgynous art deco–style artwork by Mark America, featuring the artist as beautiful Egyptian royalty, full face of makeup, smoking a long brown cigarette. The record begins with the transitional downtempo and funky "All I Need," a Wirrick track similar in style to his last Fantasy albums. The song is sung in a tenor range, no falsetto, with Jeanie Tracy and a returning Martha Wash singing backup (and credited as the Fabulashes, possibly to avoid conflict for Tracy at Honey and Wash at Columbia Records). Track two, however, is the floor-filler "Be With You," an almost seven-minute high-energy dance track sung in Sylvester's glorious, unapologetic falsetto (where he remains for the rest of the album), written and largely performed by Wirrick in the Cowley style, complete with bass gallop, psychedelic virtuosic synthesizer solos, and thick synth string pads. After Cowley and Sylvester's hit

"Do Ya Wanna Funk," the first side closes with the dance rock, radio-friendly "Hard Up."

Side two returns to high energy with the seven-minute Cowley-esque "Don't Stop." A more straightforward, sparer track than the superficially similar "Be With You," this was chosen as the first single from the album because of its clear club potential. "Tell Me" returns to the slower R&B funk of the first track, and the album closes with a final up-tempo seven-minute Cowley-inspired dance track, "Won't You Let Me Love You," this time with a burning guitar solo by Wirrick, bringing the track, and the album, to a confident and very contemporary conclusion.

The reaction to *All I Need* was extremely positive. Much of this was down to James Wirrick's inspired songwriting. His songs, like his best tunes on *Step II*, gave listeners a newly liberated Sylvester with the electronic dance rhythms and what seemed like an embrace of his gay audience. "Now that I have control over what I'm doing, I see it even more plainly," Sylvester told British publication *Blues and Soul*, in 1984. "And that freedom is now a necessity in my life. At Fantasy, I simply went along with the programme at first and as I gradually became wiser and got to know more, they started giving me less and less cooperation."[14] Several critics felt *All I Need* and "Do Ya Wanna Funk," were a return to form for the artist not heard since "You Make Me Feel (Mighty Real)," with San Francisco gay rock critic Jerry de Gracia observing that Cowley and Sylvester have "given new impetus to locally produced dance music."[15] De Gracia asserted that "this performance will undoubtedly bring back old fans who were not quite ready for his artistic turnabout on *Too Hot to Sleep* . . . It should also garner him new fans who may have missed the birth of Sylvester's unique disco styling in 1977."[16] The *Sentinel* also loved the new "old" Sylvester, calling the album "pure pop geared directly for the I-Beam crowd that wants to boogie down for seven cuts."[17] *Billboard* too welcomed the return of form for the artist: "Here's his most consistent, interesting album since late '70s high period," Brian Chin observed. "There are fast dance songs . . . and slow dance songs . . . and a couple of real killers . . . which peak in glorious gospel harmony."[18]

In December, Sylvester premiered his new album at a megaparty in the old Dreamland building, with Steve Fabus DJing, and the critical response was equally glowing. The *Bay Area Reporter*'s South of Market critic gushed that "Masterful is the only word to describe the debut of Sylvester's new material. Syl doesn't just present music, he *is* music at its dynamic best."[19]

DANCING WITH AIDS   189

Sylvester clearly struck a chord with dance listeners, and the album peaked at number 3 on the *Billboard* dance charts, staying in that position for almost two months.

Sylvester Confronts Clone Culture

While a follow-up single release, the rock "Hard Up," didn't score as a dance hit, the music video was one of the first by a Black artist to air on MTV.[20] With the momentum of a hit record pushing them forward, Megatone sent Sylvester touring, across the United States and through Europe twice. Sylvester's "return" to the fold of San Francisco gay life forced him to confront some ugly aspects of the culture he had been able to ignore. During his mainstream heyday, the majority of his audiences had been straight, mostly women and young people, but now that he was with a gay label located in the heart of the Castro, he began to express a more critical attitude of the conformity, racism, and political disarray he found there.[21] A product of the sixties, Sylvester never could understand the conformity of clone life, but while he was on tour for *All I Need*, his boyfriend dumped him. "I had to go because I wasn't butch enough," he told Adam Block in 1983, "I really thought there was something wrong with me."[22] In a moment of despair, Sylvester cut his hair, replaced his glitter for jeans and leather. "And I felt like a fool, an absolute fool. I thought, 'Fuck this. I'm not going to bother with this. I must spend $60,000 a year on clothes, and I'm *not* going to reduce myself to 501s.' I felt like *shit*. I was through with San Francisco, hated show business and wanted to quit everything."[23] But after the rapturous reception he received at San Francisco's 1983 Gay Day Parade, he realized that in the wake of AIDS the messy politics of Castro life was actually being questioned. "I get this conformist shit from queens all the time. They always want to read me. They always want me to do it their way. I am not going to conform to gay lifestyle as they see it and that's for sure—that's the very last thing I want to do."[24]

He also started to seriously critique San Francisco's gay racism problem, particularly as he was seen as something of a spokesperson for the city's gay Black population. When a reader of the *Bay Area Reporter* complained in 1982, "I swear sometimes that the only thing San Francisco white gay males know about minority relations is to shake their behinds to Sylvester," he was articulating a reality for many people of color in the city.[25] Sylvester connected this back to the petty identity politics of the Castro clone:

190   MENERGY

It seems ridiculous that nine times out of ten you can be accepted on the job even when people know you are gay when you can't be accepted in a gay bar because you have a Lacoste shirt on. Let me tell you, my shows are all E.O.Q.—Equal Opportunity Queen—shows, because they are for everyone. I've stopped shows upon hearing that people were being hassled at the door—I will not perform in a place that discriminates or segregates against anyone.[26]

The endemic racism of mainstream gay culture wasn't limited to clones, of course. Some activists who dismissed clones as racist were ironically the same people who had abandoned Black artists in lieu of the primarily white punk and rock scene. After white critic Jerry de Gracia posed the question in his weekly column, "If white musicians can capture the sound of soul and hit the soul charts, why can't Black musicians capture the sound of today's rock?," Black freelance DJ Robert T. Ford took him to task for his ignorance of contemporary artists, as well as the assumptions so common among white music critics about the importance of rock: "By asking why Black musicians *can't* do rock, Mr. De Gracia sets up an implied value judgment of rock as *the* form of modern music, and the inability to do rock as the inability to create important music."[27] For his part, Sylvester showed with his latest work that dance rock was not the exclusive domain of white artists. As he had done since the earliest days of Sylvester and the Hot Band, his new music fused a rock aesthetic with a Black gospel sensibility and a camp sense of excess that proved irresistible to gay men across the country.

Call Me

Days after recording his first Megatone album, Sylvester was back in the studio adding vocals to a new version of Cowley's 1981 hit "Menergy" to be included on a Cowley Greatest Hits record. For Sylvester's second Megatone album, *Call Me* (1983), Marty Blecman mostly kept the same production team together, with Wirrick writing four of the eight songs as well as performing nearly all the instruments. The record was previewed by the release of the first single, a 12-inch dance cover of the 1970 Freda Payne hit "Band of Gold." With high-energy synthesizers supplemented by a gospel-style piano, the self-produced track continued the drive of the previous album and was another chart success. Wirrick built on the dance rock style of "Hard Up" for the album's first two tracks, "Trouble in Paradise" (which Sylvester called "my AIDS message to San Francisco") and "Call Me."[28] "Good Feelin'" brought back Dennis Wadlington, Blecman's old friend, fellow Ohioan, and bass player from Fever, who was now a songwriter permanently relocated to the Bay Area.

The biggest stylistic change on the album was the much greater influence of the Love Center Church, founded by Walter Hawkins in Oakland in the early 1970s as a more open-minded Christian congregation that was accepting of LGBTQ believers, similar to the Glide Memorial Church. Side one ends with a straight-up gospel song, "He'll Understand," and side two opens with the downtempo *Dreamgirls* ballad "One Night Only," both featuring Love Center pianist Daryl Coley. Sylvester expanded the Fabulashes throughout to include fellow choir members Lynette Hawkins, Dennis Sanders, and Coley alongside Tracy and Wash, giving the background vocals a thick, gospel quality. The choral singing continues on the dance track "Too Late," updated with a funky vocoded voice echoing Sylvester's wailing and hip-hop–inspired record scratching. "Power of Love" is another high-energy dance rock track, and the record closes with the single, "Band of Gold."

Call Me represented an important shift away from the San Francisco sound for Sylvester. For the first time, an album sold under the idea that it was representing the San Francisco dance scene now carried a majority of sounds from other places; hip-hop, rock, funk, and Broadway. That's not to say it isn't a good record; on the contrary, it manages to successfully combine many of the most important trends in current dance music. It's just that those trends originated in other places, primarily New York City. Sylvester, and Megatone, would have to work harder than ever to find a distinctive place and sound on this increasingly crowded dance floor.

Too Much to Dream

Paul Parker's second Megatone single, "Shot in the Night," was another triumph for him and the label, strategically timed to preview his forthcoming album. At his death in November 1982, Patrick Cowley had finished the record's production, but Megatone co-owner Marty Blecman wanted to wait until the initial wave of Sylvester's success had started to wind down so the small company could give Parker's album the attention it deserved as only the fourth full-length release from the label. By the time *Too Much to Dream*

192 MENERGY

debuted in the middle of May 1983, "Shot in the Night" had risen to number 16 on *Billboard*'s dance chart. Parker was sent out on a promotional blitz, and interviews appeared in most of the major gay publications. The reviews and interviews, predictably, expended a lot of energy discussing his looks, but quite a few also complimented his ability as a singer. For Jerry de Gracia, two important questions were answered: "Whether San Francisco's handsomest Gay singer is hot enough (he is) [and] whether his first album sustains the dance energy of last year's single 'Right on Target' (it does)."[29] Donald Mclean called the album's seven tracks an "abundance of riches," and praised Parker's "strong, clear, legit voice and faultless diction."[30] The singer is helped by Cowley's songs, which showcase Parker's dramatic range, but, song for song, *Too Much to Dream* is first and foremost a Cowley production.

"Love's on the Line" opens the album with the trademark Cowley synth gallop and uses synth patches similar to his 1981 "Get a Little." Here, however, it's given an eighties rock update by local musician Mark Baum's saxophone solos and Parker's aggressive vocal style. Still, Cowley's psychedelic synthesizer break affirms the song's connection to his earlier music. As Brian Chin observed in his review of the album, Cowley "draws a direct line between techno-pop and psychedelia, and does so while remaining true to requisite disco vamping and breaking."[31] The same is true of "Baby You Can Have My Lovin' Anytime," "Shot in the Night" (the only song solely written by Parker), and a cover of the 1966 psychedelic Electric Prunes song "I Had Too Much to Dream Last Night," which in Cowley's hands are given mysterious electronic sound effects, breaks that take dancers to strange, dark places, and new enigmatic lyrics, connecting them more to *Mind Warp* than Parker's earlier hit "Right on Target." "Nighthawk" is almost a return for Cowley to the seedy cruising songs of his early years, echoing the ideas of "Thief of Love" or "I Wanna Take You Home," but whereas those songs seemed excited and visionary, here Cowley fills the lyrics with the same kind of apocalyptic imagery and compulsion as in *Mind Warp*, such as "Summer nights and a red sky over the city," and "I've got to feed this hunger, it can't be denied." Parker's thrusting vocals give this sexual hunting an air of desperation and, as if to emphasize the futility and hollowness of the search, Cowley borrows his own buzzy bassline from *Mind Warp*'s closer, "Goin' Home," itself an ironic coda to the album's attempt to reconcile his impending death with all the future plans he would now never realize.

"Travelin' Man" successfully demonstrates that the Cowley style could be adapted to other genres, in this case blues and country. The electronics seem perfectly at home with Maurice Tani's bass playing and James Wirrick's roadhouse guitar solos. Parker does his best vocal work here as well, showing real range and emotional depth. Some critics misunderstood the overall intent of the album, however. One appreciated how this song allowed Parker to explore "a richer vocal sound which stands out in contrast to the dance numbers which seem to put a strain on his voice,"[32] and the critic for *Gaze Memphis* completely missed the point with his rockist attitude when he observed that "it's not the kind of music that is any good off the dance floor."[33] That pundit did admit however that "despite the shortcomings of his music, I can't deny being overwhelmingly swayed by his good looks. He can sing to me anytime he wants."[34]

Final Cowley Projects at Megatone

When Cowley died, Marty Blecman hired old friend Audrey Joseph to help run Megatone. Born and raised in New York City, Joseph had begun her musical career in nightclubs like Brooklyn's Dynamite and Manhattan's famed Electric Circus. She eventually moved into dance music marketing and promotion, and at MK Dance Promotions helped with their commission for New York City's "I Love New York" single, the B-side of which was Chic's first release, "Dance Dance Dance (Yowsah, Yowsah, Yowsah)."[35] When the latter song was rereleased as a single in its own right, it became a massive hit and launched both the careers of Chic and disco as a mainstream phenomenon. Joseph continued to work with major dance music artists, earning more than 100 gold records with associated acts before the disco demolition of 1979.[36] Her experience in promotion was the perfect fit for Megatone, and when Blecman called, the openly gay Joseph leapt at the chance to move west.

Under Joseph's guidance, Megatone quickly released the final two projects Cowley had been working on before his death, two songs for the ex-Labelle singer Sarah Dash. Both "Low Down Dirty Rhythm" and "Lucky Tonight" were popular, commercially successful releases in 1983, but one could argue that their sales were down to Cowley's reputation and the goodwill owed the label after two years of consistent product. In interviews, Dash certainly appealed to dancers' affection for the label's line-up, namechecking James Wirrick, Sylvester, and Cowley in an interview at the time.[37] While "Low Down Dirty Rhythm" has style, "Lucky Tonight" sounds hastily assembled,

194 MENERGY

and the co-production credit by Marty Blecman and writing credit to Jeff Mehl (Jo-Carol Block's boyfriend) and Maurice Tani alongside Cowley betrays its incomplete status at the time of Cowley's death. Tani remembers, "Pat was already gone, and Marty brought in Sylvester and Sarah Dash, I think, to lay the thing down. It didn't have enough lyrics to it, and me and Jeff Mehl went to the studio and finished the stuff while they were in the other room."[38] The song's lyrics likewise attempt to return to the bacchanalian days of unproblematic, seedy sex associated with Cowley's earlier music, which sounded increasingly out of touch in the context of 1983's new reality.

SFX and Magda Dioni

Meanwhile, back at 8th and Minna—the studio shared by Cowley and Wirrick on one side, Maurice Tani and Art Adcock on the other, and Jolo upstairs—Tani and Adcock had been working with a drummer on a dance music project, the "experimental new wave band" Thump, Thump, Thump.[39] Half recorded and half live, they worked with Shigemi Komiyama, a drummer who played to a prerecorded track. "It allowed us to have a three-piece band that sounded like an orchestra," Tani recalls.[40] When the drummer had to return to his native Japan, they started including drum tapes as well, and brought in vocalists Katie Guthorn and Marthetta Blakley (singers in the Barry Beam Band). They recorded a few demos for Megatone, but by this point Blecman was swamped with material, so their first single, "She Loves the Beast (Je Taime La Bette)" was released through Hot Rocks.[41] The positive reaction to this song led them to explore more dance songs and a change of name ("Maurice hated it, but I loved it!," confesses Guthorn).[42] John Hedges suggested Shiver, and they released their next song, "Never Coming Back," under that name. A patent search by Blecman revealed someone else had already registered Shiver, however, and so they kept their eyes out for a new name. One day, Tani recalls, "the engineer we were working with gave me a cassette, and on the spine of the cassette, he scribbled 'SFX,' but the way it looked in his scrawl, it looked like he had written 'SEX.' And the nice part about it was that SFX sounded like it had something to do with San Francisco . . . and it might have had something to with sound effects, which it was."[43] "La Bête (The Beast)," kicked off the successful SFX album on Megatone, more rock pop than true high-energy dance music. The highlight of the record is a cover of the 1966 Lou Christie song "Lightning Strikes," here a wonderful mix of influences from classic disco to Klaus Nomi's 1981 new wave version.

One of Megatone's most unusual releases of 1983 was "When Will I See You Again" by Magda Layna. San Francisco clubgoers Gary Hatun Noguera and Magda Dioni were working together at a real estate company in property management, hating every minute. To relieve the boredom, they would discuss how satisfying it would be to record dance music like the kind they partied to every weekend. One night in late spring they introduced themselves to Bill Motley, standing in his usual "Bear Country" corner of the Trocadero, and shared their ideas with him. Motley encouraged them to invest in making a single. By this time Motley had left Moby Dick and formed his own Motley Productions. Motley contacted his old Popeye friends Denver Smith and Mike Guess who, with a financial investment from Noguera, wrote and recorded an arrangement of the 1973 Three Degrees' Philly Soul hit "When Will I See You Again" for Dioni to sing under the name Magda Layna. Her naïve, sultry vocals capture a sixties girl group quality, amateurish but intense and probably the closest Motley came to capturing the essence of that style, particularly as he used almost entirely acoustic instruments in his arrangement, doubling and tripling each other, to create a Phil Spector–inspired "Wall of Sound" texture. Singing backup were an uncredited Jo-Carol Block, Lauren Carter, and Linda Imperial.

The song reached number 8 on the *Record Mirror*'s "Boys Town Gay Disco" chart over the summer of 1983 and became a standard among gay club DJs for years. After this, Dioni was quite prolific as a live performer, including an invited gig at New York's Studio 54 and regular appearances up and down the West Coast. For these engagements, she rerecorded "When Will I See You Again" with an up-to-date synthesizer accompaniment and new backup by Jeanie Tracy and Linda Imperial, who sang in a contemporary R&B style more in keeping with a mainstream pop sound. Dioni's tenacity as performer was rewarded in 1985 when she achieved even greater success on Pink Glove Records with the dance rock track "Dangerous."

Moby Dick Is a Success

For the premiere of Boys Town Gang's second album, *Disc Charge*, in May 1982, Moby Dick's publicity manager Will Smith arranged events at the

196 MENERGY

Trocadero Transfer and the Saint in New York City, where the DJ played two hours of the label's music before introducing the group's new material. From Moby Dick's headquarters on Castro Street (above the luxury card shop Statements), they were releasing a steady stream of both home-grown material and reissues of imports (under their "Gold Standard" imprint), like Love International's "Dance on the Groove and Do the Funk" with "Airport of Love" and a cover of Dave Brubeck's "Unsquare Dance" on the B-side.[44]

Love International was the brainchild of Parisian musician Phillipe Chany, who drew from his experiences in the post-punk scene in New York with Lydia Lunch and the B-52s and the electronic sounds of Kraftwerk to create cool, ironic, antifunk funk. It's easy to hear what attracted Moby Dick to this Polydor import as they scouted for artists at the annual Midem international music industry conference in Cannes earlier that year. "Dance on the Groove" features no less than five "truck driver gear change" modulations up a half step, and a campy commentary throughout, including a knowing homage to Giorgio Moroder's 1979 album closer "E = Mc2," as the song's credits are recited for the last two minutes of the song.

Most of the Gold Standard releases, like the in-house artists' output, walked a fine line between old-fashioned disco and state-of-the-art electronic, high-energy dance music, and judging by sales this was clearly what gay dancers across the country wanted to hear. For example, the label released a successful cover of the 1976 Hazell Dean song "Got You Where I Want You Babe" by studio group Stereo Fun, Inc., produced by Los Angeles–based Iranian artist Elton Ahi. The San Francisco–based Crystal and the Team's "Won't You Dance With Me/Sooner or Later" (with lead singer Nina Schiller) never rose above thirty-ninth place on the dance charts, but it stayed a constant presence in US dance clubs for months. Crystal and the Team headlined the Trocadero Transfer's fourth anniversary party for the Sunday Tea Dance in March 1982.[45]

But as in 1981, local talents Lisa, Loverde, and Boys Town Gang would prove to be Moby Dick Records' biggest sellers in both 1982 and 1983. "Our Castro Street home," Will Smith told a reporter in 1982, "is a place where we can pick up on the vibrations of the street and bring them inside.[46] Boys Town Gang's second full album, *Disc Charge*, entered the *Billboard* dance charts on May 29, 1982. It peaked at number 15 on August 21, 1982, and produced the group's biggest international hit, a cover of Frankie Valli's 1967 song "Can't Take My Eyes Off You." As well as featuring their previous singles, "You're the One" and "Disco Kicks" (in a new remix), the album offered two new dance song covers: Redbone's 1973 hit "Come and Get Your Love," and Stevie Wonder's 1970 Motown classic, "Signed, Sealed, Delivered (I'm Yours)." Moby Dick was always a little "casual" about bookkeeping but managed to scrape enough money together to produce a video for "Can't Take My Eyes Off You," featuring Jackson Moore backed by Tom Morley and Bruce Carlton. The video buoyed the song, and it topped the mainstream pop listings in Belgium, the Netherlands, and Spain, reaching number 4 on the United Kingdom's pop chart.

Loverde's "Die Hard Lover"

In 1983, the Cowley name continued to keep the San Francisco sound alive at Moby Dick as well. One of the biggest hits of the year came from a track he had been working on in the last months of his life, "Die Hard Lover." Jo-Carol Block and Lauren Carter had kept the old Acapella Gold studio in the same building as Cowley and James Wirrick's studio, and Linda Imperial, from Loverde, recalls how "we were recording there and working there and that was our little club house where we would all hang out and work on music."[47] After the success Frank Loverde and Don Miley had with writing "I Got the Feeling" for Two Tons o' Fun, Cowley would occasionally approach them with material: "Patrick Cowley would come by my house after sessions in his studio with these instrumental demo tapes and ask me if I could do anything with them," Loverde recalled. "I would keep them for a few days and either write the lyrics myself or take them over to Don Miley's house and we'd write together."[48] One of these happened to be "Die Hard Lover."

The lyrics were inspired by an ad for a car battery. "I liked the idea of never running out of fuel or energy or love, so with that idea I took it over to Don and we wrote this song for Linda Imperial," Loverde remembers.[49] Thinking back on her time working with Cowley, Imperial appreciated his generosity: "There's a tendency to have a hierarchy, for those who are successful. An attitude over those not as successful. Patrick was extremely successful and never had that energy, that feeling of superiority over anyone . . . Patrick was always so nurturing . . . So giving, so loving, so real."[50] Suspecting they had a hit, Miley sold the song to Moby Dick, and hired gay jazz pianist Horus Jack Tolson to produce. Paul Parker recalls the situation slightly differently: "I

198 MENERGY

remember Marty [Blecman] saying that he [Cowley] was just throwing Moby Dick a bone by letting them put that song out . . . Of course it turned out to be one of the biggest records of the whole lot (doing especially well in Europe and Mexico)."[51]

The 12-inch single was Tolson's first project as a producer, despite years in the gay dance music scene. A little older than most of the other San Francisco artists in high energy, Tolson was a veteran of San Francisco's gay nightlife (he had been at the legendary Black Cat with José Sarria the night it closed in 1963). In his career, he had performed at the Stud with his own band, Horus, and as Sylvester's musical director for a time. He also performed as a pianist both solo and with some of avant-garde jazz's biggest names, including Pharaoh Sanders, Archie Shepp, and his first teacher, Jack DeJohnette. He had also been acting as an informal voice coach for Megatone's and Moby Dick's singers (as he had with Sylvester), so when they began the recording sessions for "Die Hard Lover," Tolson was un-sure when Bill Motley suggested using Frank Loverde instead of Imperial as lead vocal. "I was saying to Don Miley, their manager," he remembers, "I said 'Linda's really got a stronger voice, what would you think?' And he went like 'No, no, no, no, no, no, no, Frank's got the look.'"[52] At that exact moment, the brooding, sexy clone Paul Parker was topping the charts with "Right on Target," and was proof that in the more openly gay dance market, male sex appeal could trump talent (although Parker certainly had both). Frank Loverde's rugged, macho good looks were irresistible to the label. "I was crushed," Imperial admits, "but I got over it as one does in this busi-ness."[53] Despite this, Tolson recorded two versions, one with Imperial on lead vocals, and another with Loverde. "Linda did it and she did a great vocal, and I played it for Don and he went, 'No, no, no. We have to go with what we got.'"[54]

The recording took place at the Sausalito-based studio Harbour Sound, where Tolson's lover, sound engineer Patrick Duran, had installed his own special low noise faders into the mixing board, which operated by bypassing the mixer's amplifiers. Tolson, along with Boys Town Gang band member Denver Smith, arranged the song and its B-side, "My World Is Empty Without You." For "Die Hard Lover," Tolson took the staccato syncopated horn sec-tion directly from Al Green's 1971 song "Tired of Being Alone," giving the song a hint of Southern soul (something more apparent in Imperial's vocals, rather than in Loverde's rock style; see figure 10.1).

Figure 10.1 Loverde publicity photo (*left to right*: Peggy Gibbons, Frank Loverde, Linda Imperial). Reproduced with permission.

Interest in High Energy from Europe

As they suspected, "Die Hard Lover" was a hit, quickly becoming a favorite of DJs and peaking at number 3 on *Billboard*'s dance chart by the beginning of 1983 and again achieving great international success. That much of the audience for Moby Dick's (and Megatone's) releases was in Europe represented less a shift on gay American dance floors than a growing interest across the pond in high-energy dance music by a general radio audience. The trade papers noted this trend in the summer of 1982, observing that the European demand is being met "by a small but growing bunch of Los Angeles and San Francisco–based companies, among them Moby Dick, Megatone, Fusion and Neo, whose productions have turned up in dance charts and even, occasionally, pop charts worldwide. Eurodisco has emigrated, apparently, and is now being exported back to Europe."[55]

No better example of the idiosyncratic nature of the European pop charts can be found than on the August 12, 1982, episode of the UK music television program *Top of the Pops*, which featured an appearance by Boys Town

200 MENERGY

Gang. Their performance was taken from the Dutch version of the same program, and featured Jackson Moore in a billowy parachute dress cinched with a gold belt lip-syncing to their hit "Can't Take My Eyes Off You," while Tom Morley and Bruce Carlton, in full clone regalia (bare chest, black denim jeans and leather vest, close-cropped hair, mustache) awkwardly danced beside her. That week on the show, they shared the charts with two-tone group Bad Manners, the rock Steve Miller Band, new wave Toto Coelo, funk Kool and the Gang, and novelty act The Firm, with their cabaret-style single "Arthur Daley ('E's Alright)." It's clear that the early 1980s in Britain were an eclectic time for pop music, when many stylistic doors were open to musicians. Despite Boys Town Gang's success in Britain, however, the unambiguous homosexuality of the act's aesthetic was disconcerting to some in the mainstream music press, especially for the arch, knowing reporter of *New Musical Express*, who dismissed their overt gayness (and their newer single from *Disc Charge*) as a "gag," while backhandedly complimenting their own ability to bring closeted men out of the woodwork:

> How everyone sniggered and whooped at the two "gays" performing on *TOTP* [*Top of the Pops*] for the smash "Can't Take My Eyes Off You." And for why I ask? No, not in 1982. The real fun in 1982 is watching the general public on *TOTP* and trying to spot the fags still in the closet. "There's one!" is the triumphant cry most often heard in our house on Thursday evenings. For seasoned spotters like us, The Boys Town Gang are very small (ginger) beer. Bit like fishing in a two-foot pond with a three-foot net, where's the thrill of the hunt? Anyhow, SSD ["Signed, Sealed, Delivered (I'm Yours)"] won't be quite the hit the last one was– for a start the song isn't anywhere near as neglected and *good* as "Can't Take My Eyes Off You" and besides the gag has worn off.[56]

That the hypermasculine clone represented homosexuality to the critic, rather than the made-up androgynous looks of UK acts like Spandau Ballet or Visage is remarkable, considering it was those characteristics that were so intriguing and confusing to mainstream stateside audiences when the Second British Invasion landed. This is particularly fascinating since it was partially the assumption of these British acts' homosexuality, both through their adoption of traditionally feminine styles and through the use of electronic music, by many gay men in the United States that drew them to the new British music over the next few years at the expense of homegrown San Francisco acts.

British Musicians Imitate the San Francisco Sound

San Francisco's dance music had always faced comparisons with Eurodisco; Giorgio Moroder had set the terms of electronic dance music in 1977, and Germany and Italy had been exploring the implications of his experiments ever since. But by 1982, the new dance music coming out of the United Kingdom started taking up a larger and larger portion of San Francisco and America's dance floors. Some critics noticed the debt owed to San Francisco artists by this new bunch, as when *Billboard*'s Brian Chin called New Order's "Blue Monday" a "dumbfoundingly successful takeoff of the Patrick Cowley cosmic-disco sound," or when Dead or Alive's "Mighty Mix" was referred to as including "Megatone-style disco, rocked and dubbed up."[57] In the United Kingdom, some critics realized that the "new sound" coming out of their country wasn't exactly new. *Record Mirror*'s James Hamilton lamented Cowley's death only a week after his 1978 remix of "I Feel Love" was finally made available in the United Kingdom, as it "now is so much more excitingly instrumental that it's perfect again with today's electrophonic hits."[58]

But most critics (and dancers) appreciated the influx of great new songs to dance to, hearing in the British imports a good beat with a contemporary rock edge. American observers of the market noticed by the summer of 1982 that, "In the UK, London has started to make its mark somewhat belatedly with home grown disco talent starting to cross over internationally," and by 1983 hits directly imitating their San Francisco counterparts were selling better than the originals.[59] A major reason for this was the overwhelming impact of AIDS in US cities, unlike Europe where the virus was slower to gain a foothold, throwing the domestic industry into disarray. By following the model established by San Francisco musicians, British acts were able to overtake US ones, shifting the attention away from the Bay.

The story of the Weather Girls is a perfect example of this. After Martha Wash and Izora Armstead's first Fantasy/Honey album, Two Tons o' Fun was forced to shorten their name simply to "The Two Tons" because a gospel group was already registered with ASCAP under the same name. They were never overly fond of their gimmicky name in the first place, and as early as

202 MENERGY

1979 they had jokingly suggested to a reporter that they were thinking of changing it to "Grand Pianos."[60] After their attorney Steven Ames Brown helped them get out of their Honey contract, the women were approached by Paul Jabara, the superstar disco songwriter probably most famous for having written Donna Summer's "Last Dance," and musician Paul Schaeffer with a song they had written together, "It's Raining Men," in an electronic high-energy style.

They debuted the song performing still as the Two Tons at the Castro Street Fair in August 1982 with Timmy Rivers DJing, but they still didn't have a confirmed label for the track. When there was some money left over after the recording session, Brown suggested to Jabara that they press a bunch of acetate copies and send them to DJs around the country, as Brown recalls: "So we got a bunch of *Billboard* disco reporters to report 'It's Raining Men.' It had a Columbia matrix number on it that Columbia had not issued. It had nothing to do with Columbia Records, we put their name on the record, and then all of a sudden, Columbia Records had charted a turntable hit that it didn't own. So they had to come and make a deal."[61] With the label contract secured, Wash and Armstead continued to promote the song in San Francisco, performing at a megaparty in the former Dreamland space with DJ Mike Lewis in October. They premiered the song's music video at Brown's San Francisco nightclub, the Oasis.

Rising in the dance charts over the next few months, the song managed to cross over to the R&B and pop charts as well and was also an international hit. "It's Raining Men" reached the number 1 spot on *Billboard*'s dance chart on Christmas Day, 1982, sharing the top 40 with Patrick Cowley's "Mind Warp," Loverde's "Die Hard Lover," and Sylvester's first Megatone album, *All I Need*. They started a tour of gay clubs right away, playing in Denver, Dallas, Memphis, New York, Miami, and Houston. Their shows would open with older Two Tons material, then launch into the new single, and as an audience member in Memphis wrote at the time, "in the blink of an eye umbrellas were whipped out to add to the intensity of the song . . . The angelic Weather Girls almost made me run for cover!"[62] So far, so typical of the trajectory of San Francisco gay dance music.

In an important essay about the song, Mitchell Morris describes their gay appeal as owing to "an ideal situation best described as more men of more types," in which "the objectification of all those nameless men provides a powerful gay subtext."[63] Their appeal "as triply abject—women, black, fat—. . . could have been seen as repositories of all that is marginal. But

DANCING WITH AIDS   203

they . . . nevertheless seemed to exist in sublime indifference to the possibility of abjection," Morris observed. Their "acting up" was a source of power, endearing them to gay male audiences: "Constructing an identity around the value of such erotic freedom was an important post-Stonewall gay male activity, not only in the bathhouses, not only in literature and pornography both written and visual, but also in the discos as well."[64]

But this status as "triply abject" allowed for an interpretation outside of gay culture, and as their hit crossed over into the mainstream, its meaning changed. This is also because while Jabara was gay (and his music often *extremely* camp), he was very much a part of the big city, New York/Los Angeles constellation of movie stars and Broadway names, rather than the more insular gay community of San Francisco. When in February 1983 Jabara included two additional Weather Girls songs, the campy "Ladies Hot Line" and a new ballad, "Hope," alongside solo tracks by Whitney Houston and Leata Galloway on the album *Paul Jabara and Friends*, neither of the new songs could be described as high energy. Rather, "Ladies Hot Line" is comedy R&B in the style of Barbara Mason or Shirley Brown, and "Hope" comes across as a lost number from *Dreamgirls*, then reigning supreme on Broadway. Likewise, the Weather Girls' first full album, *Success*, opens with a title track that borrows liberally from *Chicago*'s "Nowadays," both in the MC introduction and the melodramatic chromatic rise. Their music, now incorporated into the mainstream, still possessed connections to gay culture but stopped filling the niche on gay dance floors that demanded a focus on the beat, concentrated electronics, and high-energy tempos.

So when UK artist Miquel Brown's "So Many Men, So Little Time" appeared in the summer of 1983, it seemed to answer the high-energy prayers of gay men across the United States. While the song was a clear rip-off of the Weather Girls' hit, British producer Ian Levine was no neophyte to dance music. A famous musician in his own country, Levine was a key figure in the Northern Soul phenomenon in the 1970s before becoming the first resident DJ at London's legendary gay disco Heaven. He produced numerous disco acts in the late 1970s, yielding few bona fide hits, but when he was asked by the owner of the Record Shack record store in London to start a high-energy dance music label (the aptly named Record Shack Records), he jumped at the chance. "So Many Men" was his first release on the new label. Levine is upfront about the West Coast gay origins of the song, recalling: "I had been at the Circus Maximus [Circus Disco] in LA and I saw a guy wearing a t-shirt that said, 'So many men, so little time,' and I was like, "One day I want to

204 MENERGY

make a record with that title."[65] Miquel Brown's voice was soulful, but had none of the gospel heft of the Weather Girls. With the electronics swirling around her and the thumping beat driving men to the dance floor, however, that didn't matter. Gay clubs in the United States made the song a huge hit, and it peaked on the *Billboard* dance charts at number 2 in August 1983.

With the success of "So Many Men, So Little Time," Levine, through Record Shack Records, continued to produce singles for the gay dance and pop markets over the next several years. He proudly boasts that, "Between 1983 and 1985 we had sales of twelve million records . . . In 1984 we brought Evelyn [Thomas] out of retirement and had a number one with 'High-Energy,' a term the USA were using for this sound."[66] His music, and others who built off the San Francisco sound, like New York's straight Bobby Orlando, gradually filled out the widening slots on DJs' playlists and became reference points for this style of music.

Having been beaten by the success of "So Many Men," Megatone Records had no choice but to join them, and toward the end of 1983 they licensed Ian Levine's latest high-energy song, Earlene Bentley's "The Boys Come to Town," for distribution in the United States alongside their own Modern Rocketry's "I'm Not Your Steppin' Stone." *Billboard* acknowledged the writing on the wall, reviewing Bentley's single as "what will likely be a long list of neo-Euro hits."[67]

While a critic could still state with confidence in February 1983 that "Between MD [Moby Dick] and Megatone, *Billboard*'s dance chart will never starve for a San Francisco hit," it was to become less true as the year passed.[68] A look at the 1983 Cable Car Award nominees for Outstanding Club Recording shows an embarrassment of riches; Patrick Cowley's *Mind Warp*, Sylvester's *All I Need*, Loverde's "Die Hard Lover," Boys Town Gang's *Disc Charge*, Paul Parker's "Right on Target," Jeanie Tracy's *Me and You*, and the Weather Girls' "It's Raining Men,"; all of them had filled the nation's gay dance floors. But by the end of 1984, AIDS had torn the heart out of gay San Francisco's music infrastructure, leaving very little for the survivors to build on.

11

Everything Falls Apart

While San Francisco's clubs, parties, and records continued to be enormously successful in 1983, HIV's long incubation period over the next few years meant illness spread gradually but overwhelmingly throughout the community. Benji Rubenstein, who opened a revamped Dreamland later in the decade, recalls the transformation of that year: "For me, '82 was the most magical, incredible year of my life in San Francisco. Shortly thereafter in '83, a lot of people were getting sick, friends of mine, and it seemed to cascade and get worse and worse as the months went on, that it was unbearable after a while. I didn't even go out for a year or two. I would not date. I wouldn't do anything. I was just scared."[1] But as the year began, optimism was running high. The music pouring out of clubs, bars, cars, and Walkmans still represented to the residents of the Castro the infinite possibilities of gay liberation in the 1980s. By 1984, however, it was clear that the party, if not ending, was again changing in radical ways. It wasn't so much that San Francisco struggled to adapt to new sounds; rather, the gay community was quite simply culled of its artists, producers, dancers, and support staff. The mass deaths of so many participants inevitably led to fundamental changes in the priorities and desires of those left to pick up the pieces. This chapter details the winding-down of the sound that came to define a city's—and the world's—gay club culture in the early 1980s. For a brief time, San Francisco was the center of the gay musical world, and the legacy of that sound continues to this day in nearly all aspects of mainstream popular music.

Castro Boy

One of the best examples of this, "Castro Boy," was a self-released dance single by DJ Lester Temple and producer Barry Beam, with assistance from John Hedges. A parody of the ubiquitous Frank and Moon Zappa hit,

Menergy. Louis Niebur, Oxford University Press. © Oxford University Press 2022.
DOI: 10.1093/oso/9780197511077.003.0012

206 MENERGY

it turned "Valley Girl" into a high-energy dance anthem. "Castro Boy" remains faithful to the original's chord changes and structure (they had asked and received permission from Zappa for the parody), but the buzzy electric bass and rock guitars and drums are replaced by the Prophet-5 and Pro One and the relentless four-on-the-floor pounding of the LinnDrum. "It was just meant to be a joke," Temple recalls, "just a silly thing for San Francisco DJs and we just threw it together. I think I wrote it on a Wednesday or Thursday. We went into Independent Sound and in two days it was done. And that was it, just thrown together basically . . . Musically, it's really sloppy."[2] Hedges's friend and former roommate, stand-up comedian Danny Williams, was invited to provide the stereotypical "Castro Boy" dialog, and in one take he managed to capture all four of clone culture's "D's":

> Castro Street is so hot! I mean, so many men, so little time! It's not pretty being easy. I mean, you can cruise for days, girl! From the Badlands to Castro Station over to Moby Dick's, check out the new wave clones at Bear Hollow, it's to die for! It's so faaaabulous! So, my friend Bill calls. Oh no, we're not lovers, we're like, you know, sisters. And anyway, he says, "come on girl, let's go dancing tonight." We always go to the Troc, but tonight I was into the Beam. You got any crystal? So all he's got is MDA. This stuff makes you horny! Wooo! For days! So like he goes, "I just got the new Viola Wills record," I mean, pu-lease, he's such a disco dolly! . . . Let me get a hit off of these poppers. Oooh! New Sylvester! Work it girl! [sings] "Do you wanna funk." Well, off to the 1808 Club, check you later. A little hanky-panky. Gag me with a cock. Faaaaaabulous![3]

They pressed 500 copies of the record, and, after an argument over the group's name (Hedges thought Temple's suggestion of "Titty and the Clamps" too risqué), they settled on "Danny Boy and the Serious Party Gods." The record was, unsurprisingly, an immediate hit on Castro dance floors, with the *Reporter* loving the "hilarious take off" of the original.[4] It may be difficult to understand how such a cheap and cheerful song made such an impact, including a nomination for Outstanding Contribution by a Recording Artist at the 1983 Cable Car Awards, but the dance track provides for the historian a snapshot of an ideal Castro clone night out in the early 1980s; on the surface silly, carefree, and frivolous, but built upon the struggles of those DJs, musicians, and dancers that made San Francisco a destination for their own liberation.

Lisa

By the end of 1983, Lisa Fredenthal-Lee, Barry Blum, and John Hedges had completed her eponymous album (figure 11.1). It had been a true collaborative effort, with their contract with Moby Dick including a clause that allowed for creative input from the singer. For the first single, "Rocket to Your Heart/Mandatory Love," Blum used his Boss Doctor Rhythm drum machine to write the initial rhythm tracks and borrowed Paul Parker's LinnDrum to program the final drum patterns. This data was transferred to a cassette and used

Figure 11.1 Lisa publicity photo. Photo courtesy of Lisa Fredenthal-Lee. Reproduced with permission.

208   MENERGY

on Peter Buffett's LinnDrum at Independent Sound.[5] Blum wrote most of the album's songs in a little closet in the back of his house on Turk Street where he had synched up the monophonic Pro One synthesizer (again borrowed from Parker, which he had himself inherited from Patrick Cowley), LinnDrum, and five-voice Prophet-5 synthesizers.[6]

While Lisa and partner Robert Lee wrote the lyrics on two of the album's six songs, their visual contributions were even more substantial. Drawing upon their skills as photographers and Fredenthal-Lee's experience as a zine publisher, they created album artwork using photocopied and overexposed photos of the singer, monochromatic but strikingly pink. To accompany her live shows, they also created several mini-zines containing song lyrics and small stickers to throw into the audience. As "Rocket to Your Heart" moved up the dance charts, peaking on *Billboard*'s at number 2 for five weeks, Lisa and Lee made a video to accompany the next single, "Invisible Love," recruiting artist friends to the project. Jim Kallet, experimental filmmaker Craig Baldwin, and award-winning video artist Denise Gallant collaborated to capture the singer's highly visual style. Gallant was a co-creator of a pioneering video synthesizer that the team employed along with digital stills made with the first video interface created for a Mac computer by Gallant's colleague Rob Schafer.[7]

Despite the massive success of "Rocket to Your Heart," Lisa's album did not lead to bigger projects. As more and more people started getting sick at the label and throughout the San Francisco dance music industry, Moby Dick's problems finally caught up with them. Projects like the "Invisible Love" video were entirely financed by the artist. She had, in fact, never been paid for her work on "Jump Shout," and by the middle of 1984, when she should have been working on her next album, the scope of Moby Dick's problems were becoming increasingly clear. She never technically "left" Moby Dick, it's just that with financial mismanagement bordering on criminal and the deaths of so many there, the label ceased to exist. As Fredenthal-Lee now observes with hindsight, "it was a very sad time indeed."[8]

Moby Dick Fades Away

Moby Dick's closure was probably inevitable, even without the AIDS epidemic. A couple of high-profile (and expensive) releases had disappointed, including Nina Schiller's album, which peaked at just 34 on the dance charts, a rereleased album by Miami-based disco singer turned high-energy diva Margaret Reynolds, and Loverde's hastily assembled follow-up single, "Backstreet Romance." With all these underperformers, cash flow was a serious problem throughout 1983. They also refused to move in new directions. Horus Jack Tolson remembers approaching the label with his new dance single "Heartstop" by Tyne Mouton (a singer with Sly Stone's band, formerly known as "Tiny Melton"): "You have to understand Moby Dick. They took themselves much too seriously and there was too much arrogance and attitude problems around there . . . So, I took some of these tracks and they were a little bit ahead of their time, they were more like what you call house music . . . And so I took these tracks to Moby Dick and I said, 'Here, this is what I'm doing. Consider putting it out. She's from Sly Stone, she's got this incredible diva voice.' 'Well Horus, you know, we don't do n***** music.'"9

Their overt racism, while unfortunately not surprising, was based in the notion that the community dancing to their records wasn't interested in newer Black music. But they had only to look at Sylvester's new top-selling releases that were increasingly embracing the New York electro and Chicago house sound to see that their vision was myopic. However, even in its final months the label was able to release a few strong records that sold well and still captured the spirit of San Francisco's scene.

BearEssense

Probably the most influential of these late singles was "The Big Hurt" by BearEssense. Chris Njirich and Bob Giudice had made their reputation as "The Lighting Bears," lighting experts for local parties and nightclubs. Socially, their particular haunt was that corner of the Trocadero Transfer known as "Bear Country," where all the big and hairy guys hung out, but bears were also popular at Victor Swedosh's Moby Dick bar. Itching to get more involved in the production side of music, they spoke to Swedosh (who was also co-owner of the record label) about their interest in recording a version of the Toni Fisher song "The Big Hurt" in the style of Sharon Redd's melancholy "In the Name of Love." Swedosh loved the idea and suggested the name "BearEssense" for the two. Njirich and Giudice asked Paul Parker if he knew of any singers who could approximate the sound they were looking for, and he suggested Marianna LoCurto, a voice student of Horus Jack Tolson

210   MENERGY

and local megaparty maven. The Bears next hired Barry Blum and his guitar player friend Richi Ray to arrange and perform the song.

Working from Truth and Beauty Studio in South San Francisco, Blum started by arranging the synthesizer parts, but after some disagreements, including LoCurto's suitability for the song, the Bears subsequently asked Ray to take over production duties. Ray had recently made his own arrangement of the song, so he already knew it well, and while staying faithful to Fisher's original he managed to also incorporate aspects of Redd's song. But when the track was finished, there were still concerns about the vocals. Although LoCurto's voice was strong, it had little in common with the soulful Sharon Redd. Swedosh suggested going back into the studio and putting Jessica Williams in, but in the end Moby Dick released the song as it was, with DJ Mike Lewis remixing the single, and, to mitigate concerns about the vocals, a prominent dub was included on the B-side. Performing as "BearEssense with Marianna," the singer had manager and party promoter Gary Roverana find solo gigs for her, including performances at the Russian River's Fife's with DJ Steve Fabus. While the song wasn't an immediate hit, underperforming on the dance charts, it had legs and slowly caught on with club DJs, particularly Lewis's dub mix, slightly slowed down and played as part of early morning sleaze sets.[10] The Bears began working on a follow-up, but the reality of AIDS put an end to that, as Njirich remembers: "It was amazing when we put out 'The Big Hurt' through Moby Dick Records, because within about a year almost everybody had died there, except for about three people. That's between ten and twenty people."[11]

The Problems with Independent Labels

Moby Dick had always had sloppy accounting practices. In the beginning, Vice President Will Smith had tried to keep accurate records, but when he left in late 1981, Larry Lustig took over and was shocked to discover that there was no formal accounting system. "Initially I had to run the business out of a folder full of 3x5 cards," Lustig told historian David Diebold.[12] "It was unbelievable." As people left the company or began to get sick, Gini Spiersch and Lustig were forced to take on their jobs as well. "Eventually there was only Larry and me left (out of the staff of sixteen or so) and we literally had to jump from desk to desk to run the office," Spiersch remembers.[13] "We did that until the day they came and closed the doors." Some outsiders perceived the label as an amateurish vanity project on the part of the bar's owners, an excuse for lavish drugged-up parties.[14] It's true that a lot of money was spent on cocaine; Mondays and Tuesdays at the Moby Dick bar were legendary for the way they just kept the weekend going past Sunday. In the end, many artists and producers were never paid by the label. This was certainly the experience of Loverde, Lisa, and Barry Blum, who never received his money for Lisa's album. He frustratingly recalled:

> "Jump Shout" went double platinum in Mexico. The estimates I've heard are up to a half a million, but we didn't get any of that. None of it . . . So "Jump Shout" was going up and [Moby Dick] said, "Do the new album," and so we're already in it and by that time, they owed everybody in town and so we couldn't afford a big lawyer and we just sort of said, "Meh," because everybody was very sick, who knows what would've happened.[15]

But it is a misperception that vast amounts of cash were flowing in and out of the company, or indeed any independent record label. The dance music industry at the time was relatively low profit, which is why the major labels dropped out in the first place. The only way to make substantial money was with a crossover hit, and that was extremely rare. Founder of independent dance label Fantasia Records Ian Anthony Stephens explains:

> To actually record a record was expensive. And then to release it was expensive. So, people who set up these businesses and record labels with a certain amount of funds, they release a record . . . And then when they get really popular and it gets released in all these countries and they get all this money, what usually happens is, they think, "Well, we'll just run the business a bit long game and when we get another record, we'll then pay everybody." And the previous record was always paying for the next one next, and they never get enough money to actually pay anybody. And while they never originally set out to be crooks, eventually that's what they were. And so the artists always felt cheated because they never got what they're promised, despite the record seeming to be popular. And so they felt exploited. The reality is, there wasn't enough money in the whole thing for everybody to do well out of it.[16]

The Closing of Moby Dick Records

Moby Dick's last single was a family affair. Mary Buffett's "My Boyfriend's Back" was produced by her husband Peter, with background vocalists including Linda Imperial, Peggy Gibbons, and Paul Parker, guitar by James

212 MENERGY

Wirrick on the B-side, and mixed and edited by Barry Blum, John Hedges, Lester Temple, and Steve Algozino. There was no money to promote the single, despite a hilarious self-financed music video, and the song spent a quiet three weeks in the bottom half of the *Billboard* dance chart in May 1984. By the time Moby Dick Records finally closed its doors that month, the label owed everyone in town, but no one came out of it rich. Most artists just accepted the reality of the situation that, as Frank Loverde put it, "most of them had either left the country or became very sick, so our plans to take legal actions against them just sort of evaporated."[17] By the end of 1986, seven of the ten core employees had died of AIDS-related illnesses: Russell Coldewey, promoter, Dennis Croteau, booking artist, Steve Hasemeier, international licenser, Tom Morley, performer, Trip Ringwald, remix engineer, and founders Stan Morriss and Bill Motley.[18] Spiersch told a journalist at the time she kept a prayer book with notes for each of the men, and the date of their death: "It's so strange to work with a group of people, build up a company with them, and then see everyone go. How do you keep them in your memory and honor what they've done? I just don't want to forget; they were too young."[19] The legacy of the label *would*, however, continue in the many independent labels that sprang up in its wake.

Splintering into Smaller Labels: Arial, C&M, ERC, Pink Glove, Zino Records

After Moby Dick's closure former employees Larry Brennan and Craig Morey still felt there was a market for the rerelease of older and import dance records. Following the model of Moby Dick's Gold Standard reissues, which included new remixes, they secured the rights to 250 in-demand but out-of-print disco classics and programmed a release schedule that stretched over three years, calling themselves Arial Records.[20] They hit pay dirt right away with Technique's "Tonight/Can We Try Again," originally released by London-based ERC Records, with a remix by Mike Lewis incorporating synthesizer by Horus Jack Tolson and percussion by David Frazier. Its success led Morey and Brennan to seek out its composer, Muff Murfin, and make plans for future releases.

But what scuttled the label was another issue that plagued so many small, independent record companies: they had no clout when it came to collecting money from distributors. Arial only ever released three recordings, the other two being Paul Sabu's "Shotgun" and Gwen Jonae's "Red Light Lover," neither of which had new mixes. Even with Arial's failure, Morey wasn't deterred, and with Leonard R. Cory Jr. set up C&M Records on Market Street. This label released Jonae's next single, "Destiny," but, again, miscalculating the time it takes for money from distributors to feed back into the company led to its closure after only three releases (the others being R&B act Danny Lugo, and the Redz, a rare new wave/rock departure mixed by Bill Motley), all of which placed in the bottom half of *Billboard*'s dance charts. At the same time, ERC Records' founder Marvin Howell relocated from London to Los Angeles. ERC distributed Moby Dick's music in the United Kingdom, and now made a similar arrangement with Megatone, and the two labels worked together to produce an album for British singer Norma Lewis, which was moderately successful, particularly in the UK.

In 1985, Gary Noguera and his brother Ramon formed their own small record label, Pink Glove Records, for the release of Magda Dioni's music (who had found success with "When Will I See You Again" on Megatone a few years earlier). Noguera hired experienced record executive Audrey Joseph as a consultant as he was starting the label, wanting to make sure he was making the right decisions. Pink Glove hired her, according to Noguera, "to consult and give us information on some of the basic components of how to make a record."[21] Among her recommendations were top quality pressing and mastering companies, such as Sterling Sound in New York, where they were able to acquire the services of mastering legend José Rodriguez. "Dangerous," the first Pink Glove release, had an aggressive rock quality more in line with Dioni's unique vocal style than the pop girl group material she worked with previously. First-time producer Leo Frappier was stunned by the transgender artist's striking looks: "She looked like a female lion with the big hair and long nails," he recalled, and he felt it was important for her breakout record as an independent artist to be "something that she could have her claws out."[22]

Leo Frappier graduated high school in 1979, so by the time he was old enough to make the Trocadero Transfer and the I-Beam his favorite hangouts, the AIDS epidemic had taken hold, and the heyday of that city's dance music was both the celebrated recent past and, to some extent, a millstone around future producers' necks. Frappier's style is very much a continuation of the San Francisco high-energy sound. He had worked as an unofficial "intern" at both Moby Dick and Megatone Records since 1982, but by 1985, the charts had already been taken over by British imitators such as Ian Levine and newcomers Stock, Aitken, and Waterman. "Dangerous" was given a boost by Alfie's DJ Tommy Williams's intense 12-inch remix and helped put the new label on the dance music map. When Frappier grew impatient with Megatone, who had taken a long time to release an earlier song he had sold them, Noguera decided to open up Pink Glove to other artists and bought Tom Anderson's "Rock Dancing," which Frappier had produced, back from Megatone and released it that same year. Tom Anderson had known Frappier for years and, as a cast member of the legendary drag show Beach Blanket Babylon in North Beach, had been the young producer's introduction to the gay musical world of San Francisco.

The song, like "Dangerous," and Barry Blum side project Blueprint's "Ritespot," captures the blend of rock and high energy that had taken over dance floors by the middle of the decade, which, while still heavily synthesized and using electronic drum machines, incorporated electric guitars in a rock style to a much greater extent. The song's kick drum pattern also shows the direct influence of New Order's "Blue Monday," a further demonstration of the lessening influence of the San Francisco sound. On the other hand, the three other 12-inch singles released by Pink Glove before shuttering—Linda Imperial's "Stranger," Joy Saint James's "Dance!" (the alias of prominent voice-over artist MJ Lalo), and Shawn Benson and Diebold and Company's "Male Fraud"—are wonderfully old-school high-energy dance tracks, without a single guitar to be heard. As the eighties progressed, Frappier's sound, such as his project as Manifestation in 1988 with Frank Loverde, reflected the culture's move away from the hedonistic and into the healing, and into a more house style. Frappier explains, "Because AIDS had really descended so quickly upon the community, some people were really just reassessing their connections, their spiritual connections, either because they were not long for this world, or they were looking for.... Perhaps there would even be some sort of cure through that.... I started listening to Chicago house and that style of these very jacked beats that were very R&B based, and that was just not part of, say, the Megatone sound, for instance."[23]

Steve Algozino, founder of Hot Tracks DJ remix service, also set up a small label in 1983. Pacific Records released three 12-inch singles, including one under his own "Zino" name. Pacific's biggest hit, however, came from Torch's "Build Me Up Buttercup." DJ Torch worked at the Rusty Nail and Drums in the gay enclave of Guerneville, California, and she introduced young producer Brian Soares to Algozino. Like Frappier, Soares would go on to release successful dance records in the San Francisco style, primarily on Los Angeles–based label Nightwave under the name Secret Ties until his death of

AIDS-related illness in 1987. When Algozino's own health began to decline in late 1985, he closed Pacific Records, turned over control of Hot Tracks to Gini Spiersch, and lived out his remaining few months in Oahu, Hawaii.

Ian Anthony Stephens and Fantasia Records

The most successful high-energy dance label to emerge in the wake of AIDS was London-based Ian Anthony Stephens' Fantasia Records. Stephens acknowledges his debt to the creators of the San Francisco sound: "I was aware of those records. They were very good. Patrick Cowley was a big influence on my taste in music. I loved what he was doing. And I wanted to make records like that. He's very, very complicated, they're quite complicated."[24] He knew that Cowley had used a Prophet-5 synthesizer, and so, although not a musician himself, he found Winston Sala's phone number in the back of a music magazine advertising instrument rental and music arranging. Armed with £5000, he hired the arranger to produce a backing track in the high-energy style. After singer Hazell Dean recorded vocals, he sold the single, "Searchin' (I Gotta Find a Man)," to Proto Records, and to TSR Records in the United States. The dance track was a huge crossover hit in the United Kingdom, rising to number 6 on the Top 10 chart, around the same time Ian Levine's follow-up to "So Many Men," Evelyn Thomas's "High Energy," was proving to be a big hit as well. Brian Chin noted the impact of British high energy on the mainstream pop charts that September:

> Judging from the British pop charts, the neo-disco work of such producers as Ian Levine and Ian Anthony Stephens has gained sudden trendy pop credibility in the UK. According to one A&R source there, the records of Hazell Dean, Evelyn Thomas, Divine, the Weather Girls and numerous others, are clearly perceived by pop music fans as—what else?—gay disco in a straight line tradition from such disco era successes as "In the Bush" and "You Make Me Feel Mighty Real." This effect has been so pronounced, we're told, that there is some apprehension among the gay crowd that the national charts have co-opted their movement.[25]

Inspired by the song's popularity but frustrated over what he felt were dishonest financial practices by Proto's managers and the lack of control he had over his own product, Stephens decided to set up his own record imprint. His

216   MENERGY

initial plan was to release Paul Parker's latest material. Stephens met Parker after a show at the Embassy Club in London in the summer of 1983. Having been frustrated with Megatone since Cowley's death six months earlier, particularly Marty Blecman's antipathy towards Parker's songwriting and production interests, Parker asked Stephens if he'd like to collaborate and invited him over to his friend Mary Buffett's mother-in-law's place in Kensington the next day. After a fun afternoon at her in-law's sprawling mansion, Mary, who owned Independent Sound studio in San Francisco, and Parker asked Stephens to come out and stay with them (Parker and partner Ken Crivello) in San Francisco so they could work on some music. When Parker picked him up from SFO a few weeks later, Stephens played him the song he'd written for him, "Desire," on the car's cassette player. Stephens ultimately stayed several months in San Francisco and recorded hours of music with Parker, Jo-Carol Block, Marianna LoCurto, Lisa, and others.

Stephens launched Fantasia Records with Parker's "Desire" in March 1984, and the singer toured the United States to promote the single. The two worked on most of the early Fantasia releases together, including Lisa's "Love Is Like an Itching in My Heart" and "Tempt Me," Debbie Jacobs featuring Jolo's "In the Heat of the Night," and a great new remix of BearEssense's "The Big Hurt," this time credited to Marianna alone. These releases were all hits on the recently renamed Hi-NRG charts (including the US-based *Dance Music Report* and UK-based *Music Mirror*). As such, London's Fantasia became a kind of British branch of the San Francisco sound's next generation; as the city itself became increasingly unable to sustain its own music scene, Stephens's label was a haven for Bay Area artists to adapt and incorporate new styles and fashions into their dance music. Fantasia issued its last single in 1988, ending a run of tracks that can be heard as a direct continuation of the high-energy San Francisco sound, relocated to friendlier shores. Parker went on to work with gay hip-hop and electro pioneer Man Parrish, releasing the freestyle record "One Look" in 1988 and other successful songs with ZYX and Almighty Records. He still enjoys a career as a popular touring artist today.

Rich and Famous

Bill Motley, the artistic heart of Moby Dick Records, had left the company in its final year after disagreements with his co-owners, and had gone into partnership with friend Steven Ames Brown. In addition to his position as an entertainment lawyer, Brown had worked with Sanford Kellman to produce live shows at the I-Beam's Sunday Tea Dances and had a real love of the local gay music scene. Together Brown and Motley created Rich and Famous Records Ltd. (named after the "standard rich and famous" contract Orson Welles offers Kermit in *The Muppet Movie*). This gave them the rights to the Boys Town Gang's back catalog and the rights to make future recordings under that name, which they did with Boys Town Gang's third and final album, *A Cast of Thousands*. Brown recalls, "Bill wanted as many people playing as possible. I always called it the Bill Motley Orchestra Chorus and Ensemble because the bills were astronomical. *Cast of Thousands* cost, like, $120,000 to make. Who spent that kind of money on a disco record in the eighties? Nobody!"[26]

Really, the project was a coming together for all the major San Francisco dance music artists of the past five years, performing a huge fifteen-minute medley of San Francisco high-energy dance hits. The list of participants is incredible (and a testament to Brown's negotiating skills), including vocalists Izora Armstead, Jo-Carol Block, Lauren Carter, Cynthia Manley, Jackson Moore, Margaret Reynolds, Sylvester, Jeanie Tracy, and Martha Wash. It also featured performances by Barry Blum, Pat Gleeson, Mike Guess and Denver Smith of Popeye, and James Wirrick. Motley filled out the rest of the album with new recordings of old girl group and soul songs, in the now-classic Moby Dick style, including his mother's favorite song, "When Will I See You Again," with a new vocal by Jessica Williams, and a version of "A Good Man Is Hard to Find," which *Billboard* called a "notably classy production."[27]

Motley remained well up until three weeks before his death. Although he had been forced for financial reasons to get rid of his San Francisco home, moving back to be with his family in Los Angeles, his heart remained in the Bay. He returned as often as he could, usually staying at Brown's place. When he was suddenly taken ill with *pneumocystis* pneumonia on one of his trips north, he was rushed to San Francisco General Hospital and died on June 15, 1985. Despite the rough legacy of Moby Dick Records, nearly all his colleagues remember him as a true artist, dedicated to dance music. John Hedges recalled him as a "fun, funny guy. He was a good guy, always joking and stuff. I remember he had a Jeep with speakers, they were so loud! He'd be riding around the Castro playing his music. He was very good at what he did. I had a lot of respect for him."[28] Likewise, Marty Blecman regarded him as a savvy taste-maker who lived for music: "Bill Motley was wonderful. Sometimes he was like a little space-puppy—so into his music that he would

218   MENERGY

get all dreamy and think that everything was beautiful. He hit hard though, with his product and did it at the right time . . . when no one else would touch disco."[29] Moby Dick and Boys Town Gang were bywords for the San Francisco sound, a label and band that perfectly captured the essence of Castro nightlife in the early 1980s.

Modern Rocketry

A year after Patrick Cowley's death, Megatone put out a "greatest hits" collection remixed primarily by Marty Blecman and Tommy Williams with new versions of several songs, including a fantastic "Menergy" with extra vocals by Sylvester. They also continued to release fresh material into 1984, including a new album by Sylvester, *M-1015*, that further emphasized his move into funk and the New York electro sound. That same year, Megatone had a string of moderate hits by established dance music artists like Queen Samantha and Scherrie Payne, and new wave band the Toons. They also released a full album by renowned keyboardist and singer Billy Preston, *On the Air*, with a track, "And Dance," mixed by Blecman and Automatt engineer Ken Kessie, which failed to generate buzz.

Without any breakout new material, and with AIDS growing worse, Megatone was certainly headed toward the same fate as Moby Dick. But a new act, Modern Rocketry, masterminded by two straight white men but filled with the spirit of the gay Castro, proved to be a surprising success. Morey Goldstein and Ken Kessie had been involved to a major extent with the San Francisco sound for several years before creating Modern Rocketry, and they used their experience to make music that embraced the sound of their gay forerunners who were now vanishing.

Like Barry Blum and Lisa, Goldstein came from San Francisco's new wave and punk scene. His father had worked for CBS Records for thirty years on their native Long Island, so Goldstein grew up surrounded by and sympathetic to music of all genres. In high school jazz band, he had won regional and state awards for his arranging, while at the same time playing in various rock groups. When he graduated high school in 1975, he and his band the Readymades moved to San Francisco where they quickly made a name for themselves, releasing their first EP in 1977. Subsequent Readymades appearances on 415 Records' 1980 punk/new wave sampler *415 Music* and the influential *Rising Stars of San Francisco* in 1981 increased the Readymades' and Goldstein's profile, as did work away from his band, especially his saxophone playing for Roy Loney and the Phantom Movers, with bass player and longtime Patrick Cowley collaborator Maurice Tani.

While recording with the Readymades at the Automatt, Goldstein met engineer Ken Kessie, who had been working extensively with Megatone Records. Together they formed Modern Rocketry, a studio project to produce high-energy dance music for a gay market using a variety of vocalists and musicians. Marty Blecman loved the idea, and the fact that both men were straight wasn't a problem for either him or the group. As Horus Jack Tolson explains, "gays broke the whole industry open with the whole late-night disco phenomenon, how you dressed, how you acted. And straight guys, you had to pretend that you were gay if you were straight . . . And so that phenomena, it was kind of amazing because so many straight guys would go out and pretend that they were gay, so they could get into the clubs."[30] Because Kessie was a staff engineer at the Automatt, he had unlimited access when no one else was there (usually from midnight until 7:00 a.m.), and the two were able to present Marty Blecman at Megatone with their first single, a cover of the Monkees' "(I'm Not Your) Steppin' Stone" in late summer 1983. *Billboard*'s critic Brian Chin now understood that high-energy dance music was the primary domain of the United Kingdom, praising the release's "wonderful New Order-ish drive and crystal clear production," and describing the song as "one of the few US products to really stand up to what's being done in Britain."[31]

For the song and its B-side, "I'm Gonna Make You Want Me," they hired vocalist Peter Dunne (aka Peter Bilt) from local new wave band Pearl Harbor and the Explosions and incorporated significant baritone saxophone work by Goldstein. Despite these rock characteristics, the driving four-on-the-floor electronic kick drum, synthesized octave bass line, and spacey synth sound effects keep the songs firmly in high-energy territory. When the 12-inch single was a surprise top 10 *Billboard* dance chart hit, Blecman quickly commissioned more from the group, releasing "The Right Stuff" and a fantastic high-energy version of "La Cage Aux Folles," under the pseudonym Le Jeté, both with Dunne as lead vocalist. Dunne performed live as Modern Rocketry for Studio West's New Year's Eve celebrations, starting a year of performing for him and the group across the country in gay venues. Through 1984, Kessie and Goldstein put an album of material together, and when *Modern Rocketry* came out, it was a major hit for Megatone. The record contained the previously released songs and new material that doubled down on the gay high-energy

220   MENERGY

content, setting its stall out right away with album opener "Homosexuality," sung by Goldstein. "Thank God for Men," with a lead vocal by Vicki Randle, a jazz singer who would find fame with the Tonight Show Band in the 1990s, and backup by Weather Girl Izora Armstead, references in its title Patrick Cowley's "Thank God for Music." Finally, "Cuba Libre" features lead vocals by Jolo (Jo-Carol Block and Lauren Carter, formerly of the Patrick Cowley Singers), only the first of several collaborations between the jazz vocalists and Rocketry over the course of the 1980s.

Blecman marketed Modern Rocketry as the gayest iteration of San Francisco dance music yet, fibbing to *Billboard* that, "Yes . . . the group and the music are gay and glad of it."[32] The gay characters Kessie and Goldstein played as Modern Rocketry evoked the utopian atmosphere they had encountered at a Galleria megaparty, where, Goldstein gushed to a reporter, "the music was hot, all these men were dancing, and it seemed as though everybody was feeling good about having a good time—it was beautiful!," and therefore, "We tried to put that feeling into 'Homosexuality.'"[33] Megatone made a music video for "Homosexuality" featuring footage of the 1984 International Mr. Leather competition, the Reno National Gay Rodeo, and the San Francisco Gay Day parade, including Sylvester dancing on a float.

This is a very specific version of homosexuality: Shots of Goldstein singing "Just flew in from San Francisco, where they take me as I am," in a black leather jacket and jeans, with short-cropped hair and a cigarette, intercut among the documentary footage, his clone look, white, muscular, and macho, matches that of nearly all the other men shown at these events. This subculture was on its way out by 1985, but its successful imitation by a straight musician shows how firmly this stereotype was holding on in the face of the community's devastation. Goldstein's wife, SFX singer Katie Guthorn, loved the passionate response he would receive when on tour, particularly in Europe and Mexico, where she remembers "Morey singing Homosexuality on a stage to 1,500 basically 15-year-old boys. It was amazing. They were throwing stuff, throwing socks at him, and trying to climb up on the stage."[34] After most of the gay performers had left the scene, Modern Rocketry was able to reproduce for Megatone the sound that had put San Francisco on the map. But it was the good intentions of Blecman that nearly brought Megatone down in the end.

Patrick Cowley Megamedley

Six months after Patrick Cowley's death, surviving Megatone owner Marty Blecman wanted to do something to benefit people with AIDS and hit upon

EVERYTHING FALLS APART   221

the idea of a special memorial 12-inch "megamix" of Cowley's hits. He announced on May 7, 1983, that "100% of Megatone's worldwide profits from this record will be donated to GMHC [Gay Men's Health Crisis] to help fight AIDS," and solicited direct donations as well as matching contributions from foundation sources.[35] Tommy Williams's megamix was an unremarkable medley that nevertheless sold well, more than 15,000 copies by the end of 1983. Blecman's next moves were serious errors in judgment. In September 1983, he sent the GMHC a check for $735.08, reporting that only 5,800 copies had been sold, earning a gross of $13,000 and a profit of 12 cents per record.[36] "We thought the amount he sent us originally seemed like a reasonable amount. We didn't know how much he sold," GMHC public relations director Mark Chataway told a reporter later.[37] An investigation by the *Bay Area Reporter* in January 1985, however, uncovered a different story. In addition to the higher number of records sold, profits were more like $1.70 per record. Two sources close to Blecman told the *Reporter* that total profits were closer to $35,000; one said "Marty told me 'there must be at least $35,000 I owe AIDS in royalties,'" and another that Blecman said "I hope they never catch me . . . I only made a token payment to AIDS."[38]

Megatone, like Moby Dick and most other independent dance labels, was hurting throughout 1984, and not just from the growing AIDS crisis. The major labels had decided, after a five-year break, to return to the 12-inch dance market, and a shift in aesthetics from high-energy to rock in mainstream dance music found independents struggling to compete.[39] By the time the GMHC sued Megatone and Blecman, the business was faltering and, as Blecman acknowledged, "I just took them as another creditor."[40] In January 1985, Blecman made a good-faith payment of $1,000 to the charity, promising to continue equal payments each month, but after three months, the amount decreased to $250, and in June 1985, he was arrested at his home (which was also the Megatone office) and his records were seized from his accountant's office on upper Market Street.[41] He paid the group $11,156 on August 8, 1985, selling his car and taking out a personal loan, but the prosecutor continued the case, stating at the time, "We are not clear that he has paid the full amount owed to the charity."[42]

Blecman eventually pled guilty to a charge of "false representation concerning the purpose for which money is solicited for a charitable purpose."[43] He was given a six-month suspended county jail sentence with three years probation, 1,000 hours of community service to the Shanti Project (a local AIDS organization), and a $1,000 payment to the GMHC. The entire situation could have been prevented if Blecman had just been more careful about his wording. As lawyer Steven Ames Brown observed, "All he had to say was,

'A portion of the proceeds will be given to charity.' Instead, the idiot said '100% of the profits' and then he didn't pay. So what he did was really stupid, just completely stupid. He wanted to do something, but he was in over his head, and he did it in a way that was reckless, and it led to criminal liability."[44]

With the case over, Blecman returned to the running of Megatone, but he found that, understandably, public sentiment in the gay community had turned against him and Megatone. John Hedges and Barry Blum had produced a new single for Jolo, "Last Call," and it entered *Billboard*'s dance chart at the beginning of December 1984. "That record was extremely well-received and flying up the charts," Hedges recalls, "and then there was the big Megatone scandal . . . And so everybody's boycotting anything on Megatone, all our records dropped off the charts and none of the DJs would play it and took a while to get back on our feet, took years. We never really recovered from that, quite frankly."[45]

While San Francisco continued to produce the occasional hit dance record, their heyday at the center of the scene was over. Bay Area dance music increasingly seemed to be retrospective in nature, wistfully nostalgic, as in the conclusion to Boys Town Gang's "Dance Trance Medley," where a chorus gradually fades over the words, repeated as if lost in a dream, "When I was young, I'd go out to the disco, dancing . . . So fine, so fine." For the generation that had found in dance music a manifestation of their newfound freedom, the comfort of memory was like a respite in the face of the hell they now faced. The next and final chapter reckons with the legacy of the San Francisco sound, a legacy still very much with us today.

12

In Retrospect

Sylvester's Ten-Year Retrospective

On February 4, 1984, Sylvester performed at the Castro Theatre. The two shows, at 8:00 p.m. and midnight, were the first time he'd performed live in the city in over two years, and were a celebration of his "ten years as a recording artist" (although he had actually been recording for fourteen).[1] At his midnight concert, which Sylvester dedicated "to the gay people of San Francisco and to a city that he loves very much," Allen White presented him with a Cable Car award commemorating his placement in the Hall of Fame.[2] Sylvester's triumph that night, manifested in the hometown hero's welcome he was given, belied the retrospective nature of this praise.[3] These concerts marked an unconscious acknowledgment that the forward-looking sounds of the future for which San Francisco's dance music had been known now could be understood as part of its past.

Dance music had moved on, taking its influences from other places, from Chicago, New York, and further afield. Not that anyone in San Francisco was overly concerned at the time. In 1984, most urban gay men had more important things to worry about, and a comforting revel in the glories of the past was exactly what they needed. Despite the appearance of a party guest quietly going out the side door, or of a star gradually fizzling out, the reality was that the sound created in San Francisco had simply immigrated overseas. Its artists could be proud knowing that the club sound they had created (hewn of its more subversive gayness) permeated mainstream popular music around the world. Artists such as Kylie Minogue, Dead or Alive, Rick Astley, Pet Shop Boys, and Erasure to a large extent owed their success to the music first created in the gay mecca, in the dark and dirty bathhouses and late-night discos, the gloriously debauched megaparties, but most of all in the minds of those for whom the music represented their own liberation.

Menergy. Louis Niebur, Oxford University Press. © Oxford University Press 2022.
DOI: 10.1093/oso/9780197511077.003.0013

224 MENERGY

By the middle of the decade most people outside of the Bay had already forgotten San Francisco's place in high energy's creation. In November 1985, British newsletter *Dance Music Report* stated, "It is generally regarded in the United Kingdom that two people gave rise, development and direction to what we today call 'high energy' disco," giving credit to Ian Levine and Record Shack Records financier Geoff Weston.[4] Levine's "So Many Men (So Little Time) "became the example from which all other productions of this new brood would be measured."[5] Levine, adopting like most other scenesters the new term "Hi-NRG" coined by British music journalist James Hamilton, proudly boasted that "he and the Northern Soul fraternity of old who are active in NRG production today contribute 90% of all product to the market."[6] In the United Kingdom, the aesthetic of high-energy music was assimilated into mainstream pop throughout 1984 and 1985, particularly through the output of producers Stock, Aitken, and Waterman, and its association with gay culture would be further diluted by an industry name change to "Eurobeat" in 1986. As New York DJ and music critic Casey Jones noted, "With the fear and loathing generated by the paranoia that has been born of AIDS, the association with the fatal condition and anything gay-served or spawned like Hi-NRG has come under scrutiny as being a wart whose potential spread is thwarted," so despite the sounds permeating most contemporary pop music, any music that emphasized the gay origins of the style was considered undesirable.[7]

In the intervening years, with very few surviving San Francisco musicians left to claim their legacy, British artists and producers have been only too happy to continue to erase high-energy dance music's gay San Francisco past. For example, in 2002, Jeremy Norman, the founder of legendary London nightclub Heaven, claimed his club "started the craze for high energy music, which transferred itself to the Saint in New York, and became a popular dance genre," ignoring the Trocadero Transfer's three-year head start on that front. Fiachra Trench, songwriter and frequent collaborator of Ian Levine, also claimed in 2002 that after the death of disco in 1979, "within a matter of a few years we came up with the high energy concept, and the first big hit we had . . . was with Miquel Brown, "So Many Men, So Little Time," restating the mistaken notion that Brown's song was the first high-energy song.

Levine himself has been the most blatantly misleading in interviews since the start of the new millennium. In a self-directed documentary film claiming to be a "history of high energy dance music," Levine proudly holds himself up as single-handedly inventing the genre:

I was fortunate enough in the eighties to be able to pioneer a whole movement in dance music. [After the death of disco] I longed to get back into
making records again, and an old record I made in the seventies, by a
group called D'llegance called "Chanson D'llegance" which I'd done with a
partner of mine in Los Angeles called Rick Gianatos, that was put out, like
three years after we made it [1982], and it made a bit of a buzz not only on
the club charts in America, but also on the new, what was known as the Gay
Disco Boys Town Gang, er, Boys Town market in England.[8]

I'm unable to find "Chanson D'llegance" on any US dance charts in 1982
or '83 before Miquel Brown's May 1983 chart success, which is unsurprising
given its very 1970s, classic disco sound, completely alien to the electro,
dance rock, and high-energy sounds dominating those charts at the time. But
retroactively positioning that song as "high energy" is essential to Levine's
historical project, one he is keen to have associated with "Boys Town Gang,
er, Boys Town" dance charts (the slip of the tongue is telling), named not only
after the common nickname given to many big city's gay ghettos but also to
the San Francisco group that made that brand of high-energy dance music
popular in the first place.

Ken Alan

Despite the intense competition from abroad, there were several notable
successes from San Francisco after the mid-eighties, and Megatone Records
lasted to the end of the decade. A minor Megatone miracle arrived in 1986
in the form of fitness instructor and DJ Ken Alan. Since the late 1970s in
Provincetown, Alan had made his own tapes of disco and dance music in a
continuous mix for his fitness classes—one of the first instructors to do so.
By the mid-1980s, he had relocated to Los Angeles and was teaching classes
in area gyms, flying up to San Francisco frequently for the nightlife, particularly the Trocadero Transfer. He approached Marty Blecman one night with
the notion of putting together a compilation for fitness classes, an album of
specially sequenced songs from Megatone's back catalog chosen to conform
to the format of a standard aerobics class. Alan persuaded Blecman by telling
him, "it won't cost you anything other than printing the records. We can
start off with a thousand, and I will buy them from you wholesale."[9] Working
with fellow DJ Randy Sills, Alan chose older Megatone tracks by Sylvester

226   MENERGY

and Modern Rocketry, and newer releases by Billy Preston, Scherrie Payne, and Jeanie Tracy. They were all pleasantly surprised when the album sold out quickly, as did the next few reprints. A sequel came out in 1988, which also sold well.

Blecman Takes a Back Seat

Even with this success, and the influx of new, talented producers and performers such as Nick John, Ernest Kohl, and David Diebold, in the aftermath of the GMHC debacle (see Chapter 11), Blecman began to take a back seat in the running of Megatone, and increasingly devoted his time to AIDS activism and ACT UP. After the death of roommate Terry Sutton, he protested the US Food and Drug Administration's delays in providing access to experimental drugs and participated in a disruption of the opening night at the San Francisco Opera in fall 1989, where activists were attacked and maced by police.[10] He also, perhaps improbably, enjoyed success as a stand-up comedian, appearing numerous times alongside his old friend and former roommate Danny Williams at the El Rio club.

In 1988, Megatone hosted a launch party at the reopened Dreamland for David Diebold, whose self-published book, *Tribal Rites*, was the first attempt to tell the story of the San Francisco sound.[11] Everyone healthy enough attended: Frank Loverde, Jo-Carol Block, John Hedges, Sylvester, Linda Imperial, Marty Blecman, and many others. It was very much a celebration of their legacy, and something of a last hurrah for many of these artists. In the summer of 1989, Blecman appointed Diebold General Manager of Megatone, who in addition to continuing to release Hi-NRG recordings, set up two sublabels, Megatone House Records and Mega-Tech Records.[12]

The writing was on the wall, however, and after the AIDS-related deaths of Sylvester in 1988, and his manager Tim McKenna and Frank Loverde a little over a year later, Blecman sold the entire Megatone catalog to John Hedges.[13] Blecman died in 1991. The label was in disarray, and, like many other small imprints, they still owed money to several of their musicians, particularly Morey Goldstein and Ken Kessie. McKenna managed most Megatone artists, and his death only confused the financial situation further. Katie Guthorn recalls the air of defeat that hung over the label in its final years: "When everybody at Megatone died, except Leo [Frappier], that just sort of crushed us. And Morey and Ken were really demoralized by Sylvester and McKenna dying and owing them so much money. And I think the last few records on Megatone, it was us girls singing them, but they were almost like disco aerobics records."[14] Indeed, the only releases keeping the label afloat at the very end were the Alan fitness compilations and the occasional new single, such as Jo-Carol Block and Leo Frappier's "Jump Up for Love," with its "Aerobic" and "Go for the Burn" mixes in 1990.

House

Sylvester continued to perform until just before his death, but by second half of the decade, a shift from high-energy to house music in gay clubs demonstrated a fundamental change in the meaning of clubgoing and dancing for many gay people, and a parallel change in the meaning of the Castro itself. As Joshua Gamson explains, "By 1986, the Castro had become almost seedy. Restaurants were emptier; clubs were emptier. There were blocks and blocks of empty parking spaces. People stayed in a lot. No one really knew what to say."[15] Gay men weren't dancing as they once had. In Jerry de Gracia's words at the time, "The tweaked to the tits 'popper in each nostril' discophiles have been supplanted by a more cautious crowd these days."[16] AIDS seemed inescapable for those who were involved in the scene. People were dying everywhere. "Everybody at Trocadero, too," Chris Njirich remembers. "You'd read a different obituary every week. You became afraid to open the paper. But what is weird is the shock you would get every time. 'I just saw him yesterday and he's gone.' It really felt like the end of everything. Nothing ever recovered from it and the parties were never quite what they had been before."[17] And for those involved in making the music so intimately associated with this community, as John Hedges noted, "Watching sales drop—that was us losing our friends."[18]

And for those who did continue to go out, the musical transition from high energy to house represented a turn from the sound of individual liberation shared with a community to one of eschewing individuality for the comfort of solidarity in a time of crisis. As Barry Walters wrote in 1988, "For a while, the politics of dancing shifted from moving ahead to holding onto the small freedoms of pleasure. Now the party lives on in picket lines, in benefits and in rallies to keep those like Sylvester alive."[19] House tracks such as "Strings of Life," "The Promised Land," and "Musical Freedom" offered consolation and hope amid the desolation of AIDS. In such an environment, Megatone's

228   MENERGY

old-fashioned "cruising songs," like Jolo's "Last Call" and Sisley Ferré's "Give Me Your Love," just seemed out of place.

The Final San Francisco Records: Shawn Benson, David Diebold, Kim Cataluna

In his last year, Sylvester's financial situation was precarious as his health expenses mounted, and many people were shocked by his appearance at the 1988 Gay Freedom March where his manager Tim McKenna, sick himself, pushed the singer's wheelchair in front of the "People with AIDS" banner down the parade's route. But just as people were saddened by Sylvester's appearance, they were inspired by his bravery and strength as he smiled and waved to his adoring fans. "A lot of people wanted us to put out a greatest hits LP," McKenna told a reporter in 1988, "I've been resistant because those albums can be so tasteless. But we had to put out something, because Sylvester has nothing to live on . . . There were times when I thought I could bring a mobile recording studio to his home, but I realized that was just me trying to continue like nothing was changed. It's hard to let go sometimes."[20] So many projects, like James Wirrick and Frank Loverde's collaboration, "Crazy Love," Steve Algozino's successful "Zino" alter ego, a full Loverde album, and Lisa's follow-up album, just to name a few, remained unfinished with the deaths of so many artists.

But the survivors and walking wounded never stopped making music, and some great dance records were made in San Francisco in the second half of the decade. Jeanie Tracy's "Don't Leave Me This Way," released on Megatone in 1985 in a remix by Sylvester, served as a direct influence on the UK's Communards' chart-topping version a year later, and was a massive hit in its own right, reaching number 1 on the Hi-NRG dance charts. Tracy would go on to reinvent herself as "Technodiva" in the 1990s, working with Brian Soares to release a series of popular house tracks before his AIDS-related death. David Diebold even opened a new company in 1985, Tunespeak Productions, to produce parties and make dance records, including Soares's high-energy remake of the Olivia Newton John track "Magic."

Tunespeak's greatest contribution to San Francisco dance music, however, was its discovery of singer Shawn Benson, a Trocadero regular who many remembered because he would sing on the dance floor at the top of his lungs. Tunespeak released his first single in 1985, "Male Fraud," a campy, openly

IN RETROSPECT 229

gay track in the tradition of old First Choice songs like "Double Cross" or "Armed and Extremely Dangerous." "I'm a victim of male fraud, taken in by a boy in a man's disguise," Benson wails, in a style not a million miles from Moby Dick's earliest releases. The song was so popular it was remixed and rereleased a year later on Pink Glove Records. His biggest hit was "Seclusion" (1986), produced by John Hedges and Barry Blum, which rose to the number 1 spot on *Dance Music Report*'s Hi-NRG chart.

As late as 1991, Megatone artists were still winning awards; David Diebold and Kim Cataluna were honored as Best Mixed Group/Duo at the Third Annual Hi-NRG Dance Music Awards in New York City for their cover of "White Rabbit," where they were also the event's closing act, joined on stage by another Megatone artist, Ernest Kohl.[21] It was Megatone and Diebold's final victory lap before his death of AIDS-related illness a year later.

The label's last official release was Kohl's techno house 12-inch "Hold On to Life," in 1993, which featured Linda Imperial, Jo-Carol Block, and Jeanie Tracy (credited as "The Original Fabulashes," a name bestowed on them as Sylvester's backup singers on several of his Megatone albums), and special remixes by John Hedges and Lester Temple. "When the world seems endless and long, and all your friends are gone," Kohl and the Fabulashes sing, "find the strength within, 'cause you know you can win." The song is both a fitting tribute to and acknowledgment of the loss of so many and the effort required to continue in the face of such tragedy. The magnitude of the plague only struck singer Linda Imperial much later: "I didn't really understand until everyone, I mean, the president of our label, my manager, my singing partner for 30 years. Everyone just went off across the board."[22]

The Legacy of the San Francisco Sound

When San Francisco emerged as a center for high-energy dance music, it was but one expression of the city's place as the world's leader in gay liberation. AIDS served to concentrate the political power and drive of the city's population, and subsequent generations of activists have continued the struggle alongside the desire to move their bodies together in dance. With a series of owner and format changes throughout the 1990s and 2000s, the Trocadero Transfer also moved with the times, and the building survived when many of its inhabitants did not. DJ Mike Lewis remembered in the late 1980s, "A lot of people . . . just will not go back to Troc due to the AIDS situation . . . A lot

230 MENERGY

of people can't face the old feelings, the intimacy we once shared because of vague feelings of guilt for friends passed away."[23] By 1984, with the death of so many party promoters, the megaparties had been reduced to only a few each year, and the I-Beam had faced such a drop in gay business that it was only gay on Sunday nights.

But, just as music production shifted to other places, new centers picked up on the model perfected by San Francisco party planners. The circuit party, the worldwide phenomenon of massive gay dance parties headlined by the world's leading DJs, is a direct descendent of the San Francisco megaparties hosted by Conceptual Entertainment and Michael Maletta's Gay Community Center events starting in the late 1970s. The similarities are striking, including the continuing and familiar criticism of the circuit party's exclusivity and physical and racial homogeneity, while still capitalizing on the financial privilege of the participants to raise huge amounts of money for AIDS research and other charitable causes. House music from Chicago, Detroit, and New York supplanted high energy on the queer dance floors of America in the second half of the 1980s and has dominated ever since, but since 2000, as spinners have started digging into our collective musical past, they have also begun to incorporate high energy's swirling electronics and camp sensibility. The various forms of house that emerged on the circuit party scene are only a small step away from the electronic dance music of Megatone and Moby Dick. The tribal house sounds of Junior Vasquez in the 1990s and his protégés DJ Paulo and DJ Abel (with his trademark "tribal cha-cha" sound), the swirling diva house sets of Kitty Glitter, and Corey Craig and the West Coast's DJ Dan all carry on the tradition of synthesizer-rich, diva-heavy, driving four-on-the-floor dance beats for a mostly queer audience.

And the sound has certainly filtered through to mainstream pop. In fact, it's hard to find current music not influenced by disco, and the hypersexualized high-energy sound of San Francisco is a frequent go-to for postmodern pop artists. Musicians such as Dua Lipa, Steps, Róisín Murphy, Robyn, and Alex Newell have all interpreted disco through an electronic high-energy lens. On Kylie Minogue's 2020 release, *Disco*, songs like "Starstruck" and "Where Does the DJ Go" bypass the "cleaned up" British form of Hi-NRG her original producers Stock, Aitken, and Waterman used to launch her into the pop world in the mid-1980s for the sensual, proudly discofied hedonism of San Francisco. For gender-nonconforming singer Alex Newell, DJ Cassidy wrote the song "Kill the Lights" as a tribute to Sylvester's spirit, and the music video for that chart-topping song recreated the iconic "You Make Me Feel (Mighty Real)" video, complete with sequined singer and dancing cocktail waitresses.[24] Sylvester's musical legacy has also been honored in a more official capacity. The US Library of Congress selected "You Make Me Feel (Mighty Real)" for inclusion in the National Recording Registry, which selects recordings that are "culturally, historically, or aesthetically significant." Pet Shop Boys, whose appreciation for the San Francisco sound goes back decades, openly acknowledged the debt their music owes to Patrick Cowley, specifically on their 2013 track "Axis," which emulates the buzzy, warm synths of "Menergy."

The rediscovery of Patrick Cowley by a new generation began in earnest in 2009 with the first of (to date) eight collections of his previously unreleased music by Dark Entries Records and Honey Soundsystem, which have received glowing reviews in the press across the spectrum, including the *New York Times*, the *Guardian*, and many others.[25] Pitchfork critic Jesse Dorris's writing has been typical of the modern reevaluations of Cowley, positioning him as "a trailblazer: a gay man making gay music for a gay audience and their admirers."[26] Journalist Matt Cotsell has similarly called Cowley's music "the sonic equivalent of opening a bottle of amyl nitrate."[27] And, indeed, the education of young queer people provided a fundamental motivation for those reissuing his music as Honey Soundsystem producer Jacob Sperber has noted: "It's a way to reconnect with an awful but important part of queer history, the onset of AIDS. It's our responsibility to tell that story, because there's a generational gap; there are young people getting into these records now, but only so many people who were actually there."[28] The 2019 publication of Cowley's diary, a guide to his sexual exploits throughout the San Francisco of the 1970s, only added to his reputation as one of that decade's most important gay artists.[29] At least outside of academia, the reevaluation of the San Francisco sound is well underway.

On May 26, 2021, as the world began to reemerge from the COVID-19 pandemic, the SoMa drag and cabaret nightclub Oasis unveiled a mural of Sylvester facing onto busy 11th Street. At the dedication ceremony Supervisor Matt Haney and aide Honey Mahogany introduced artist Josh Katz, who explained, "I wanted to create a mural dedicated to San Francisco's vibrant queer history, and that could uplift folks after an incredibly challenging year. Sylvester is so loved in this city, I knew painting his portrait would remind us of the good times we've had, and those that are sure to come again soon."[30] Dance has always seen us out of dark times. Brian Jones, writing in the early days of AIDS, understood the necessity of dancing, the almost religious freedom it provided, no matter how bleak the situation: "But

232 MENERGY

Disco! Disco could save us in these trying times. Anybody who's bumped and humped and shimmied and shaked as the deejay gooses the spin from 119 up to 126 up to (gasp) 136 beats per minute knows what we're talking here. We're talking Disco Orgasm. And if you ask me, it's every bit as dizzy as the other kind."[31] For Jones though, the solution was not to go to a club, but to retreat into memory, to remind himself of the times before everything fell apart. Putting on his copy of Sylvester's live *Living Proof* album from 1978, he danced alone: "And I shimmie and shake and kick the shit out. And there in the middle when the neighbors are closing their windows and I'm dripping sweat all over the floor and the dishes are rattling and Sylvester announces Patrick Cowley on the piano I burst into tears. But I don't stop dancing no I never stop dancing I couldn't do that or somehow I am afraid actually I am sure, I would not be alive anymore."[32]

The need to dance never went away, and through Cowley's releases, the Remember the Party tributes to the Trocadero Transfer, the Go BANG! events at the Stud and f8, the work of DJ Jim Hopkins and his San Francisco Disco Preservation Society digitization project, and the post–Drag Race emergence of Sylvester as "drag icon" (a label he would have hated, while loving the attention), a new generation of queer people are learning that, despite the passing of so much time and so many forgotten souls, their lost comrades shared the same passion to move their bodies as they do. They are learning that they too want to be a part of a community that dishes together, parties together, and most of all dances together.

Notes

Introduction

1. Martin H. Levine, *Gay Macho* (New York: New York University Press, 1998), 53.
2. Edmund White, *States of Desire: Travels in Gay America* (New York: Plume, 1980), 37.
3. White, *States of Desire*, 37.
4. Sherrie Tucker, *Dance Floor Democracy: The Social Geography of Memory at the Hollywood Canteen* (Durham, NC: Duke University Press, 2014), xxi.
5. *A Different Beat*, September 2, 1976.
6. Alice Echols, *Hot Stuff: Disco and the Remaking of American Culture* (New York: W. W. Norton, 2010).
7. Donald Cameron Scot, *A Different Beat*, August 5, 1976.
8. Scot, *Different Beat*.
9. *A Different Beat*, August 5, 1976.
10. "Gratify Yourself," *A Different Beat*, November 1976.
11. Davitt Sigerson, "Sounds Goes Gay," *Sounds*, August 26, 1978.
12. David Diebold, *Tribal Rites: The San Francisco Dance Music Phenomenon 1978–88* (San Francisco: Time Warp Publishing, 1988), 7.
13. Diebold, *Tribal Rites*, 7.
14. *Gay Life*, September 1978, 70.
15. *Gay Life*, 30.
16. Diebold, *Tribal Rites*, 21.
17. "The Tempest," *Data-Boy* 258, September 18, 1980, 8.
18. Diebold, *Tribal Rites*, 95.
19. Think of Vanessa's "Upside Down (Dizzy Does It Make Me)" (1982) or Digital Emotion's "Go Go Yellow Screen" (1983) for examples of Italodisco's less intensely erotic version of electronic dance music.

Chapter 1

1. Allan Bérube, *Coming Out Under Fire: The History of Gay Men and Women in World War II—Twentieth Anniversary Edition* (Chapel Hill: University of North Carolina Press, 2010).
2. Nan Alamilla Boyd, *Wide Open Town: A History of Queer San Francisco to 1965* (Berkeley: University of California Press, 2003), 53.

234 NOTES

3. George Chauncey, *Gay New York: The Making of the Gay Male World, 1890–1940* (London: Flamingo Press, 1994), 23.
4. Randy Shilts, *The Mayor of Castro Street* (New York: St. Martin's Press, 1982), 173.
5. For the definitive account of the establishment of New York's gay dance scene of the late 1960s and early 1970s, see Tim Lawrence, *Love Saves the Day: A History of American Dance Music Culture, 1970–1979* (Durham, NC: Duke University Press, 2003).
6. John Hedges, interview with author, September 20, 2017.
7. Peter Fisher, *The Gay Mystique: The Myth and Reality of Male Homosexuality* (New York: Stein and Day, 1972), 44.
8. Hedges, interview.
9. "Interview with Bob Damron," *Cruise: The National Magazine of Gay Travel and Entertainment* 4, no. 9, 1979, 12.
10. Hedges, interview.
11. Hedges, interview.
12. Marty Blecman, "Roamin' the Forum, Raising Kane, and Rising Hits," *Advocate*, August 9, 1978.
13. Marty Blecman, *Coast Times*, 1977, 45, GLBT Historical Society, San Francisco.
14. John Geraldo, "Interview: John Hedges and Marty Blecman," *Baseline: Bay Area Disco Report*, February 1979.
15. Hedges, interview.
16. Geraldo, "Interview," 13.
17. Geraldo, "Interview," 13.
18. Janel Bladow, "A Man of Passion," *Villager*, June 2–8, 2010, https://www.amny.com/news/a-man-of-passion-from-fine-food-to-chic-design-jean-denoyer-has-a-zest-for-life/.
19. W. Pate McMichael, "In the Name of the Father," *St Louis*, April 17, 2007, https://www.stlmag.com/In-The-Name-of-The-Father/.
20. "Club: Loverde," *Bay Area Reporter*, March 18, 1976.
21. Review in "Frank Loverde," folder, n.d., source unknown, GLBT Historical Society.
22. "Loverde Returns to the City," *Bay Area Reporter*, June 9, 1977, 32.
23. Ad, *Bay Area Reporter*, October 4, 1972.
24. Ad, *Bay Area Reporter*, July 26, 1972.
25. *Bay Area Reporter*, March 3, 1977, cover.
26. Henri Leleu, "Oil Can Harry's Expands," *Bay Area Reporter*, March 17, 1977, 17.
27. Leleu, "Oil Can Harry's," 17.
28. "Gratify Yourself," *Different Beat*, June 17, 1976.
29. Ad, *Bay Area Reporter*, June 9, 1977, 5.
30. *Bay Area Reporter*, November 19, 1977.
31. Susan Stryker and Jim Van Buskirk, *Gay By the Bay: A History of Queer Culture in the San Francisco Bay Area* (San Francisco: Chronicle Books, 1996), 64.
32. All-American Boy was a clothes store owned by Tim Oviatt at 463 Castro Street, popular among fashionable gays, and according to Randy Shilts was "the quartermaster depot of the 'Castro clone' look." Mick Sinclair, *San Francisco; A Cultural and Literary History* (Northampton, MA: Interlink Publishing, 2013), 219.

NOTES   235

33. Andrew Holleran, "The Petrification of Clonestyle," *Christopher Street*, no. 69, 1982, 14.

34. Benjamin Heim Shepard, *White Nights and Ascending Shadows: An Oral History of the San Francisco AIDS Epidemic* (London: Cassell, 1997), 21.

35. Shilts, *Mayor of Castro Street*, 174.

36. Richard Dearborn, "Hop at the Frog Palace," *San Francisco Gay Life*, no. 1, 1977, 21.

37. "What's New," *San Francisco Gay Life*, no. 4, 1977, 14.

38. Barry Walters, "Sylvester: Staying Alive," *Village Voice*, originally published November 8, 1988. Reprinted online: https://www.villagevoice.com/2020/06/22/sylvester-staying-alive/.

39. "San Francisco The Balcony: Welcome to the Fun House, " *Blueboy*, September 1980, 28–31.

40. Martin P. Levine, *Gay Macho* (New York: New York University Press, 1998), 21. Quoting William Simon and John H. Gagnon, "Sexual Scripts: Permanence and Change," paper presented at American Sociological Association, Detroit, 1973.

41. Levine, *Gay Macho*, 29.

42. Levine, 28.

43. Quoted in Brandon Judell, "Sexual Anarchy," in *Lavender Culture*, ed. Karla Jay and Allen Young (New York: NYU Press, 1994), 138.

44. Judell, "Sexual Anarchy," 139.

45. "Disco Delirious," *Alternate*, February 1978, 14–15.

46. "National Tea Dance," *Different Beat*, August 5, 1976.

47. Wayne Sage, "Disco Fever: What's Behind the Boom of the Super Bars Called Discos?," *Cruise*, August 1976, 15.

48. Sage, "Disco Fever," 16.

49. Richard Dearborn, "The Future of Gay Disco," *American Gay Life*, September 1978, 12.

50. Patricia Nell Warren, *The Front Runner* (New York: Bantam Books, 1974), 66.

51. Walter Hughes, "Mighty Real," *Rock and Roll Quarterly*, Summer 1993.

52. Dan Vojir, *The Sunny Side of Castro Street* (San Francisco: Strawberry Hill Press, 1982), 71–72.

53. Shepard, *White Nights*, 24.

54. Marty Blecman, "Disco Beat Says," unlabeled undated photocopy in Marty Blecman files, GLBT Historical Society.

55. Benji Rubenstein, interview with author, August 30, 2017.

56. Rubenstein, interview.

57. Ira Kamin, "Easy Days, Disco Nights," *San Francisco Chronicle*, August 10, 1979, 35.

58. "Poppers: The Disco 'Drug,' " *Cruise*, April 1978, 53–56.

59. Oscar Quine, "Poppers: How Gay Culture Bottled a Formula that has Broken Down Boundaries," *Independent*, January 2016, https://www.independent.co.uk/life-style/poppers-how-gay-culture-bottled-a-formula-that-has-broken-down-boundaries-a6828466.html.

60. "Rushing to a New High: Poppers with a Risky Bang," *Time*, July 17, 1978, 16.

61. Dearborn, "Hop at the Frog Palace," 21.

236 NOTES

62. Alex Espinoza, *Cruising: An Intimate History of a Radical Pastime* (Los Angeles: Unnamed Press, 2019), 97.

63. Martin Hoffman, *The Gay World* (New York: Basic Books, 1966), 56.

64. Evelyn Hooker, "The Homosexual Community," in *Sexual Deviance*, ed. John H Gagnon and William Simon, with the assistance of Donald E. Carns (New York: Harper & Row, 1967), 175.

65. Hooker, "Homosexual Community," 178.

66. Donald Webster Cory, *The Homosexual in America: A Subjective Approach* (New York: Greenberg, 1951), 121. Hooker, "Homosexual Community," 181.

67. Shepard, *White Nights*, 25.

68. George Heymont, "Opera Companies and Opera Queens," *Christopher Street* 6, no. 9 (1983), 53.

69. Mr. Marcus, "The Star Wore Spurs," *Bay Area Reporter*, August 31, 1978, 33.

70. "Music Review," *Alternate*, December 1977, 42.

71. Mr. Marcus, "The Endangered Species," *Bay Area Reporter*, February 15, 1979, 29.

Chapter 2

1. Steve Fabus, interview with author, October 2, 2016.

2. As Mike Weiss convincingly explores in his analysis of the assassinations. Mike Weiss, *Double Play: The Hidden Passions Behind the Double Assassination of George Moscone and Harvey Milk*, 2nd ed. (San Francisco: Vince Emery Productions, 2010).

3. Bruce Pettit, "Does Improved Housing Displace Blacks?," *Bay Area Reporter*, February 1, 1979, 4.

4. Pettit, "Does Improved Housing Displace Blacks?," 4.

5. Pettit, 4.

6. Pettit, 4.

7. Blackberri, interview with author, December 4, 2017.

8. Kurt Lawson, interview with author, August 30, 2017.

9. Chrysler Sheldon, interview with author, January 20, 2020.

10. Lawson, interview.

11. Sheldon, interview.

12. Sheldon, interview.

13. Mr. Marcus, "Smile 'til It Hurts," *Bay Area Reporter*, March 17, 1977, 13.

14. Pearl Heart was a drag musician who performed mostly Janis Joplin covers. Referred to as "rude, trashy, and much too loud' (*After Dark*, August 1974), she recorded most of an album of Joplin songs, but died of AIDS-related illness in the early 1980s before they could be released. These songs ultimately emerged as a white label pressing in the 1980s. A promotional red flexi-disc was also released promoting the upcoming release of the album. Joey Amoroso was her birth name.

15. "Gratify Yourself," *Different Beat*, July 1977.

16. Lawson, interview.

NOTES   237

17. Lawson, interview.

18. "Castro Disco Refused by Planning Commission," *Bay Area Reporter*, August 31, 1978, 16.

19. Wayne A. Schotten, "Discoteque of the Present," *San Francisco Gay Life*, no. 4 (1977): 29–31.

20. Those seven bars were Gus's Pub (1974–1980), Bradley's Corner (1965–1987), Bones, Maud's Study (1964–1989), and the I-Beam, with two unnamed bars opening in the fall. Noel Hernandez and Ferris Fischer, "Haight: The New Castro?," *Bay Area Reporter*, April 27, 1978, 12.

21. Jack McDonough, "Unprecedented Boom Enlivens the Bay Area," *Billboard*, July 15, 1978, 53.

22. David Diebold, *Tribal Rites: The San Francisco Dance Music Phenomenon 1978–88* (San Francisco: Time Warp Publishing, 1988), 144.

23. The Bolt was a relatively short-lived bar at 1347 Folsom Street, but that location has been the home of many gay bars over the years, including the In-Between, the Cow Palace Saloon, the No-Name Bar, and later the Brig and Powerhouse.

24. Ira Kamin, "Easy Days, Disco Nights," *San Francisco Chronicle*, August 10, 1979, 35.

25. Diebold, *Tribal Rites*, 146.

26. "Castro Disco Refused by Planning Commission," *Bay Area Reporter*, August 31, 1978, 16. The Shed was located at 2275 Market. The owners of Oil Can Harry's, Dan Turner and Bob Charrot, proposed the opening of a disco here, the Village Cabaret, when the Shed closed in 1977. The proposal was unanimously denied by the Planning Commission.

27. Fabus, interview.

28. Schotten, "Discotheque of the Present," 31.

29. *San Francisco Gay Life*, December 21, 1977, 47.

30. David Markham, "They Aren't Dancin'," *Gay American Life*, September 1978, 50.

31. Fabus, interview.

32. Maria Sanchez, "The Beat Steams On!," *Baseline: Bay Area Disco Report*, February 1979.

33. Sanchez, "Beat Steams On!".

34. Andy Thomas, "Nightclubbing: San Francisco's Trocadero Transfer," *Red Bull Music Academy Daily*, September 1, 2014, https://daily.redbullmusicacademy.com/2014/09/nightclubbing-trocadero-transfer.

35. "All-Nite Gay Disco Approved by Appeals Board," *Bay Area Reporter*, January 19, 1978, 7.

36. McDonough, "Unprecedented Boom," 53.

37. McDonough, 53.

38. *San Francisco Gay Life*, December 15, 1977.

39. Ad, *Bay Area Reporter*, August 3, 1978, 27.

40. *Wrecked for Life: The Trip and Magic of Trocadero Transfer*, 1993, dir. John C. Goss.

41. Lester Temple, interview with author, October 1, 2016.

42. Diebold, *Tribal Rites*, 129.

43. *Wrecked for Life*.

238 NOTES

44. *Wrecked for Life*.
45. *Wrecked for Life*.
46. Kamin, "Easy Days," 34–37.
47. Kamin, 34.
48. Kamin, 36.
49. Kamin, 35.
50. Kamin, 35.
51. *Wrecked for Life*.
52. Kamin, "Easy Days," 37.
53. Michael Bronski, *A Queer History of the United States* (Boston: Beacon Press, 2011), 112.
54. Peter Fisher, *The Gay Mystique: The Myth and Reality of Male Homosexuality* (New York: Stein & Day, 1972), 60.
55. George Chauncey, *Gay New York: The Making of the Gay Male World, 1890–1940* (London: Flamingo Press, 1994), 280.
56. Marc Stein, "Rizzo's Raiders, Beaten Beats, and Coffeehouse Culture in 1950s Philadelphia," in *Modern American Queer History*, ed. Allida M. Black (Philadelphia: Temple University Press, 2001), 147.
57. Chauncey, *Gay New York*, 278–279.
58. Chauncey, 257.
59. Chauncey, 259.
60. Fabus, interview.
61. Benjamin Heim Shepard, *White Nights and Ascending Shadows: An Oral History of the San Francisco AIDS Epidemic* (London: Cassell, 1997), 30.
62. "Night Flight," *Alternate* 1, no. 3 (February), 7.
63. Diebold, *Tribal Rites*, 167.
64. Diebold, 167.
65. "Night Flight," *Alternate*, 9.
66. "Night Flight," 9.
67. Shepard, *White Nights*, 62.
68. Mr. Marcus, "Bay Area Rapid Tripe-Writer," *Bay Area Reporter*, January 5, 1978, 27.
69. Ad, *Bay Area Reporter*, April 13, 1978, 40.
70. Mark Abramson, "Friday, April 21, 1978," in *Sex, Drugs and Disco: San Francisco Diaries from the Pre-AIDS Era* (Minnesota Boy Press, 2017), 134.
71. Wakefield Poole, *Dirty Poole* (Maple Shade, NJ: Lethe Press, 2011), 233.
72. Mr. Marcus, "The Good Ole Summertime," *Bay Area Reporter*, August 3, 1978, 35.
73. Shepard, *White Nights*, 30.

Chapter 3

1. Susan Barnes, "Records: The State of the Art in the Bay Area—Can Fantasy Records Break into the Big Time?," *San Francisco Chronicle*, July 6, 1978.

NOTES 239

2. Barnes, "Records."
3. Cliff White, "Harvey Fuqua: The Man Behind Sylvester," *Black Music and Jazz and Disco Music Review*, November 1978, 24–31.
4. Archie Ivy, "Sylvester Is Real," *Soul*, March 18, 1974.
5. Michelle Kidd, "Makin' It: Sylvester/Entertainer," *Journal Unknown*, 1974, Joshua Gamson's private collection.
6. Ad, *Bay Area Reporter*, August 5, 1976, 24.
7. Joshua Gamson, *The Fabulous Sylvester* (New York: Picador, 2005), 114.
8. Gamson, *Fabulous Sylvester*, 116.
9. "Two Tons of Fun," Fantasy publicity material, January 1980.
10. "The Two Tons," *Ebony*, June 1981, 104; and Ruth Stein, "The Bigger the Better," *San Francisco Chronicle*, June 27, 1980.
11. Stein, "Bigger the Better."
12. Gamson, *Fabulous Sylvester*, 117.
13. Stein, "Bigger the Better."
14. This short-lived venue became the Different Strokes disco from 1978 to 1980. Ad, *Bay Area Reporter*, March 3, 1977, 9.
15. Gamson, *Fabulous Sylvester*, 121–128.
16. "The Coquettes," *Advocate*, October 19, 1977.
17. White, "Harvey Fuqua," 24–31.
18. Joel Selvin, "At the Old Waldorf: Sylvester's Potent Combination," *San Francisco Chronicle*, July 22, 1977.
19. Gamson, *Fabulous Sylvester*, 121.
20. Gamson, 119.
21. Richard Dearborn, "Sylvester," *San Francisco Gay Life*, no. 1, 1977, 5–6.
22. "Sylvester: Biography," Fantasy Records, June 1977, Joshua Gamson's private collection.
23. "Sylvester: Biography."
24. Vince Aletti, "July 23, 1977," *The Disco Files 1973–1978* (London: DJHistory.com, n.d.), 310.
25. "No, No Cockettes!," unknown journal, n.d, Joshua Gamson's private collection.
26. Russell Gersten, "Sylvester," *Rolling Stone*, October 6, 1977.
27. Aletti, "July 23, 1977," 310.
28. Vince Aletti's "Essential Disco Discs of 1977" puts Donna Summer's *I Remember Yesterday* at number 3, Village People's debut at number 5, and Kebekelektrik's "Magic Fly" comes in at 27, while the original Space album ranks as the twenty-seventh best album. *Sylvester* doesn't even make it into the top sixty albums, but the "Over and Over" 12-inch does merit fifty-fourth place in the singles list.
29. For example, "DaArla's Disco," *Cruise Atlanta* 2, no. 8, 31.
30. Mark Abramson, "Thursday, February 10, 1977," *Sex, Drugs and Disco: San Francisco Diaries from the Pre-AIDS Era* (Minnesota Boy Press, 2017), 112.
31. Aletti, "July 16, 1977," 308.
32. Disco Central, "Meet the Disco Stars!," *San Francisco Disco News*, December 1977, 5. Publication of Disco Central, record store located at 356 Hyde at Ellis.

240 NOTES

33. Disco Central, "Meet the Disco Stars!," 5.
34. Marty Blecman, "Disco Beat," *San Francisco Disco News*, December 1977, 7.
35. Blecman, "Disco Beat," 7.
36. Andrew Holleran, "The Petrification of Clonestyle," *Christopher Street*, no. 69, 1982, 16.

Chapter 4

1. Kenneth Cowley interview, *Buffalo News*, 1984, taken from Daniel Heinzmann's Patrick Cowley website, as of September 23, 2021 archived at https://web.archive.org/web/20181019030249/http://webs.advance.com.ar/dheinz/.
2. Maurice Tani, "Synths, Sex and San Francisco in the 1970s: Pat, Art, HiNRG and Me," accessed April 4, 2019, http://www.darkentriesrecords.com/synths-sex-san-franci sco-in-the-1970s-pat-art-hinrg-me-by-maurice-tani/.
3. Quote taken from Heinzmann website, as of September 23, 2021 archived at https://web.archive.org/web/20181019030249/http://webs.advance.com.ar/dheinz/.
4. Maurice Tani, interview with author, May 18, 2018.
5. Tani, "Synths."
6. Tani.
7. Short Circuit Productions, c/o Blossom Studios, P.O. Box 5953, 1360 Howard Street, San Francisco, CA, 94103. From letterhead on Heinzmann website, as of September 23, 2021 archived at https://web.archive.org/web/20181019030249/http://webs.adva nce.com.ar/dheinz/.
8. Tani, interview.
9. This material was released in 2016 by Dark Entries Records. *Patrick Cowley and Candida Royale*, Dark Entries, DE-140.
10. They did eventually release his remix, after his success with Sylvester, as Casablanca—FEEL 12 (1982).
11. Tani, interview.
12. Tani, interview.
13. Patrick Cowley, *Mechanical Fantasy Box: The Homoerotic Journal of Patrick Cowley* (San Francisco, CA: Dark Entries Editions, 2020).
14. Sharon Davis, "Sylvester: Master of Divine Decadence," *Blues and Soul & Disco Music Scene*, June 5–18, 1979, 12.
15. Josh Cheon, interview with Linda Imperial for Dark Entries Records and Honey Soundsystem, 2009, accessed June 3, 2021, https://soundcloud.com/darkentriesreco rds/linda-imperial-interview.
16. David Diebold, *Tribal Rites*, 2nd ed. (San Francisco: Time Warp Publishers, 1988), 4. "Kickin' In" was eventually released in 2015 on Honey Soundsystem Records—HNY-009.
17. Ad, "Up, Coming, and Choice," *Bay Area Reporter*, May 25, 1978, 25, 30.

NOTES   241

18. Barney Hoskyns, "Woofers and Tweeters," *New Musical Express*, September 25, 1982, 27; and Michael Branton, with photos by Phil Bray, "Step Two: Disco Dandy Lured to Hollywood," *City Adventure (San Francisco)*, June 1978.

19. D. Lawless, "Sylvester," *San Francisco Sentinel*, June 2, 1978.

20. Branton, "Step Two."

21. Thank you to Erik Leidal for this metaphor used in an unpublished analysis of Sylvester's song.

22. George Lakoff and Mark Johnson, *Metaphors We Live By* (Chicago: University of Chicago Press, 1980), 18–19.

23. Sharon Davis, "Truckin' with Sylvester. . . ," *Blues and Soul & Disco Music Review*, September 12–15, 1978, 16–17.

24. Cliff White, "Harvey Fuqua: The Man Behind Sylvester," *Black Music and Jazz Review*, November 1978, 23.

25. Barbara Graustark with Janet Huck, Peggy Clausen, and Ronald Henkoff, "Disco Takes Over," *Newsweek*, April 2, 1979, 63.

26. Vince Aletti, *The Disco Files 1973-1978* (London: DJHistory.com), 409.

27. Pablo Yoruba Guzman, "Pop Music: Saturday Night Sashay," *New York Daily News*, May 27, 1979.

28. Robert Christgau, "Sylvester Is a Star," *Village Voice*, June 11, 1979, 73.

29. "Album Breakouts," *Cash Box*, July 22, 1978.

30. Brian Chin, "Feeling Mighty Real; Feeling Disco Good," *Gaysweek*, July 17, 1978.

31. Simon Frith, "No Business Like Show Business," *Melody Maker*, July 1979.

32. Frith, "No Business."

33. White, "Harvey Fuqua," 23.

34. Branton, "Step Two."

35. Susan Barnes, "Can Fantasy Records Break Into the Big Time?," *San Francisco Bay Guardian*, July 6, 1978, 13.

36. John E. Abbey, "Sylvester: The Living Proof of Disco's Heat," *Blues and Soul & Disco Music Review*. no. 291, November 20–December 3, 1979, 6.

37. White, "Harvey Fuqua," 23.

Chapter 5

1. "Oil Can Harry's Bash—A Smash" *Bay Area Reporter*, May 26, 1977, 4.

2. Ad, *Bay Area Reporter*, June 9, 1977, 22–23.

3. Roc Sands, "Celebrating Our Third Year: Yesterday, Today, & Tomorrow," *Baseline Bay Area Disco Reporter*, April 1979, 4–5.

4. Marty Blecman, "Disco San Francisco," *Coast to Coast Times*, 1977, 45, photocopy in Marty Blecman file, GLBT Historical Society.

5. Chrysler Sheldon, interview with author, January 20, 2020.

6. Richard Dearborn, "The Future of Gay Disco," *Gay American Life*, September 1978, 10.

242 NOTES

7. Sheldon, interview.
8. Marty Blecman, "Grace Hits SF," *Coast to Coast Times*, n.d., 23.
9. Blecman, "Disco San Francisco," 45.
10. John Hedges, interview with author, September 20, 2017.
11. Susan Barnes, "Can Fantasy Records Break into the Big Time?," *San Francisco Bay Guardian*, July 6, 1978.
12. *Santa Ana Register*, March 20, 1975, and August 8, 1974; *Pasadena Star News*, January 20, 1977.
13. *Arkansas City Traveler*, January 11, 1979.
14. Hedges, interview.
15. Barry Lederer, "Disco Mix," *Billboard*, February 10, 1979, 36.
16. *Arkansas City Traveler*, January 11, 1979.
17. Hedges, interview.
18. Martha Reeves, "Paradise Express: Fantasy," *Blues and Soul & Disco Music Review*, March 13–26, 1979, 12.
19. Barnes, "Fantasy Records," 13.
20. Hedges, interview.
21. Barnes, "Fantasy Records," 11.
22. Barry Lederer, "Disco Mix," *Billboard*, January 13, 1979, 60.
23. Joseph Bomback, interview with author, July 17, 2017.
24. Bomback, interview.
25. Bomback, interview.
26. Bomback, interview.
27. Hedges, interview.
28. In his defense, Tighe was almost certainly anticipating Deborah Washington's live appearance at the Trocadero on October 28 and 29, alongside Divine, Denise McCann, and DJ Tom Savarese as part of "The Monster Party," a "No on 6" anti–Anita Bryant Halloween fundraiser sponsored by the nightclub. Ad, *Bay Area Reporter*, October 26, 1978, 23; Aletti, "October 28, 1978," *The Disco Files 1973–1978* (London: DJHistory. com, n.d.), 438.
29. Richard Dearborn, "Disco Gold," *American Gay Life* 2, no. 1, Marty Blecman file, GLBT Historical Society.
30. John Geraldo, "Interview: John Hedges and Marty Blecman," *Baseline: Bay Area Disco Report*, February 1979.
31. Mr. Marcus, "Have a Cool Yule (& a Frantic 'First')," *Bay Area Reporter*, December 21, 1978, 36.
32. Aaron Whittle, "BADDA Bits," *Baseline: Bay Area Disco Report*, May 1979, 9.
33. Cliff White, "Harvey Fuqua: The Man behind Sylvester," *Black Music and Jazz Review*, November 1978, 23.
34. John E. Abbey, "Sylvester: Step Three . . .," *Blues and Soul & Disco Music Review*, March 13–26, 1979, 10.
35. "Creative Power Does the Circus," *Bay Area Reporter*, August 16, 1979, 20.
36. Barry Lederer, "Disco Mix," *Billboard*, March 17, 1979, 89.
37. Lee Horning, "Tempo Tunes," *Baseline: Bay Area Disco Report*, May 1979, 10.

NOTES 243

38. Barry Lederer, "Disco Mix," *Billboard*, April 21, 1979, 57.
39. Joshua Gamson, *The Fabulous Sylvester* (New York: Picador, 2005), 174.
40. Lederer, "Disco Mix," *Billboard*, April 21, 1979, 57.
41. Gamson, *Fabulous Sylvester*, 170.
42. Jack McDonough, "At S.F. Opera House Sylvester Takes Act into Sacred Ground," *Billboard*, April 14, 1979, 54.
43. Jeanie Tracy, interview with author, May 5, 2017.
44. Tracy, interview.
45. Gamson, *Fabulous Sylvester*, 177.
46. Gamson, 176.
47. Gamson, 176.
48. Martha Wash interview, https://www.youtube.com/watch?v=qURgltat-jw&t=26s, accessed May 6, 2020.
49. Tracy, interview.
50. Tracy, interview.
51. Barry Lederer, "Disco Mix," *Billboard*, October 27, 1979, 62.
52. *New Musical Express*, review, n.d., Gamson personal collection.
53. Tim Rivers, "DishCo," *Baseline Bay Area Disco Report*, April 1979, 7.
54. Barry Lederer, "Disco Mix," *Billboard*, January 26, 1980, 35.
55. Lederer, "Disco Mix," 35.
56. Bomback, interview.
57. Dennis Wadlington, interview with author, April 10, 2017.
58. Bomback, interview.
59. Wadlington, interview.
60. Bomback, interview.
61. Bomback, interview.
62. Bomback, interview.
63. Bomback, interview.
64. Barry Lederer, "Disco Mix," *Billboard*, September 22, 1979, 58.

Chapter 6

1. Disco Demolition organizer DJ Steve Dahl denies that racism, homophobia, and misogyny were a part of his motivation. "I'm worn out from defending myself as a racist homophobe for fronting Disco Demolition at Comiskey Park. This event was not racist, not anti-gay. It is important to me that this is viewed from the lens of 1979. That evening was a declaration of independence from the tyranny of sophistication. I like to think of it as illustrative of the power that radio has to create community and share similarities and frustrations. It is for that magic that I wish to keep the memory severed from those who ascribe hateful motives to a wildly successful radio promotion. We were just kids pissing on a musical genre." Steve Dahl with Dave Hoekstra and Paul Natkin with a foreword by Bob Odenkirk, *Disco Demolition: The Night Disco Died* (Chicago: Curbside Splendor Publishing, 2016), 16.

244 NOTES

2. Mel Cheren, *Keep on Dancin': My Life and the Paradise Garage* (New York: 24 Hours for Life Inc., 2000), 246.

3. Mr. Marcus, "Ah, Leather!," *Bay Area Reporter*, March 13, 1980, 31.

4. "Disco Riot in Massachusetts," *Bay Area Reporter*, May 24, 1979, 14.

5. Cynthia Gorney, "The Legacy of Dan White: A Stronger Gay Community Looks Back at the Tumult," *Washington Post*, January 4, 1984, D13.

6. Fred Rogers, "Elephant Walk Took Brunt of Police Attack in the Castro," Uncle Donald's Castro Street, accessed February 25, 2020, http://thecastro.net/milk/rogers.html).

7. Ad, *Bay Area Reporter*, April 12, 1979, 35; Les Ledbetter, "San Francisco Tense as Violence Follows Murder Trial," *New York Times*, May 23, 1979; Kim Corsaro, "Remembering "White Night": San Francisco's Gay Riot," *San Francisco Bay Times*, May 18, 2006.

8. Steve Fabus, interview with author, October 2, 2016.

9. Fabus, interview.

10. Dennis Hunt, "Disco Clubs: Down But Not Out," *Los Angeles Times*, April 9, 1980, G1.

11. "Disco Clubs."

12. Bill Brewster, "Dancer-Turned-Producer Chris Njirich on the Highs and Lows of San Francisco Disco," DJ History, March 15, 2018, https://daily.redbullmusicacademy.com/2018/03/chris-njirich-interview.

13. Jerry de Gracia, "Dreamland: A Progressive Move," *Bay Area Reporter*, July 30, 1981, 26.

14. Radcliffe Joe, "Disco Survives Its Dip; Future's Bright," *Billboard*, January 5, 1980, 55.

15. Jan Carl Park, "The A-Gay's Disc Jockey: Robbie Leslie and the Politics of the Turntable," Mario Z, *New York Native*, June 1983, 36–37.

16. Jim Farber, "From Disco Sucks to Disco Rocks," *After Dark*, December 1979, 32.

17. Roman Kozak, "Rock Disco Pops in New York Houses," *Billboard*, July 14, 1979, 46, 66.

18. Hunt, "Disco Clubs," G1.

19. Adam Block, "Beyond Disco," *Bay Area Reporter*, February 14, 1980, 28.

20. Lee James, "As I See It," *Cruise Atlanta*, March 6–13, 1980, 20–21.

21. Chrysler Sheldon, interview with author, January 20, 2020.

22. Michael Goldberg, "The Gays and the San Francisco Sound," *San Francisco Examiner*, November 11, 1983.

23. Richard M. Nusser, "Query: Can You Dance To It?," *Billboard*, February 16, 1980, 42, 48.

24. Tim Lawrence, *Life and Death on the New York Dance Floor 1980–1983* (Durham, NC: Duke University Press, 2016), 7.

25. Adam Block, "Dance to New Wave 'n' Rock," *Bay Area Reporter*, August 30, 1979, 21.

26. Jack McDonough, "Bay Area's Disco Craze Seen in Peril with 2 New Rock Venues," *Billboard*, November 10, 1979, 34.

27. Ad, *Bay Area Reporter*, October 11, 1979, 28.

28. Jerry de Gracia, "Old Loves and the 'New Romance,'" *Bay Area Reporter*, October 21, 1981, 33.

NOTES 245

29. Gary Hatun Noguera, interview with author, April 26, 2021.

30. Adam Block, "Rock Dirt," *Bay Area Reporter*, June 19, 1980, 27.

31. Randall Schiller, interview with author, March 10, 2020.

32. Ken Maley, "The Story behind the 1980 Muni Metro Party," Muni Diaries website, January 7, 2013, https://www.munidiaries.com/2013/01/07/the-story-behind-the-1980-muni-metro-party/.

33. Adam Block, "Rock Dirt," *Bay Area Reporter*, July 3, 1980, 26.

34. Radcliffe Joe, "Disco DJ Re-Mix Experts Look to More Flexibility," *Billboard*, November 10, 1979, 61.

35. Paul Grein, "S. F. Disco Pool Split," *Billboard*, April 19, 1980, 72.

36. Grein, "S. F. Disco," 72.

37. David Diebold, *Tribal Rites*, 2nd ed. (San Francisco: Time Warp Publishers, 1988), 155.

38. Dick Nusser, "The Music: It's Evolving, Changing Rapidly," *Billboard*, March 3, 1979, 90.

39. Bernard Lopez, "Bobby Viteritti," Discomusic.com (2002, updated 2017), https://www.discomusic.com/15-bobby-viteritti.

40. Andy Thomas, "Nightclubbing: San Francisco's Trocadero Transfer," *Red Bull Music Academy Daily*, September 1, 2014, https://daily.redbullmusicacademy.com/2014/09/nightclubbing-trocadero-transfer.

41. Thomas, "Nightclubbing."

42. Lopez, "Bobby Viteritti."

43. Lopez.

44. Robbie Leslie, Facebook post, February 22, 2020.

45. This recording and many other DJ sets are available at the San Francisco Disco Preservation Society website, sfdps.org.

46. Dennis Croteau would become a party planner in his own right, as co-producer of Night Shift Productions' parties, and briefly worked for Moby Dick Records. He died of AIDS in 1985 at twenty-seven.

47. Bobby Viteritti, interview with author, February 15, 2019.

48. Viteritti, interview.

49. Viteritti, interview.

50. Viteritti, interview.

51. Viteritti, interview.

52. Thomas, "Nightclubbing."

53. Lopez, "Bobby Viteritti."

54. Maria Sanchez, "Under the Tables," *Baseline: Bay Area Disco Report*, May 1979, 21.

55. Lopez, "Bobby Viteritti."

56. "This is. . . Bobby Viteritti," website of Claes "Discoguy," accessed February 20, 2020, http://disco-disco.com/djs/bobby-v.shtml.

57. Chris Njirich, interview with author, July 29, 2019.

58. Njirich, interview.

59. Njirich, interview. Bobby Viteritti remembers the array as belonging to the J. Geils Band.

246 NOTES

60. Lopez, "Bobby Viteritti."
61. Ad, *Bay Area Reporter*, July 5, 1979, 22.
62. Ads, *Bay Area Reporter*, May 10, 1979, 3; and June 7, 1979, 23.
63. "New Disco Opens," *Bay Area Reporter*, June 7, 1979, 32.
64. Mr. Marcus, "Quo Vadis," *Bay Area Reporter*, June 7, 1979, 34.
65. Mr. Marcus, "Black Dawn: A Party in Leather," *Bay Area Reporter*, May 8, 1980, 32.
66. Barry Lederer, "Disco Mix," *Billboard*, March 8, 1980, 46.
67. Mr. Marcus, "And the Winner is . . .," *Bay Area Reporter*, February 14, 1980, 32.
68. Diebold, *Tribal Rites*, 141.
69. Jack McDonough, "SF Scene: Far from Moribund: Dreamland Setting the Pace," *Billboard*, August 2, 1980, 43, 45.
70. Diebold, *Tribal Rites*, 142.
71. Allen White, "Dreamland Folds Its Wings," *Bay Area Reporter*, October 8, 1981, 8.
72. Diebold, *Tribal Rites*, 141.
73. Brewster, "Dancer-Turned-Producer Chris Njirich."
74. Brewster.
75. Diebold, *Tribal Rites*, 141.
76. Lopez, "Bobby Viteritti."
77. Diebold, *Tribal Rites*, 142.
78. Lopez, "Bobby Viteritti."
79. Lopez.
80. Diebold, *Tribal Rites*, 143.
81. Lopez, "Bobby Viteritti."
82. Lederer, "Disco Mix," 46.
83. Chris Njirich, interview.
84. Block, "Beyond Disco," 28.
85. De Gracia, "Dreamland,", 26.
86. White, "Dreamland Folds," 8.
87. Lopez, "Bobby Viteritti."
88. Lawrence, "White Gay Aesthetic," 10.
89. Lawrence, 10.

Chapter 7

1. Disconet *DJ News*, September 1983.
2. Sylvester, dedication on back cover of Two Tons o' Fun, *Two Tons O' Fun*, Fantasy Honey Records, 1980.
3. Unpublished interview, Gamson personal collection.
4. "Division I-Beam Presents Maneuvers," ad, *Bay Area Reporter*, February 25, 1982, 3; Mr. Marcus, "Bob's Bazaar," *Bay Area Reporter*, March 11, 1982, 29.
5. "Victor Swedosh," *Bay Area Reporter*, December 1, 2005.
6. Disconet *DJ News* 3, program 6, April 1980.

7. Barry Lederer, "Disco Mix," *Billboard*, April 26, 1980, 41.
8. Michael D. Dwyer, *Back to the Fifties: Nostalgia, Hollywood Film, and Popular Music of the Seventies and Eighties* (Oxford University Press, 2015), 10.
9. Dwyer, *Back to the Fifties*, 97.
10. Michael Pickering and Emily Keightley, "The Modalities of Nostalgia." *Current Sociology* 54, no. 6 (2006): 919–941.
11. Dwyer, *Back to the Fifties*, 10; Lawrence Grossberg, "Is Anyone Listening? Does Anybody Care?: On 'The State of Rock,'" in *Microphone Fiends: Youth Music and Youth Culture*, ed. Tricia Rose, 41–58 (New York: Routledge, 1994).
12. Mike Gymnaites, interview with author, November 14, 2019.
13. Gymnaites, interview.
14. Cynthia Manley, email to author, September 9, 2017.
15. The original version of the song on both the Disconet and the *Cruisin' the Streets* albums has not been included on the digital rereleases since 1981. Instead, it has been replaced by a probably contemporary, slightly rearranged, embellished version with added "steel drum" synthesizer filling out the song's once-open texture.
16. *DJ News*, Disconet Volume 4, Program 2, June 1981.
17. Manley, email.
18. Manley, email.
19. "Sex Rock," *Time*, December 29, 1975, 39.
20. Michael Reiss, "It Had to Happen...," *Alternate*, December 1980, 18; "Off the Record," *Bay Area Reporter*, May 21, 1981, 24.
21. Barry Lederer, "Disco Mix," *Billboard*, April 25, 1981, 52.
22. Manley, email.
23. Manley, email.
24. Manley, email.
25. Allen White, "The 1981 Parade: What's Up and What's Missing," *Bay Area Reporter*, June 4, 1981, 15.
26. David Diebold, *Tribal Rites*, 2nd ed. (San Francisco: Time Warp Publishers, 1988), 74.
27. Diebold, *Tribal Rites*, 74.
28. Bobby Viteritti, interview with author, February 15, 2019.
29. Chrysler Sheldon, interview with author, January 20, 2020.
30. Disconet *DJ News*, Volume 4, Program 5, September 1981.
31. Viteritti, interview.
32. "Disco Mix," *Billboard*, August 22, 1981, 48.
33. Richard M. Nusser, "Indies Find Sweet Success on Disco's Top 100 Chart," *Billboard*, February 14, 1981, 44, 47.
34. Barry Lederer, "Disco Mix," *Billboard*, January 30, 1982, 66.
35. "Vinyl by Michoacan," *Castro Times*, February 1982, 26.
36. "Vinyl," 26.
37. Joshua Gamson, *The Fabulous Sylvester* (New York: Picador, 2005), 210.
38. Maurice Tani, "Synths, Sex and San Francisco in the 1970s: Pat, Art, HiNRG and Me," Dark Entries Website, accessed March 3, 2020, http://www.darkentriesrecords.com/synths-sex-san-francisco-in-the-1970s-pat-art-hinrg-me-by-maurice-tani/.

248 NOTES

39. Tim Rivers, "Dish-Co," *Baseline Bay Area Disco Report*, February 1979.
40. Barry Lederer, "Disco Mix," *Billboard*, June 13, 1981, 54.
41. Including Carl Carlton, Stacy Lattisaw, and Angela Bofill. For Bofill's album *Tropical Love*, Cowley added "Sweep-claps" to the first track, "Something about You," and "percussion sound effects" to "Holdin' Out for Love." For Lattisaw, he added "effects" to "Attack of the Name Game." Automatt owner David Rubinson also gave Cowley twenty free hours in the studio (which he ultimately stretched to eighty) in exchange for contributing synthesizer to Carl Carlton's new album *The Bad C.C.* Riding high with his recent hit, "She's a Bad Mama Jama (She's Built, She's Stacked)," Carlton was probably most famous in disco circles for his 1974 floor-filler "Everlasting Love," but he temporarily abandoned his boogie funk sound for pop R&B on the new album.
42. Diebold, *Tribal Rites*, 95.
43. Jon Sugar, "Cocaine for Christ: The Bobby Kent Story," *Bay Area Reporter*, March 28, 1985, 33.
44. Sugar, "Bobby Kent," 33.
45. Bobby Kent, interview with author, October 3, 2018.
46. Kent, interview.
47. Kent, interview.
48. Barry Lederer, "Disco Mix," *Billboard*, January 24, 1981, 46.
49. Lederer, "Disco Mix," *Billboard*, January 24, 1981, 46.
50. Kurt B. Reighley, "Queer to Stay: Megatone Records Keeps on Dancin'," *Outweek*, July 3, 1991, 92.
51. Diebold, *Tribal Rites*, 66.
52. Diebold, 66.
53. Barry Lederer, "Disco Mix," *Billboard*, September 12, 1981, 68.
54. Wally Wallace, flyer, quoted in Jack Frischer, *Gay San Francisco: Eyewitness Drummer*, ed. Mark Hemry (San Francisco: Palm Drive Publishing, 2008), 457–458.
55. Diebold, *Tribal Rites*, 7.
56. Steven Ames Brown, interview with author, November 19, 2019.
57. Ad, *Billboard*, November 7, 1981, 35.
58. "120 Dance Name Change in N.Y. Move," *Billboard*, September 5, 1981, 46; Ad, *Billboard*, November 28, 1981, 60.
59. This is a controversial version of events, but plausible. Viteritti explains that when Unidisc bought the record, they replaced his name on the back with Marty Blecman's, and copies of the record with Viteritti's credit do exist.

Chapter 8

1. David Diebold, *Tribal Rites*, 2nd ed. (San Francisco: Time Warp Publishers, 1988), 6.
2. Jorge Socarrás, "The Man Behind the Menergy," liner notes to *School Daze* DE-052, Dark Entries Records, 2013.

NOTES 249

3. See John Brackett's presentation "Sound, Structure, and Narrative Designs in Patrick Cowley's Synthesizer Soundtracks for Gay Porn," Music and Moving Image Conference, New York University, May 26, 2018, https://www.youtube.com/watch?v=axDRC3bz7M8.

4. Daniel Dylan Wray, "Getting Deep Inside Patrick Cowley, the Greatest Gay Pornography Soundtracker of all Time," *Vice*, December 9, 2015, https://www.vice.com/en_us/article/ez7zkn/getting-deep-inside-patrick-cowley-the-greatest-gay-pornography-soundtracker-of-all-time.

5. All three soundtracks have since been released by Dark Entries Records. *School Daze* DE-052, 2013; *Muscle Up* DE-106, 2015; and *Afternooners* DE-185, 2017.

6. Diebold, *Tribal Rites*, 38.

7. Diebold, 4.

8. John Hedges, interview with author, September 20, 2017.

9. Hedges, interview.

10. Disconet *DJ News* 3, program 7, 1980.

11. Bill Stevenson and Susan Smith, "Megatone—Keeping 'em Dancing," *Gaze Memphis*, August 1982, 13.

12. "Biography of Marty Blecman, One of the Nation's Most Successful Disc Jockeys and Record Producers," publicity document, in Marty Blecman file, GLBT Historical Society.

13. Diebold, *Tribal Rites*, 95.

14. Stevenson, "Megatone," 13.

15. Hedges, interview.

16. Diebold, *Tribal Rites*, 95.

17. Diebold, 6.

18. Barry Lederer, "Disco Mix," *Billboard*, December 5, 1981, 65.

19. Lederer, "Disco Mix," 65.

20. And, besides, only "Menergy" was rerecorded. The version of "I Wanna Take You Home" on the Megatone album was the same as on the Fusion 12-inch.

21. Steven Ames Brown, interview with author, November 19, 2019.

22. Diebold, *Tribal Rites*, 7.

23. Madonna Cowley interview, 2009, Dark Entries Records, https://soundcloud.com/darkentriesrecords/sets/patrick-cowley-interviews.

24. Diebold, *Tribal Rites*, 7.

25. Ian Anthony Stevens, interview with author, May 28, 2020.

26. Stevenson, "Megatone," 13.

27. Jeryl Thompson, interview with author, May 25, 2021.

28. Diebold, *Tribal Rites*, 66.

29. Ad, *Bay Area Reporter*, June 18, 1981, 5.

30. John F. Karr, "Sharon McNight: San Francisco, Bye-Bye," *Bay Area Reporter*, October 29, 1981, 26.

31. Ad, *Cruise Weekly* 6, no. 52 (1981). Acapella Gold, meanwhile, continued a successful career, recording with Tee Carson and the Basie Bandsmen in October 1981, and had a four-month engagement at that venue on December 10 at the Tivoli, capped

250 NOTES

by an appearance at Amnesty International's celebration of Human Rights Day. They had performed at the Berkeley Jazz Festival and the Feather River Festival of Jazz in Marysville and were meant to be one of the headliners at the Conceptual Entertainment party "Safety in the Streets," a benefit for the Community United Against Violence organization, on December 16, 1981, alongside gay rock group David Kelsey and Pure Trash and other prominent local cabaret artists. This party fell through when funding dried up from the sponsoring organization.

32. Diebold, *Tribal Rites*, 67–68.
33. Diebold, 69.
34. Joshua Gamson, *The Fabulous Sylvester* (New York: Picador, 2005), 207.
35. Mr. Marcus, "Chicago: A Leather Odyssey," *Bay Area Reporter*, April 29, 1982, 26.
36. Ad, *Bay Area Reporter*, May 20, 1982, 13.
37. Barry Lederer, "Disco Mix," *Billboard*, March 20, 1982, 59.
38. Cable Car Awards folder, GLBT Historical Society.
39. The other new award, "Outstanding Community Contribution by a Recording Artist," had nominees Meg Christian, the San Francisco Gay Men's Chorus, Paul Parker (for his song "Welcome to Freedom"), Conan, Holly Near, David Reighn, Sharon McKnight, and Teresa Trull. Sylvester won in two categories: "Entertainer of the Year" and a special award created for the occasion, "Outstanding Contribution to Entertainment."
40. Jerry de Gracia, "Cable Car Awards to Honor Outstanding Recording Artist," *Bay Area Reporter*, December 30, 1981, 20.
41. Allen White, "Mammoth Disco Rocks Moscone Center," *Bay Area Reporter*, January 21, 1982, 3.
42. Since the complex opened in 1981, there have been two expansions. The original building is today known as Moscone South.
43. Mr. Marcus, "Starting All Over Again," *Bay Area Reporter*, January 7, 1982, 23.
44. Bob Murphy, "Beyond Another First Encounter," *Bay Area Reporter*, January 21, 1982, 7.
45. Murphy, "First Encounter," 7.
46. Jerry de Gracia, "Tone Deaf," *Bay Area Reporter*, January 28, 1982, 23.
47. Barry Lederer, "Disco Mix," *Billboard*, January 30, 1982, 66.
48. Konstantin Berlandt, "First Encounter," *Bay Area Reporter*, February 4, 1982, 15.
49. Berlandt, "First Encounter," 15.
50. Danielle Goldman, *I Want to Be Ready: Improvised Dance as a Practice of Freedom* (Ann Arbor: University of Michigan Press, 2010), 1–4.
51. Quoted in Sherrie Tucker, *Dance Floor Democracy: The Social Geography of Memory at the Hollywood Canteen* (Durham, NC: Duke University Press, 2014), xxi.
52. Harry Britt, "Saturday Night at Moscone Center," *Bay Area Reporter*, January 21, 1982, 14.
53. Andrew H. Ward, "Dancing in the Dark: Rationalism and the Neglect of Social Dance," in *Dance, Gender and Culture*, ed. Helen Thomas, 16–33 (New York: St. Thomas Press, 1993), 18.

NOTES 251

54. Hot Tracks profile, Steve Algozino, in Hot Tracks notes, author's personal collection.

55. "Hot Tracks Offers Subscription Service," *Billboard*, November 21, 1981, 83; Steffen Spranger, "Do Ya' Wanna dance . . . ?," accessed March 19, 2020, hotdiscomix.de.

56. "Hot Tracks," *Billboard*, 83.

57. Hedges, interview.

58. Barry Blum, interview with author, July 27, 2017.

59. Blum, interview.

60. Blum, interview.

61. Katie Guthorn, interview with author, February 14, 2018.

62. Barry Blum, text message, April 6, 2020.

63. Blum, interview.

64. Blum, interview.

65. Blum, interview.

66. Blum, interview.

67. Hedges, interview.

68. "DJ's Dilemma: Indie or Label Staffer?," *Billboard*, October 3, 1981, 39.

69. Disconet *D. J. News*, July 1981.

70. Blum, interview.

71. Blum, interview.

72. Lisa Fredenthal-Lee, letter to author, May 19, 2020.

73. Diebold, *Tribal Rites*, 46.

74. Blum, interview.

75. Diebold, *Tribal Rites*, 50.

76. Hot Tracks notes, Series 1, Issue 1.

77. Hedges, interview.

78. Hedges, interview.

79. Barry Lederer, "Disco Mix," *Billboard*, February 20, 1982, 33.

80. Robert Lee, interview with author, May 4, 2020.

81. Fredenthal-Lee, letter.

82. Diebold, *Tribal Rites*, 50.

83. Diebold, 50.

84. Jerry de Gracia, "Paul Parker: Mr. Nice Guy and the Dream of Success," *Bay Area Reporter*, April 22, 1982, 23.

85. "Before Dance Music . . . ," The Official Site of Paul Parker, last modified January 20, 2010, http://www.utmosis.net/paulparker/memories/the-early-days.html.

86. Diebold, *Tribal Rites*, 38.

87. Jerry de Gracia, "Gay Music: A Continuing Saga," *Bay Area Reporter*, August 27, 1981, 23.

88. De Gracia, "Gay Music," 23.

89. D. Lawless, "Rock Records," *San Francisco Sentinel*, July 24, 1981, 20.

90. Diebold, *Tribal Rites*, 39.

91. Diebold, 39.

92. Brian Chin, "Dance Trax," *Billboard*, June 5, 1982, 36.

252 NOTES

Chapter 9

1. Randy Shilts, *And the Band Played On, 20th Anniversary Edition*, 2007. "Ch. 4: Foreshadowing," ebook.
2. John Hedges, interview with author, September 20, 2017.
3. David Diebold, *Tribal Rites*, 2nd ed. (San Francisco: Time Warp Publishers, 1988), 10.
4. Nancy E. Stoller, *Lessons from the Damned: Queers, Whores, and Junkies Respond to AIDS* (New York: Routledge, 1998), 34.
5. Frank Howell, "Books," *Bay Area Reporter*, July 6, 1978, 36.
6. Robert K. Bolan, "Medicine, Activism and the Gay Community in San Francisco," in Sally Smith Hughes, *The AIDS Epidemic in San Francisco* Vol. 3, *The Response of Community Physicians, 1981–1984* (Berkeley: University of California, 2000), 10, https://oac.cdlib.org/view?docId=kt1489n6h0&brand=calisphere&doc.view=enti re_text.
7. It appeared over several issues in the *Bay Area Reporter*, for example, through July 1981, just as the first announcements of HIV-related illnesses were reported.
8. Bolan, "Medicine, Activism and the Gay Community," 10–11.
9. Donald I. Abrams, "The KS Clinic, Lymphadenopathy and AIDS-Related Complex, and the County Community Consortium," in Hughes, *AIDS Epidemic in San Francisco* Vol. 2, *The Medical Response, 1981–1984*, 4–5.
10. Abrams, "KS Clinic," 15.
11. Bolan, "Medicine, Activism and the Gay Community," 32–33.
12. Bolan, 32–33.
13. Victoria A. Harden, *AIDS at 30: A History* (Washington, DC: Potomac Books, 2012), loc. 384 of 7086, Kindle.
14. Harvey Thompson, "SF Gay Medical Symposium: Two New Gay Illnesses," *Mom . . . Guess What!*, August 1981, 19; Alvin E. Friedmann-Klein, "Kaposi's Sarcoma in Gay Males," *Baphron* 3, no. 7 (July 1981): 99.
15. CDC, "Kaposi's Sarcoma and *Pneumocystis* Pneumonia among Homosexual Men— New York City and California," *Morbidity and Mortality Weekly Report* 30, no. 25 (1981): 305–308.
16. Friedmann-Klein, "Kaposi's Sarcoma," 99.
17. "Rare Viral Cancer Rouses Fear and Hope," *Campaign*, October 1981, 14.
18. Robert Bolan, "Your Gay Health: New Bugs . . . No Alarm," *Bay Area Reporter*, August 13, 1981, 16.
19. Bolan, "Your Gay Health," 16.
20. "Rare Viral Cancer," *Campaign*, 14.
21. "Gay Cancer," *Gay Community News*, July 18, 1981, 2.
22. Bolan, "Medicine, Activism and the Gay Community," 19.
23. Abrams, "KS Clinic," 4–5.
24. "Rare Viral Cancer," *Campaign*, 14.
25. "New 'Gay' Cancer?," *Gaze*, August 1982, 7.
26. "Acquired Immune Deficiency behind Kaposi's Sarcoma?," *Gaze*, September 1982, 8.
27. "Acquired Immune Deficiency," *Gaze*, 8.

NOTES   253

28. "Acquired Immune Deficiency," *Gaze*, 8.
29. Jean L. Marx, "New Disease Baffles Medical Community," *Science* 217, no. 4560 (1982): 618–621.
30. Marx, "New Disease," 620.
31. Marx, 620.
32. "Health Shorts: 'Gay Men's' Pneumonia," *Bay Area Reporter*, July 2, 1981, 34.
33. Abrams, "KS Clinic," 9.
34. Abrams, 9.
35. Abrams, 9.
36. Bolan, "Medicine, Activism and the Gay Community," 21–22.
37. Bolan, 22.
38. "Stonewall Topics: Gay Cancer and Unregulated Poppers," *Bay Area Reporter*, November 5, 1981, 3.
39. "Stonewall Topics," 3.
40. David T. Durack, "Opportunistic Infections and Kaposi's Sarcoma in Homosexual Men," *New England Journal of Medicine* 305, no. 24 (1981): 1466.
41. Durack, "Opportunistic Infections," 1466–1467.
42. Arthur Evans, "Poppers Are Serious," *Bay Area Reporter*, January 7, 1982, 6.
43. "The Year of the Plain Brown Bottle," *Bay Area Reporter*, January 14, 1982, 3.
44. Harden, *AIDS at 30*, 789–802.
45. "Health Update," *Bay Area Reporter*, January 28, 1982, 26; Arthur J. Ammann, "Pediatric AIDS Immunologist: Advocate for the Children," in Hughes, *AIDS Epidemic*, 3: 19.
46. Charles Everett Koop, *Koop: The Memoirs of America's Family Doctor* (New York: Random House, 1991), 250.
47. Wayne April, "Is the Party Over?," *Bay Area Reporter*, August 19, 1982, 6.
48. Ann Japenga, "Gays Trying to Deal with Fear of Cancer," *Los Angeles Times*, September 28, 1982.
49. Japenga, "Fear of Cancer."
50. Marcus A. Conant, "Founding the KS Clinic, and Continued AIDS Activism," in Hughes, *AIDS Epidemic*, 2: 116–117.
51. Stanley Ross Specht, "Coming Home," *Bay Area Reporter*, June 3, 1982, 3.
52. Japenga, "Fear of Cancer."
53. The product appeared in ads in prominent gay publications, including *Bay Area Reporter*, April 22, 1982, 17; and the *San Francisco Sentinel*, April 29, 1982, 12.
54. Ad, *Bay Area Reporter*, April 22, 1982, 17.
55. Jason Serinus, "Home Remedies," *Bay Area Reporter*, January 14, 1982, 7.
56. Japenga, "Fear of Cancer."
57. Charles Kaiser, *The Gay Metropolis* (New York: Grove Press, 1997), 283.
58. Wayne April, "Is the Party Over?," *Bay Area Reporter*, August 19, 1982, 6.
59. Arthur Evans, "A Smashed Dream," *Bay Area Reporter*, December 30, 1982, 9.
60. Evans, "Smashed Dream," 9.
61. Eric Hellman, "The Tyranny of the Mental Ghetto," *San Francisco Sentinel*, September 18, 1981, 4.

254 NOTES

62. Rick Weatherly, "Pecs, Fuchsia Jockstraps and the Spirit of God," *Bay Area Reporter*, May 27, 1982, 13.

63. Paul Lorch, "How Does It Go with AIDS: Part II—Life with AIDS," *Bay Area Reporter*, May 26, 1983, 6.

64. David L Heranney, "I Pass, This Time," *Bay Area Reporter*, May 26, 1983, 6.

65. Benjamin Heim Shepard, *White Nights and Ascending Shadows: An Oral History of the San Francisco AIDS Epidemic* (London: Cassell, 1997), 61.

66. Diebold, *Tribal Rites*, 9.

67. Diebold, 9.

68. Diebold, 9.

69. Both Sylvester and the Two Tons o' Fun sued Fantasy/Honey Records for money they never received. Sylvester eventually won the suit against Harvey Fuqua and Nancy Pitts for a judgment of $218,112.50. While he never received the full amount they eventually agreed to sign over all publishing rights to the music recorded at Fantasy and Fantasy/Honey. Joshua Gamson, *The Fabulous Sylvester* (New York: Picador, 2005), 212; John E. Abbey, "Life after Disco," *Blues and Soul and Disco Music Report*, March 27–April 9, 1984, 15.

70. Gamson, *Fabulous Sylvester*, 209.

71. Abbey, "Life after Disco," 15.

72. Diebold, *Tribal Rites*, 10.

73. The melody itself dates back to the mid-nineteenth century, in the musical *Grand Chinese Spectacle of Aladdin or The Wonderful Lamp*, and has no connection at all to any preexisting Asian melody.

74. Brian Chin, "Dance Trax," *Billboard*, July 24, 1982, 44.

75. Jerry de Gracia, "Megatone Dance Tracks Hit Charts," *Bay Area Reporter*, August 5, 1982, 21.

76. De Gracia, "Megatone Dance Tracks," 21.

77. Hedges, interview.

78. Diebold, *Tribal Rites*, 10.

79. Hedges, interview.

80. Diebold, *Tribal Rites*, 10.

81. Jan Carl Park, "The Party Will Still Be There When You Get Back: A Conversation with Sylvester," *Christopher Street*, December 1982, 45.

82. Allen White, "Conceptual Entertainment Launches New Projects," *Bay Area Reporter*, February 25, 1982, 8.

83. Tom Waddell, "Update '82 Olympics: Gathering for August," *Bay Area Reporter*, April 8, 1982, 25; Allen White, "Big Shows Set for Summer," *Bay Area Reporter*, April 22, 1982, 4.

84. Mike Hippler, "Walking a Tightrope: People behind the Big Parties," *Bay Area Reporter*, May 19, 1983, 18.

85. John Carollo, interview with author, August 2, 2019.

86. Diebold, *Tribal Rites*, 11.

87. Diebold, 11.

NOTES   255

88. Linda Imperial, interview with Josh Cheon for Dark Entries Records and Honey Soundsystem, 2009, https://soundcloud.com/darkentriesrecords/linda-imperial-interview.
89. Chris Njirich, interview with author, July 29, 2019.
90. Diebold, *Tribal Rites*, 13.
91. Linda Imperial, interview, 2009.

Chapter 10

1. John E. Abbey, "Sylvester's Transition," *Blues and Soul and Disco Music Review*, March 11–24,1980, 18.
2. Abbey, "Sylvester's Transition," 18.
3. As did, predictably, the gay music critics invested in rock and R&B, such as D. Lawless, who wrote that "Sylvester butches it up a bit" in a production that "moves out of the straightjacket of disco redundancy and into the Doobie Brothers–like neo-Motown sunniness that's become synonymous with California pop/soul." D. Lawless, "Rock Records," *San Francisco Sentinel*, June 12, 1981, 20; Guy Trebay, "I, a Man: Sylvester's Story," August 19, 1981, Joshua Gamson's personal collection (probably published in the *Village Voice*). Mainstream rave reviews also include Brian Chin, "Disco File," *Record World*, May 23, 1981, 20; and Barry Lederer, "Disco Mix," *Billboard*, May 23, 1981, 59.
4. John E. Abbey, "Sylvester without Frills," *Blues and Soul and Disco Music Review*, August 11–24, 1981, 20.
5. Patrick Dieli, "Taking It to the Street: A Conversation with San Francisco's Very Own, Sylvester," *Castro Times*, August 10, 1981, 20.
6. Dieli, "Taking It to the Street," 20.
7. Dieli, 20.
8. Adam Block, "Sylvester: There's Trouble in Paradise," *The Advocate*, December 8, 1983, 52.
9. Joshua Gamson, *The Fabulous Sylvester* (New York: Picador, 2005), 194.
10. Gamson, *Fabulous Sylvester*, 192.
11. Joel Selvin, "Castles, Churches for a Star," November 26, 1980, Joshua Gamson's personal collection.
12. Gamson, *Fabulous Sylvester*, 194.
13. Jerry de Gracia and Jon Seifer, "A Decade of Faaabulous Falsetto," *Bay Area Reporter*, January 19, 1984, 20.
14. John E. Abbey, "Life after Disco," *Blues and Soul and Disco Music Review*, March 27–April 9, 1984, 14.
15. Jerry de Gracia, "Megatone Dance Tracks Hit Charts," *Bay Area Reporter*, August 5, 1982, 21.
16. de Gracia, "Megatone Dance," 21.

256 NOTES

17. Donald Mclean, "Donald Mclean's Critic's Corner," *San Francisco Sentinel*, January 6, 1983, 9.
18. Brian Chin, "Dance Trax," *Billboard*, January 8, 1983, 60.
19. Karl Stewart, "My Knights in Leather," *Bay Area Reporter*, December 30, 1982, 28.
20. Sylvester claimed at different times he was "the first Black artist to have a video shown on MTV," or the "third by an African-American to be on MTV," but neither of these were the case. It *is* true that he was among the first though. De Gracia and Seifer, "A Decade of Faaabulous Falsetto," 20; Block, "Trouble in Paradise."
21. Sylvester discusses his audience in a radio interview from January 1984, "Trouble in Paradise Remix," Joshua Gamson's personal collection.
22. Block, "Trouble in Paradise," 53.
23. Block, 53.
24. Jan Carl Park, "The Party Will Still Be There When You Get Back: A Conversation with Sylvester," *Christopher Street*, December 1982, 42.
25. Romeo Holloway, "Values Misplaced," *Bay Area Reporter*, December 30, 1982, 7.
26. Park, "Party Will Still Be There," 42.
27. Jerry de Gracia, "Tone Deaf," *Bay Area Reporter*, April 15, 1982, 21; Robert T. Ford, "Rock and Soul," *Bay Area Reporter*, May 6, 1982, 13.
28. Block, "Trouble in Paradise."
29. Jerry de Gracia, "Dreaming with Mr. Parker," *Bay Area Reporter*, May 19, 1983, 24.
30. Donald Mclean, "Critic's Corner," *San Francisco Sentinel*, May 12, 1983, 6.
31. Brian Chin, "Dance Trax," *Billboard*, May 21, 1983, 45.
32. De Gracia, "Mr. Parker," 24.
33. Bill Johnson, "If Looks Were Everything . . . ," *Gaze Memphis*, November 1982, 6.
34. Johnson, "If Looks Were Everything," 6.
35. Joel Selvin, "Club Townsend's Grand Finale: Audrey Joseph Closing Doors of Popular Venue," *SFGate*, May 21, 2002, https://www.sfgate.com/entertainment/article/Club-Townsend-s-grand-finale-Audrey-Joseph-2820397.php.
36. Selvin, "Club Townsend's Grand Finale."
37. "Sarah Dash: Low Down Dirty Rhythm," *Cruise Atlanta* 8, no. 47 (December 1983): 38.
38. Maurice Tani, interview with author, May 18, 2018.
39. Tani, interview.
40. Tani, interview.
41. Tani, interview.
42. Katie Guthorn, interview with author, February 14, 2018.
43. Tani, interview.
44. Barry Lederer, "Disco Mix," *Billboard*, February 20, 1982, 33.
45. Ad, *Bay Area Reporter*, March 25, 1982, 23.
46. Allen White, "Moby Dick's High Energy: Local Company Has Global Success," *Bay Area Reporter*, May 27, 1982, 21.
47. Linda Imperial, interview with author, October 15, 2018.
48. David Diebold, *Tribal Rites*, 2nd ed. (San Francisco: Time Warp Publishers, 1988), 55.

49. Imperial had been singing a lot of backup outside of Loverde, including on Sylvester's latest Megatone album and on Cowley's *Mindwarp* album.
50. Linda Imperial, interview with Josh Cheon for Dark Entries Records and Honey Soundsystem, 2009, https://soundcloud.com/darkentriesrecords/linda-imperial-interview.
51. Diebold, *Tribal Rites*, 39.
52. Horus Jack Tolson, interview with author, September 28, 2017.
53. Diebold, *Tribal Rites*, 61.
54. Tolson, interview. Linda Imperial's version ultimately was released on Megatone Records in 1985.
55. Brian Chin, "Dance Trax," *Billboard*, June 19, 1982, 48.
56. Danny Baker, "Singles," *New Musical Express*, September 25, 1982, 19.
57. Brian Chin, "Dance Trax," *Billboard*, March 26, 1983, 43; and April 28, 1984, 40.
58. James Hamilton, "Odds 'n' Bods," *Record Mirror*, November 20, 1982.
59. Jerry Gilbert, "Disco Lives: Technological Advances Lead Way as Genre Experiences Growth in Europe," *Billboard*, June 19, 1982, 46.
60. *Cash Box*, February 24, 1979, 42.
61. Steven Ames Brown, interview with author, November 19, 2019.
62. Collin Lane, "Heavyweight Crash Barracks," *Gaze Memphis*, January 1983, 7.
63. Mitchell Morris, "It's Raining Men": The Weather Girls, Gay Subjectivity, and the Erotics of Insatiability," in *Audible Traces: Gender, Identity, and Music,* ed. Elaine Barkin and Lydia Hamessley, 213–229 (Zürich: Carciofoli Verlagshaus, 1999), 221.
64. Morris, "It's Raining Men," 224, 226.
65. Peter Shapiro, *Turn the Beat Around: The Secret History of Disco* (London: Faber & Faber, 2005), 72.
66. "DJ Legends: Ian Levine," accessed June 29, 2020, http://www.dmcworld.net/interviews/dj-legends-ian-levine/.
67. Brian Chin, "Dance Trax," *Billboard*, September 17, 1983, 37.
68. Jerry de Gracia, "The Art of Falling Apart," *Bay Area Reporter*, February 24, 1983, 28.

Chapter 11

1. Benji Rubenstein, interview with author, September 28, 2017.
2. Lester Temple, interview with author, October 1, 2016.
3. "Castro Boy," no label, 1982.
4. Jerry de Gracia, "Music for Boys," *Bay Area Reporter*, September 23, 1982, 21.
5. Barry Blum, text to author, June 6, 2020.
6. Ian Anthony Stephens, interview with author, May 18, 2020.
7. The video for "Invisible Love" can be seen at https://www.youtube.com/watch?v=2jJFQBwVZ-g&feature=youtu.be.
8. Lisa Fredenthal-Lee, letter to author, May 19, 2020.

258 NOTES

9. Horus Jack Tolson, interview with author, September 28, 2017. Mouton's "Heartstop" was released by Hot Tracks in 1984.

10. Lewis himself would incorporate his dub into his own Trocadero Transfer sleaze sets, slowed down to a stultifying 104 BPM, as in a December 1983 set where he followed this by an equally lethargic "Magnifique."

11. Bill Brewster, "Dancer-Turned-Producer Chris Njirich on the Highs and Lows of San Francisco Disco," March 2018, https://daily.redbullmusicacademy.com/2018/03/chris-njirich-interview.

12. David Diebold, *Tribal Rites*, 2nd ed. (San Francisco: Time Warp Publishers, 1988), 109.

13. Diebold, *Tribal Rites*, 109.

14. Diebold, 104–113.

15. Barry Blum, interview with author, July 27, 2017.

16. Stephens, interview.

17. Diebold, *Tribal Rites*, 109.

18. Edward Guthmann, "AIDS Artists Remembered," *San Francisco Examiner: Datebook*, December 7, 1986.

19. Edward Guthmann, "Record Company Devastated by AIDS: Seven Key Men are Dead," *San Francisco Examiner: Datebook*, December 7, 1986.

20. Brian Chin, "Dance Trax," *Billboard*, March 12, 1983, 45.

21. Gary Hatun Noguera, interview with author, April 21, 2021.

22. Leo Frappier, interview with author, March 28, 2018.

23. Frappier, interview.

24. Stephens, interview.

25. Brian Chin, "Dance Trax," *Billboard*, September 1, 1984, 49.

26. Steven Ames Brown, interview with author, November 19, 2019.

27. Brian Chin, "Dance Trax" *Billboard*, November 24, 1984, 54.

28. John Hedges, interview with author, September 20, 2017.

29. Diebold, *Tribal Rites*, 15.

30. Tolson, interview.

31. Brian Chin, "Dance Trax," *Billboard*, September 17, 1983, 37.

32. Kim Freeman, "Grass Route," *Billboard*, June 22, 1985, 77.

33. Jeffrey Wilson, "That Reviewer Was Opinionated!," *Bay Area Reporter*, December 4, 1986, 7.

34. Katie Guthorn, interview with author, February 14, 2018.

35. Brian Chin, "Dance Trax," *Billboard*, May 14, 1983, 34.

36. Brian Jones, "Record Company Keeps Fund-Raising Profits: Megatone Withholds 20,000 Promised to NY AIDS Charity," *Bay Area Reporter*, January 24, 1985, 2.

37. Ira Kleinberg, "GMHC Gets Check from SF's Megatone," *Sentinel USA*, January 31, 1986, 2.

38. Jones, "Record Company," 2.

39. Fred Goodman, "12-Inchers: Majors Move In. Indies Express Concern," *Billboard*, July 28, 1984, 1, 66.

40. Kleinberg, "GMHC Gets Check," 2.

NOTES 259

41. Brian Jones, "Cops Arrest Marty Blecman; D.A. Charges Charity Scam," *Bay Area Reporter*, June 27, 1985, 2, 4.
42. Brian Jones, "Blecman Pays Up; Charity Gets Cash," *Bay Area Reporter*, September 12, 1985, 4, 11.
43. Kleinberg, "GMHC Gets Check," 2.
44. Brown, interview.
45. Hedges, interview.

Chapter 12

1. Jerry de Gracia and Jon Seifer, "A Decade of Faaabulous Falsetto, " *Bay Area Reporter*, January 19, 1984, 19, 20. 19.
2. De Gracia and Seifer, "Faaabulous Falsetto," 19; Karr, "Dancing the Sylvester Two-Step," *Bay Area Reporter*, February 23, 1984, 22.
3. Jesse Hamlin, "A Deserved Hero's Welcome for Sylvester at the Castro," *San Francisco Chronicle*, February 6, 1984.
4. Casey Jones, "Hi-NRG," *Dance Music Report*, November 16–29, 1985, 9.
5. Jones, "Hi-NRG," 9.
6. Casey Jones, "Hi-NRG," *Dance Music Report*, August 16–September 7, 1985, 20.
7. Jones, "Hi-NRG," November 16–29, 1985, 16.
8. *The Story of High Energy Music*, dir. Ian Levine, unreleased, recorded in 2002, https://www.youtube.com/watch?v=sa8oyDTA18c.
9. Ken Alan, interview with author, July 18, 2017.
10. Dennis McMillan, "Activists Demand Access to Experimental Treatments," *Bay Area Reporter*, June 29, 1989, 5; Marty Blecman, "Why We Zapped the Opera," *Bay Area Reporter*, September 14, 1989, 7.
11. David Diebold, *Tribal Rites: The San Francisco Dance Music Phenomenon 1978–88* (San Francisco: Time Warp Publishing, 1988).
12. David Taylor-Wilson, "Megatone Coming on Strong," *Bay Area Reporter*, August 10, 1989, 29.
13. Mr. Marcus, "B.A.R. Bazaar," *Bay Area Reporter*, August 9, 1990, 53.
14. Katie Guthorn, interview with author, February 14, 2018.
15. Joshua Gamson, *The Fabulous Sylvester* (New York: Picador, 2005), 247.
16. Jerry de Gracia, "From a Whisper to a Scream," *Bay Area Reporter*, April 26, 1984, 28.
17. Bill Brewster, "Dancer-Turned-Producer Chris Njirich on the Highs and Lows of San Francisco Disco," March 2018, https://daily.redbullmusicacademy.com/2018/03/chris-njirich-interview.
18. San Lefebvre, "Waking the Spirit of a Disco Innovator," *New York Times*, August 5, 2016, https://www.nytimes.com/2016/08/07/arts/music/patrick-cowley-disco-reissues.html.
19. Barry Walters, "San Francisco's Disco Diva," *San Francisco Examiner*, November 20, 1988.

260 NOTES

20. Walters, "Disco Diva."
21. David Taylor-Wilson, "'Rabbit' Leads the Pack," *Bay Area Reporter*, August 22, 1991, 35.
22. Linda Imperial, interview with author, October 15, 2018.
23. Diebold, *Tribal Rites*, 136.
24. Pollo Del Mar, "DJ Cassidy Talks New Single 'Honor,' Compares Out Star Alex Newell to Sylvester," *Huffington Post*, https://www.huffpost.com/entry/dj-cassidy-talks-new-single-honor-compares-out-star_b_59166adde4b00ccaae9ea2ee.
25. Lefebvre, "Disco Innovator"; Jude Rogers, "Patrick Cowley's Pioneering Electronic Disco Music," *New Statesman*, October 30, 2019, https://www.newstatesman.com/patrick-cowley-pioneering-electronic-disco-music-mechanical-fantasy-box-review.
26. Jesse Dorris, "Patrick Cowley Is One of Disco's Most Important Producers. These Are His Must-Hear Deep Cuts." *Pitchfork*, accessed May 26, 2021, https://pitchfork.com/thepitch/patrick-cowley-is-one-of-discos-most-important-producers-these-are-his-must-hear-deep-cuts/.
27. Matt Cotsell, "Do It Any Way You Wanna: An Introduction to Patrick Cowley," *Spotlights*, October 19, 2020, https://www.musicomh.com/features/spotlights/patrick-cowley-some-funkettes-introduction.
28. Lefebvre, "Disco Innovator."
29. Patrick Cowley, *Mechanical Fantasy Box: The Homoerotic Journal of Patrick Cowley* (San Francisco: Dark Entries Editions, 2019).
30. "Sylvester Mural Livens Up SOMA," *Bay Area Reporter*, May 26, 2021, https://www.ebar.com/news/news//305277.
31. Brian Jones, "Mary-Louise and Gertrude at the Disco," *Bay Area Reporter*, August 23, 1984, 33.
32. Jones, "Mary-Louise and Gertrude," 34.

Suggested Reading

Abramson, Mark. *Sex, Drugs and Disco: San Francisco Diaries from the Pre-AIDS Era*. n.p.: Minnesota Boy Press, 2017.

Aletti, Vince. *The Disco Files 1973–1978*. London: DJHistory.com, n.d.

Boyd, Nan Alamilla. *Wide Open Town: A History of Queer San Francisco to 1965*. Berkeley: University of California Press, 2003.

Brewster, Bill. "Dancer-Turned-Producer Chris Njirich on the Highs and Lows of San Francisco Disco." Red Bull Music Academy, 2018, https://daily.redbullmusicacademy.com/2018/03/chris-njirich-interview.

Diebold, David. *Tribal Rites: The San Francisco Dance Music Phenomenon 1978–88*. San Francisco: Time Warp Publishing, 1988.

Echols, Alice. *Hot Stuff: Disco and the Remaking of American Culture*. New York: W. W. Norton, 2010.

Espinoza, Alex. *Cruising: An Intimate History of a Radical Pastime*. Los Angeles: Unnamed Press, 2019.

Gamson, Joshua. *The Fabulous Sylvester*. New York: Picador, 2005.

Goldman, Danielle. *I Want to Be Ready: Improvised Dance as a Practice of Freedom*. Ann Arbor: University of Michigan Press, 2010.

Goss, John C., dir. *Wrecked for Life: The Trip and Magic of Trocadero Transfer*. 1993. Private release, digital file, 60 mins.

Harden, Victoria A. *AIDS at 30: A History*. Washington, DC: Potomac Books, 2012.

Lawrence, Tim. "The Forging of a White Gay Aesthetic at the Saint, 1980–84." *Dancecult* 3, no. 1 (2011): 4–27.

Lawrence, Tim. *Life and Death on the New York Dance Floor: 1980–1983*. Durham, NC: Duke University Press, 2016.

Lawrence, Tim. *Love Saves the Day: A History of American Dance Music Culture, 1970–1979*. Durham, NC: Duke University Press, 2003.

Levine, Martin H. *Gay Macho: The Life and Death of the Homosexual Clone*. New York: NYU Press, 1998.

Lopez, Bernard. "Bobby Viteritti." Disco Music. Updated 2017. https://www.discomusic.com/15-bobby-viteritti.

Morris, Mitchell. "'It's Raining Men': The Weather Girls, Gay Subjectivity, and the Erotics of Insatiability." In *Audible Traces*, edited by Elaine Barkin and Lydia Hamessley, 213–229. Zurich: Carciofoli Verlagshaus, 1999.

Shepard, Benjamin Heim. *White Nights and Ascending Shadows: An Oral History of the San Francisco AIDS Epidemic*. London: Cassell, 1997.

Shilts, Randy. *And the Band Played on, 20th Anniversary Edition*. New York: St. Martin's Press, 2007.

Shilts, Randy. *The Mayor of Castro Street*. New York: St. Martin's Press, 1982.

Sinclair, Mick. *San Francisco; A Cultural and Literary History*. Northampton, MA: Interlink Publishing, 2013.

262 SUGGESTED READING

Stryker, Susan, and Jim Van Buskirk. *Gay by the Bay: A History of Queer Culture in the San Francisco Bay Area.* San Francisco: Chronicle Books, 1996.

Tani, Maurice. "Synths, Sex and San Francisco in the 1970s: Pat, Art, HiNRG and Me." Dark Entries Records. December 10, 2015. http://www.darkentriesrecords.com/synths-sex-san-francisco-in-the-1970s-pat-art-hinrg-me-by-maurice-tani/.

Thomas, Andy. "Nightclubbing: San Francisco's Trocadero Transfer." Red Bull Music Academy Daily. September 1, 2014. https://daily.redbullmusicacademy.com/2014/09/nightclubbing-trocadero-transfer.

Vojir, Dan. *The Sunny Side of Castro Street.* San Francisco: Strawberry Hill Press, 1982.

Ward, Andrew H. "Dancing in the Dark: Rationalism and the Neglect of Social Dance." In *Dance, Gender and Culture*, edited by Helen Thomas, 16–33. New York: St. Thomas Press, 1993.

Selected Discography

The entries in this list are organized by record label and include the key San Francisco Sound songs. All recordings are 12-inch singles unless otherwise indicated. More complete discographical information can be found at discogs.com.

Aim Records
    Beam, Barry. *Barry Beam*, 1982. (album)
      "Radio Head (Party Mix)," 1981.

Arial Records
    Jonae, Gwen. "Red Light Lover," 1983.
    Sabu, Paul. "Shotgun," 1983.
    Technique. "Can We Try Again/Looking for Someone to Love Tonight," 1983.

Fantasia Records
    Jacobs, Debbie. "In the Heat of the Night," 1985.
    Lisa. "Tempt Me/Love Is Like an Itching in My Heart," 1985.
    Marianna. "The Big Hurt (Remix)/Just One More Touch," 1985.
      "Feels Like a Dream," 1986.
    Parker, Paul. "Don't Play with Fire," 1985.
      "Ready or Not/Time After Time," 1986.
      "Without Your Love," 1984.
    Shanghai Lil' featuring Perri Halevy. "Groove Boy (Come to Lotus Land)," 1986.

Fantasy Records/Fantasy Honey Records
    Aragorn Ballroom Orcestra. "(Theme from) The Lord of the Rings," 1978.
    Blueprint (Barry Blum). "Ritespot," 1983.
    Fever, *Dreams and Desires*, 1980. (album)
      Fever, 1979. (album)
      "Standing in the Shadows of Love," 1978.
    Hurtt, Phil. "Boogie City (Rock and Boogie Down)," 1979.
    Paradise Express. *Let's Fly*, 1979. (album)
      Paradise Express, 1978. (album)
    Side Effect. *Goin' Bananas*, 1977. (album)
      What You Need, 1976. (album)
    Sylvester. *Living Proof*, 1979. (album)
      Sell My Soul, 1980. (album)
      Stars, 1979. (album)
      Step II, 1978. (album)
      Sylvester, 1977. (album)
      Too Hot to Sleep, 1981. (album)
    Tracy, Jeanie. *Me and You*, 1982. (album)

264 SELECTED DISCOGRAPHY

Two Tons o' Fun. *Backatcha*, 1980. (album)
 "I Got the Feeling (The Patrick Cowley MegaMix)," 1980.
 Two Tons o' Fun, 1980. (album)

Fusion Records
 Cowley, Patrick. *Menergy*, 1981. (album)
 "Menergy/I Wanna Take You Home," 1981.
 Kent, Bobby. *Juice*, 1980. (album)

Megatone Records
 Alan, Ken. *Aerobic Beat: Music for Working Out*, 1986. (album)
 Aerobic Beat 2: Music for Working Out, 1988. (album)
 Bentley, Earlene. "The Boys Come to Town," 1983.
 Cowley, Patrick. *Megatron Man*, 1981. (album)
 Mind Warp, 1982. (album)
 Patrick Cowley's Greatest Hits Dance Party, 1984. (album)
 12 x 12: The Patrick Cowley Collection, 1988. (album)
 Cowley, Patrick, featuring Sylvester. "Do Ya Wanna Funk," 1982.
 Dash, Sarah. "Low Down Dirty Rhythm," 1983.
 "Lucky Tonight," 1983.
 Diebold and Cataluna. *Sex Technology*, 1990. (album)
 Diebold and Co. featuring Kim Cataluna. "The Way We Were," 1989.
 Faulkner, Joan. "I Don't Wanna Talk (about the Weather)," 1986.
 Imperial, Linda and Patrick Cowley. "Diehard Lover," 1986.
 John, Nick. "Lost in a Dream," 1987.
 "Planet Nine," 1986.
 Jolo. "Last Call," 1984.
 "Soul," 1986.
 "Violation/On Hold," 1983.
 Kohl, Ernest. "Hold On to Life/Can We Try Again," 1993.
 Layna, Magda. "When Will I See You Again," 1983.
 Le Jeté [Modern Rocketry]. "La Cage Aux Folles," 1983.
 Lewis, Carl. "Goin' for the Gold," 1984.
 Modern Rocketry. "Homosexuality (Remix)," 1986.
 "(I'm Not Your) Steppin' Stone/I'm Gonna Make You Want Me," 1983.
 Modern Rocketry, 1985. (album)
 "Thank God for Men," 1985.
 "The Right Stuff," 1983.
 Norma. *It's Gonna Happen*, 1983. (with ERC Records) (album)
 Parker, Paul. "Right on Target/Pushin' Too Hard," 1982.
 Too Much to Dream, 1983. (album)
 Payne, Scherrie. "One Night Only," 1984.
 Preston, Billy. *On the Air*, 1984. (album)
 Queen Samantha. "Close Your Eyes (Remix)/Summer Dream," 1983.
 SFX, *Special Effects*, 1983. (album)
 Sylvester. *All I Need*, 1982. (album)
 Call Me, 1983. (album)
 Immortal, 1989. (album)
 M-1015, 1984. (album)
 Mutual Attraction, 1986. (album)

SELECTED DISCOGRAPHY   265

Toons, The. *Looking at Girls*, 1982. (album)
    "Video Games/Japanese Kids," 7-inch, 1983.
Tracy, Jeanie. "Don't Leave Me This Way (mixed by Sylvester)," 1985.
    "Let's Dance," 1988.
    "Time Bomb/Sing Your Own Song," 1984.

Moby Dick Records
BearEssense. "The Big Hurt," 1983.
Boys Town Gang. *A Cast of Thousands* (Rich and Famous Records), 1984. (album)
    Cruisin' the Streets, 1981. (album)
    Disc Charge, 1981. (album)
Buffett, Mary. "My Boyfriend's Back," 1984.
Crystal and the Team. "(Won't You) Dance with Me/Sooner or Later," 1982.
Elliman, Yvonne. "Love Pains (special DJ edited version)," 1982.
Griffin, Peter. "Step by Step/Devil's Reception," 1981.
Hot Posse, "An American Dream (Medley)," 1981.
Imortals, The. "The Ultimate Warlord," 1981.
Jiani, Carol. "Hit n' Run Lover (Moby Mix version)," 1981.
    "The Woman in Me/Mercy," 1981.
Laser. "His Name Is Charlie/Laser," 1981.
Lisa. "Invisible Love (R.E.M.I.X.)/Sex Dance (R.E.M.I.X.)," 1984.
    "Jump Shout," 1982.
    Lisa, 1983. (album)
    "Rocket to Your Heart (Remix)," 1983.
Love International. "Dance on the Groove and Do the Funk," 1981.
Loverde. "Backstreet Romance," 1983.
    "Die Hard Lover," 1982.
Partners, The. "Give It to Me All Night Long," 1982.
Passengers, The. "Hot Leather (Moby Mix version)," 1981.
Reynolds, Margaret. *Keep on Holdin' on*, 1982. (album)
Schiller, Nina. *Stay the Night*, 1983. (album)
Spyyce. "My Baby Loves Lovin'/Movin' (with the Rhythm)," 1983.
Stereo Fun Inc. "Got You Where I Want You Babe," 1983.

Nightwave Records
Diebold and Co. "Your Eyes," 1987.
Diebold and Co. featuring Brian Soares. "Rock It Down to Midnight," 1986.
Loverde, Frank, and Manifestation. "Manifestation of Love," 1988.
Secret Ties. *All through the Night*, 1987. (album)
Soares, Brian. "Magic," 1985.
Not on Label
Danny Boy and the Serious Party Gods, "Castro Boy," 1983.

Pacific Records
Torch. "Build Me Up Buttercup," 1983.
Zino. "Lovin' Is Really My Game," 1984.
Zino with Jayne Edwards. "Walk Away Satisfied," 1985.

Pink Glove Records
Anderson, Tom. "Rock Dancing!," 1985.

266   SELECTED DISCOGRAPHY

Benson, Shawn, and Diebold and Co. "Male Fraud," 1986.
Dioni, Magda. "Dangerous," 1985.
Imperial, Linda. "Stranger," 1985.St. James, Joy. "Dance!," 1985.

Prism Records
Loverde. "Iko Iko/San Francisco Serenade," 1980.

TSR Records
Benson, Shawn. "Seclusion," 1986.

Index

For the benefit of digital users, indexed terms that span two pages (e.g., 52–53) may, on occasion, appear on only one of those pages.

Figures are indicated by an italic *f* following the page number

Abrams, Donald, 166–67, 168–69, 170
Abramson, Mark, 45, 58–59
Acapella Gold, 130–31, 135–37, 150–51, 197
Adams, Arthur, 49
Adams, Patrick, 125–26
Adams, Terry, 89
Adcock, Arthur, 62–63, 131, 133, 194–95
Ahi, Elton, 196
AIDS/HIV, 1–2, 9, 165, 166–71, 172–76, 184–85, 189, 190–91, 201, 204, 205, 208–9, 210, 211–12, 213–15, 218, 220–22, 224, 226–30, 231–32, 236n.14, 245n.46
Aim Records, 159
Alan, Ken, 225–27
Aletti, Vince, 56, 57, 59
Alexander, Ken, 104
Alfie's, 5, 33–34, 40–41, 43, 80, 104, 143, 150, 213–14
Algozino, Steve, 155–56, 211–12, 214–15, 228
All-American Boy, 21–22, 234n.31
Allen III, Paul B, 49
Allen, Richard, 120
Almighty Records, 216
Ambush, 20
America, Mark, 187–88
Ammann, Arthur, 172
Anderson, Tom, 213–14
Andreadis, Ted, 122–23
Andromeda, 52
Angels of Light, 21–22, 65
April, Wayne, 172, 174
Aragorn Ballroom Orcestra, 84
Arena, 20
Arial Records, 212–15
Ariola Records, 128–29
Armstead, Izora (*see* Rhodes, Izora)
Arroyo, Armando, 45
Ashford and Simpson, 53–54, 122
Atlantic Records, 79–80

Automatt Recording Studio, 131–33, 144, 177, 218, 219, 248n.41

B-52s, The, 157–58, 196
Backstreet (Atlanta bar), 150–51
Badlands, 33, 119–20, 143, 160, 206
Baer, Marti, 63
Bailey, Michael, 179–80
Balcony, 21–22
Baldwin, Craig, 208
Bandy, David, 46, 87, 89, 152, 181
Barracks, 29
Bathhouses, 7, 20, 29, 36–39, 66–67, 99, 100, 136, 141–42, 174, 202–3, 223
Baum, Mark, 192
Bay Area Disco DJ Association (BADDA), 79–81, 87, 104
Bay Area Physicians for Human Rights, 167
Beach Blanket Babylon, 52, 213–14
Beach Boys, 138
Beachdell, Marianna (*see* Marianna LoCurto)
Beam, Barry (*see* Blum, Barry)
Bear subculture, 39, 118–19, 195, 209–10
BearEssense, 209–10, 216
Beautiful Bend, 38–39
Beck's Motor Lodge, 1
Beckwith, Catherine, 157, 158
BeeGees, 82–83, 106–7
Bell, Beckie, 133
Bellotte, Pete, 129–30
Benjamin, Benny, 120
Benson, Shawn, 113, 214, 228–29
Bentley, Dale, 35
Bentley, Earlene, 204
Berlandt, Konstantin, 153
Bérube, Allan, 11
Bilt, Peter (*see* Dunne, Peter)
Black Cat, 11, 198
Black Sabbath, 145

268 INDEX

Blackberri, 32
Blackbyrds, 49, 56–57, 81
Blakley, Marthetta, 157, 194–95
Blecman, Marty, 5–6, 8–9, 12, 13, 15–18, 26–27, 46, 59–60, 61, 69, 77, 83–84, 101–2, 118–19, 133, 135, 142–43, 150, 156–57, 163, 176–77, 197–98, 215–16, 217–18, 248n.59
 Blecman and Hedges, 78–87, 88–89, 91–95, 143
 Lawsuit, 220–22
 Megatone Records, 8, 139, 144, 147–48, 149, 163–64, 187, 190–92, 193–95, 218, 219–20, 225–27
Block, Adam, 102–3, 189
Block, Jo Carol, 39, 130–31, 135–36, 145–46, 147–48, 150–51, 180–81, 193–94, 195, 197, 215–16, 217, 219–20, 226–27, 229
Blue Thumb Records, 50–51, 53–55
Blueprint (see Barry Blum)
Blum, Barry, 139, 156–59, 194–95, 209–12, 217, 218–19, 222, 228–29
 Barry Beam (as alter ego), 157–58, 159
 Blueprint, 214
 Castro Boy, 205–6
 Lisa, 159–62, 207–8
Board of Permit Appeals, 32
Bojangles, 2, 21, 22
Bolan, Robert, 166–68, 170
Bolt (San Francisco), 35–36, 237n.23
Bomback, Joseph "Joe," 84–86, 93–94
Bones, 43, 59–60, 237n.20
Bonham, Jerry, 1
Boyd, Nan Alamilla, 11
Boys Town Gang, 9, 116, 122–29, 128f, 130, 136, 137, 184, 195–97, 198, 199–200, 204, 216–18, 222, 225
Bradley, Wes, 56–57
Bradley's Corner, 237n.20
Brass Rail (Sunnyvale bar), 89–90
Bray, Phil, 74
Brenda and the Tabulations, 105
Brennan, Larry, 212
Brewster, Mickey, 125–26
Bridges, Lloyd, 147–48
Brig, 20, 237n.23
Britt, Harry, 89, 154
Bronski, Michael, 41–42
Brooks, Pattie, 87
Brown Door Records, 89–90
Brown, Ian Anthony, 147–48, 211, 215–16
Brown, Miquel, 203–4, 224, 225
Brown, Steven Ames, 126–27, 137, 147–48, 201–2, 216–18, 221–22

Brown, Willie, 112
Brubeck, Dave, 195–96
Bruce, Lenny, 48–49
Bryant, Anita, 56, 78, 106–7, 242n.28
Bryant, Mel, 3
Buena Vista (band), 43
Buffett, Mary, 162, 179–80, 211–12, 215–16
Buffett, Peter, 179–80, 207–8
Burke, Kevin, 104, 111–12
Buzzby's, 2, 21–22, 155

C&M Records, 212–15
Cable Car Awards, 7–8, 151–52, 163, 204, 206, 223
Cailleau, John, 44–45, 46, 176
Carleo, Vincent, 45, 104, 111–12
Carlton, Bruce, 127, 128f, 196–97, 199–200
Carollo, John, 181–82
Carpenter, Richard, 120–21
Carter, Lauren, 130–31, 135–36, 145–46, 150–51, 177–78, 195, 197, 217, 219–20
Casablanca Records, 66, 67–68, 70–71, 148–49, 240n.10
Casell, Paul, 79
Cashman, Frank, 111
Castro Planning Commission, 34, 237n.26
Castro Station (bar), 101–2, 206
Castro Street Fair, 21–22, 46, 202
Castro Theatre, 223
Cataluna, Kim, 228–29
Cave, The, 125–26
CBS Records, 218–19
Centers for Disease Control and Prevention, 167–68, 172
Cerrone, 8, 38–39, 59–60, 125–26
Chany, Phillipe, 196
Charin, Robin, 127
Charot, Bob, 21
Chataway, Mark, 220–21
Chauncey, George, 11–12, 42
Chavala (St. Louis club), 18–19
Chic, 79–80, 83, 86, 193
Chicago, 95, 96, 118–19, 169, 209, 214, 223, 230
Chicago (musical), 203
Chin, Brian, 74–75, 188, 192, 201, 215, 219
Christgau, Robert, 74–75
Christian, Meg, 151–52, 163, 250n.39
Christie, Lou, 194–95
Christo, 44–45
Crystal and the Team, 196
Circus Disco (Los Angeles), 100, 118–19, 122, 203–4

INDEX 269

City Cabaret and City Disco, 5–6, 12, 17–18, 19, 43, 59–60, 69, 79, 80, 102
Clifford, Linda, 175–76
Clone culture, 2, 21–24, 31, 32–34, 39–41, 44, 46–47, 55, 58, 60, 72–73, 95, 124–25, 126, 127–28, 136, 139, 141–42, 153–54, 163–64, 165, 172–76, 184–85, 189–90, 199–201, 205–6, 220
Club Baths, 35
Club San Francisco, 36–37
Cockettes, 21–22, 50, 56, 57, 89
COCO (Cleveland Ohio Comes On), 84–85
Cohen, Jeffrey E., 117, 131–33
Coldewey, Russell, 211–12
Cole, David, 122–23
Coletti, John, 141
Coley, Daryl, 191
Collier, Dick, 37–38, 107–8, 152
Collins, Rodger, 89–90
Columbia Records, 187–88, 202
Communards, 228
Compton's Cafeteria, 20
Conant, Marcus, 170–71, 172–73
Conceptual Entertainment, 46–47, 97, 103, 127, 152–53, 181, 230, 249–50n.31
  Let it Snow, 87
  Salute to the Men of San Francisco, 46
  Summer Heat, 175–76
  Sylvester at the Opera House, 89, 90–91
Conan (band), 163, 250n.39
Continental Baths (New York bathhouse), 36–37
Cooper, Robb, 161–62
Cory, Donald Webster, 29
Cory Jr, Leonard R, 212–13
Cosby, Henry (Hank), 49, 81
Costandinos, Alec R., 59–60, 150
Council on Religion and Homosexuality, 133–34
Cowley, Madonna, 147–48
Cowley, Patrick, 1, 5–6, 9, 12–13, 61–77, 83–84, 92–94, 106, 113–14, 116–17, 131–32, 139, 140*f*, 141–43, 156–58, 162–64, 165, 176–78, 181–83, 184, 191–93, 197–98, 201, 207–8, 215, 218–20, 230–32
  Fusion Records, 133, 135–38, 139–43, 147–50
  "gallop," 71–72, 71*f*, 93–94, 116–17, 137, 142–43, 144–45, 146, 146*f*, 161, 178–79, 187–88, 192
  "Masculine Music," 139–43
  Megatone Records, 8, 147–52, 163–64, 193–94, 215–16, 218, 220–21
  Megatron Man, 143–50, 161–62

"Menergy," 8–9, 135–38, 190–91, 209
Mind Warp, 178–83, 182*f*, 202, 204, 257n.49
  Studio at 8th and Minna, 116–17, 130–31, 194–95
  With Jorge Socarrás, 64, 133, 139–41, 148
  With Sylvester, 5–6, 68–77, 78–79, 87–89, 131, 176–78, 187–88, 190–91
Creative Power Foundation, 43
Creative Source, 105–6
Creedence Clearwater Revival, 48–49
Crivello, Ken, 111–12, 163–64, 183, 215–16
Crockett, Greg, 116–17
Croteau, Dennis, 106–7, 211–12, 245n.46

Dahl, Steve, 95, 243n.1
Damron, Bob, 15
Danae (DJ), 25
Dance Your Ass Off, 38, 102
Danny Boy and the Serious Party Gods, 205–6
Dante's Inferno, 13
D'Aquisto, Steve, 79
Dark Entries Records, 231
Dash, Sarah, 193–94
Dead or Alive, 201, 223
Dean, Hazell, 196, 215
Dearborn, Richard, 25, 28
Dearie, Blossom, 57
De Gracia, Jerry, 100, 102, 152–53, 163, 188, 190, 191–92, 227
DeJohnette, Jack, 198
DePaulo, Nino, 18–19
DePre, Jimmy, 1
Deserio, Pat, 58
Diebold and Co., 214
Diebold, David, 210–11, 226, 228–29
Different Fur Studios, 93–94
Dioni, Magda, 194–95, 213
Disco Demolition Night (Disco Sucks), 95, 96–97, 193
Disconet, 116–17, 119–21, 122–24, 129, 142–43, 151, 155, 156, 158–59
Divine, 101, 215, 242n.28
Dolby, Thomas, 157
Douglas, Carol, 38–39, 86, 150
Drayton, Leslie, 53, 74–75
Dreamgirls, 191, 203
Dreamland, 5, 104, 111–15, 119–20, 127–29, 134–35, 160, 188–89, 202, 205, 226
Droney, Maureen, 180–81
Drummer, 112, 151
Drums (Guerneville club), 214–15
Dunne, Peter, 219–20
Dunstan, John, 53, 54

270 INDEX

Durack, David T., 171
Duran Duran, 102
Duran, Patrick, 198
Dynamic Superior, 56–57

Echols, Alice, 4
El Rio, 226
Electric Circus (New York club), 193
Electric Prunes, 192
Electrola Records, 130
Elephant Walk, 19, 50–51, 97–98
Elyria, Ohio, 13, 14, 84–85
Emmitt, 39–41
End Result, 81–82
Endup, 20, 25–26, 32–33, 39–40, 104,
    151, 161–62
ERC Records, 212–15
Espinoza, Alex, 28
Etting, Emlen, 42
Evans, Arthur, 171, 174–75

Fabulashes, 187–88, 191, 229
Fabus, Steve, 1, 31, 36–38, 43, 188–89, 210
    At I–Beam, 12, 36, 104
    Red Hanky Party, 99–100
Fantasia Records, 211, 215–16
Fantasy Records, 48–50, 52–53, 58, 61, 81, 82–
    83, 92–93
    Blecman and Hedges, 5–6, 78–79, 80–81, 83–
        87, 91–92, 94, 143
    Sylvester, 53–57, 59–60, 68–69, 74–75, 76,
        87–89, 91–92, 131, 151–52, 177, 185–88,
        254n.69
    Jeanie Tracy, 90, 152, 177
    Two Tons o' Fun, 116–17, 201–2, 254n.69
Fat Larry's Band, 49
Fe–Be's, 20
Fedasz, Sergio, 1
Feinstein, Dianne, 7–8, 89, 99–100
Ferré, Sisley, 227–28
Ferren, George, 104
Fever, 84–87, 92–95, 123–24, 190–91
Fife's (Russian River bar), 210
Finden, Michael C, 6, 69, 88, 130–31, 132, 135–
    36, 150, 183
First Choice, 38–39, 228–29
First Encounter megaparty, 139, 152–54
Fisher, Peter, 14, 41–42
Fisher, Toni, 209–10
Fisk, Peter, 111–12
Flamingo (New York disco), 25, 112
Flunder, Yvette, 54–55
Folsom Fantasies, 111

Fonda, Jane, 78, 177–78
Forbes, Steve, 100, 107
Ford, Mel, 35–36
Ford, Robert T., 190
Foreman, Chuck, 82–83
415 Records, 218–19
Four Seasons, 120–21
Four Tops, 84–85
Fox, The (Oakland bar), 90
Fox Studios, 141, 179
Foxy, 119–20
Frampton, Peter, 84–85
Frappier, Leo, 213–15, 226–27
Frazier, David, 53, 54, 82, 116–17, 179–80, 212
Freedland, Nat, 74
Freedom Day Parade, 5, 25, 45–46, 112, 127,
    189, 220, 228
Friedman–Kein, Alvin E., 168, 169–70
Frith, Simon, 75
Fuqua, Harvey, 49–50, 52–54, 55, 56–57, 68,
    75–76, 80–81, 87–89, 90, 116–17, 131, 185,
    254n.69
Fusion Records, 116, 133–35, 137–38, 139–40,
    144–45, 147–50, 199, 249n.20

Gadson, James, 74
Galaxy, 89–90
Gallant, Denise, 208, 257n.7
Galleria Design Center, 43, 46, 87, 127, 152–53,
    165, 181–82, 220
Galloway, Leata, 203
Gamson, Joshua, 51–52, 186, 227
Garrett, Michael, 36, 43, 59–60, 104, 181–82
Gassner, Dennis, 74
Gay Community Center, 44–45, 99, 230
Gay Freedom Day Marching Band and Twirling
    Corps, 111
Gay Games, 181
Gay Men's Health Crisis, 169–70, 220–21
Gaye, Marvin, 49–50, 123
Gaynor, Gloria, 39
Gentle Giant, 84–85
Gentrification, 20, 31, 32–34
Gibbons, Peggy, 18, 19, 130–31, 199f, 211–12
Gideon and Power, 51–52
Gilded Cage, 20
Gildemeister, Jerry, 13, 14
Ginsburg, Allan, 48–49
Giudice, Bob, 114, 209–10
Glayzer, Glynda, 52
Gleeson, Pat, 93–94, 217
Glide Memorial United Methodist Church,
    133–34, 191

INDEX   271

Go Bang!, 1, 232
Goldberg, Stu, 38
Goldman, Douglas, 142–43
Goldstein, Morey, 218–20, 226–27
Gomez, Presley, 153
Goodstein, David, 2
Gordon, Conni, 63
Gordon, Huntly, 144
Gospel Pearls, 133–34
Gotham, 18
Goya, Francis, 156
Graebar Sound System, 37–38, 107–8, 111–12
Graham, Larry, 8
Graham, Nicholas, 131
Gramophone Records, 15
Grand Theft, 49–50
Green, Al, 198
Gregg's Blue Dot Lounge (Los Angeles), 155
Griffin, Peter, 130
Griff's, 118–19
Groubert, Peter, 22
Grove Street Band, 49–50
Guerneville, California (*see* Russian River)
Guess, Mike "Rudy," 122–23, 129–30, 195, 217
Gus's Pub, 237n.20
Guthorn, Katie, 157, 194–95, 220, 226–27
Gymnaites, Mike, 122–23
GZR Productions, 181

Hamilton, James, 201, 224
Hamilton Lodge Ball, 42–43
Hancock, Herbie, 64–65, 93–94, 131–32
Handball Express, 99
Harbour Sound, 198
Harold Melvin and the Blue Notes, 8, 53–54
Hartman, Dan, 152–53
Hasemeier, Steve, 211–12
Hawaiian Hut (Sacramento disco), 32–33
Hawkins, Lynette, 191
Hawkins, Walter, 191
Hedges, John, 5–6, 7–8, 12–18, 43, 59–60, 61, 77, 78, 79–81, 104, 118–20, 139, 142–44, 165, 179–81, 187, 194–95, 217–18, 226–27, 229
   Blecman and Hedges, 78–87, 88–89, 91–95, 143
   With Barry Beam, 156–62, 157f, 205–6, 207–8, 211–12, 222, 228–29
Hell Storm, 49–50
Hellman, Eric, 175
Hendrix, Jimi, 61–62, 67
Hepatitis B, 166, 167–69
Heranney, David L., 175

Herbaugh, Richard, 174
Hermes, Wolfgang (Laser), 130
Hernandez, José, 49–50
HIM (Health and Immunity for Men) Vitamins, 173
Hinte, Terry, 186
Hodges, Pat, 87–88, 148–49
Hoffman, Martin, 28
Holloway, Loleatta, 142–43
Holmes, Marvin, 89–90
Honey Productions, 52–53, 55–57, 58, 59–60, 131, 185–87, 201–2, 254n.69
Hong Kong Bar, 81–82
Hongisto, Richard, 78
Hooker, Evelyn, 28–29
Hopkins, Jim, 232
Horning, Lee, 88–89
Horton, Gretchen, 84
Horus, 198
Hot Classics, 155–56
Hot Posse, 143, 153, 158, 164
Hot Rocks, 155–56, 194–95
Hot Tracks, 155–56, 160–61, 214–15, 258n.9
Hotel Bonaventure, 81–82
Houston, Whitney, 203
Howell, Marvin, 212–13
Hues Corporation, 105
Hughes, Walter, 25–26
Hurrah (New York disco), 101
Hymes, Sharon, 82, 89

Ian Dury and the Blockheads, 101–2
I–Beam, 1, 5, 7–8, 12–13, 27, 30, 34–36, 37, 40–41, 59–60, 103–4, 187, 188, 206, 213–14, 229–30, 237n.20
   Live music, 102, 114, 117, 118f, 151, 216–17
Imperial, Linda, 18–20, 39, 69, 130–31, 141–42, 183, 195, 197–98, 199f, 211–12, 214, 226, 229, 257n.49, 257n.54
Importe/12 Records, 129
Independent Sound Studio, 162, 179–80, 205–6, 215–16
Indoor Life, 133
International Mr. Leather, 220
Invertebrates, The, 160

Jabara, Paul, 82, 83, 201–2, 203
Jacksom, Dianne, 85
Jackson, Clydine, 87, 94
Jacksons, The, 38–39, 155
Jacobs, Debbie, 150, 216
Jaguar Books, 140–41
Jamerson, James, 74

272 INDEX

James, Denita, 87–88
James, Lee, 101–2
James, Toni, 134
Jarreau, Al, 84–85
Jaubert, Pierre, 65–66, 71–72, 133
J. Geils Band, 245n.59
Jiani, Carol, 129–30, 156
Jimmerson, Herb, 81–83, 92–93, 94
Jimmerson, Vi Ann, 81–83
Joe Boxer, 131
John Castelli's Tangerine, 106
John Davis and the Monster Orchestra, 66
John, Nick, 226
Jolly Roger Inn, 81–82
Jolo, 12–13, 151, 194–95, 216, 219–20,
    222, 227–28
Jonae, Gwen, 187, 212–13
Jones, Brian, 231–32
Jones, Casey, 104–5, 146–47, 224
Jones, Cleve, 97–98
Jones, Grace, 80
Jones, Jim, 78
Jones, Phil, 81, 82, 83–84, 186
Joplin, Janis, 50–51, 123, 134, 236n.14
Judell, Brandon, 24
Judnick, Jerry, 62

Kaffel, Phil, 85–86
Kallet, Jim, 208
Kano, 119–20
Kaposi's sarcoma, 165, 167, 170–71, 172, 173–74
Kaposi's Sarcoma Clinic, 170–71
Kat Mandu, 129–30
Kebekeletrik, 58, 239n.28
Keepnews, Orrin, 81
Keith's Cruise Room, 105–6
Kellman, Sanford, 35–36, 49, 216–17
Kent, Bobby, 133–35
Kessie, Ken, 218–20, 226–27
KFRC Radio, 63–64
Kimbel, Rob, 61, 155–56
King, Barry, 78
King, Ben E., 87–88
King, Evelyn, 107–8
King, Clydie, 148–49
Kingson, Bob, 69, 116–17, 132
Kitt, Eartha, 18
Klein, Howie, 102–3
Knight, Gladys, 4
Kohl, Ernest, 226, 229
Koldwyn, Scrumbly, 21–22, 64
Komarek, Jim, 39
Komiyama, Shigemi, 194–95

Koplar, Harold, 18
Kraftwerk, 58, 74–75, 104–5, 132, 196
Kreiner, Marc, 86

LaBelle, Patti, 28, 55, 131–32
La Greca, Joe, 129–30
Lane, Bill, 133–34
Langenheim, Billy, 108–10, 110*f*, 114
La Pietra, Gene, 100
LaRue, Larry, 102–3
Laser, 130
Laws, Ronnie, 49
Lawson, Kurt, 32–34
Layna, Magda (*see* Dioni, Magda)
Lear, Amanda, 177–78
Lebonte, Richard, 173
Lederer, Barry, 38, 84, 88–89, 136, 151
Lee, Michael, 59–60, 61
Lee, Robert, 162, 208
Le Jeté, 219–20
Le Page, Denis, 129–30
Le Page, Denyse, 129–30
Leslie, Robbie, 101, 106
Levine, Ian, 203–4, 213–14, 215, 224–25
Levine, Martin H., 2
Lewis, Mike, 114, 118–20, 122, 129–30, 143,
    152, 153, 155–56, 158–59, 202, 210, 212,
    229–30, 258n.10
Lewis, Norma, 212
Liberty Baths, 36–37
Lime, 129–30
Lisa (Lisa Fredenthal–Lee), 9, 12–13, 39, 156,
    159–62, 184, 196–97, 207*f*, 215–16, 218–
    19, 228
    "Jump Shout," 153, 156, 159, 160–62, 210–11
    Lisa, 207–8, 210–11
Little Richard, 57
Little Sister, 127–28, 129
LoCurto, Marianna, 209–10, 215–16
Loft (New York club), 79
Logan, Bob, 155
Lone Mountain College, 135–36
Lopez, Ross, 155–56
Lorch, Paul, 175
Lord of the Rings, 84
Los Angeles, 5, 15–17, 18, 19, 21, 49, 77, 79,
    81–82, 87–88, 100, 107, 108, 116, 118–26,
    127, 165, 167, 169, 196, 199, 203, 212–13,
    214–15, 217–18, 225–26
Love Center Church, 191
Love International, 195–96
Love Tracks, 155–56
Love Twins, 150

INDEX 273

Loverde (band), 5–6, 9, 12–13, 18–20, 46, 61, 112, 116, 117, 130–31, 141–42, 184, 196–97, 199*f*, 208–9, 210–11, 228
   "Die Hard Lover," 197–98, 202, 204
   "Iko Iko," 131–32, 151–52
Loverde, Frank, 18–20, 69, 117, 131–32, 139–40, 142, 197–98, 199*f*, 211–12, 214, 226–27, 228
Lowe, Helen, 49
Lugo, Danny, 212–13
Lunch, Lydia, 196
Luscious Lorelei, 21
Lustig, Larry, 210–11
Lygizos, Nick, 104

Macho (band), 125–26
Magnifique, 134–35, 258n.10
Maier, Michael, 111–12
Maletta, Michael, 43–44, 46, 165, 176, 230
   Abracadabra, 45–46
   Night Flight, 43–45, 46–47
   Stars, 45, 88–89
Maley, Ken, 103
Mambar, Alan, 91–92
Mamou, Jimmy, 89–90
Mancuso, David, 79
Man's Country (Los Angeles), 155
Marcello's Pizza, 1
Manley, Cynthia, 123, 124–27, 150, 217
Markham, David, 37
Marlin Beach Hotel (Poop Deck), 105, 106
Marshall University, 155
Martha and the Vandellas, 92–93
Martinez, Ray, 134–35, 142–43
Marx, Jean L., 169–70
Mason, Barbara, 203
Matra Records, 129–30
Matuchek, Christine, 21, 61
McAdams, Pat, 15, 33
McBride, Gerry, 13–14, 15–17
McKenna, Tim, 177–78, 226–27, 228
McKuen, Rod, 125–26
McMacken, Carol, 130–31, 135–36
McMahon, Charlie, 141
McNight, Sharon, 102
Mega–Tech Records, 226
Megatone House Records, 226
Megatone Records, 1, 9, 12–13, 89, 115, 116, 138, 139, 144–45, 147, 150, 151, 177–78, 193–94, 198, 199, 201, 202, 204, 212–14, 218, 219–20, 225–28, 229, 230, 257n.54
   founding, 8, 144, 150, 163–64
   lawsuit, 220–22

Paul Parker, 9, 163–64, 191–93, 215–16
   "Previews," 165, 181–83, 182*f*
   Sylvester, 184, 185, 187–89, 190–91
Mehl, Jeff, 194–95
Melton, Tiny (*see* Tyne Mouton)
Merritt, Randy, 69
Metro Madness Party, 102–10
Metropolitan Community Church, 183
Michele, 65–66, 76
Mickey's 7, 125–26
MIDEM Conference, 196
Midler, Bette, 101–2
Miley, Don, 34, 43, 79–80, 112, 117, 132, 197–98
Milk, Harvey, 31, 89, 97–100, 154
Miller, David, 104
Mind Shaft, 5, 12, 15, 16*f*, 17, 33–34, 80
Mineshaft (New York bathhouse), 136
Mistake, 22
Mitchell, Brenda, 71–72
Moby Dick (bar), 22, 118–19, 122, 209–10
Moby Dick Records, 1–2, 5–6, 8, 9, 12–13, 115, 116, 118–19, 122–24, 126–29, 130–31, 137, 143, 144, 155–56, 160–62, 184, 195–98, 204, 206, 207–8, 210, 212–14, 216–18, 221, 228–29, 230, 245n.46
   Closing, 208–9, 211–12
   Gold Standard releases, 129–30
Modern Rocketry, 204, 218–20, 225–26
Monkees, 219
Montreal, 58, 129–30, 163–64
Moore, Jackson, 127, 128*f*, 151–52, 196–97, 199–200, 217
More, Juanita, 1
Morey, Craig, 8, 114, 118–20, 122, 124–25, 127–28, 129–30, 143, 152, 153, 155–56, 212–13
Morley, Tommy, 127, 128*f*, 196–97, 199–200, 211–12
Moroder, Giorgio, 9, 38–39, 57–58, 66–67, 75, 106–7, 129–30, 196, 201
Morriss, Stan, 118–19, 122, 124–25, 162, 211–12
Moscone Convention Center, 139, 152–53, 154
Moscone, George, 31, 78, 89, 97–100
Motley, Bill, 8, 9, 116, 118–19, 120–21, 122–28, 129–30, 143, 160–61, 195, 198, 211–13, 216–18
Moulton, Tom, 105
Mouton, Tyne, 208–9, 258n.9
Mr. S Leather, 125–26
MTV, 189, 256n.20
Mueller, Jerry, 62
Mueller, Madeleine, 62
Munich Machine, 70–71
Murfin, Muff, 212

274 INDEX

Murphy, Eddie, 177–78
Music Hall (disco), 104, 111, 113
Musique, 125–26

National Disco Tea Dance, 4
National Gay Task Force, 24–25
Near, Holly, 163, 250n.39
Neo Records, 199
New Bell Saloon, 20
New Body Center, 46, 181
New Order, 201, 214, 219–20
New York City, 4–6, 11–12, 17–18, 25, 27,
    36–38, 41–42, 43–45, 50, 68, 70, 77, 79,
    101–2, 107–8, 111–12, 114–15, 132,
    134–35, 136, 138, 150–51, 160, 161–62,
    165, 167, 169–70, 174, 191, 193, 195–96,
    202, 203, 204, 209, 213, 218, 223, 224, 229,
    230, 234n.5
New York Record Pool, 79
Newman, Randy, 157
Newton John, Olivia, 228
Niagara College, 61–62
Nicholson, Carla Ann, 39, 40
Nightwave Records, 214–15
Njirich, Chris, 100, 109, 112–13, 114, 136–37,
    209–10, 227
Noguera, Gary, 195, 213–14
Noguera, Ramon, 213
Nomi, Klaus, 194–95
NOW (News of the World), 51–52
N'Touch, 2
Nubs, The, 159–60
Nyland, Thomas, 169, 172

Oasis (band), 85
Oasis (disco), 202
Oil Can Harry's, 5, 12, 17–18, 21, 33, 59–60, 78,
    79–80, 93, 102, 104, 237n.26
Old Waldorf, 53, 102
Olympia Records, 133–34
One Flew Over the Cuckoo's Nest, 48–49, 84
Ono, Yoko, 156
Opus (New York club), 18
Orlando, Bobby, 204

Pacific Records, 214–15
Palms Café, 20, 51, 52
Paradise Express, 8, 81–84, 92–93, 94, 117,
    123–24, 125–26
Parente, Edward, 44–45
Parker, Paul, 12–13, 135–36, 139, 142, 146–47,
    150, 162–64, 177, 178–79, 197–98, 207–8,
    209–10, 211–12, 215–16
  "Right on Target," 9, 163–64, 204

Too Much to Dream, 144, 165, 181–82,
    184, 191–93
Parrish, Man, 216
Patrick Cowley Singers, 96, 136–37, 145,
    146–47, 150–52, 179, 181, 219–20
Payday, 48–49
Payne, Freda, 190–91
Payne, Sherrie, 218, 225–26
Pearl Harbor and the Explosions, 219–20
Pearl Heart, 33–34, 236n.14
Pendergrass, Teddy, 74, 186
Pendulum, 22, 33–34
Peoples Temple, 78
Perceptive Audio Productions, 35–36
Perea, Ray, 151
Philadelphia International Records, 8, 12
Philly Cream, 49
Phuckem, Canya, 125–26
Pierce, Charles, 18
Pink Glove Records, 195, 213–14, 228–29
Pitts, Nancy, 50, 52, 56–57, 74, 89, 185, 254n.69
Pneumocystis carinii pneumonitis, 167, 170,
    172, 217–18
Polk Gulch, 15, 20, 32
Pollock, Jeff, 102
Polydor Records, 196
Poole, Wakefield, 45–46, 140–41
Popeye (band), 122–23, 124, 127, 195, 217
Pople, Phil, 102
Poppers, 7, 27, 60, 146–47, 148–49, 206
    and AIDS, 167–68, 170–71, 172, 173, 174
Post-punk, 96–97, 100, 133, 148, 161
Poussez, 142–43
Presley, Elvis, 121
Previews megaparty, 165, 181–83, 182f
Prism Records, 132
Preston, Billy, 218, 225–26
Probe, 155–56
Prophet-5 synthesizer, 149, 158, 205–6,
    207–8, 215,
Proposition 6, 32, 78
Proto Records, 215–16
P.S., 79
Punk, 29, 35–36, 96–97, 100, 125–26, 156,
    157–58, 159–60, 190, 196, 218–19

Queen (band), 119–20
Queen Samantha, 218
Question Mark, 176

Racism in San Francisco Gay Culture, 19, 25,
    32–34, 39–40, 79–80, 189–90, 208–9
Rae, Jesse, 142–43
Ramrod, 125–26

INDEX 275

Randall, Jon, 163
Randazzo, Jon, 5, 24–25, 79, 80, 101–2, 104
Randle, Vicki, 219–20
Ray, Don, 88
Ray, Lynn, 157, 158
Ray, Richi, 209–10
RCA Records, 49–50
Readymades, 157–58
Reagan, Ronald, 162–63, 172
Record Shack Records, 203–4, 224
Red Onion Restaurant, 122
Redbone, 196–97
Redd, Sharon, 209–10
Redz, The, 212–13
Reed, Dale, 84–85, 87, 93
Reese, Danny, 85
Reich, Dan, 53, 69
Reiner, Sandyjack, 53–54
Remember the Party, 232
Rendezvous, 12, 15
Reno National Gay Rodeo, 220
Reynolds, Margaret, 208–9, 217
Rhodes, Izora, 5–6, 50, 51–52, 72, 73, 116–17, 201–2, 217, 219–20
Rich and Famous Records Ltd, 216–18
Richardson, Gladys M., 85
Rick, Louie, 122–23
Rickshaw Lounge, 55
Ridgeway, Tommy, 104
Ringwald, Trip "Tripper," 118–19, 120, 121, 122–23, 124–25, 129–30, 211–12
Ritz, Kreema, 21–22
Rivers, Timmy, 33, 34, 36, 40, 43, 61, 79–80, 104, 132, 141–42, 202
Robinson, Alan, 102
Robinson, Eric, 74, 90, 116–17
Roderick, William "Rod," 34, 35, 36–37, 38, 41–42, 43, 44, 99–100
Rolling Stones, 109, 163
Romeo Void, 151–52
Ross, Diana, 122
Rossiello, Larry, 111–12
Roverana, Gary, 46, 87, 89, 152, 157–58, 210
Roy Loney and the Phantom Movers, 219
Royale, Candida (*see* Candice Vadala)
Rubinson, David, 131–32, 133, 144, 248n.41
Rubenstein, Benji, 27, 205
Rushin' River, 133–34
Russian River, 138, 181, 210, 214–15
Rusty Nail (Guerneville bar), 214–15

Sabu, Paul, 187, 212–13
Sage, Wayne, 24–25

Saint, The (New York disco), 97, 101, 106, 111, 114–15, 150–51, 160, 174, 195–96, 224
Saint James, Joy, 214
Salgado, Sean, 46
Salty Dog Studios, 122–23
Sam and Dave, 162
San Francisco AIDS Foundation, 172
San Francisco Art Institute, 159–60
San Francisco Black Leadership Forum, 32
San Francisco City College, 49, 64, 131, 141
San Francisco Disco Preservation Society, 232, 245n.45
San Francisco Conservatory, 51–52
San Francisco State University, 162–63
San Francisco War Memorial Opera House, 7–8, 87–91, 185–86, 226
San Francisco Vocoder Choir, 179–80
Sanchez, Maria, 37, 107–8
Sanders, Dennis, 191
Sanders, Pharoah, 198
Sands, Roc, 34, 79
Sanford, Tom, 17–18
Sarria, José, 52, 198
Saturday Night Fever, 29, 32–33, 84, 112
Schaeffer, Paul, 202
Schafer, Rob, 208
Schiller, Nina, 196, 208–9
Schiller, Randy, 103, 181
Scot, Donald Cameron, 4
Scott, David, 32, 38
Sea Witch, 150–51
Secret Ties, 214–15
Sedaka, Neil, 120–21
Sex Pistols, 29
SFX, 194–95, 220
Shanti Project, 221–22
Shapiro, Roy, 111–12, 114
Shed, The, 36–37, 237n.26
Sheldon, Chrysler, 33, 34, 79–80
Shepp, Archie, 198
Shilts, Randy, 12, 22, 103
Shiver, 194–95
Short Circuit Productions, 63–65, 240n.7
Side Effect, 49
Sills, Randy, 128–29, 225–26
Sister Power, 187
Sleeping Lady, 158
Slick, 49
SMC TV, 109–10
Smith, Alan, 134
Smith, Jessica, 87–88
Smith, Denver, 122–23, 129–30, 195, 198, 217
Smith, O.C., 105–6
Smith, Will, 122, 195–97, 210–11

276 INDEX

Soares, Brian, 214–15, 228
Socarrás, Jorge, 64, 133, 139–41
Soccio, Gino, 58
Society for Individual Rights (SIR), 43
Sound Genesis, 45
Southern California Disco DJ
    Association, 118–19
Space (band), 58, 59–60, 239n.28
Sparr, Peter, 111–12
Specht, Stanley Ross, 173
Spectrum, 69
Spence, Timmy, 157–58
Spero, Chuck, 124
Spider's Webb, 49
Spiersch, Gini, 39, 112–13, 155–56, 210–12,
    214–15
Stanton, Holly, 157–58
Staple Singers, 48–49
Star Wars, 58, 59–60, 93–94, 145
Starlight Sound, 160
Starr, Bobby, 64
Starr, Chico, 34
Starr, Edwin, 148–49, 150
Statements, 195–96
Stax Records, 48–49, 81
Stereo Fun, Inc., 196
Stevens, Rick, 89–90
Stevenson, William "Mickey," 87–88
Stewart, Bob, 90
Stewart, Keith, 127
Stingers, 157
Stokes, Rick, 78
Stone, Henry, 119
Stone, Sly, 127, 208–9
Stracke, Billy, 133, 134–35, 137, 138, 139–40
Strayhorn, Danny, 19–20
Stud, The, 1–2, 20, 27, 40, 50–51, 102, 103,
    198, 232
Studio 54 (New York disco), 195
Studio One, 100, 107, 108, 114, 118–19,
    148–49, 160
Studio West, 111–12, 151, 219–20
Summer, Donna, 129–30, 201–2
    Bad Girls, 94
    "I Feel Love," 9, 57–58, 66–68, 76,
        104–5, 106
    I Remember Yesterday, 239n.28
    "Love to Love You Baby," 8, 125–26
    Once Upon a Time, 59–60
Sunshine (musician), 125–26
Supremes, The, 120, 124, 129–30
Sutro Baths, 36–37
Sutton, Terry, 226

Swedosh, Victor, 118–19, 122, 123, 124,
    126, 209–10
Sylvester, 1, 5–6, 12–13, 18, 19, 46, 48, 50–53,
    55–57, 61, 78, 80–81, 82–85, 93–94, 97–98,
    102–3, 104, 112, 116–17, 123–24, 130–32,
    133–34, 135, 137, 139, 141, 150, 152, 153,
    165, 176–78, 179–83, 182*f*, 184, 189–90,
    191–92, 193–94, 198, 206, 209, 217,
    218, 220, 223–28, 229, 230–32, 250n.39,
    254n.69, 256n.20, 257n.49
    All I Need, 187–89, 202, 204
    Blue Thumb albums, 50, 51, 53–54
    Call Me, 190–91
    With the Cockettes, 21–22, 50, 56, 89
    Living Proof, 87–92
    M-1015, 218
    Sell My Soul, 185–87, 255n.3
    Stars, 87–89, 130–31, 141
    Step II, 68–77, 130–31
    Sylvester, 53–55
    Sylvester Day, 7–8, 89
    Too Hot to Sleep, 151–52, 185–87
    "You Make Me Feel (Mighty Real)," 38–39,
        46, 71–73, 71*f*, 74–75, 83–84, 90–91, 136
    "Dance (Disco Heat)," 73, 75, 90–91
Symptoms (band), 157–58

Talking Heads, 101–2
Tani, Maurice, 62–64, 67, 131, 141, 142, 144–45,
    192–95, 218–19
Technique (band), 212
Technodiva, 228 (*see* Jeanie Tracy)
Temple, Lester, 32–33, 38–39, 93, 104–5,
    205–6, 229
Teramani, Franl, 39
Thode, Roy, 97, 105
Thomas, Evelyn, 204, 215
Thompson, Frank, 42
Thompson, Jeryl, 148–50
THP Orchestra, 59–60
Three Degrees, 195
Thump, Thump, Thump, 194–95
Tichane, Robin, 26, 29, 43–44
Tighe, Gary, 38–39, 61, 86, 107–8, 242n.28
Tina Freeman's Voices of Harmony, 90
T.K. Records, 119–20
Toad Hall, 14–15, 17, 22, 40, 104
Tolson, Horus Jack, 197–98, 208–10,
    212, 219
Tom Tom Club, 101–2
Tool and Die, 159–60
T.O.P. 25, 104, 151
Top of the Pops, 199–200

INDEX 277

Torch, 214–15
Tower of Power, 89–90
Trading Places, 177–78
Tracy, Jeanie, 89–92, 116–17, 185, 187–88, 191, 195, 217, 225–26, 228, 229
  Me and You, 152–53, 177, 204
Trax, 176
Trench, 125–26
Trench, Fiachra, 224
Tripp, C.A., 24
Trocadero Transfer, 1, 5, 7–8, 12, 27, 30, 32–33, 34–35, 36–39, 40, 74, 86, 98*f*, 104–5, 107–10, 110*f*, 111–14, 115, 119–20, 127–29, 134–35, 152, 155, 160, 195–96, 206, 209–10, 213–14, 224, 225–26, 227, 228–30, 232, 242n.28, 258n.10
Troy, Doris, 105
Truth and Beauty Studio, 210
TSR Records, 215
Tucker, Sherrie, 2
Toons, The, 218
Tunespeak Productions, 228–29
Turner, Dan, 21, 237n.26
12 West (New York disco), 17–18, 37–38, 107–8
Two Tons o' Fun, 5–6, 52, 53, 54–55, 57, 73–75, 82, 83–84, 87–88, 89, 90, 91, 118*f*, 151–52, 197, 201–2, 254n.69
  Two Tons O' Fun, 116–17, 130–32

University of California, Berkeley, 118–19
University of Michigan, 159–60
University of Nebraska, Omaha, 134
University of Rochester, 61–62
University of Wisconsin, 118–19

Vadala, Candice, 64, 65, 240n.9
Valli, Frankie, 196–97
Van de Laar, Bart, 156
Vandross, Luther, 186
Vangelis, 35–36
Vapors, The, 177–78
Village Cabaret, 237n.26
Village People, 9, 58, 59–60, 122, 124, 136, 239n.28
Viteritti, Bobby, 12, 38, 49, 98*f*, 104–10, 113–15, 119–20, 127–29, 133, 134–35, 138, 142–43, 245n.59, 248n.59
Voeller, Bruce, 24–25
Vojir, Dan, 25–26
Vukas, John, 152, 153

Wadlington, Dennis, 85, 93–94, 190–91
War Bride Records, 157–58

Warner Brothers Records, 117
Warped Floors, 64, 65
Warren, Patricia Nell, 25
Warwick, Dionne, 20
Wash, Martha, 5–6, 50, 51–52, 72, 73, 116–17, 118*f*, 187–88, 191, 201–2, 217
Washington, Deborah, 86, 242n.28
Washington, Tony, 57
Water Drinkers, 159–60
Waters, Julie, 87, 94
Waters, Maxine, 87, 94
Watson, Johnny "Guitar," 48–49
Weather Girls, The (*see* Two Tons o' Fun)
Weather Report, 84–85
Weatherly, Reverend Rick, 175
Weiner, Gerald, 147
West, Belinda, 150–51
West End Records, 65–66
Westbook, Idaree, 32
Western Association of Rock DJs, 104
Wharton, Bob, 35
White, Allen, 223
White, Barry, 5
White, Dan, 31, 78, 97–98
White Night Riots, 97–98
Whitehead, Michael, 36
Wilkinson, Mike, 129, 142–43
Williams, Reverend Cecil, 133–34
Williams, Danny, 15–17, 205–6, 226
Williams, Jessica, 150, 210, 217
Williams, Tommy, 104, 213–14, 218, 220–21
Wilson, Hank, 170–71
Wilson, Ruby, 153
Wirrick, James "Tip," 51, 53–55, 69, 93–94, 116–17, 131–32, 187–89, 190–91, 192–95, 197, 211–12, 217, 228
WMOT (We Men of Talent), 49
Wolf, Prince, 1
Wonder, Stevie, 81, 196–97
Wood, Don, 127
Woods, The (Marin County club), 15–17

X (club), 102
Xtravaganza, Hector, 1

Yellowfingers (New York club), 18
Young, Earl, 8, 12, 53–54, 120

Zaentz, Saul, 48–49, 84
Zappa, Frank, 205–6
Zappa, Moon, 205–6
Zino, 214–15
ZYX Records, 216

Printed in the USA/Agawam, MA
June 12, 2023

811418.016